Construction Safety

Jimmie W. Hinze

Director,
M. E. Rinker, Sr., School of Building Construction
University of Florida

Prentice Hall
Upper Saddle River, New Jersey   Columbus, Ohio

Library of Congress Cataloging-in-Publication Data
Hinze, Jimmie W.
     Construction safety / Jimmie W. Hinze.
          p.   cm.
     Includes bibliographical references and index.
     ISBN 0-13-377912-2
     1. Building—Safety measures. 2. Building—Superintendence.   I. Title.
TH443.H55   1997
690'.22—dc20   96-19486
                                                                                          CIP

Cover image: © Ewing Galloway
Editor: Ed Francis
Production Editor: Rex Davidson
Design Coordinator: Julia Zonneveld Van Hook
Text Designer: Susan E. Frankenberry
Cover Designer: Russ Maselli
Production Manager: Deidra M. Schwartz
Electronic Text Management: Marilyn Wilson Phelps, Matthew Williams, Karen L. Bretz,
     Tracey Ward
Illustrations: Christine Marrone

This book was set in Transitional 511 and Zurich by Prentice Hall and was printed and bound by
Quebecor Printing/Book Press. The cover was printed by Phoenix Color Corp.

© 1997 by Prentice-Hall, Inc.
Simon & Schuster/A Viacom Company
Upper Saddle River, New Jersey 07458

Printed in the United States of America

10 9 8 7 6 5 4 3 2 1

ISBN: 0-13-377912-2

Prentice-Hall International (UK) Limited, *London*
Prentice-Hall of Australia Pty. Limited, *Sydney*
Prentice-Hall of Canada, Inc., *Toronto*
Prentice-Hall Hispanoamericana, S. A., *Mexico*
Prentice-Hall of India Private Limited, *New Delhi*
Prentice-Hall of Japan, Inc., *Tokyo*
Simon & Schuster Asia Pte. Ltd., *Singapore*
Editora Prentice-Hall do Brasil, Ltda., *Rio de Janeiro*

Construction Safety

To Maxine, Jacob, and Justin

Preface

One of my first jobs in the construction industry took place in the early 1970s. I was a green engineer and was hired primarily as the construction scheduler for the firm. I also had the title of safety director. It was in the position as safety director that I became familiar with OSHA, workers' compensation, and the general issue of safety on the job-site. I kept track of safety statistics and required reporting. Two of our construction projects were very similar in scope, and they were only about two miles apart. The workforce on one of the projects sustained four injuries, while the workforce on the other project sustained 37 injuries. Since the projects were very similar in type of construction, location, etc., I began to suspect that the difference was attributable to the roles played by the superintendents. Since then, I have conducted research and have examined the research conducted by others, and I am convinced that superintendents and those in other management or supervisory positions play key roles in influencing project safety.

Through nearly 20 years of teaching experience, I always made a specific point of incorporating safety into every course. Until recently, I had thought that this was the way safety should be taught. I recently offered a course devoted entirely to the topic of construction safety. I then began questioning the merits of my previous method of addressing safety. I still feel that safety should be incorporated into every subject on construction, but I also feel that it is most appropriate to devote an entire class to the subject of safety in order to provide students with the full scope of the material.

In comparison with the limited number of construction safety texts that exist, several distinguishing features will become apparent. This text is a compilation of construction safety research studies conducted in the past 25 years. The information has been compiled in a manner that lends the information to implementation. The effort reflected by these research studies is enormous. Some very credible research studies have been completed in the construction industry, and I have attempted to highlight the more relevant information. No other text on construction safety has drawn on such a vast number of safety references.

This text delves into topics not commonly addressed by textbooks on construction safety. These are the theories on accident causation, contract provisions that address safety, the role of project coordination in safety, and the role played by designers in construction safety.

The Introduction presents historical information on the safety record demonstrated by the construction industry over the years. Chapter 1 enumerates various theories of accident causation, including one developed by me. Subsequent chapters address the timing of the occurrence of most construction injuries, the total costs of injuries, the fundamental aspects of the operation of OSHA, and summary information on OSHA investigations. Chapter 6 presents an overview of the basic components of a safety program. The following chapters address more specific aspects of the components of a safety program, including jobsite safety assessment, safety meetings, safety incentives, safety as addressed in construction contracts, substance abuse testing, and safety record keeping. The remaining chapters, beginning with Chapter 13, address specific information on safety pertaining to workers, first-line supervisors, superintendents, top managers, safety personnel, subcontractors, owners, and designers. The role of coordination on safety performance is summarized in Chapter 19.

An attempt has been made to address all major aspects of construction safety that relate to behavioral issues. While OSHA is discussed specifically in two chapters, no attempt has been made to familiarize the reader with the various standards that pertain to the construction industry. Much of this information can be obtained directly by reading the OSHA standards pertaining to construction and by referencing the many brochures and safety digests that have been published.

No author can complete a text without the help of others. This is certainly true in this case. Much of what I know about safety was taught to me by many of the students whom I advised over the years. Some specific students to be thanked include James Brown, Derek Brown, Robert Blegen, Christine Engan, Kevin Stover, Lisa Applegate, David Maxwell, Mohammad Banki, Paul Raboud, Peggy McShane, Donna Talley, Lori Figone, Francis Wiegand, Anne Kusaka, Timothy Burns, James Van de Voorde, Debra Russell, Scott Hinton, Robert Hymel, Mark Lawless, Nancy Piepho, Thomas Rodgers, Ricardo Indradjaja, David Bren, Katherine Bren, John Heckmann, Darryl Creasy, Bernadine Thomson, Curtis Nakamura, Kevin McMeel, Raymond Chou, Charles Harrison, John Gambatese, and many others. While all those contributing cannot be named here, many are referenced in the text. I would like to also thank Carm Sherlock and Abe Mutawe, personnel at the OSHA Region 10 office in Seattle, who were very helpful in providing information about OSHA on numerous occasions. Tremendous effort was expended by Ann Colowick in the primary editing of the text, and I very much want to acknowledge her contribution. In the final editing and proofreading, I had some excellent assistance from Barbara Eickhoff, who has helped over the years on many other matters and her efforts are certainly appreciated.

In finalizing this text, many constructive suggestions were offered which helped to improve the final version. I would like to thank the many reviewers of the text as their comments were very helpful. The comments provided by Professor D. A. Wahlstrom were very helpful. Professor Richard Coble was extremely helpful in his review. He utilized the manuscript as a text in a safety class at the University of Florida and had the students provide independent reviews. My sincerest thanks go to those students who provided many insightful comments. I would also like to thank Professor Coble for his many comments of encouragement. With his comments, I was able to discern which material was in greatest need of change. The final version of the text is much improved, because others gave their earnest comments on changes needed as this was being developed.

Lastly, I must thank my wife, Maxine, who was so encouraging throughout the entire process of writing the text. After listening to my ramblings about some aspect of safety, she often provided me with uncanny insights that I had previously failed to recognize. She, more than anyone, keeps reminding me to be safe.

Contents

Introduction   *1*

     The Time for Safety Awareness Has Arrived   1
     Construction Worker Injuries   2
     Safety in Construction versus Safety in Other Industries   3
     What Is an Accident?   6
     Is Accident Prevention a Realistic Objective in Construction?   7

1

Injury Accidents and Their Causes   *11*

     Why Do Accidents Occur?   11
     The Accident-Proneness Theory   12
     The Goals-Freedom-Alertness Theory   14
     The Adjustment-Stress Theory   15
     The Distractions Theory   17
     Mental Stresses   21
     The Chain-of-Events Theory   21

2

When Do Injuries Occur?   *31*

     Hour of the Day   31
     Day of the Week   33

Season of the Year   36

The Effect of Shift Work   37

The Effect of Lunar Cycles   39

The Effect of Biorhythm Cycles on Safety Performance   42

Research Involving Biorhythms   42

A Study of Biorhythm Cycles and Construction Worker Injuries   43

3

The True Costs of Construction Worker Injuries   *49*

Direct Costs of Injuries   50

Workers' Compensation (Prepayment Premium or Postpayment Penalty)   50

Indirect (Hidden) Costs of Injuries   52

Previous Studies of the True Costs of Injuries   54

Recent Research on the Costs of Injuries   55

Costs of Injuries Quantified   57

Application of the True Costs of Injuries   58

Additional Analysis of the Costs of Injuries   60

Application of Injury Cost Models   62

Indirect Costs Are Significant   64

Some Costs Are Not Known   65

The Next Step   65

The Cost of Safety   66

Workers Compensation Fraud   66

4

OSHA   *71*

Key OSH Act Provisions   71

OSH Act Agencies   72

OSHA Standards   72

Promulgation of New Standards   76

Variances   76

Informing Employees   77

Compliance Inspections   77
OSHA State-Plan States   80
OSHA Consultation Services   80
Other OSHA Programs   81

5

Problem Areas in Construction Safety 85

Problem Areas   85
Problem Regulations   86
Problems with Injury Coding   91
The Focus of OSHA Inspections   92

6

Elements of an Effective Safety Program 99

Establishing Your Company's Safety Philosophy   100
Statement of Policy or Mission   100
The Scope of the Safety Program   101
The Responsibility of the Company   101
The Safety Director   102
Preconstruction Meeting or Conference   102
Preconstruction Checklist   102
The Project Safety Program   102
Training   104
Safety Standards and Regulations on Owner's Premises   104
OSHA Regulations   105
Hazard Analysis   106
Safety Meetings   106
Safety Committees   107
Safety Budgets   107
Substance Abuse Programs   107

Subcontractor Compliance   108
Inspection of the Work Site by Regulatory Personnel   108
Safety Performance Evaluations   108
Emergency Plans   109
Accident Reporting   109
Investigation of Accidents and Incidents   110
Avoiding Liability   110
Selection of an Insurance Carrier   112
Other Elements   112

7

Job-Site Safety Assessment   *115*

Job Hazard Analysis   115
   Assessment of General-Conditions Hazards   116
   Assessment of Hazards of Specific Operations   117
   Documenting the Hazards   118
   Corrective Measures   118
   Being Ever Vigilant   120
OSHA Consulting   120
Safety Committees   121
Job-Site Safety Inspections   122
   Mock OSHA Inspections   123
   Insurance Carrier Job Inspections   123

8

Safety Meetings   *133*

When Should the Safety Training Sessions Be Held?   135
Who Should Attend the Safety Training Sessions?   136
Who Should Conduct the Safety Training Sessions?   136
What Topics Should Be Addressed?   136
Preparation for Safety Training Sessions   137

Documentation of Safety Training Sessions   137
Supervisory Safety Meetings   139
Company Safety Meetings (Dinners)   139

9

Safety Incentives   141

Disincentives for Unsafe Behavior   144
Incentives for First-Line Supervisors   146
Incentives for Superintendents   147
Project Safety Incentives   148
An Example   149

10

Safety in Construction Contracts   151

Compliance with Existing Laws and Regulations on Safety   152
Statement of Policy or Mission   155
Scope   155
Responsibility of the Contractor   156
Preconstruction Checklist   156
Contractor's Safety Program   157
Construction Checklist   159
Requirement to Follow Safety Standards and Regulations on Owner's Premises   159
Hazard Analysis   160
Safety Meetings   161
Substance Abuse Programs   162
Subcontractor Compliance   162
Inspection of the Work Site by the Contractor   162
Inspection of the Work Site by the Owner   162
Inspection of the Work Site by Regulatory Personnel   163
Contractor Failure to Comply with Safety Standards or Regulations   163

Safety Performance Reports to the Owner   164
Emergency Plans   164
Accident Reporting   165
Safety Officer   165
Accident Prevention Plan   166
Detailed Safety Requirements   166
Specific Items   167
Confined Spaces   *167*
Traffic Supervisor   *168*
Traffic Plan   *168*
Engineer's Authority   *168*
Indemnification   *169*
Incentives for Safety   170

11

Substance Abuse   *173*

The Incidence of Substance Abuse   173
Drug Testing   174
Consequences of Testing Positive for Drugs   179
Effect of Substance Abuse Programs on Safety Performance   181

12

Safety Record Keeping   *185*

Log of Occupational Injuries and Illnesses (OSHA No. 200)   186
Supplementary Record of Occupational Injuries and Illnesses (OSHA
No. 101)   189
Maintenance of OSHA Records   191
Annual OSHA Summary Report   191
Incident Reports   191
Accident Investigation Reports   193
The Level of Reporting in Safety Reports   196

13

Safety Culture 201

Safety Must Be a Sustained Effort on All Fronts   203

14

Safe Workers 207

New Workers   208
Working with Friends   210
Job Satisfaction and Loyalty to the Company   212
Experience in the Industry   213
Worker Safety and Job Pressures   213
Treating Workers with Respect   215

15

Safety and First-Line Supervisors (Foremen) 219

Foremen and New Workers   220
Considering Motivational Approaches   221
Job Pressures   222
Managerial or Supervisory Style   223
Safety and Project Constraints   225
A Good Attitude about Safety   227

16

Safety and Middle Managers (Superintendents) 231

Superintendents and New Workers   232
Safer Superintendents Are Good Managers   234
Superintendents Keep Job Pressures Down   236

17

Top Management Practices, Company Activities, and Safety 243

Company Size   244

Why Do Different-Sized Companies Have Different Safety Records?   244
Small Company Operations   247

Project Control and Safety Performance   247

Company Turnover and Safety Performance   250

Competitive Work Environment   251

Policies on Safety That Include Top Managers   251

A Top-Management Model of Safety   255

An Example   256

Model Company   257
Poor Communication   258
A New Title for the President   259
Insurance as a Partner   259

18

Safety Personnel 263

OSHA's Personnel Requirements   263

Safety Responsibility of Job-Site Personnel   264

Safety Personnel   265

19

Subcontractor Safety 271

Subcontractor Safety Begins in the Selection Process   274

Influence of General Contractors on Subcontractor Safety   275

Subcontractor Safety on Medium-Sized Projects   276

Project Pressures   276
Project Coordination   277

Emphasis on Safety   *278*
Concern for Workers   *279*
Compliance with Safety Regulations   *279*
Subcontractor Safety on Large Projects   279

20

Project Coordination and Construction Safety   *283*

The Importance of Coordination   284
Conflict between Scheduling and Safety?   285
The Relationship of Coordination to Safety Performance   286
Short-Interval Schedules and Safety   290
Project Complexity   294

21

Owners and Construction Safety   *297*

Owner Involvement in Construction Safety   298
Selecting Safe Contractors   299
Injury Incident Rates   *299*
Experience Modification Rates   *300*
Loss Ratio   *303*
Record of OSHA Citations and Fines   *304*
Litigation Related to Injuries   *304*
Performance Records of Key Personnel   *305*
Project Safety Plan   *306*
Contractor Qualification Safety Survey   *306*
Starting a Construction Project Safely   306
Owner Involvement in Site Safety   307
Designer Selection   308
Owners and Subcontractor Safety   308

22

Designer Influence on Construction Worker Safety   313

Owner Attitudes about Designing for Safety   316
Design Decisions That Affect Construction Safety   318
Construction Managers and Safety   321

Key Terms   325

Index   327

Introduction

Safety is no luxury; it is a necessity.

Attention to safety in the construction industry has increased dramatically in the United States over the past few decades. The 1990s can properly be called the "decade for construction safety." Several factors have led to the greater emphasis on safety. Although construction work has become safer, there is still much to be accomplished. Since there is now a strong concern for safety in the construction community, one can hope that further improvements will continue to reduce the numbers of fatalities and serious injuries in the industry.

The Time for Safety Awareness Has Arrived

The involvement of the government in worker safety has gone through major changes in the past 200 years. During the Industrial Revolution of the nineteenth century, employers were seldom held responsible for the work-related injuries of their employees. The common law defenses of assumption of risk (the worker knew the job was dangerous), contributory negligence (the worker's actions helped cause the accident), and the fellow-worker doctrine (the accident was precipitated by another worker, not the employer) gave considerable relief to employers. Thus, industrial workers were often responsible for their own job-site well-being and for any injuries they might receive during the course of their employment.

During the first half of the twentieth century, the common law defenses gradually gave way to statutory workers' compensation laws, which transferred the responsibility for worker injuries from the employee to the employer. Unfortunately, many employers regarded worker injuries as a necessary cost of doing business. They did not consider that perhaps injuries could be prevented.

Despite workers' compensation legislation, unacceptable levels of worker injuries persisted in the 1960s and led to the passage of legislation mandating that employers provide their employees with a safe work environment. An employer's failure to provide for the safety and health of employees could result in citations and fines. Employers were charged with the maintenance of worker well-being in addition to the financial responsibility for worker injuries. Such legislation is epitomized by the Occupational Health and Safety Act (OSH Act) of 1970.

Part 5A of the OSH Act's general duty clause imposes a broad obligation on employers, stating, "Each employer shall furnish to each of his employees employment and a place of employment which are free from recognized hazards that are causing or are likely to cause death or serious physical harm to his employees." The OSH Act is particularly relevant to the construction industry, where the need for safety legislation may be greater than in most other industries. A disproportionately high number of industrial injuries and fatalities are incurred by construction workers.

Following the passage of the OSH Act, efforts by the courts to protect injured construction workers led to an extension of the responsibility for safety to others involved in construction projects. With the expanded responsibility, general contractors were held accountable, to some extent, for injuries sustained by subcontractors' employees, and owners began to carry some of the burden for *all* construction site injuries. In short, safety responsibilities were extended beyond the traditional employer-employee relationship. The courts generally maintained that although other parties are not the direct employers of an injured worker, their presence on the job site and involvement in the work sequence may justifiably transfer some of the responsibility for worker safety onto their shoulders. As a result, mounting liability litigation led to a liability crisis in the mid-1980s. Premiums on liability insurance skyrocketed, and many employers faced the difficult choice of whether or not to carry any liability insurance coverage. Some firms failed to qualify for liability coverage and were forced to operate "bare," or without insurance coverage. In response to the liability crisis, much work and in-depth research has been performed to investigate accident causes, address job-site hazards, and propose appropriate safety measures.

As these events were taking place, a parallel phenomenon was taking place in the health care industry; that is, health care costs were escalating at nearly uncontrollable rates. Coupled with liability suits with high settlements, rising health care costs led industry leaders to recognize that the owners of facilities being constructed were the parties on whom the ultimate indebtedness for worker injuries would fall. By the early 1990s many private owners were taking a keen interest in safety. They began to demand assurances from their contractors that their construction sites would be safe.

By examining some simple statistics, many facility owners came to realize that some companies are consistently safe while others seem to incur unacceptable levels of injuries among their workers on a regular basis. As contractors were sought for projects, it became common to consider only those firms with a demonstrated history of good safety performance.

Interest in safety is continuing to spread. The interest on the part of facility owners has now caught the attention of many contractors. Those contractors have begun to recognize that the only way to stay in business is to provide safe construction services. With a concerted effort, they will succeed in that objective.

Construction Worker Injuries

Safety is or should be a major concern of any employer in any industry. In the construction industry, the need for such concern may be greater than in most other industries. The greater need stems primarily from the disproportionately high number of industrial injuries incurred by construction workers. The statistics have remained reasonably constant over the past several years: the construction industry employs approximately

5% of the industrial work force, but has generally accounted for nearly 20% of all industrial worker fatalities, as reported in *Accident Facts,* an annual publication of the National Safety Council (NSC). Although some construction leaders claim that construction has more inherent hazards, others claim that construction site hazards can be eliminated and that they need not be a part of construction work. The fatality rate (deaths per 100,000 workers) in construction is regularly exceeded only by worker fatality rates in mining and agriculture. Table 1 shows that the number of fatalities and, especially, the death rate have declined over the past few years, a trend that is observable in injury statistics of all industries. Note that a sharp decline in fatalities is shown from 1991 to 1992. The 1992 statistics are those reported by the Census of Fatal Occupation Injuries (CFOI). The CFOI data, excluding homicides and suicides, have been adopted by the NSC, beginning with 1992.

The statistics presented in Table 1 are those compiled by the NSC. Similar statistics are also compiled by the United States Bureau of Labor Statistics (BLS). When past BLS statistics are compared with data compiled by the NSC, a statistical analysis reveals a striking difference. The two agencies use different methods to generate the fatality statistics. The NSC used a program called the "three-way split." Under this program non-motor-vehicle deaths were allocated by predetermined percentages into work, home, and public classes. That method was used for data from 1928 to 1994. In 1995 the NSC decided to use the CFOI data. The injury and fatality statistics were then readjusted, back to 1992. The change will be further described later in this chapter.

In the early 1990s, in an effort to provide more accurate fatality statistics, the BLS created the Census of Fatal Occupational Injuries (CFOI). That census is more thorough than the efforts of the NSC or the method previously used by the BLS. In the CFOI all fatalities are carefully examined. To be included in the CFOI data, a fatality must have double verification. The data may initially come from the Occupational Safety and Health Administration (OSHA); however, each death must be verified by a second source, such as a death certificate or a coroner's report. Newspaper clippings are also scanned for occupational fatalities. Thus, fatalities that OSHA may not record are included in the CFOI data. The CFOI data appear to be quite accurate because they are the result of an attempt to track every fatality. The NSC and the BLS had not previously made such an attempt.

The NSC's data on worker injuries and deaths in the construction industry are shown as a graph in Figure 1. Despite the significant differences between the NSC's statistics on injuries and fatalities and the CFOI data, the historical trends depicted by the NSC data present valuable information on general changes in safety performances over the years. Care must be taken, however, if trends are to be evaluated for data reported before 1992 as well as for data reported in 1992 and thereafter.

Safety in Construction versus Safety in Other Industries

The evidence is clear from Table 1 and Figure 1 that worker injuries in the construction industry are a serious issue. Comparisons have been made between the construction industry and other industrial sectors. Over the years, the construction industry has consistently been among those industries with the highest injury and fatality rates. The

Table 1

Construction Injury and Fatality Data

Year	Workers	Deaths	Death Rate*	Disabling Injury Rate**
1958	3,200,000	2,400	75	5.8
1959	3,200,000	2,100	78	6.6
1960	3,300,000	2,300	73	6.1
1961	3,400,000	2,300	68	5.9
1962	3,200,000	2,400	75	6.6
1963	3,400,000	2,500	74	6.2
1964	3,600,000	2,600	72	6.1
1965	3,700,000	2,700	73	6.1
1966	3,800,000	2,800	74	6.3
1967	3,800,000	2,700	71	6.0
1968	3,800,000	2,800	74	6.3
1969	4,000,000	2,800	70	6.0
1970	3,900,000	2,800	72	6.2
1971	3,800,000	2,700	71	6.3
1972	4,000,000	2,800	70	6.5
1973	4,100,000	2,900	71	6.8
1974	4,100,000	2,600	63	5.6
1975	3,600,000	2,200	61	5.6
1976	3,700,000	2,100	57	5.4
1977	4,200,000	2,500	60	5.7
1978	4,600,000	2,600	57	5.2
1979	5,000,000	2,600	52	5.0
1980	5,600,000	2,500	45	4.3
1981	5,500,000	2,200	40	3.8
1982	5,200,000	2,100	40	3.8
1983	5,400,000	2,000	37	3.7
1984	5,700,000	2,200	39	3.9
1985	6,000,000	2,200	37	3.7
1986	6,300,000	2,100	33	3.5
1987	6,300,000	2,200	35	3.0
1988	6,500,000	2,200	34	3.2
1989	6,500,000	2,100	32	2.9
1990	6,400,000	2,100	33	3.3
1991	5,900,000	1,800	31	3.0
1992[†]	5,900,000	840[†]	14[†]	5.1
1993	5,900,000	840	14	4.8
1994	6,200,000	910	15	4.8

* Deaths per 100,000 workers.

** Disabling injuries per 100 workers (or 200,000 hours of worker exposure).

† Beginning with the 1992 data, the NSC abandoned its method of estimating fatalities and injuries and adopted the values determined by the Bureau of Labor Statistics program called the Census of Fatal Occupational Injuries (CFOI). The NSC data exclude the homicides and suicides included in the CFOI data.

Source: National Safety Council, annual

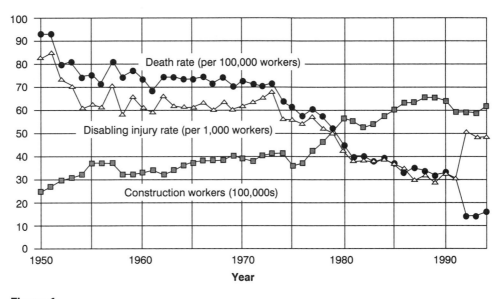

Figure 1
Injury and Fatality Statistics since 1950
Source: National Safety Council, annual

only industries that rival construction are agriculture and mining. Statistics developed for agriculture, however, are not always comparable with those for construction. The rates are based on worker hours of exposure. If workers live on the premises, as is common in agriculture, how can comparisons be realistically made? Obviously, the extent of exposure is much greater than the number of hours actually worked each day. Comparisons with mining may be valid.

What features of construction make it an industry in which so many workers are injured and killed? A common response to that question is simply, "Construction work is inherently dangerous and injuries are more likely to occur." That answer reflects a fatalistic view of construction and essentially excuses the industry for its dismal safety record. It is appropriate to consider construction work as inherently dangerous if no proactive steps are taken to improve the work conditions and to ensure that the work is undertaken in a safe manner. One need only look at the history of safety performance in the construction industry to realize that the incidence of injuries and fatalities has been reduced by more than 50% in the past three decades. Those who took a fatalistic view in the mid-1960s would have argued that the level of injuries was commensurate with the hazards in the work environment and that the injuries were unavoidable. They have been proven wrong.

Is the level of incidence of injuries and fatalities now the lowest we can expect? Further examination of current safety performance data indicates that substantial improvements can be made. Many construction firms now boast of having worked millions of worker hours on some projects without incurring any lost-time injuries. Those firms report such statistics with great regularity. Does that mean that firms with high injury rates can also achieve better safety performances? With a proactive stance on safety, the answer is surely yes.

Safety should be viewed, not in a fatalistic manner, but in a positive manner. The objective of every employer should be to have no worker injuries. Coupled with that objective must be a deep-seated conviction that the goal is attainable. Firms must be prepared for the occurrence of injuries, but they should, at the same time, plan to have none.

It should be clear that the construction industry has not had a favorable safety record over the years. Granted, improvements have been made, but comparisons with all industries continue to show that further improvements can be made. Why does the construction industry have such a dismal record when compared with most other industries? The answer is not a simple one. Explanations would have to include such issues as the changing nature of the work site as the construction project evolves, the changing composition of the work team, and the adverse weather conditions of outside work. The following example may help to clarify this point.

Example: A worker has been working on the construction of a five-story office building for a few weeks. Last week this worker was laying decking with two carpenters who were his personal friends. Today, Monday of the following week, the worker returned to the project at the beginning of the workday. When he got to the work area, he was told that he was being reassigned to another crew, which is building concrete forms. He is to work with three other carpenters, workers he does not know. He was reassigned because heavy rains over the weekend have made conditions on the site quite muddy. The forms cannot be set on schedule by a crew the size of the one that worked on the forms last week. Thus, the reassigned worker is suddenly placed in an environment in which the conditions are quite different from those he worked under last week. For example, he is working with strangers, working in muddy conditions, working at a different task, working to meet a tighter schedule, and working under a different foreman or supervisor. Any of those conditions might render the worker more susceptible to injury if the appropriate steps are not taken.

What Is an Accident?

An accident can be defined as an unplanned event. The terms *undesirable*, *unexpected*, and *noncontrolled* have also been used to describe such events (DeReamer 1958, National Safety Council 1985). An accident does not necessarily result in an injury. Accidents that result in damage to equipment and materials and especially those that result in injuries receive the greatest attention. All accidents, regardless of the nature of the damage or loss, should be of concern. Accidents that do not cause damage to materials or equipment or injury to personnel may foretell future accidents with less desirable results.

The use of the term *accident* presents some problems in the area of accident prevention. First of all, the term *accident* is commonly associated with events that are assumed to be out of the control of the persons involved. Consider the situation in which a small child spills a glass of milk at the supper table. The child's defense, "But,

Daddy, it was an accident," is used to imply that blame or fault should not be placed on the child. Although some may argue that the only implication is that the act was not perpetrated on purpose, the inference may be made that no action is required to prevent future spills. Regardless of the way accidents are viewed, the healthiest approach to prevention is to focus on the causal factors (Suchman 1961).

A second problem presented by the use of the term *accident* is the common assumption that an accident involves damage or injury. Many unplanned events take place from which no damage or injury results. Such events are not treated in the same way as occurrences of property damage or bodily injury. Those so-called near misses, which may be more frequent than one realizes, can be very effective signals about specific areas that need safety improvement. From the standpoint of safety, it would be most prudent to document as many near misses as possible and to develop plans to reduce or eliminate the chance of reoccurrence. Near misses are inexpensive "wake-up calls," warning of future accidents that may occur if the appropriate measures are not taken. The key to accident prevention may be in recognizing near misses when they occur and then taking prudent steps to make the work environment safe.

Is Accident Prevention a Realistic Objective in Construction?

Many construction personnel will argue that successful accident prevention efforts in construction are different from those of typical manufacturing facilities. They contend that the effort required is different because the work environment in manufacturing is reasonably consistent from day to day whereas the work environment in construction is in a constant state of change. Despite their argument, the changing work environment may make accident prevention a more challenging task, but it does not mean that safety objectives in a construction setting must be any lower than in manufacturing. It may even be argued that it is the changing nature of construction projects that makes this type of work such a rewarding experience. The vitality provided by change in the work environment may even be regarded as healthy for safety.

It is often postulated that the work force in construction is ever changing whereas the work force in manufacturing remains relatively constant. High turnover, many will argue, has adverse implications when it comes to training. Efforts to train a worker are assumed to be lost when that worker leaves the firm. If a worker will be on the job for a short while, some may feel that safety training is not worth the effort. Such arguments are unconvincing. The costs of safety training are far less than the consequences should a serious injury occur.

The sense that workers do not remain with a single construction firm long enough to justify serious safety training is often unfounded. One of the early studies on construction safety was conducted by Lance deStwolinski (1969). His study focused on the Operating Engineers' Local Union No. 3 in northern California. One interesting finding of his research was that 57% of the workers had worked for their current employers for at least one year out of the previous five. Additionally, 20% of the workers had worked for their current employers for the entire five years.

Turnover appears to be low in some segments of the construction industry. It is especially low in construction firms that confine most of their operations to a specific geographic location. For example, utility contracting firms tend to be relatively small, and they tend to restrict the bulk of their operations to a particular region. It was observed in one nationwide study of utility contractors that more than two-thirds of the firms had employed more than 60% of their workers for more than one year and that nearly one-third had employed more than 60% of their workers for more than five years (Hinze 1978).

Since a significant number of workers are often rehired by the same construction firms, it stands to reason that training efforts are not in vain. The workers tend to be employed long enough to have made significant investments of their time in specific firms. It stands to reason that those firms can readily justify a greater investment in their employees. Even if a worker will be employed on a project for only a few hours, a thorough orientation to the project is still warranted.

Final Comments

Among industries, construction is unique in that it affords great opportunities for workers to be involved in many projects of interest. The work requires diverse skills. Additionally, construction work must often take place outdoors, in conditions that may not be completely favorable for health and safety. In addition to constant change in the nature of the work and in the mix of workers on construction projects, the location of the work frequently changes for the workers. Although the special attributes of construction may be attractive to some workers, the safety record amassed in the industry is not to be envied. Those attributes need not result in injuries and fatalities. Managers and supervisors must simply take a strong role in controlling their projects. Safety performance can be improved. A unified effort by the industry is warranted.

Review Questions

1. Historically, how can the safety performance of the construction industry be characterized?
2. How many disabling injuries occur in the construction industry each year? How many fatalities?
3. What is an accident?
4. How does the safety performance of the construction industry compare with other industries? Explain why.
5. Does the nature of construction work justify a greater frequency of accidents?
6. Discuss the argument that safety training has a minimal payoff because workers are not employed very long by construction firms.
7. For those tracking safety performance over a period of several years or even decades, what are the implications of the fatality statistics generated by the Census of Fatal Occupational Injuries?

References

DeReamer, R. 1958. *Modern Safety Practice.* New York: John Wiley.

deStwolinski, L. 1969. *A Survey of the Safety Environment of the Construction Industry.* Technical Report No. 114, Department of Civil Engineering. Stanford, Calif.: Stanford University.

Gilmore, C. 1970. *Accident Prevention and Loss Control.* New York: American Management Association.

Haddon, W., E. Suchman, and D. Klein. 1964. *Accident Research Methods and Approaches.* New York: Harper and Row.

Hinze, J. 1977. "Effective Job Control Improved Job Safety." *National Utility Contractor* 1, no. 3:23–25.

———. 1977. "How Dollar Volume Changes a Company." *National Utility Contractor* 1, no. 2:26–27.

Hinze, J., and J. Pannullo. 1978. "Safety: Function of Job Control." *Journal of the Construction Division, ASCE* 104, no. 2:241–49.

Hinze, J. 1978. "Turnover, New Workers, and Safety." *Journal of the Construction Division, ASCE* 104, no. 4:409–17.

National Safety Council. Annual. *Accident Facts.* Chicago: National Safety Council.

National Safety Council. 1985. *Supervisors Safety Manual.* 6th ed. Chicago: National Safety Council.

Suchman, E. 1961. "A Conceptual Analysis of the Accident Phenomenon." In *Behavioral Approaches to Accident Research.* New York: Association for the Aid of Crippled Children.

Toscano, G., and J. Windau. 1993. "Fatal Work Injuries: Results from the 1992 National Census." *Monthly Labor Review,* October. Vol. 116:39–48.

U.S. Department of Labor. Occupational Safety and Health Administration (OSHA). 1970. *Safety and Health Regulations for Construction.* Code of Federal Regulations, Part 1926. Washington, D.C.: Department of Labor.

Injury Accidents and Their Causes

Accidents don't just happen; they are caused.

Why Do Accidents Occur?

Effective accident prevention depends on an understanding of the reasons accidents occur. The accidents of primary interest are those in which personal injuries are sustained. In this book the term *accident* will usually refer to a personal-injury incident.

Bear in mind that injuries are generally sustained by persons who do not want to be injured. That is, injuries occur even though people really do not want to be involved in accidents and will normally take steps to avoid them. Why, then, do accidents occur? Some of the theories of accident causation will be discussed in this chapter to answer this question. The theories to be described include accident-proneness, goals-freedom-alertness, adjustment-stress, chain-of-events, and distractions theories. The accident-proneness theory has been the subject of considerable research, but the other theories have not been subjected to rigorous testing. Though largely untested, the theories do appear to help explain accident causation.

The Accident-Proneness Theory

Perhaps the oldest and best-known theory of accident causation is the accident-proneness theory. This theory is focused on personal factors related to accident causation. It is based on the assumption that when several individuals are placed in similar conditions, some will be more likely than others to sustain an injury. Essentially, the advocates of the theory contend that accidents are not randomly distributed or that sustaining an injury is not simply a chance occurrence. They assert that some persons have permanent characteristics that predispose them to a greater probability of being involved in accidents. One of the first researchers on this topic stated that accident proneness could be traced to personality traits (Vernon 1918). Farmer and Chambers (1929) defined accident proneness as "a personal idiosyncrasy predisposing the individual who possesses it in a marked degree to a relatively high accident rate." This theory has the underlying assumption that even when exposed to the same conditions, some people are more likely to be involved in accidents because of "their innate propensity for accidents" (Shaw and Sichel 1971).

Numerous research studies have been conducted to determine the validity of the accident-proneness theory. The studies have generally consisted of an examination of a given population and an assessment of the distribution of injuries in that population. Several researchers have concluded from such studies that injuries are not randomly distributed and that some individuals sustain more injuries than would be predicted by chance alone (Farmer and Chambers 1929). Accident proneness, as the dates of the studies indicate, was once a much debated phenomenon. It is no longer the favored accident theory.

There have been numerous critics of the research purporting to affirm the accident-proneness theory. Although some accident-proneness researchers tried to account for differences in work hazards, the researchers were generally remiss in addressing factors that might make some workers more susceptible to injury than others. Factors related to personal problems and the contributions of fellow workers were generally ignored in the research. The critics do not necessarily refute the accident-proneness theory, but they criticize the methodology by which the conclusions were formed. Others acknowledge that there may be some validity to the accident-proneness theory, but they believe that the theory explains only a small proportion of accidents, perhaps 10–15%.

The fact that some persons are injured more often than others is frequently cited as support for the theory of accident proneness. The persons who sustain more injuries are then called accident-prone. From a purely statistical viewpoint, one might assume that the occurrence of injuries is randomly distributed. For example, suppose there is a chance of 1 in 1000 of being injured on any given day. With a work force of 1000, it would be reasonable to expect an injury each day. In most cases, if a worker is injured and receives treatment, that worker returns to the work force. The injured worker then faces the same risk of being injured as the other workers. With this "sampling with replacement," it would not be uncommon for a worker to sustain several injuries from pure chance.

Schulzinger (1956) examined the records of a hospital near a small plant over an 18-year period (1930–48). A total of 35,000 accidents (27,000 industrial and 8000 nonindustrial) were examined. The injuries were sustained through accidents in homes, on the highways, at play, and at work. Schulzinger concluded that "most of the accidents were due to a large number of individuals with single accidents and not to a small group of highly 'accident prone' persons or accident repeaters." Patients with more than one injury accounted for less than 30% of the total number injured. That finding was consistent among males and females and for each year examined.

DeReamer (1958) examined the injury records of 10,964 people. Using a statistical analysis, he determined that by chance alone 79 of those people would be expected to have five or more injuries. For the data he examined, there were 90 persons with five or more injuries. He recognized that exposure to hazards is ignored in the statistics. In fact, it had previously been assumed by most accident proneness researchers that the injured worker was at fault in all cases. That assumption may not be valid for many injuries. Thus, the study by DeReamer offered little support for the accident-proneness theory.

It has been suggested that accident proneness may be a real phenomenon but that it is of a transitory nature. That is, people may be "maladjusted" for a short period of time for some reason. It can be determined statistically that a small percentage of the work force can be expected to account for virtually all the accidents. Although those with three or more injuries might be labeled accident-prone, that characterization is unfair when viewed from a purely statistical perspective.

A more recent work associated accident proneness with the propensity to take risks. Dahlback (1991) referred to accident proneness as a personality trait. Since risk taking is not a permanent or fixed trait, accident proneness might then change over time. For example, a young, single man may feel comfortable riding a motorcycle without a helmet, but his attitude may change once he becomes a husband or father. A young man may have poor driving habits with his peers in the car, but he may drive quite safely when children or older adults are with him. He will not view the nature of the risk itself any differently, but he will assess the consequences of a mishap differently. In fact, a young father may very well decide that riding a motorcycle offers too many risks even with a helmet and thus give up riding a motorcycle altogether. The propensity for risk taking may also decline with age. This trend may stem from the recognition of one's own mortality that may accompany the maturing process. For persons who experience such a decline, the propensity for risk taking is a passing phenomenon. It should be recognized that even if a worker has a propensity for risk taking, that worker's behavior may be influenced sufficiently to result in safe performance. Denning (1983) found that workers who were more impulsive in their actions had more injuries.

Dahlback conducted a study that offered support for the hypothesis that some people are more accident-prone than others. Note that this study was based on the propensity to take risks. Thus, it took a different view from many past studies on accident proneness. Although Dahlback found support for the hypothesis, his view is not the conventional view of the phenomenon.

From the standpoint of safety, Dahlback's findings show a reason for optimism. Risk taking can be influenced through proper motivational techniques. Thus, an "accident-prone" worker need not be regarded as someone who will eventually be involved in an accident. He or she must be trained in making the proper choices. Workers who regard it as "macho" to take risks cannot be tolerated on construction sites. Unsafe behavior jeopardizes not only their own safety, but also the safety of other workers. Denning (1983) found that industrial workers who attended a safety clinic had fewer accidents than those who did not attend such clinics.

Many research studies have examined accident proneness by investigating personality traits. One personality trait that has been examined is the extent of control that individuals believe they have over their involvement in accidents. It has been found that those who believe they have control over the events taking place in their places of work sustain fewer injuries than those who believe they have little control (Suchman 1965; Hoyt 1973; Dalhauser 1982). Studies have shown that persons who are extroverted have more accidents than those who are introverted (Fine 1963; Smith and Kirkham 1981). Still other studies have found that persons who exhibit aggressive attitudes are involved in more accidents (Schenk and Rausche 1979). Social maladjustment has also been correlated with a greater frequency of accidents (Hansen 1986; Wellman 1982). Social maladjustment includes such traits as resentfulness, hostility, antisocial behavior, and belligerence.

Although some people are involved in more accidents than others, there has been no substantiation of the accident-proneness theory. Although the subject has been researched extensively, little evidence exists to conclusively validate the theory. For such research to be effective, some adjustments must be made for differences in exposure to hazards. Careful examination must also be made of the actions leading to an accident. The employment of an unsafe practice instead of a safe one might explain some accidents. A distinction should also be made between accidents in which the injured worker is at fault and those in which a fellow worker is at fault.

The Goals-Freedom-Alertness Theory

One theory that has been described to explain accident causation is the goals-freedom-alertness theory, which was first suggested by Kerr (1950, 1957). The goals-freedom-alertness theory states that safe work performance is the result of a psychologically rewarding work environment. Under the goals-freedom-alertness theory, accidents are viewed as low-quality work behavior occurring in an unrewarding psychological climate, which does not contribute to a high level of alertness. He believed that "great freedom to set reasonable attainable goals is accompanied typically by high quality work performance." He claimed that a climate "richer" in diverse economic and noneconomic opportunities will be associated with the achievement of a higher level of alertness. That alertness will result in high-quality work and accident-free behavior.

The essence of the theory is that management should let a worker have a well-defined goal and should give the worker the freedom to pursue that goal. The result will be that the worker focuses on the task that leads to that goal. The worker's attentiveness to the job will reduce the probability of being involved in an injury. In other words, a worker who knows what to do on a job will be well focused on the task to be performed and therefore will be safe. Thus the goals-freedom-alertness theory dwells on the positive aspects of safety.

According to Kerr's theory, a rewarding psychological climate is one in which workers are encouraged to participate in setting attainable goals and choosing methods to attain these goals. They must have opportunities to participate in raising problems and solving them. Kerr stated that such participation would lead to alertness habits that would in turn promote high-quality production, safe behavior, and fewer accidents.

Kerr felt that there was considerable evidence to support the theory; however, the substantiation of that evidence as solid support for the theory is debated.

Haddon, Suchman, and Klein (1964) believed that most of the sources cited as supporting the theory contributed only circumstantial evidence. Hitchcock and Sanders (1974) criticized the methodology and the conclusions that Kerr tried to substantiate. In all, few studies have actually tried to test the theory.

In one study, Kerr (1950) concluded that more injuries in one firm occurred in the departments with the lowest intercompany transfer rates and those with the lowest promotion potential. He concluded that workers with little chance of transfer or promotion would develop attitudes of relative indifference to their work environment. That indifference would lead to lowered alertness and more accidents. He did not disclose if the more hazardous jobs were in those departments with lower intercompany transfer mobility or lower promotion potentials.

According to the goals-freedom-alertness theory, managers and supervisors should be trained to make the work more rewarding for workers. They might do so through various managerial techniques, including participative management, clear work assignments, positive reinforcement, and goal setting.

The Adjustment-Stress Theory

Kerr postulated a second theory to explain accident causation: the adjustment-stress theory. The adjustment-stress theory states that safe performance is compromised by a climate that diverts the attention of workers. Kerr believed that the goals-freedom-alertness theory explained much about accident causation not covered by the accident-proneness theory but that additional unexplained variance still existed. The adjustment-stress theory was developed to explain the remaining variance, that is, to complement the goals-freedom-alertness theory. Whereas the goals-freedom-alertness theory states that workers will be safe in a fulfilling or positive work environment, the adjustment-stress theory sets forth the conditions under which a worker will not be safe.

The adjustment-stress theory contends that "unusual, negative, distracting stress" placed on workers increases their "liability to accident or other low quality behavior" (Kerr 1957). As does the goals-freedom-alertness theory, this theory emphasizes the nature of the work climate as a major factor in accident occurrence. Kerr referred to the theory as a climate theory. The climate, or environmental conditions, can be assumed to be either internal or external. According to the theory, any complications or negative stresses imposed on an individual either by the internal environment (fatigue, alcohol consumption, loss of sleep, drugs, disease, or such psychological stresses as worry, personal problems, or anxiety) or by the external environment (noise, illumination, temperature, or excessive physical strain) will increase accident occurrence. If the worker cannot adjust to the stress, the chance of injury is increased. In other words, stress diverts a worker's attention during work hours and that diversion increases the susceptibility to injury.

This theory states that negative factors in the worker's environment create diversions of attention and that the lack of attention can be very detrimental to safety. Examples may be offered in other work environments in which preoccupation with non-work-related matters makes individuals more susceptible to being injured. For example, it is generally accepted that it is not safe to read a road map while driving a car. Also, a driver may be very safe when going to a casual event when there is time to spare, but that same driver may be considerably less safe if he or she is already very late for an important meeting. Various types of mental diversions occur in our everyday lives that decrease our attention and focus on a particular activity; for construction workers, the same types of diversions exist. The mental diversions are the result of stresses that preoccupy the minds of the workers and increase their probability of being injured.

According to the adjustment-stress theory, the factors that divert attention and increase the probability of an accident may be brought to the job, or they may be generated on the job. The mental diversions created or generated on the job are of primary importance to managers, as it is the practices and policies of managers that are often the source of such on-the-site job stress. Such stress may arise from unrealistic demands placed on workers. Two common sources of such mental diversions include pressure to keep costs below some level that may not be realistic and pressure to meet an unrealistically tight deadline. Note that many of the sources of stress are directly attributable to management in many cases. Consequently, they are the easiest for management to minimize and control. Any pressures related to threats to job security are potential catalysts for injuries. A stressful situation can arise between a worker and a supervisor who have incompatible personalities or between one worker and another worker who abuses him or her. Stress is imposed when workers are asked to work in an obviously unsafe environment.

It must be recognized that much of the stress on workers may be brought to the job. The family can be a source of such stresses as divorce, the death of a loved one, the illness of a child, and financial problems. Personal sources of stress include substance abuse, bodily pain, fatigue, and lack of sleep. When such stresses are brought to the job, they may affect the worker's ability to remain safe in the workplace. Although management may not be able to detect the nature of such stresses, supervisors should be sensitive to their workers and should be able to tell when a worker appears to be particularly distraught.

The adjustment-stress theory is not to be confused with the accident-proneness theory. Note that the accident-proneness theory postulates that there is an inherent inadequacy in the individual, whereas the adjustment-stress theory assumes that the increased probability of an accident is due to temporary conditions that influence a worker.

Kerr, who developed the goals-freedom-alertness theory and the adjustment-stress theory concluded that they were complementary theories. He felt that, along with the accident-proneness theory, they could explain virtually all variance in accident rates. Although no empirical research study has examined the relative merits of the three theories, Kerr postulated that the importance of the theories in explaining accidents was approximately as shown in Figure 1.1.

From the pie chart it is evident that Kerr felt that the adjustment-stress theory was the best single model for explaining accident occurrence. Of course, it cannot go unnoticed that the adjustment-stress theory and the goals-freedom-alertness theory are actually related. The adjustment-stress theory says that accidents occur when negative influences exist in the job environment, and the goals-freedom-alertness theory states that safety performance is best when the job environment is of a positive nature.

Figure 1.1
Kerr's Estimates of the Relative
Merits of Different Accident
Theories in Explaining Accident
Occurrence

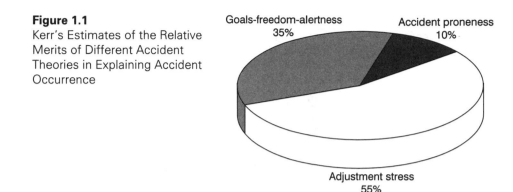

Goals-freedom-alertness
35%

Accident proneness
10%

Adjustment stress
55%

The Distractions Theory

The distractions theory states that safety is situational. Because mental distractions are varied in nature, the responses to those distractions may have to differ for safe performance to result. Hazards may exist in many forms. Normally, hazards are thought of as physical conditions with inherent qualities that can cause harm to a person. Such hazards may be those that the person recognizes as dangerous. The distractions theory is an accident-causation theory that can be applied to situations in which a worker undertakes a particular work task in an environment in which recognized hazards exist. I developed the distractions theory to apply to a situation in which the following two factors exist: (1) a recognized safety hazard or a mental distraction and (2) a well-defined work task.

It can generally be assumed that workers want to succeed in accomplishing their assigned tasks. In the absence of hazards, there is often little to prevent workers from completing their assignments. The presence of hazards, however, greatly complicates tasks and frustrates workers in the completion of their assignments.

From Figure 1.2 it can be observed that a worker has a greater probability of achieving a particular task if the distractions from a known hazard are minimal. It must be stressed that this theory specifically focuses on task accomplishment in the absence of an injury-causing incident; work task achievement will stop once an injury occurs. Note that, according to these constraints, the worker has the greatest probability of accomplishing a given task when the worker's focus on the distractions is minimal. Conversely, the probability of task achievement is minimal when there is a high level of focus on the distractions posed by the hazards.

On initial observation of Figure 1.2, it may appear that productivity (high task achievement) and safety (low probability of injury occurrence) are in direct conflict with each other. That may very well be the case when serious hazards exist in the workplace, but productivity and safety need not be in conflict. Distractions theory simply points out that productivity is compromised when the distraction due to hazards is high. Naturally, when the hazard level is high, it is understandable and even preferable for the worker to have a high level of awareness of those hazards. The attention paid to the hazards, however, is a distraction. What should be done if productivity is to be improved? The answer lies, *not* in reducing the focus on the hazards, but in the

Figure 1.2
Distractions Theory Applied to a
Work Condition with Serious
Hazards

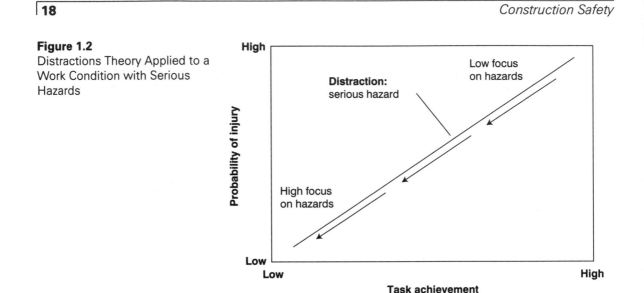

removal or reduction of those hazards. For example, if the work can be performed in an environment in which the work has fewer serious hazards, the distractions theory predicts that task achievement will be high even if the worker is focused on the hazards. (See Figure 1.3.) Since the hazards are no longer posing a serious threat to the worker, the distraction is not as intense, and consequently task achievement is not compromised to any great extent.

The information presented in Figures 1.2 and 1.3 shows that safety and productivity can be achieved simultaneously. However, that is possible only when the serious hazards have been removed from the work environment.

Figure 1.4 is perhaps a more realistic portrayal of a situation that might exist in the workplace. It shows several hazards existing in the workplace. Note that the slopes of

Figure 1.3
Distractions Theory Applied to a
Work Condition with Minor
Hazards

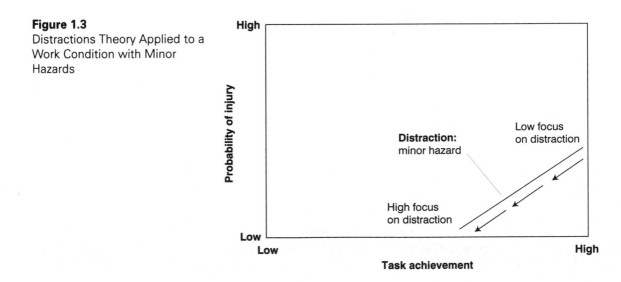

Figure 1.4
Distractions Theory Applied to a Work Condition with Numerous Hazards

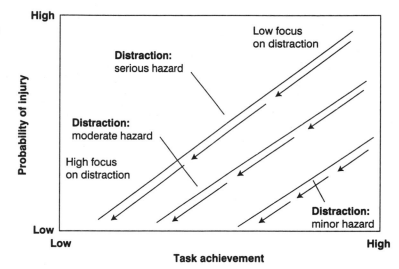

the lines associated with the hazards are indicative of the potential risks posed by the hazards. For example, the steepest line in Figure 1.4 might represent a missing guardrail (a serious hazard) on the 10th floor of a building where a worker is laying brick. The shallow line in the same figure might represent the hazard posed by working without gloves while laying the bricks (a minor hazard). Naturally, the missing guardrail poses the threat of a fall that could be fatal, whereas working without gloves poses the threat of an abrasion or some other type of skin problem. From a safety perspective, the greatest hazard should receive the most attention, and its elimination should be of greater importance.

Figure 1.5 shows how the distractions theory can be applied to an actual job situation. In this example, a painter is to paint a soffit on a one-story building. The painter is

Figure 1.5
Distractions Theory Applied to the Choice of a Support for Painting Soffits

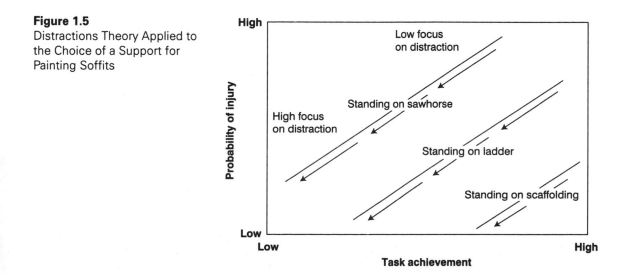

not tall enough to reach the soffit without some means of elevated support. Three means of support are under consideration: a sawhorse, a ladder, and scaffolding. Each of the means of support will enable the painter to reach the soffit; however, the safety of the three options varies quite a bit. From the figure it is apparent that the sawhorse presents the greatest risk. Note also that the job will probably not be done as efficiently with the sawhorse as it would with some form of scaffolding. Although it is important to remain focused on hazards in the workplace, it is even more important to utilize those work techniques that have the fewest inherent hazards.

As stated at the beginning of the discussion of the distractions theory, hazards are typically defined or thought of as physical conditions with inherent qualities that can cause harm to a person. That is a narrow interpretation of hazards. Hazards can also exist if the worker is not in the proper frame of mind when work is being performed. Thus, the worker (more specifically, the mental state of the worker) might be considered the possible source of a hazard. The magnitude of that hazard is dependent on the nature of the mental distractions that preoccupy the worker's mind. The seriousness of any accident that might arise as a consequence of the mental distractions is dictated to a large degree by the nature of the work being performed.

Figure 1.6 is an illustration of the influence of mental distractions on two workers performing the same task. The figure shows that the workers have the same probability of accomplishing the task if they do not think about the events that could potentially occupy their minds and compromise their work. If both are distracted, the worker with the "heavier mental baggage" (in this case, the recent death of a parent) will be much less likely to succeed in the work assignment. Note that as the worker is distracted to a greater extent, the probability of being injured increases. That effect is different from what is shown in Figures 1.2, 1.3, and 1.4, where the chance of being injured decreases as the worker focuses on the distractions, which are the physical hazards.

In the situation illustrated in Figure 1.6, there is no conflict between safety and high productivity. In fact, both can be achieved at the same time. The mental distrac-

Figure 1.6
Distractions Theory Applied to a Work Condition with Serious Hazards

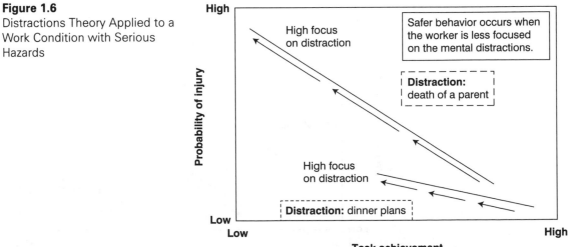

tions must be avoided both to achieve high levels of productivity and to perform safely. The mental distractions can be of various types, including financial worries, a dispute with a spouse, the illness of a child, an auto accident involving a loved one, competition at work, personality conflicts at work, and drug abuse.

The mental distractions posed by worries or even by positive events (such as anticipated parties, celebrations, and anniversaries) are detrimental to both productivity and safety. If a worker's distractions are of considerable magnitude, the worker might be referred to as an "accident waiting to happen." Workers with problems that occupy their minds may be difficult to detect or identify. If their problems are serious, their altered behavior may be readily identified. Such workers are best sent off the job site. If kept on site, they should be reassigned to tasks in which they will not pose a serious threat to themselves or other workers.

The distractions theory has essentially two components. One deals with hazards posed by unsafe physical conditions. The other deals with workers' preoccupation with issues not directly related to the task being performed (although the issues might be work related—e.g., a tight deadline or unduly close supervision).

Mental Stresses

The distractions described in the preceding section were noted as consisting of both positive and negative events. Two early psychological researchers of such events were Holmes and Rahe (1967), who examined the relationship between various life stresses and the onset of illness. Their work followed that of others who had provided evidence that stressful life events played a strong causative role in the onset of diseases. Those stressful events tended to be changes in the social structures of people's lives, including marriage, employment, education, and religion. Holmes and Rahe noted that stress was evoked by both positive and negative factors. Positive events included success, achievement, and an improvement in the quality of life. Holmes and Rahe developed a scale of stressful events in which they gave each type of event a value. The values of all the events that apply to a given person are added up. A higher score indicates a more stressful condition and a greater likelihood of contracting an illness. The scoring might be similarly applied to the distractions theory. Table 1.1 is a list of various potentially stressful events and the scores assigned to each.

The Chain-of-Events Theory

Accidents are occasionally characterized as occurrences that are the results of series of events. The events in a series are all linked in that each event is followed by yet another event. This portrayal of accident occurrence is referred to as the *chain of events*. The occurrence of all the events in the series, or chain, ultimately results in the accident. Furthermore, if any event in the chain had not occurred, the accident might have been averted.

The last event preceding many worker injuries is some action performed by the injured worker. Thus, it is common for many injuries to be blamed on worker behavior,

Table 1.1
Social Readjustment Rating
Scale of Holmes and Rahe

Life Event	Value
Death of spouse	100
Divorce	73
Marital separation	65
Jail term	63
Death of close family member	63
Personal injury or illness	53
Marriage	50
Fired at work	47
Marital reconciliation	45
Retirement	45
Change in health of family member	44
Pregnancy	40
Sex difficulties	39
Gain of new family member	39
Business readjustment	39
Change in financial state	38
Death of close friend	37
Change to different line of work	36
Change in number of arguments with spouse	35
Mortgage over $10,000	31
Foreclosure of mortgage or loan	30
Change in responsibilities at work	29
Son or daughter leaving home	29
Trouble with in-laws	29
Outstanding personal achievement	28
Spouse begins or stops work	26
Begin or end school	26
Change in living conditions	25
Revision of personal habits	24
Trouble with boss	23
Change in work hours or conditions	20
Change in residence	20
Change in schools	20
Change in recreation	19
Change in church activities	19
Change in social activities	18
Mortgage or loan less than $10,000	17
Change in sleeping habits	16
Change in number of family get-togethers	15
Change in eating habits	15
Vacation	13
Christmas	12
Minor violations of the law	11

if for no other reason than that the worker is often the last party involved in the chain of events. However, stopping the occurrence of any event in the chain will break the chain; that is, breaking any link will break the chain. If safety is to be promoted, it is important to consider the other events in the chain, not just the final action of the worker who becomes injured. To simply blame injured workers for many of their own injuries is to ignore the roles that other parties play in influencing worker behavior.

Every link in the chain is a vital component of accident causation, so every link is a potential target for accident prevention. The links may relate to physical working conditions, first-line supervisors, various levels of management, company policies, or other factors beyond the control of the injured worker. The parties associated with the various links in the chain have the opportunity to alter the course of events and thereby prevent accidents.

The chain-of-events theory is best used as a means of preventing accidents. It is not intended to be used to establish blame for accidents that occur. Nonetheless, that is occasionally the exact use made of the theory—for example, in tort liability suits. A party to a suit may try to establish that another party was in a position to act (break the chain) and had a duty to act to prevent the injury. A court may impose liability on a party if it finds that the party had a duty to act and failed to act.

Serious consideration of the events in the chain and their role in an accident can be helpful in accident prevention. Such consideration addresses factors other than simply the action or actions of the party that is ultimately injured. Focusing on the chain of events focuses attention on the physical working conditions that might contribute to the risk of an accident. Furthermore, other means of averting accidents can be identified, including worker training, supervisory instructions, project planning, corporate policies, and improved project designs.

The chain-of-events theory does not conflict with the distractions theory. In fact, the two theories can be used in concert to help explain accident occurrence.

Although the chain of events has been labeled a "theory," it may be more accurate to call it a conceptualization of the way accidents occur. In fact, the description of a chain of events encompasses all preventable causes of an accident. The chain of events does not focus on or identify any specific link in the chain that causes accidents. Nevertheless, it can be very helpful in understanding accidents and in devising means of accident prevention.

The following situation is an example of a chain of events leading to an accident: A worker was seriously injured when he fell off the third story of a building. He was not protected by a safety lanyard. Is this a simple matter of the worker's not wearing safety equipment, or can a chain-of-events analysis be applied? Further examination revealed that, because of an oversight by one of the field supervisors, rails had not been installed around the perimeter of the third floor to provide fall protection. Regarding the safety lanyard, it was discovered that the company had an ample supply of lanyards on the project but that a worker wishing to use one had to fill out a long requisition form to be issued one. Because of the paperwork, many workers simply did not feel it was worth the effort. Also, the workers inferred that the company did not want them to use the lanyards; otherwise, the company would have made the lanyards more readily available. The worker who was injured had been on the project for two weeks. He had not seen anyone use a lanyard in those two weeks, so he assumed that lanyards were not available.

It is easy to see how the chain-of-events theory can be applied to this injury. Although the injured worker may have been responsible for the last event before the injury, numerous other parties played a role. Events that could have broken the chain include the following: proper orientation of the worker regarding available safety equipment, easy access of workers to all safety equipment, stringent company policy on safety compliance, site safety inspections to identify hazards, and safety awareness training. Obviously, many issues can be identified that should be addressed by managers in the company.

The *healthy* use of the chain-of-events theory is for management to assume that it is *in a position to act to prevent virtually all accidents.* With that attitude, management will aggressively seek out areas in which improvements can be made.

Consider another example: A worker reported to the foreman that a small piece of a hammer had chipped off and had lodged in his eye. An investigation revealed that the worker had not worn his safety goggles. Were the goggles available? Had the wearing of goggles been stressed to the workers? Further investigation disclosed that the hammer was defective. The worker had known the hammer was defective, but he stated that it was too difficult to obtain a new hammer from the warehouse (papers to fill out, etc.). Are hand tools regularly checked for safety? Can defective hand tools be replaced with ease? The questions point to links in the chain. The most important links are those over which management has some degree of control or influence.

A study conducted at the Naval Surface Weapons Center in Silver Spring, Maryland, applied the concept of the chain of events. Although its report did not specifically utilize the term *chain of events*, the concept was the same. The study focused exclusively on management's role in injury accidents and was based on the premise that "all accidents and hazards are indicators of management failures" (Fine 1975). The hypothesis for the study was as follows: "In the investigation of any accident, there can always be found some degree of management involvement or activity that might in some way have prevented the accident. Therefore, it is arbitrarily assumed that management will be responsible for the causes of every accident, as well as for the existence of every hazard." With this underlying premise, accidents were investigated to seek the means that might have been available to management to change the course of events so as to avert the accident.

The Navy study included the investigation of accidents with seemingly clear-cut causes. Upon closer examination, managerial opportunities to avoid or minimize the hazards began to emerge. One case consisted of an incident in which a hammer with a defective handle was being used because the inventory of replacement hammer handles had been kept too low. Another case involved a back strain suffered by a worker who was carrying a heavy load up a flight of stairs (as was required several times daily) because a mechanical lift (costing about $2,000) had been considered too expensive. In yet another case, makeshift scaffolding was used because the cost of properly manufactured scaffolding (about $1,000) was considered prohibitive. A housekeeping violation was noted to be the result of management's failure to recognize that temporary storage space was not available for materials that should have been disposed of, resulting in waste materials' being left in an aisle (a tripping hazard).

When each accident or hazard had been carefully evaluated, virtually every investigation revealed a failure by management. Management was found to have failed in the following ways:

Failure to enforce procedures	Inadequate training
Inadequate facilities	Inadequate coordination
Failure to recognize hazard	Unclear operational procedures
Failure to motivate	Inadequate warnings
Poor design or selection	Inadequate supply
Poor maintenance	Lack of comprehension
Inadequate instructions	Low morale
Poor attitude	Inadequate supervisory proficiency
Inadequate planning and layout	Poor worker placement
Failure to enforce safety	

The failures, as can be seen, were quite varied. Once management recognized its failures, it was in a position to remedy them. The corrective actions included simple procedural changes, additional training, and changes in policies. Economically, the effect of the corrective measures proved to be positive. That is, the steps taken to improve safety at the facility yielded higher productivity. In the long term, implementing the safety suggestions resulted in overall reductions in the costs of the Navy operations.

Effective safety management begins with the premise that management can influence or affect at least one link in every chain of events leading to an accident. Management should view every accident as having been preceded by a chain of events. What is more, management does have control over some of the links in virtually every chain. If management takes such a posture, it will view essentially every accident as being preventable through management's efforts.

Consider the evolution of a project. Projects have their beginnings as dreams or ideas. If an idea for a project appears sufficiently realistic and practical, the potential owner of the project will consider the pros and cons of pursuing the project. If the project is one that is to be built, the owner typically obtains the services of an outside design firm. Once the design is well defined, the design firm assists the owner in selecting a general contractor. The general contractor, the firm with direct responsibility for the completion of the project, employs some workers directly, and the remainder of the work is performed by subcontractors. Before the project is eventually completed, many parties will have been involved in it. What presents unique problems is that often many of the parties involved have never worked together before. Thus, the working relationships of the various contracting parties are usually established specifically for a particular construction project.

Consider the typical general contractor's organizational structure on a project (illustrated in Figure 1.7). The parties shown include the project manager, the project superintendent, the general foreman, the foreman, and the worker. According to the chain-of-events theory, each of those parties could play a role in the causation of an accident in which a worker is injured, and conversely, each party could play a role in thwarting a series of events that would otherwise lead to an accident.

The chain-of-events theory suggests that each party in the organizational structure is in a position to perform some task that might eventually result in an injury to a worker. At the same time, each party is also in a position to initiate certain actions that might help to prevent injury to a worker. In fact, it might even be possible for one party to create a situation that might result in an injury and, at the same time, for another

Figure 1.7
Typical Project Organizational
Structure of a General Contractor

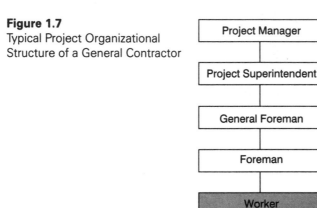

party to take the appropriate actions to reduce the possibility of an injury. Thus, concern should not focus purely on the causation of injuries by parties in the organizational structure, but should also focus on the prevention of injuries by those parties.

The project manager has overall control of a project. That is especially true of situations in which the project manager is regarded as the contractor's top representative on the project. The company's philosophy about how a project is to be undertaken is reflected in the actions of the project manager. The project superintendent has the specific objective of providing directions for the performance of the actual construction work. The general foreman, a position not found on some smaller projects, is typically more focused on work being carried out by a particular craft. The general foreman provides support for several foremen. The foremen are the first-line supervisors; they have direct and ongoing contact with the various workers they oversee. The workers are the parties most often injured on construction projects. To some extent workers may appear to be pawns who are being manipulated by the various levels of supervision. That would not be an accurate portrayal of workers, however, as they too bear a responsibility for their own actions. There are laws and regulations that clearly give workers the right to refuse to perform work if they determine that the conditions are unsafe. That issue will be explored in greater detail later. For now, suffice it to say that each party in the project organizational structure plays a role in worker safety.

Another organizational chart is presented in Figure 1.8. It is much broader in scope than the contractor's project organizational chart shown in the previous figure. It includes all the major parties in a project.

The focus of the organizational chart is initially on the owner, the party at the top of the chart. Does the owner control any of the players? The answer is a definite yes. More specifically, how can the owner play a role in the chain of events? The owner can set the tone on a project. The owner can begin by using past safety performance as a qualifying criterion when selecting the general contractor and when approving the general contractor's choices for subcontractors. There are various other ways that owners can be proactive in the area of safety that will enhance job safety. That is not to imply that the owner is responsible for everything that happens on the project, regardless of the actions of other parties involved. The chain-of-events theory suggests that the

Figure 1.8
Organizational Chart on a Construction Project

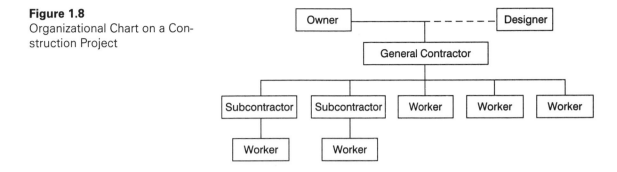

owner might implement certain programs that would directly influence worker safety. This topic will be discussed in greater detail in a later chapter.

Clearly, the designer, the general contractor, the subcontractors, and even the workers have some responsibility for safety. However, no party can take the view that safety is solely someone else's responsibility. Every party plays a role.

One cannot seriously address project safety without considering the general contractor. The general contractor ostensibly exerts control over the entire project. As such, the general contractor has considerable control over the subcontractors and the workers. What means or methods might the general contractor employ to control the subcontractors, particularly as pertains to safety?

If every party involved in a construction project recognized its power to alter or influence the chains of events that result in injuries, safety would surely improve. Every party should accept responsibility for worker safety. Saying that is quite different from stating that every party causes accidents or is liable for accidents that do occur. Note that the emphasis is on the prevention of accidents.

To summarize, the general contractor directs, or controls, the subcontractors. In a similar manner, the owner directs the general contractor. General contractors have a major influence on the safety performance of their subcontractors. Similarly, owners exert considerable influence on the safety performance of general contractors. Although to a lesser degree, every other party involved in the construction of a project may be one of the links in the chain of events that might lead to an injury.

Final Comments

There have been many attempts to explain the causes of worker accidents. Of the various theories that have been posited, there is general agreement that accidents do not just happen. The physical conditions in the workplace and the states of mind of the workers are invariably the primary factors under consideration. Managers and supervisors certainly have the ability to influence the physical conditions. They are also in a position to influence to some degree the mental state of each worker. The mental state of a worker may not be conducive to conducting work safely. Managers and especially supervisors should try to identify such situations and respond accordingly. It is also incumbent on managers and supervisors to recognize that their actions can exert an unfavorable influence on the mental states of workers. Workers do not want to be injured, so a cooperative spirit should exist with regard to safety.

Review Questions

1. Defend and criticize the past research that has attempted to test the validity of the accident-proneness theory.
2. Explain how the distractions theory can be used to point out management's role in accident prevention.
3. Describe the different theories of accident causation.
4. Which theory of accident causation gives the most consideration to the physical conditions at the place of work?
5. Compare the adjustment-stress theory with the distractions theory.
6. Does the chain-of-events theory place the blame for accidents on management?
7. How are the goals-freedom-alertness and adjustment-stress theories related?
8. Describe conditions under which the distractions theory would suggest that safety and productivity are in conflict. Conversely, describe conditions under which the distractions theory would suggest that safety and productivity are not in conflict but are simultaneously achievable.
9. Why is the chain of events considered a conceptualization of accident causation rather than a theory?
10. How does management play a role in the chain of events of accident causation? Give examples.

References

Dahlback, O. 1991. "Accident-Proneness and Risk-Taking." *Personality and Individual Differences* 12, no. 1: 79–85.

Dahlhauser, M. 1982. "Visual Disembedding and Locus of Control as Variables Associated with College Football Injuries." *Dissertation Abstracts International* 42:4985A.

Denning, D. 1983. "Correlates of Employee Safety Performance." Paper presented at the Southeastern I/O Psychology Association Meeting, Atlanta.

DeReamer, R. 1958. *Modern Safety Practice.* New York: John Wiley.

Farmer, E., and E. Chambers. 1929. *A Study of Personal Qualities in Accident Proneness and Proficiency.* London: His Majesty's Stationery Office.

Fine, B. 1963. "Introversion-Extroversion and Motor Vehicle Driver Behavior." *Perceptual and Motor Skills* 16:95–100.

Fine, W. 1975. *A Management Approach in Accident Prevention.* Technical Report 75-104 (July). Silver Spring, Md.: Naval Surface Weapons Center, White Oak.

Haddon, W., E. Suchman, and D. Klein. 1964. *Accident Research Methods and Approaches.* New York: Harper and Row.

Hansen, C. 1988. "Personality Characteristics of the Accident Involved Employee." *Journal of Business and Psychology* 2, no. 4:346–65.

Hitchcock, L., and M. Sanders. 1974. *A Comprehensive Analysis of Safety and Injuries at NAD Crane.* RDTR no. 279. Crane, Ind.: Naval Weapons Support Center.

Holmes, T., and R. Rahe. 1967. "The Social Readjustment Rating Scale." *Journal of Psychosomatic Research* 11, no. 2: 213–18.

Hoyt, M. 1973. "Internal-External Control and Beliefs about Automobile Travel." *Journal of Research in Personality* 7:288–93.

Kerr, W. 1950. "Accident Proneness of Factory Departments." *Journal of Applied Psychology* 34:167–70.

Kerr, W. 1957. "Complementary Theories of Safety Psychology." *Journal of Social Psychology* 43:3–9.

McKenna, F. 1983. "Accident Proneness: A Conceptual Analysis." *Accident Analysis & Prevention* 15:65–71.

Schenk, J., and A. Rausche. 1979. "The Personality of Accident-Prone Drivers." *Psychologie und Praxis* 23:179–86.

Schulzinger, M. 1956. *Accident Syndrome.* Springfield, Ill.: C. C. Thomas.

Shaw, L., and H. Sichel. 1971. *Accident Proneness.* Oxford: Pergamon Press.

Smith, D., and R. Kirkham. 1981. "Relationship between Some Personality Characteristics and Driving Record." *British Journal of Social Psychology* 20:229–31.

Suchman, E. 1965. "Cultural and Social Factors in Accident Occurences and Control." *Journal of Occupational Medicine* 7:487–92.

Vernon, H. 1918. "An Investigation of the Factors Concerned with the Causation of Industrial Accidents." Health and Munitions Workers Committee, Memo no. 21.

Wellman, R. 1982. "Accident Proneness in Police Officers: Personality Factors and Problem Drinking As Predictors of Injury Claims of State Troopers." *Dissertation Abstracts International* 43:538B.

When Do Injuries Occur?

Accidents are no accident.

Although injuries may be regarded as random occurrences, a statistical review of injuries suggests that they are not always random. Injuries may be more likely to occur during certain hours of the day or on certain days of the week. To a large extent, the timing of injuries can often be explained by the work activities taking place on a project or the mental disposition of workers at differing times of the day or week. There are no hard and fast rules that tell when most injuries will occur on a particular project; however, some generalizations about the industry can be made. Those generalizations are supported by data accumulated by the Department of Labor and Industries of the State of Washington over a period of five years. Although that information related to the work force in a single state, it has been compared with information reported by other states, and the generalizations made from it are quite valid.

Hour of the Day

It is most common for construction work to be performed during regular daytime hours. Labor agreements often stipulate that the workday will start at 8:00 A.M. If there is an eight-hour workday with one-half hour for lunch, the workday typically ends at about 4:30 P.M. Most construction projects have similar hours.

The timing of injuries in the workday can often be explained by the levels of work activity taking place at different times. To more fully understand the connection, examine the normal sequence of events during a day on a typical construction project. The workday begins at 8:00 A.M. During the first 15–30 minutes, most of the effort is focused on requisitioning tools and materials, organizing the work area, and planning the activities to be performed. As those preparations proceed, the pace of work begins to pick up. After a while, all the workers on the project have been assigned to specific tasks, and supervision becomes focused on maintaining the work pace. That pace of work prevails for some time (possibly attaining a peak about 10:00 A.M.), and then at about 11:30 A.M., the pace of work begins to slow down markedly as workers prepare for the lunch break. Tasks that cannot be completed before lunch may be deferred until after lunch. Workers may put away some of the tools and may clean up the work area. By noon, the workers are ready to cease all work efforts.

After the lunch break, workers regroup at their respective work areas. Although the preparations for work are not as involved as they were when the workday started, the work does not return to the peak morning pace until some time has passed. On some types of work, particularly physically demanding work, the work pace may not return to the peak level attained during the morning. The work pace attains an acceptable level of productivity after a period of about a half hour. The pace may remain at that level for the rest of the afternoon. On some projects the work pace may reach a peak level about 2:00 P.M. About a half hour before quitting time, however, the project effort begins to change. Efforts are expended on cleaning up the work areas, securing the work in place, organizing the materials, and returning tools and equipment to storage areas.

In the sequence of work just outlined, it is evident that the least productive periods are those immediately after the beginning of the workday, just before lunch, just after lunch, and just before quitting time. To a lesser degree, similar reductions in work effort occur in the periods preceding and following any organized morning or afternoon breaks.

It is most common for accidents to occur during the most intense work periods, namely, at midmorning and in the early afternoon. At those times, when workers are most intent on accomplishing their tasks, accidents are more likely to occur and workers more likely to be injured. This pattern of accident occurrence is depicted in Figure 2.1, which is based on construction worker injury data collected by the Department of Labor and Industries of the State of Washington. Since the data cover a five-year period, they have considerable credibility. The information depicted was provided to me by the Data Integrity Unit of the state Workers' Compensation Division. I assembled the data and formatted the information to develop the figures.

The pattern of distribution of injuries in the workday, as depicted in Figure 2.1, includes two distinct peak hours during which a greater number of injuries occur. The morning peak, the larger one, occurs between 10:00 and 11:00 A.M., and the afternoon peak occurs between 2:00 and 3:00 P.M. The number of injuries reported between 2:00 and 3:00 P.M. was only slightly above the number occurring between 11:00 A.M. and noon. In general, the data indicate that a greater number of injuries occur during the morning hours than during the afternoon hours. Those data suggest that fatigue is not an overriding factor in injury occurrence, as workers are generally more fatigued in the afternoon.

The same general pattern of injury occurrence can be observed for each of the five years included in the data. Thus, the pattern does not appear to change appreciably

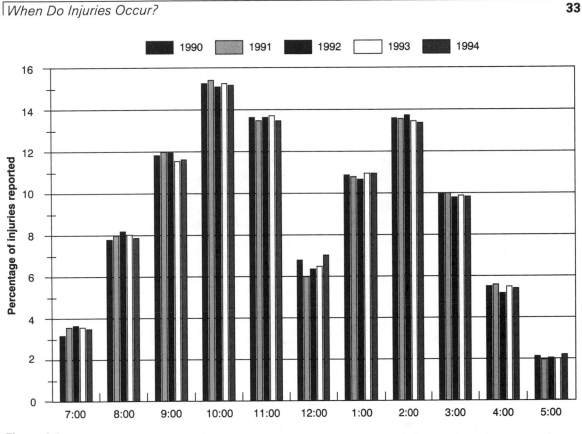

Figure 2.1
The Distribution of Injuries by Hour of the Day

from year to year. Although the data reflect the occurrence of construction injuries only in the state of Washington, this general pattern of injury occurrence during the workday is consistent with the distribution-of-injury data in other states.

When peak levels of productivity are attained, it is important for safety that all the work be carefully planned.

Day of the Week

Because injuries are not distributed evenly throughout the day, it is reasonable to expect injuries not to be distributed evenly throughout the week. Just as the general pattern of work activity changes during the workday, so, too, the general pattern of work activity changes during the week. To some extent, the change in the pace of work that is realized during a morning or during an afternoon is realized on a larger scale during the workweek. On most construction projects, work is performed during the regular workweek, Monday through Friday. Monday is the day on which the work for the week is planned. The pace of work builds on the following days, with peak production typically occurring on Wednesday or Thursday. Friday is the day on which the work for the week is finished.

If work activity is assumed to be the driving factor in injury occurrence, one may reasonably expect the greatest number of injuries to occur on Wednesday, commonly called "hump day." A review of injury distribution by day of the week fails to bear out that expectation. (See Figure 2.2.)

More injuries tend to occur on Mondays than on other days. The total number of injuries then follows a steady decline through Friday. The explanation generally offered for the peak occurrence of injuries on Monday is that workers must make the greatest mental transition, from the weekend to the workweek, on Monday. That is, workers are mentally the least ready for the workday on Monday. It is that rationale which often prompts supervisors to plan safety meetings for Monday mornings. Despite the general injury statistics that suggest that more injuries occur on Mondays, it is wise to evaluate specific project conditions to determine whether Monday is in fact the day on which more accidents occur.

The data presented in Figure 2.3 show that the hour of the day during which the most injuries occur may also vary during the week. That is particularly true of the three hours that are worked on Monday morning. On Monday mornings the number of

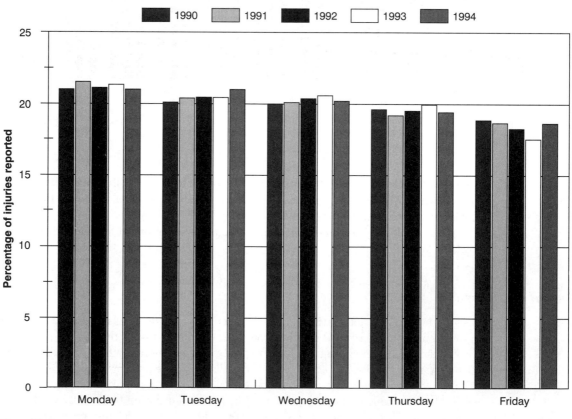

Figure 2.2
The Distribution of Injuries by Day of the Week

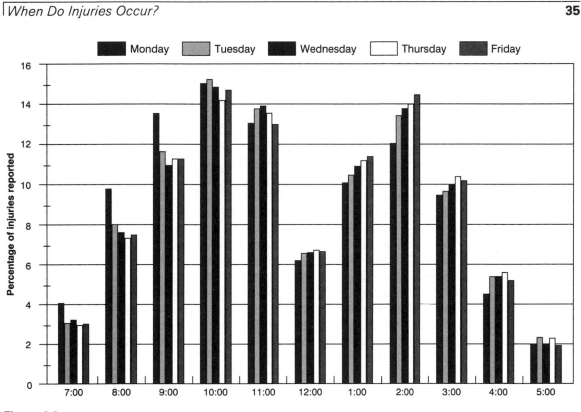

Figure 2.3
The Distribution of Injuries By Hour and Day of the Week

injuries is particularly elevated in comparison with the other days. In fact, if only the afternoon hours are considered, the occurrence of injuries tends to increase progressively toward the end of the week. The high incidence of injuries on Monday mornings lends support to the idea that workers are not fully prepared for the workweek just after the weekend.

There has been speculation that some workers may get injured over the weekend, show up on Monday morning to report for work, and then shortly thereafter claim that they were injured while working. A work-related injury would be covered by workers' compensation insurance. Although such practices are fraudulent, some workers may feel that they do not have the financial resources to pay for injuries they incur at home. Some insurance companies aggressively fight claimants when evidence suggests the claims are fraudulent.

On large construction projects, particularly those involving the placing of large quantities of concrete, the work is frequently scheduled around a weekly cycle. On such projects, it is common for large concrete placements to be scheduled for the same day each week. For example, Mondays may consist of work being laid out for the week. On Tuesdays, the primary effort is devoted to setting forms. On Wednesdays, the work on the forms will be completed, and the reinforcing steel will be installed. The day might end with the plumbing and securing of the forms. On Thursdays, the workday begins with checking the forms (making sure they are properly oiled and all inserts have been installed). The major effort will be devoted to the placing of concrete. Depending on the nature of the project, the forms may be stripped and cleaned on Fridays. The type of project and the type of concrete elements being constructed (walls, beams, columns, elevated slabs, etc.) will dictate to a large degree the amount of time required for concrete curing before the concrete forms can be stripped or removed.

If the work is planned and performed on a weekly cycle, it seems logical for the occurrence of injuries to be related to that work cycle. If the concrete work is most intense on Thursday, one may expect that to be the day on which more injuries occur. Thus, injury frequency may be related more to work intensity on a given day rather than to the Monday transition from the weekend to the workweek.

On some projects the frequency of injuries has been noted to relate to still other factors. For example, on some projects injury rates are highest on the workday that immediately follows the day on which wages are paid. Many workers celebrate payday until late at night and are not fully functioning when the next workday begins. One project consisted of wood-frame construction of several small buildings. Most of the framing work was performed by college students who were hired for the summer. Many injuries were recorded on that project. A review of the injury records showed that the day with the most injuries was Thursday. It was a local custom among the college students to "party" on Wednesday nights. The custom took its toll on Thursdays.

Rather than relying on general statistics about when in the workweek injuries tend to occur, firms would be well advised to evaluate the actual timing of injuries on their own projects. If any noticeable patterns are observed, a strategy can then be developed to help reduce the occurrence of injuries.

Season of the Year

Injuries may also be related to the time of year when work is performed. That is particularly true of work performed in the elements. The weather extremes of primary concern tend to be those of temperature—extremely cold temperatures or extremely hot temperatures. In regions where flash flooding is a possibility, rainfall is also a major concern.

Cold weather does affect the ability to perform certain tasks, particularly those that require considerable dexterity. Of particular concern with regard to safety is cold weather accompanied by precipitation, which can make walking treacherous. Ice and snow on construction sites are the causes of numerous falls and serious injuries.

Most outside work is planned to take place during the spring and summer months. They tend to be the drier months, times when the greatest productivity can generally be realized. When the summer temperatures are extreme, however, the safety and health of construction workers can be seriously jeopardized. Heat exhaustion and dehydration are real dangers, and care must be exercised to minimize any of those ill effects. It is important that workers have ample drinking water available and that proper safeguards be utilized to avoid excessive exposure to the sun. Proper headgear, shirts, and long pants should be worn at all times.

The distribution of injuries during the year is presented in Figure 2.4. Injury occurrence is lowest during the months of December and February and highest during the summer months, peaking in August. The February low can best be explained by

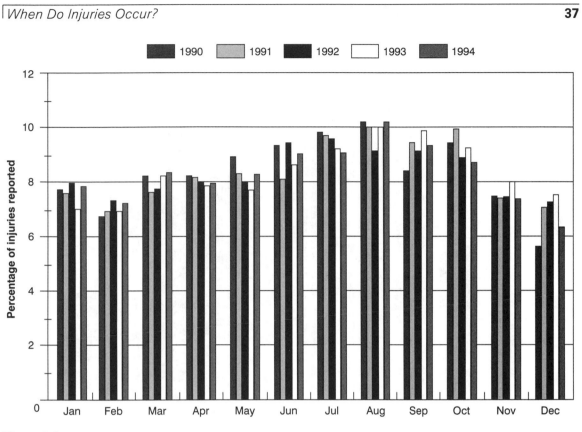

Figure 2.4
The Distribution of Injuries by Month of the Year

slower work activity, due to the cold weather. The December low can best be explained by a reduced number of workdays, due to the extended holiday season. The elevated number of injuries during the summer closely parallels the increased amount of construction work performed then.

Figure 2.5 shows the distribution of injuries by hour of the day during the different construction seasons. There is a slight increase in injuries between 7 and 8 A.M. during July and August when compared with other months, but it is probabaly attributable to earlier starting times during the summer months. In general, no noticeable pattern seems to distinguish one season from the next with respect to hours of injury occurrence.

The Effect of Shift Work

When the managers of a company use or contemplate using shift work on a project, it is important for them to understand how circadian rhythms function in the human body. Natural biological clocks function in each of us, whether on some hourly interval, an annual cycle (circannual rhythm), or a 24-hour cycle (circadian rhythm). The rhythms corresponding to the daily cycle (24 hours) are the most common. They regulate various functions in our bodies throughout our lives. In many organisms, the 24-hour cycle per-

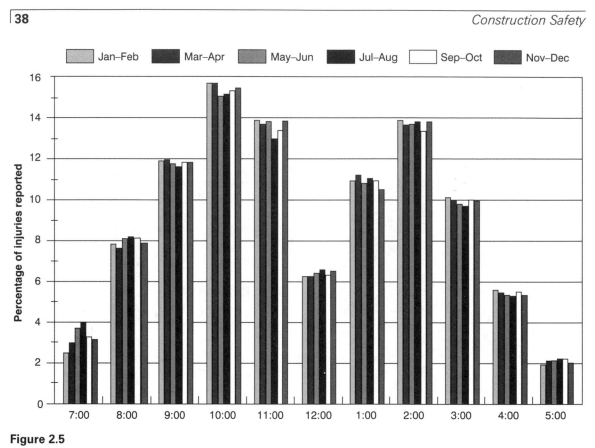

Figure 2.5
The Distribution of Injuries By Hour and Time of the Year

sists even in the absence of any day (light) and night (dark) clues. When the rhythms are maintained without such clues, they are said to be generated by the internal clock. Such internal rhythms have been observed in plants and animals placed in laboratory environments, but have not been observed in humans. It is more typical for circadian rhythms in humans to be synchronized to an external stimulus, namely, the day-and-night cycle.

The 24-hour light-dark cycle is said to entrain, or synchronize, the internal biological clock to 24 hours. That entrainment causes the internal clock to regulate, systematically and predictably, certain functions in our bodies. As long as the external stimuli are maintained, the biological clock performs in an orderly fashion. During the circadian cycle, body temperature fluctuates predictably within a small range.

The circadian rhythm is synchronized with the 24-hour day, in which the body expects to eat at given times and to sleep at given times each day. Changing the external environment will upset the cycle. For example, when people travel by jet across time zones, particularly across several time zones, it is common for them to experience "jet lag." That phenomenon occurs because the body expects to eat and sleep according to the established circadian cycle while external influences are trying to entrain the body to the conditions of the new time zone. Although a traveler who crosses only 1 time zone may sense no effect, a traveler crossing 8 or 10 time zones must make quite an adjustment, one that will take several days to complete. Most travelers also find that westward travel across time zones is easier on the body than eastward travel across the same time zones. Apparently, the body can adjust or entrain more readily when the body time is shifted to an earlier time rather than to a later time.

Although most construction work does not adversely affect the circadian rhythms of workers, shift work can. If a worker has been working a regular day shift and is suddenly asked to work a night shift, that worker's circadian rhythm will be affected. The body wants to stay entrained to the day-and-night cycle, which directs the body to sleep at night. The adjustment of the worker's circadian rhythm to the night-work routine will take some time. Eventually, after several weeks, the worker's body will adjust to working nights and sleeping during the day. If the new routine is maintained, the biological clock will become adjusted to it.

For many night workers, the circadian rhythm is adversely affected on a regular basis. That occurs on weekends, when a worker attempts to conform to the "normal" routine of other family members, who sleep at night and are more active during the day. Some day napping on weekends is important to help maintain the cycle entrainment.

Managers should not schedule shift work without understanding the effect that it may have on the circadian rhythms of the workers. Workers can adjust to shift work, but the adjustment generally takes some time. Shift work can be particularly devastating to workers when the shifts are constantly rotated. The circadian rhythm never fully adjusts when the routine keeps changing from working days, to working evenings (swing shift), to working nights (graveyard shift), and so on.

In some work settings, shift work is inevitable. It is often inevitable under "turn-around" contracts, in which contractors are asked to move quickly into an operating facility and make necessary construction modifications with minimal shutdown time. Such contracts are common in some process plants. The cost of shutting down a process is often so high that shift work is deemed imperative. Projects on which completion dates cannot be met without an acceleration of the work may also be planned with shift work. Shift work may pose the only viable means of undertaking a project, but its adverse effects must not be ignored.

From the standpoint of safety, shift work may introduce new considerations. Since entrainment does require some time, it is prudent to stress safety during the first few days of shift work or after a shift change. Shift work may be more stressful when the work is performed under artificial lighting. That stress is magnified by the pressure imposed by the circadian rhythm to remain entrained on the day-and-night cycle. Extra precautions are warranted.

The Effect of Lunar Cycles

Research has shown that lunar cycles do not have a significant influence on worker injury rates. Initially, it may seem absurd to even suggest that injury occurrence might be associated with the cycles of the moon. An examination of various occurrences in nature that are linked to the lunar cycles demonstrates that the comparison of lunar cycles and injury occurrence is quite rational. A quick review of some of those phenomena may help to clarify the point.

A number of events in nature occur predictably during specific lunar phases. Perhaps the most well known is the variation in the tides. It is commonly accepted that the highest tides occur immediately after the full moon and the lowest tides occur shortly after the new moon (Schuessler 1951). Another phenomenon is that the transmission of radio broadcasts is affected by "atmospheric tides," which are influenced by the position of the moon. Some living creatures also exhibit behaviors that coincide with the lunar cycles. Certain oysters are known to open their shells when the moon is in specific phases. It is during the waning period of the moon that eels begin their migration from European rivers to spawning grounds in the Sargasso Sea. Fishermen have reported that the largest herring catches occur during the full moon. It has also been observed that certain tropical worms emerge from their coral habitat twice a year on precisely the first day, in both October and November, that the moon enters the last quarter of its phase (Cottrell 1969). The reproductive cycles of certain marine animals are also linked to the lunar phases. Note that the events described in this paragraph take place whether the moon is visible or is completely hidden by cloud cover.

Although the effect of the lunar cycle on many natural events and on the behavior of many creatures is well established, the alleged link between other events and lunar cycles has not been scientifically documented. Many of those events are from folklore. For example, in Central America it is believed that mahogany trees should be cut during the full moon or they will become infested with termites (Middleton 1978). Many farmers, even in the United States, believe that root crops should be planted during a full or waning moon and that flower and vegetable crops (those bearing above the ground) should be planted between the new moon and the full moon. Some women in Greenland believe that they will become pregnant if they sleep in moonlight. Other people contend that the moon determines the sex of unborn babies. In some primitive societies, weddings are conducted in moonlight for fertility (Cottrell 1969). Such beliefs are quite numerous. The source of the beliefs is not fully understood; however, the beliefs do attest to the widespread acceptance of the influence the moon has on our lives.

Some argue that the lunar phases influence the way some people behave. Personnel at health facilities often report that patients act differently during the full moon. Dade County, Florida, documented lower numbers of psychiatric emergency room admissions during the new and full moons, periods during which more homicides occurred (Lieber 1978). Cuyahoga County, Ohio, reported similar observations. Patna Medical College Hospital in India observed more poisonings on full-moon days (Thakur 1980). The Phoenix fire department reported a higher number of calls on full-moon nights than during any other phase of the moon (Middleton 1978). More violent crimes have been noted to occur during the waxing of the moon (Snoyman and Holdstock 1980).

Although some studies have shown a clear link between lunar positions and individual behavior, some researchers have failed to find that association. In one study moods did appear to change with the changing phases of the moon, but the causal relationship was never confirmed. Another study failed to show any significant relationship between the phase of the lunar cycle and the number of people seeking emergency psychiatric help (Cottrell 1969).

It has been suggested that the lunar influence may be akin to tides of the mind, which may cause individuals to act differently at different times during the lunar cycle.

That premise is based on the fact that the human body is more than 50% water (Hartley and Hartley 1972).

The influence of the moon on worker injury occurrence was examined in a study of all job-related injuries in Missouri that were reported to the Missouri Division of Worker's Compensation in 1980 and 1981 (Hinze and Roxo 1984). A total of more than 200,000 worker injuries were reported in the two-year period. The study included all worker injuries, not just those in construction work. The data were examined to determine if the frequency of injuries fluctuated in any predictable fashion with the different phases of the moon. Only regular workdays were considered. That is, Saturdays, Sundays, holidays, and the Christmas holiday season were excluded from the study.

The results of the study failed to show that more or fewer injuries occur when the moon is full or new. In fact, the occurrence of injuries relative to the lunar cycle appeared to be completely random. (See Figure 2.6.) The frequency of injuries did not appear to be unusually high or unusually low on any particular day in the lunar cycle.

Author's note on the lunar cycle study: One might ask why research was conducted to examine injury occurrence in relation to the lunar cycles. In retrospect, it does seem a bit silly. However, construction contractors planted the seed that grew into the idea for the study. Twice, after I had spoken to a group of contractors about safety, some of the contractors asked me whether any research had been done on injury occurrence

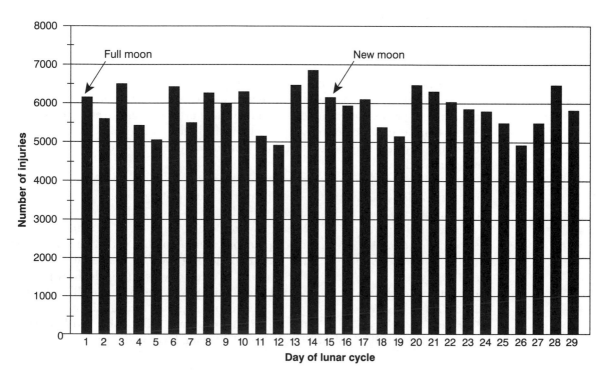

Figure 2.6
The Distribution of Injuries during the Lunar Cycle

and lunar cycles. Since contractors had suggested the study, I felt compelled to find an answer. I was pleased to discover no relationship. One can readily imagine the frustrations for managers who had to address safety issues raised by phases of the moon.

The Effect of Biorhythm Cycles on Safety Performance

With regard to accident occurrence, the issue of biorhythms may seem as strange a topic to consider as that of lunar cycles. The literature linking the positions of biorhythm cycles with various events is fairly extensive, however, and thus warrants some discussion of biorhythms.

Interest in biorhythm cycles seemed to peak in the 1970s and 1980s. There are three basic biorhythm cycles (Bolch 1977; Kagan 1974; Mackenzie 1973; O'Neil and Phillips 1975; Parlee 1978). Those cycles have several characteristics in common. All three cycles begin at the same point in time, precisely at the moment of birth. Each cycle has a sinusoidal shape, and the key difference among the cycles is the period of time required to complete a full cycle. The first cycle, which is called the physical cycle, is completed every 23 days. The second cycle, the emotional cycle, is completed in 28 days. The third cycle, the intellectual cycle, is completed in 33 days.

Since the cycles are sinusoidal in form, each cycle has a positive component and a negative component. Although the negative portions of the cycles appear less desirable, the times that are of particular concern are the points where a cycle crosses from positive to negative or from negative to positive. Those points are known as *critical days,* as they are days when the person is going through a rapid transition. According to the theory, an accident is more likely to occur on a critical day.

A variety of other scenarios associated with biorhythm cycles might make someone more accident-prone. For example, if the intellectual cycle is negative and the physical and emotional cycles are positive, a person may feel quite athletic and optimistic, but intellectual alertness may be lacking. Such a condition might make one more prone to having an accident.

It is a simple procedure to determine a person's position on the biorhythm cycles for any given day. The computation can be made by calculating the age of the person in days. For the emotional cycle, that age is divided by 28 days. If the computed number is an integer, the person is on a critical day in the emotional cycle, as a full cycle has been completed on that day. If the computation yields a number with a remainder, the remainder represents the number of days into the next cycle. If the remainder in the emotional cycle is 14 days, that also represents a critical day, as it is the halfway point in the emotional cycle, where the cycle changes from positive to negative (Blount 1978; Kagan 1974; Lutus 1977). The computations can be simplified through the use of calculators, commercially available computer programs, charts and graphs, and biorhythm consultants (Blount 1978; Chan 1978; Lutus 1977; Lyon, Dyer, and Gary 1978).

Research Involving Biorhythms

Researchers have been debating for decades the validity of the theory that biorhythm cycles influence human behavior. Several studies have supported the theory. In 1939,

Hans Schwing, a student at the Swiss Federal Institute of Technology in Zurich, conducted an extensive study of biorhythms and accident statistics. Of the 700 accidents he examined, he found that 401 of the injured persons were on critical days at the time of the accident. When he examined the data for 300 deaths, he found that 197 occurred on critical days (Mackenzie 1973). In Berlin in 1953, Reinhold Bochow investigated 500 agricultural machinery worker injuries and found that nearly 98 percent of the accidents occurred on critical days (Thumann 1977).

Advocates of the theory that biorhythms influence accident occurrence frequently refer to the experience of the Ohmi Railway Company in Japan. The company employed 500 drivers. Each driver was told when his or her biorhythm cycles were critical, and the drivers were admonished to be particularly careful on those days. The program was implemented in the late 1960s. In the first year of the program, the accident rate was reduced by 50%. The accident reductions continued in subsequent years (Chan 1978; Kagan 1974; Mackenzie 1973; O'Neil and Phillips 1975; Parlee 1978; Scott 1978; Thumann 1977). According to rumor, some airlines had biorhythm charts prepared for their pilots and scheduled the pilots' flying days accordingly. When asked about the practice, the airlines have either denied it or refused to comment (Chan 1978; O'Neil and Phillips 1975; Scott 1978; Thumann 1977).

Despite the seemingly strong evidence in support of the influence of biorhythms on human behavior, several studies have refuted any such direct association. A 20-year study of 112 lost-time accidents at Oak Ridge National Laboratory failed to show any correlation between the occurrence of the accidents and the critical days of the biorhythm cycles. It must be remembered that each person has two critical days in the physical cycle of 23 days, two critical days in the emotional cycle of 28 days, and two critical days in the intellectual cycle of 33 days. In fact, over the long term, each person has a critical day in one of every six days (Lyon, Dyer, and Gary 1978; Mackenzie 1973).

In a study of 205 automobile crashes in which driver error was determined to be a contributing cause, no pattern in the biorhythm positions was apparent. In a study of 4,279 aircraft accidents involving pilot error, the biorhythm cycles of pilots at the time of the crashes were examined. The study provided no support for the biorhythm theory (Lyon, Dyer, and Gary 1978; Thumann 1977).

A Study of Biorhythm Cycles and Construction Worker Injuries

I conducted a study in the construction industry to test the biorhythm theory (Hinze 1981). The study was of injury data collected on a single construction site, a large multiyear construction effort in which approximately 3,000 workers were employed. Although various sources of accident statistics exist, few can provide the birth dates of the injured persons, from which positions on the biorhythm charts can be determined. In fact, the date of birth is not information typically collected on an injury report. Because the study was of a large construction project and the birth dates were available from the personnel files, I was able to obtain from a single source sufficient information to conduct a useful study.

I computed the biorhythm cycle positions at the time of the injury for each of the injured construction workers. The injury data, covering a seven-month period, included both first-aid cases and reportable cases (those for which the services of a doctor were obtained). The study included a total of 1,575 injury cases.

The distribution of injuries was considered in relation to positions on each of the three cycles. The analysis also considered the frequency of injuries on days that were critical for the injured worker on two of the biorhythm cycles. The results showed no pattern in the frequency of injuries to suggest that injury occurrence is associated with positions on the biorhythm cycles. The results are depicted in Figures 2.7, 2.8, and 2.9.

Author's note on the biorhythm cycle study: The methodology of the study produced clear evidence that biorhythm cycles have, at best, no significant influence on accident causation.

Final Comments

When injury data are examined over a period of time, patterns of occurrence can often be identified. The most common patterns relate to the hour of day, the day of the week, and the season of the year. It is important to recognize that patterns may vary among companies. Effective managers should examine their firms' own injury records to determine whether any patterns appear. The timing of injuries may be different on different projects. Once a pattern has been identified, it is then appropriate to assess the possibility of altering that pattern. The timing of accidents may point to the possible

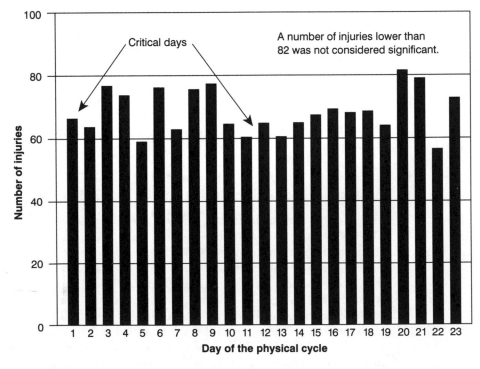

Figure 2.7
The Distribution of Injuries during the Physical Cycle

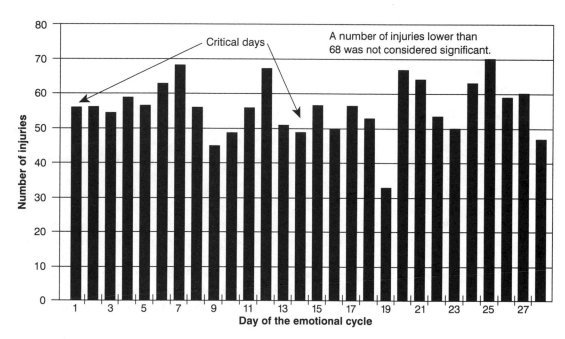

Figure 2.8
The Distribution of Injuries during the Emotional Cycle

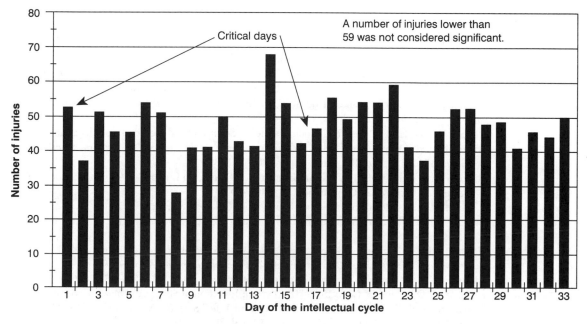

Figure 2.9
The Distribution of Injuries during the Intellectual Cycle

causes of those accidents. When it does, steps can be taken to reduce or eliminate the injuries by addressing the causes.

Review Questions

1. During which hours of the day do more injuries occur? During which days of the week? During which months of the year? Explain why those patterns of injury occurrence seem to exist.
2. How might a construction firm logically determine when it should conduct its jobsite safety meetings?
3. Describe major elements of safety that managers should consider before implementing shift work on a project.
4. Suppose a project manager examined injury data on a particular construction project and discovered that a disproportionately high number of injuries occurred on Thursdays. Many of the workers were college students who were employed for the summer. The project manager recognized that Wednesday was payday on that particular project and that the local college students had a tradition of "partying" on Wednesday nights. What course of action might the project manager take with this knowledge of the timing of accidents?
5. What has research shown about injury occurrence in relation to various phases of the moon?
6. What has research shown about injury occurrence in relation to biorhythm cycles?

References

Bedard, P. 1978. "I Got Rhythm, Biorhythm." *Car and Driver*, October, 138.

Blount, R., Jr. 1978. "Biorhythm and the Big Game." *Esquire*, March 14, 28.

Bolch, J. 1977. "Biorhythm: A Key to Your Ups and Downs." *Reader's Digest*, September, 63–67.

Chan, J. 1978. "Biorhythm: Charting Your Ups and Downs." *McCall's*, April, 55–56.

Cottrell, J. 1969. "Moon Madness: Does It Really Exist?" *Science Digest*, October. Vol. 66, no. 4:24–29.

Encyclopedia Britannica. 15th ed., s.v. "moon."

Hartley, W., and E. Hartley. 1972. "Moon Madness." *Science Digest*, September. Vol. 72, no. 3:28–33.

Hinze, J. 1981. "Biorhythm Cycles and Injury Occurrences." *Journal of the Construction Division*, ASCE 107, no. CO1, Proc. Paper 16085, 21–33.

Hinze, J., and J. Roxo. 1984. "Is Injury Occurrence Related to Lunar Cycles?" *Journal of the Construction Division*, ASCE 110, no. CO4, 409–19.

Kagan, J. 1974. "Plotting Your Ups and Downs." *McCall's*, January, 29.

Lieber, A. 1978. "Human Aggression and the Lunar Synodic Cycle." *Journal of Clinical Psychiatry* 39, no. 5.

"Link Mind and Cosmos." 1951. *Science News Letter*, November 17. Vol. 60, no. 20:311.

Louis, M. 1978. "Should You Buy Biorhythms?" *Psychology Today*, April, 93–96.

Lutus, P. 1977. "Biorhythm Forecast." *Popular Electronics*, June. Vol. 11, no. 6:45–46.

Lyon, W., F. Dyer, and D. Gary. 1978. "Biorhythm: Imitation of Science." *Chemistry* 51, no. 3: 5–7.

Mackenzie, J. 1973. "How Bio Rhythms Affect Your Life." *Science Digest*, August, 18–22.

Medical Notes. 1951. *Newsweek*, November 19. Vol. 38, no. 21: 63–64.

Michelson, L., J. Wilson, and J. Michelson. 1979. "Investigation of Periodicity in Crisis Intervention Calls over an Eight-Year Span." *Psychological Reports*. Vol. 45:420–22.

Middleton, T. 1978. "Light Refractions: Do We Ebb and Flow by the Moon?" *Saturday Review,* September 16. Vol. 5, no. 24, 57.

"The Moon and Moods." 1951. *Newsweek,* April 23. Vol. 37, no. 17, 94–95.

O'Neil, B., and R. Phillips. 1975. *Biorhythm: How to Live with Your Life Cycles.* Pasadena, Calif.: Ward Ritchie Press.

Parlee, B. 1978. "The Rhythms in Men's Lives." *Psychology Today,* April, 82–91.

Schuessler, R. 1951. "Does the Moon Influence Your Moods?" *Science Digest,* November. Vol. 30, no. 5, 23–26.

Schweich, C. 1981. "Full Moon Madness." *McCall's,* July, 41.

Scott, E. 1978. "Staying Well—What to Believe about Biorhythms." *Seventeen,* May. Vol. 37, no. 6, 90.

Snoyman, P., and T. Holdstock. 1980. "The Influence of the Sun, Moon, Climate, and Economic Conditions on Crisis Incidence." *Journal of Clinical Psychology* 36, no. 4, 884–93.

Stephens, G. 1976. "Periodicity in Mood, Affect, and Instinctual Behavior." *Nursing Clinics of North America* 11, no. 4, 595–607.

Thakur, C. 1980. "Full Moon and Poisoning." *British Medical Journal* 281 (December 20–27), 1684.

Thumann, A. 1977. *Biorhythms and Industrial Safety.* Atlanta: Fairmont Press.

The True Costs of Construction Worker Injuries

Injuries cost; safety pays.

Construction workers, like all workers, do not want to be injured as a consequence of their employment. If injuries are to be curtailed or diminished, however, safety cannot be left solely under the control of the workers, because the safety environment consists of many factors over which workers have little or no control. Those factors include the expenditure of funds to make the physical conditions safer. The effective coordination of work activities, which is vital to safety, also relies heavily on managerial personnel. That task is made more complex when the workers are employed by numerous subcontractors. Responsibility for the orientation and training of workers to improve safety also lies with each employer.

In general, accident prevention is accepted as the responsibility of management. However, not all construction firms commit the same amount of effort or funds to accident prevention. The differences may stem partially from differences in the perception of the degree of influence that management can actually have on reducing worker injuries. They may also be the result of different perceptions of the actual costs associated with worker injuries. If the true costs of injuries were well defined, management would be in a better position to make informed decisions concerning safety. Rather than addressing safety solely from an altruistic point of view, construction managers should also consider safety from a more purely economic perspective.

Direct Costs of Injuries

The costs of injuries can be roughly categorized as either direct or indirect. The direct costs are those directly attributed to or associated with injuries. They are typically the costs covered by workers' compensation insurance policies. Examples of direct costs include ambulance service, medical and ancillary treatment, medication, hospitalization, and disability benefits, including a percentage of the lost wages of injured workers. Historical records can be reviewed to determine the expenditures attributed to each injury. Thus, the direct costs of injuries tend to be those associated with the treatment of the injury and any unique compensation offered to workers as a consequence of being injured. Direct costs are well understood and can be quantified with accuracy.

Workers' Compensation (Prepayment Premium or Postpayment Penalty)

Workers' compensation laws have existed in all 50 states for nearly 50 years. Many employers regard workers' compensation as an insurance policy for their employees when they are "on the clock." That is, worker's compensation is not designed to cover employees when they are away from the site or when they are not involved in company activities.

Viewing worker's compensation as an insurance policy is generally accurate; however, workers' compensation differs from some other policies. For example, it is not analogous to fire insurance on a residence, in which the insurance holder's claims history may not influence premiums. If it were, there would be less incentive to be safe. Workers' compensation is more akin to automobile insurance in that a poor claims history results in higher premiums. The number and cost of injury claims directly influence the premiums to be paid in future years.

The premiums paid by an employer are based on two numbers. The first is the manual rate established for a particular craft in the state and published in the workers' compensation manual. The second is a multiplier or modifying value that reflects the past experience of the particular employer. The manual rate is stated as the cost of insurance per $100 of payroll or simply as a percentage of payroll. For example, the workers' compensation manual rate for carpenters in a particular state might be $18.40 per $100 of payroll, while in another state it might be 11.8% of payroll. The manual rate applies uniformly to a particular craft in an entire state. The rate may be as low as 4% or 5%, but it may also exceed 100%, a situation in which the cost of workers' compensation for a trade exceeds the actual cost of wages. Although the rates have considerable variation, the industry average is nearly 30% of the cost of wages.

The computation of the manual rate is based on the past experience of claims for that craft in that state. The manual rate for a particular craft will be high in a state where several very bad accidents have been incurred by that craft. Thus, the differences in the manual rates between two states may reflect the differing accident histories in those states. Since the manual rates are based largely on the costs of claims, rate differences between states may also be due to differences in compensation plans. One of the costs of claims is the compensation paid to workers for lost wages when they cannot immediately return to work. A worker begins to receive such compensation after losing a certain number of days because of the injury. For example, in one state an injured worker may receive compensation for lost wages after losing three days of work. In another state a worker may not receive compensation until he or she has lost five days. States that have longer periods before compensation is due for lost wages have lower claims costs than states that have shorter periods. The rate at which lost wages are compensated also varies by state. One state may compensate injured workers at 60% of regular wages, while another may compensate injured workers at 90% of regular wages. Many such factors cause the manual rates to differ between states.

Just as the manual rate reflects the claims history of a particular craft in a state, a similar factor is used to reflect the claims history of a particular employer. The factor applied to individual employers is referred to as the *experience modification rate (EMR)*. The EMR, which is employer-specific, is a complex formulation that takes into account both the frequency and the severity of injuries. It is designed so that a major accident will not severely alter it. At the same time, it is designed to be severely altered by the occurrence of many minor injuries. The presumption is that many minor injuries will eventually lead to a severe one. Thus, there is an incentive to keep minor injuries to a minimum.

The EMR is computed by a rating bureau. Different agencies perform the computations, depending on the specific state. Nonetheless, the essence of the computation is relatively constant. In all cases, the EMR reflects the claims history of the employer for a three-year period that does not include the immediately preceding year. Thus, an EMR computed for 1997 reflects the claims history of an employer for the years 1993, 1994, and 1995. The rationale commonly given for not including the immediate past year is that too many of the injury cases will not have been closed at the time of the computation of the EMR. If the cases are not closed, the EMR computations will include the amounts set aside as reserves for those cases. Reserve amounts may or may not be accurate. They may bear little or no resemblance to the actual costs to be incurred. Thus, it is desirable to have injury cases closed before they are used in computing the EMR.

The following table shows how the EMR changes over time for an employer:

Year	Loss Ratio	EMR
1991	1.08	0.98
1992	1.05	0.97
1993	0.36	0.92
1994	0.24	0.96
1995	0.22	0.72
1996	0.37	0.66
1997	0.63	0.58

In this example, the contractor had a series of very bad years (up to and including 1992) followed by years of steadily declining injury claims (1993–1995). The injury or claims history is shown as the loss ratio, which is computed by dividing the cost of claims by the premiums paid. Thus, a loss ratio greater than 1.0 for a particular year means that the insurance company paid more in claims for a firm than the firm paid in premiums. In this example, the loss ratio exhibited a steady decline over the years, indicating that the firm was becoming a lower risk to the insurance carrier. Despite that decline, note that the EMR rose in 1994. Since the EMR for 1994 was based on the experience recorded for 1990, 1991, and 1992, it is not surprising that the EMR was still quite high. Note also that although the loss ratio rose in 1997, the EMR continued to decline. That is because the claims history only for 1993, 1994, and 1995 was considered when the EMR was computed for 1997.

Suppose a project owner wanted to evaluate the safety of the company whose experience is set forth in the table. The loss ratio trends and the EMR trends present contradictory evidence. It is most common to review the EMR of a firm to assess its safety performance. An examination of the given firm's EMR trend would suggest that the firm is getting progressively better in its safety performance. If the owner evaluated the firm solely on the basis of the loss ratio, the conclusion would be that the firm's safety performance improved from 1991 to 1995, but that it appears to have begun to diminish. Of course, the apparent discrepancy exists because of the lag and the averaging that occur in the computation of EMRs. The loss ratio reflects information on the current year. Note that the loss ratio computed for a given year does not overlap with any of the claims data used to formulate the EMR value for that year.

Indirect (Hidden) Costs of Injuries

The indirect costs are the most elusive component of the costs of construction worker injuries. To some extent, the elusiveness of the indirect costs lies in the lack of a clear definition. The indirect costs can be considered as those that are hidden, or for which no historical record is kept. That is, indirect costs are those for which there is no retrieval mechanism to accurately associate them with injuries. Thus, it is not a matter of whether a particular cost has been identified, but rather a matter of whether the cost has been attributed to the injury. Indirect costs are then "hidden" only in that they are not attributed to injuries in a bookkeeping sense.

For example, suppose a concrete wall form is being set by a crane and two carpenters. As the wall form is being adjusted near its final location, one of the carpenters, feeling that the form is reasonably secure, lets go of the tag line to get a pry bar from his toolbox. When the wall form is lifted slightly, it suddenly begins to rotate and strikes the other carpenter. The injury is not serious; however, the work is stopped for about 20 minutes for first-aid treatment. During those 20 minutes, each of the carpenters is paid at the rate of $22 per hour, and the crane operator is paid a similar wage. With benefits, the cost of each worker's time to the company is about $35 per hour. The crane is being rented at a rate of $100 per hour. All those costs are customarily tracked by construction firms as part of their cost control effort. The cost of the 20 minutes would probably be recorded as part of the cost of forming. In truth, the cost should really be applied to the first-aid injury. The true cost of the injury is hidden.

From the definition given earlier of indirect or hidden costs, it is clear that the indirect costs of injuries cannot be conventionally retrieved or quantified with accuracy. A description of some of the indirect costs of injuries will clarify the types of costs that are hidden. Although the direct costs of construction worker injuries are very similar to those of workers in manufacturing facilities, the indirect costs may be somewhat different because of the different work environments.

The most obvious indirect costs are those associated with the injured construction worker. When the worker is injured, it is standard practice for the injured worker to continue to be paid while receiving treatment. If the injury is minor, the injured worker may return to work within two to three hours, depending on the distance to the medical treatment facility. When the worker returns to work, it is very likely that as a direct result of the injury, the worker will not function at maximum productivity. For example, bandages may hamper movement, and pain may cause the worker to be more cautious in performing tasks.

Another indirect cost of an injury is the cost of transporting the injured worker to a medical facility for treatment. Unless the injury is quite severe, the transportation cost generally consists of the use of a company vehicle and the time taken by a staff member or a fellow worker to accompany the injured worker until treatment is received. The staff member or fellow worker earns regular hourly wages during that time, and the company vehicle is not available for any other purposes. Therefore, the cost of the vehicle and the wages of the accompanying individual during that time are incurred as a direct result of the injury.

An injury also has an adverse effect on the injured worker's crew. The productivity of the entire crew usually comes to a complete stop when an injury occurs. The next few minutes are devoted to attending to the injured worker, primarily to administering first aid and summoning the appropriate personnel to arrange prompt transportation to a health care facility. Once the injured worker leaves the site, the crew tries to return to work. However, work activities do not generally resume as normal. The crew members may first discuss the circumstances surrounding the accident. They may then be required to restore the physical work conditions to preinjury status, particularly if equipment damage or material damage accompanied the accident.

Since the crew must work "short-handed" after an injury, its productivity is often below normal, as now the crew must rearrange the work activities to compensate for the decreased crew size. If the injury was severe or dramatic, the crew members may feel particularly uneasy about the accident, reducing productivity even more.

If the injured construction worker does not return to work on the day following the injury, or if the worker must be reassigned to a different task as a result of the injury, the crew will feel further effects. If the worker cannot return to the crew, a replacement construction worker must be hired. The hiring will consume administrative time on the project, and it will require additional orientation and training for the replacement worker. The productivity of the crew will be compromised or decreased as the replacement worker adjusts to the sequence and assignment of tasks being performed by the different crew members.

The effect of an injury can extend beyond the crew of the injured worker. For example, two construction crews may work sequentially, with one crew able to perform its work only after the other crew has completed its task. If the first crew halts work, the second crew is immediately affected. Even if one crew merely works in close proximity to another, an injury accident will surely have an effect on both crews. Even if an injury does not directly interfere with the work of a crew, observation of the injury may have a long-lasting influence on the workers. The workers may initially try to help the injured worker. Possibly, the workers in the second crew will only observe what is being done for the injured worker. Regardless of their actions, the productivity of the nearby crew is likely to come to a complete stop for at least a short while. Later, as the crew returns to work, the uneasiness experienced by the workers will continue to retard the productivity of that crew.

Shortly after an injury occurs, a supervisor on the construction project is generally summoned. The initial task of the supervisor is to ensure that prompt first aid is provided and that a responsible party is assigned to accompany the injured worker to obtain medical treatment. Subsequently, the supervisor investigates the conditions leading up to the accident. The information the supervisor gathers is required for the completion of government-mandated or company reports regarding the injury. On more serious injuries, the supervisor typically makes long-distance telephone calls to the home office to inform them of the accident. With the great demand placed on the supervisor, the supervisor's effectiveness is compromised by accidents that divert his or her attention to the injured workers.

If an injury is particularly severe or dramatic, it attracts media attention. Dealing with the media consumes considerable supervisory time. If an injury attracts media attention, it will undoubtedy also attract the attention of regulatory personnel. Working with regulatory personnel can drain considerable amounts of construction managers' time, time that would otherwise be devoted to productive construction activities.

The cost of damage to equipment and materials in injury accidents was examined in one study of U.S. Army Corps of Engineers construction projects (Brown 1988). In the study, conducted in 1987, the investigator estimated the average cost of damage to equipment and materials at approximately $750 per accident, whether paid by the contractor or by the contractor's risk carrier. That average was computed from the costs of 11,472 injury accidents, including 10,596 injuries for which no significant equipment or material damage was reported. The premiums for the builders' risk insurance were not included in the costs. In actuality, the builders' risk coverage paid for much of the damage. For the major damage incidents, it was assumed that the only costs to the contractors were the deductible amounts on their risk policies, typically set at around $2,500. On cases involving little damage, the contractors were assumed to absorb the entire cost of the damage, up to the deductible amount. Using those conservative assumptions, the investigator determined that the average out-of-pocket expenditure by the contractor for property damage was about $100 to $125 per incident. Note that the average cost was estimated from data that included numerous injury accidents for which no property damage was reported. Note also that it does not include the cost of the builders' risk coverage.

Little else has been published about the cost of material and equipment damage. It is the injury cases that receive the most attention. There are many cases in which serious injuries occur with little equipment or material damage. There are also many cases in which significant equipment or material damage occurs with no associated worker injury.

Previous Studies of the True Costs of Injuries

Safety professionals have recognized the presence of indirect, or hidden, costs of injuries for decades. One of the early texts on the subject was written by Heinrich in 1941. He listed the following indirect costs:

1. cost of lost time of injured worker
2. cost of lost time of other workers who stop work
3. cost of time lost by foreman, supervisors, or other executives
4. cost of time spent on the case by first-aid attendant and other staff
5. cost due to damage to equipment, tools, property, and materials
6. incidental cost due to interference with production
7. cost to employer under employee welfare and benefit systems
8. cost to employer for continuing wages of injured worker
9. cost due to loss in profit due to reduced worker productivity
10. cost due to loss in profit due to idle equipment
11. cost incurred because of subsequent injuries partially caused by the incident
12. cost of overhead (utilities, telephone, rent, etc.)

A few safety research efforts have been made to quantify the true costs of worker injuries. Instead of actually quantifying the costs in monetary terms, however, it has been common for researchers to compare the indirect, or hidden, costs of injuries with the direct costs. The most common means of expressing that relationship is as a ratio of the indirect costs to the direct costs. The first estimate of that ratio was made more than 50 years ago by H. W. Heinrich (1941), an employee of Traveler's Insurance. He determined the ratio of the indirect costs of injuries to the direct costs to be approximately 4, a value that is frequently quoted. The ratio computed by Heinrich was based on data collected from various industrial facilities in the United States. That ratio was computed before the relatively steep escalation of the costs of health care (direct costs), so the ratio might reasonably be expected to be lower now.

Although the factor of 4, estimated by Heinrich, was widely accepted for many years as the ratio of the indirect costs of injuries to the direct costs, computations in the 1980s became less conservative. Sheriff (1980) showed that the ratio may be as high as 10. Bird and Loftus (1976) computed a ratio as high as 50. Although the numbers calculated were quite varied, the researchers were convinced that the indirect costs were significant.

Subsequent research studies have attempted to ascertain the validity of Heinrich's results. Leopold and Leonard, in a study conducted in 1987, concluded that the indirect costs were essentially insignificant, too small to serve as a motivator for safety. It is noteworthy that the definition of direct costs was considerably broader than described earlier. Their definition of direct costs included several items commonly referred to as indirect costs. Thus, their conclusions cannot be compared readily with those of Heinrich.

A study conducted at Stanford University (Robinson 1979) resulted in projections of the ratio of the indirect costs of construction worker injuries to the direct costs; however, that study was based on only 49 construction injuries. With such a small sample size, no firm conclusions could be drawn from the research effort.

Recent Research on the Costs of Injuries

A subsequent study was conducted by the Construction Industry Institute (CII) in conjunction with the University of Washington (Hinze and Appelgate 1991). The study was a large undertaking focused on a very important safety issue. Because of the significance of this study, it will be described in greater detail.

The CII is a consortium of approximately 100 firms, representing both owner and contractor interests. Each firm commits a stipulated amount of money each year to sustain the administration of the institute and to fund selected research studies. Founded in 1983 under the leadership of Dr. Richard Tucker of the University of Texas, the CII has been instrumental in sponsoring a number of significant construction research studies. Several construction safety studies have been conducted through the CII.

The purpose of the research to be described here was to quantify the true costs of construction worker injuries, with particular emphasis on the indirect, or hidden, costs. The study was restricted to short-term indirect costs that can be observed within the first few months of the occurrence of an injury. Long-term costs were too difficult to quantify with accuracy, and the cost of monitoring expenditures for several years was prohibitive.

The essence of the study was to meticulously monitor the costs of a large number of injuries. The study was conducted with data provided by companies in the United States that were willing to participate in the study. Participation was solicited from members of the Construction Industry Institute, the Associated Builders and Contractors, the National Constructors Institute, other contractor associations, and specifically identified contractors.

The researchers gave each participating company numerous copies of a four-page questionnaire on which to record information about the direct costs of injuries and the indirect costs, as defined earlier. Participants were to use a separate form for each construction worker injury. The researchers asked them to begin keeping information on injury costs immediately after an injury occurred and to continue to record information concerning those costs until most indirect and direct costs had been quantified. The data on most injuries were considered complete when the workers' compensation claim amounts were received from the insurance carriers. As the forms were being completed, the participants had to estimate the costs of the reduced productivity of the injured worker's crew after an injury occurred, the reduced productivity of an injured worker upon returning to work, and the lower productivity of any replacement worker in comparison with the injured worker.

Although the research effort was extensive and thorough, the researchers did not attempt to quantify each and every indirect cost of an injury, especially those not directly related to the construction effort. Some indirect costs cannot be accurately quantified. One such cost is that of the pain and suffering of the injured worker. Another is the financial and emotional hardship that the injury imposes on the family members. No attempt was made to accurately quantify the effect that a worker's reduced wages would have on the community. Although job costs would be directly affected, the long-lasting decreased morale of workers as a result of serious injuries was not quantified. Estimates of those costs would have been rough approximations at best.

Another indirect cost that is highly variable relates to the repercussions that an injury has on the project or the firm. Injuries can have an adverse effect on a firm if many injuries or a few serious injuries take place. The initial damage is to the general reputation of the firm. A reputation of being unsafe can result in a firm's inability to attract or retain some of the better crafts workers. The general goodwill of the firm also suffers if the firm is labeled unsafe. Such a reputation may also cause the firm to be removed from the bidding or tendering lists of clients who are conscious of the merits of contracting only with firms that are focused on the safety of workers.

Costs of Injuries Quantified

More than 100 construction firms cooperated in the study, submitting injury cost data from 185 construction projects in 34 states. The projects ranged in size from less than $1 million to more than $500 million. Although 56% of the projects were constructed under either fixed-price or unit-price contracts, the remainder were cost-reimbursable. Of the projects, 14% were classified as new construction, 15% as maintenance projects, and 71% as renovation projects. Although most projects were being constructed for private owners, rather than for public agencies, there was diversity in the types of projects. Most were buildings and industrial facilities.

The participating firms returned completed survey forms on 834 construction worker injuries. The injuries reported involved workers associated with 19 different trades. Pipe fitters, laborers, and carpenters made up 52% of the total sample.

In the analysis of the data, a distinction was made between medical-case injuries (those requiring only a doctor's attention before the injured worker returns to work) and lost-workday cases (those in which the injured worker could not return to work the following workday or where the worker had to be reassigned to a different type of work because of the injury). For the medical-case injuries, the average indirect cost was $442.40, and the average direct cost was $519.15. For the lost-workday cases, the average field indirect cost (total indirect cost minus liability claims) was $1,613.21, and the average direct cost was $6,909.98. The breakdowns of the indirect costs of the injuries are illustrated in Figures 3.1 and 3.2, and all the costs are tabulated in Table 3.1. Note that the average total cost of restricted-activity or lost-workday cases was $21,133, a value that closely approximates the estimates that DuPont's Safety Services Division regularly computes.

The ratios of field indirect costs to direct costs were computed for the two categories of injuries. For medical-case injuries, the ratio was 0.85, and for lost workday cases, the ratio was 0.23. That is, for every dollar spent directly on medical treatment for an injured worker, a medical-case injury costs an additional 85 cents that remains

Figure 3.1
Job-site Cost Breakdown of
Medical-Case Injuries

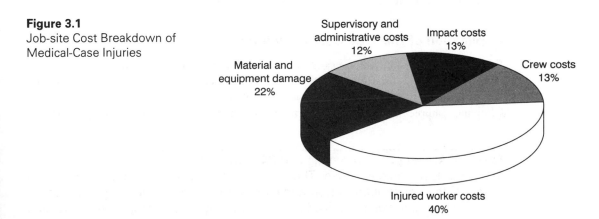

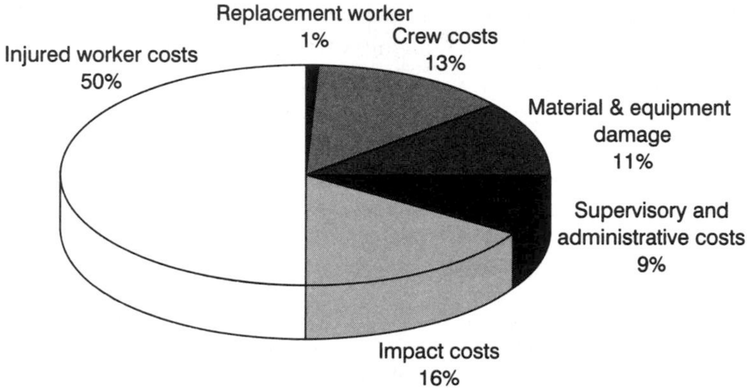

Figure 3.2
Job-site Cost Breakdown of
Restricted-Activity or Lost-Work-
day Cases

hidden and is not charged against the injury. A lost-workday case costs an additional 23 cents in hidden charges for every dollar spent on medical treatment. The ratios relate to the indirect costs only at the job site itself.

In the United States it is common for lawsuits to be filed in conjunction with serious injuries. Third-party liability lawsuits may be filed against the owner of a project or, when a subcontractor's employee is injured, against the general contractor. When the owner is sued, the suit commonly affects the general contractor as well, through a contractor indemnity clause in the construction contract.

One safety expert has stated that in California 1 in every 8 lost-workday cases results in a liability suit. In other states, the number may be as low as 1 in 20. In a few states, such liability suits are not permitted by law. In the CII study, the investigators consulted experts in construction safety on the numbers and costs of such suits in the construction industry. From the estimates of various experts, the investigators concluded that the average cost of the liability claims associated with construction worker injuries in the United States is not trivial. For medical-case injuries, liability claims were estimated to make up 28% of the indirect cost, and for lost-time or restricted-activity cases, liability claims were estimated to make up about 90% of the indirect cost. For medical-case injuries, the ratio of indirect costs to direct costs increased to 1.18, and for lost-workday cases, the ratio increased to 2.06.

Application of the True Costs of Injuries

For many managers and supervisors in construction, the findings about the relative magnitude of the true costs of injuries will serve as sufficient incentive to be proactive on safety. Others might want to make more accurate estimates of the costs of injuries. The following examples show how the information on the true costs of injuries can be applied.

Example A: Suppose a project had 34 medical-case injuries and 8 restricted-activity or lost-workday cases. The project, which was competitively bid, consisted of the construction of an addition to a refinery, primarily new construction. The contract was for a fixed price of $20 million. The project was originally

Table 3.1
Costs of Construction Worker Injuries

Source of Injury Costs	Medical Case Only		Restricted Activity/Lost Workday	
Injured worker				
Lost productivity on the day of injury	$54.65		$81.31	
Lost productivity due to follow-up care	58.64		490.05	
Lost productivity after resuming work	44.90		203.43	
Cost of transporting injured worker	18.74		40.79	
Subtotal		$176.93		$815.58
Worker's crew				
Assisting injured worker	20.97		43.73	
Completing added work due to accident	2.26		6.68	
Lost productivity due to accident	28.17		122.16	
Lost productivity due to inspection	0.00		6.33	
Subtotal		51.40		178.90
Crew in vicinity of accident				
Watching events and discussing accident		4.19		34.27
Replacement worker				
Reduced productivity of replacement	0.11		1.81	
Training the replacement worker	0.60		19.93	
Subtotal		0.71		21.74
Supervisory and administrative staff				
Assisting injured worker	16.76		42.00	
Investigating accident	16.09		53.23	
Preparing reports	17.56		35.94	
Time with media, project owner, and/or regulatory inspector	0.89		4.73	
Subtotal		51.30		135.90
Damaged property				
Repairing damage	0.80		74.62	
Material damage	100.00		100.00	
Subtotal		100.80		174.62
Other costs		57.07		252.20
Long distance telephone calls				
Supervisor diverted from production tasks				
Total field indirect costs		$442.40		$1613.21
Claims costs		$171.20		$12,610.15
Total indirect costs		$613.60		$14,223.36
Direct costs of injuries		$519.15		$6,909.98
Total cost (direct and indirect costs)		$1,132.75		$21,133.34
Ratio: field indirect costs to direct costs		0.85		0.23
Ratio: total indirect costs to direct costs		1.182		2.058

expected to last two years, but because of construction problems and engineering delays, it took almost three years to complete. During the project, the average total employment was about 110 workers. An estimate can be made of the true costs of the project injuries as follows:

Medical-case injury costs:

$$34(\$614 + \$519) = \$38,522$$

Restricted-activity or lost-workday injury costs:

$$8(\$14,223 + \$6,910) = \$169,064$$

Total cost of project injuries = $207,586

Example B: On a $46 million pulp mill addition, a construction contractor's employees incurred 67 medical-case injuries and 21 restricted-activity or lost-workday injuries. The insurance carrier reports showed that the direct costs of those injuries totaled $183,000. No other information is available about the injuries or their costs. If the ratio of indirect costs to direct costs is 1.18 for medical-case injuries and 2.06 for restricted-activity or lost-workday cases, the true costs of the project injuries can be estimated as follows:

Direct costs = $183,000

Indirect costs = 2 X $183,000 = $366,000

(A multiplier of 2 is used because the 21 restricted-activity or lost-workday cases are assumed to account for most of the indirect costs.)

Total estimated cost of injuries = $549,000

Another approach is to base the estimate solely on the average costs of injuries, as done in Example A.

Medical-case injury costs:

$$67(\$614 + \$519) = \$75,911$$

Restricted-activity or lost-workday injury costs:

$$21(\$14,223 + \$6,910) = \$443,793$$

Total cost of project injuries = $519,704

Additional Analysis of the Costs of Injuries

In the CII study, the investigators conducted additional analysis of the data to identify other patterns or relationships. When they focused the analysis on the trade of the injured worker, they noted no statistically significant differences between the indirect-to-direct cost ratios of different crafts. When they considered project size, they noted that the cost ratio appeared to increase with project size. Projects that were constructed under cost-reimbursable contracts also tended to have higher cost ratios. Closer examination revealed that the cost-reimbursable contracts were among the larger projects. There were no clearly discernible patterns of cost ratios with respect to type of project (new construction, renovation, or maintenance). In summary, the cost ratios appeared to be higher on cost-reimbursable contracts and on larger projects.

Considerable analysis was conducted in order to explain any other aspects of the cost ratios. One objective of the analysis was to formulate models for estimating the field indirect costs of injuries, one model for medical-case injuries and another for lost-workday injuries. Ideally, the models sought would simplify estimates of the indirect costs associated with construction worker injuries. In developing the models, the investigators used multiple regression analysis.

In the multiple regression analysis, all available variables were initially considered for inclusion. The variables that did not contribute significantly to the formulation were excluded. Through various iterations, many different models were developed. However, the value of a model lies in the degree to which it explains the relationship of different variables to the dependent variable being defined (in this case, field indirect costs). The investigators assessed the ability of each model to explain the field indirect costs of construction worker injuries. The best model for estimating the field indirect costs of medical-case injuries was as follows:

$$\text{Field indirect costs} = \$150 + \$15F + \$30H + \$100A$$

where

$F =$ the number of hours lost by the injured worker to receive follow-up care

$H =$ the number of hours lost by the injured worker on the day of the injury

$A =$ the number of hours spent by administrative and supervisory personnel to assist the injured worker on the day of the injury

When that equation was applied to the injury data, the linear regression analysis revealed an R-square value of 0.79, which means that the equation successfully explains 79% of the field indirect costs. Since an R-square value of 1.00 would mean that all the variation was explained, a value of 0.79 indicates that the model is a fairly good one. To obtain the total indirect costs of medical-case injuries, one must increase the field indirect costs by about 40%, or simply multiply them by 1.4.

A slightly different model was developed for the field indirect costs of lost-workday injuries. The model is as follows:

$$\text{Field indirect costs} = \$625 + \$20F + \$20H + \$50V$$

where

$F =$ the number of hours lost by the injured worker to receive follow-up care

$H =$ the number of hours lost by the injured worker on the day of the injury

$V =$ the number of hours spent by administrative personnel to investigate the injury

When applied to the injury data, that equation successfully explains 81% of the field indirect costs of lost-workday injuries. To obtain the total indirect costs of lost workday injuries, one must multiply the field indirect costs by a factor of 9. Given the considerable variability that was noted in the raw data, the models provide considerable accuracy in estimating the indirect costs.

Attempts were made to develop other models that would be accurate for estimating indirect costs. One model sought was one that did not require information on the number of hours lost for follow-up care. Information on follow-up care is often not available until a considerable time after an injury has occurred. The time lapse is not ideal, as an estimate may be desired shortly after an injury occurs. Models were developed in which the hours lost for follow-up care were not included in the formulation. The best-fit model for estimating the field indirect costs of medical-case injuries was as follows:

$$\text{Field indirect costs} = \$150 + \$80H + \$80A$$

where H and A are as previously defined. The best-fit model for estimating the field indirect costs of lost-workday injuries was as follows:

$$\text{Field indirect costs} = \$625 + \$100H + \$100V$$

where H and V are as previously defined.

Testing of those models (without the hours of follow-up care) revealed that the model for estimating the field indirect costs of medical-case injuries had an R-square value of 0.37. The model for estimating the field indirect costs of lost-workday injuries had an R-square value of 0.43. It is evident from these R-square values that accuracy diminishes considerably when the hours lost for follow-up care are excluded from the formulation. Despite efforts to improve the predictive capacity of these models, no variables could be added to the formulation that made any significant contributions to the estimation of field indirect costs.

Application of Injury Cost Models

The models developed to estimate the field indirect costs of injuries might be used in a variety of ways. They provide greater accuracy than the use of the generic information allows. The following two examples demonstrate how costs can be estimated from the model equations.

Example C: A laborer fell from a wall form and incurred some serious cuts. The worker was absent for 6 hours on the day of the injury and was unable to return to work for 10 days. A fellow worker also was absent from the project for 6 hours because he took the injured worker to the emergency room, returned to the project to collect the laborer's personal belongings, and then took the laborer home. Other time committed to this lost-time injury was as follows:

Superintendent's time to investigate the accident = 2 hours

Injured worker's time lost for follow-up treatment = 30 hours

$$\text{Field indirect cost} = \$625 + \$20(F + H) + \$50V$$
$$= \$625 + \$20(30 + 6) + \$50(2)$$
$$= \$1,445$$
$$\text{Total indirect cost} = \$1,445 \times 9 = \$13,005$$
$$\text{Total direct cost} = \$13,005/2.058 = \$6,319$$
$$\text{Total cost (direct + indirect)} = \$19,324$$

Example D: A carpenter was injured slightly while adjusting a pneumatic nailer. The worker received medical treatment and was able to return to work after treatment. The worker was absent for 4 hours on the day of the injury. The foreman was also absent from the project for 4 hours to assist the injured worker. The superintendent took 3 hours to investigate the accident, fill out a report, talk to the company safety director, and develop a safe procedure to discuss at the next toolbox meeting. The worker was able to work the next day. The cost of the injury was estimated at the end of the day as follows:

$$\text{Field indirect cost} = \$150 + \$80(H + A)$$
$$= \$150 + \$80(4 + 4)$$
$$= \$790$$
$$\text{Total indirect cost} = \$790 \times 1.4 = \$1,106$$
$$\text{Total direct cost} = \$1,106/1.182 = \$936$$
$$\text{Total cost (direct + indirect)} = \$2,042$$

The actual computation of the costs of injuries may need little accuracy. The general intent of considering such costs is for management to get a better idea of the general magnitude of the costs of injuries. Taking administrative time to actually track the time involved in assisting workers, investigating accidents, and performing other tasks arising from the injury may provide little benefit if the details are not really that important. It may be more important to recognize that the costs are high. That point can be driven home easily just by directing attention to some of the average cost figures shown earlier. For example, the indirect costs of medical-case injuries are about $600, and the indirect costs of restricted-activity or lost-workday cases are about $14,000 (refer to Table 3.1).

More detailed injury cost estimates are clearly possible. Estimates of the indirect costs could be made individually; however, the issue of bias may result in some disagreement. Work performed by Robinson (1979) resulted in the development of a cost schedule for injuries of different types. In the schedule, different specific costs were established for a leg amputation, a leg fracture, a leg strain, a leg puncture, a leg burn, a leg bruise, and many other specific types of injury. The work was ambitious, and the final result is somewhat complex. In addition, the cost estimates tend to be of limited accuracy when based on "best guesses," and the accuracy quickly diminishes with time unless the appropriate factors are applied to them to adjust for inflation.

Robinson's cost schedule for injuries was intended to be used as the basis for a system of accounting for the costs of injuries. Essentially, when an injury was reported, the cost schedule would be used to determine the appropriate amount to allocate for the injury. That figure would be used irrespective of the actual costs that would eventually be incurred. Thus, it would be possible to allocate a cost for an injury shortly after the injury occurred. That immediacy is considered a strong benefit, as most of the costs cannot be known with accuracy until after the cases have been closed.

Why have an accounting system for the costs of injuries? The answer will be apparent to firms that have safety incentive programs. For example, a company may have an upcoming project for which the total worker hours have been estimated. Company statistics and industry averages can be used to determine an estimate of the number of injuries that may be incurred. From the average costs of injuries, discussed earlier, the company can estimate the total costs to be incurred if those injuries take place. From that figure, the company determines an appropriate amount to be set aside as an incentive. Suppose the company estimates the potential cost of injuries at $375,000 for a project. The company may decide to set aside $250,000 in the budget as a line item for safety. As injuries occur, the set-aside amount is reduced. The amount remaining in the account at the end of the project may be allocated among the workers, the supervisors, or both in some predetermined manner.

Although a great deal of study has been devoted to quantifying the true costs of injuries, the question becomes academic if no injuries occur. With a clear understanding of the true costs of injuries, perhaps more managers of construction will adopt the zero-accidents goal.

Indirect Costs Are Significant

The results of the CII study indicate that the indirect costs of injuries are not trivial and that perhaps greater attention should be given to them. The indirect costs examined were those that were associated with the job site and with liability suits. As stated earlier, no attempt was made to quantify the costs associated with the adverse impacts on the family members of the injured worker or the long-term impact of injuries on a company. In addition, the liability costs were only estimated for the study, as they are generally not incurred until long after an injury has occurred.

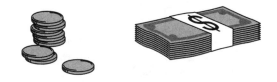

The researchers were successful in developing a model that could be used to estimate the field indirect costs of injuries. The best predictive models were those that included information on the number of hours lost by the injured worker because of follow-up care. Estimating models that did not include the variable on follow-up care were also developed, but accuracy was compromised when that variable was omitted. Since the models without the follow-up–care variable still explained about 40% of the indirect costs, some consideration should be given to their use. For some uses, they may be sufficiently accurate.

Some Costs Are Not Known

Although the costs of injuries have been shown to be significant, computations still have not addressed various actual costs. For example, no studies have developed reasonable estimates of the following cost items:

loss of pay for the injured worker
pain and suffering of the injured worker
adverse effects of the injury on other family members
personal negligence suits
damage to the company image
reduced profit margins for the firm
removal of the firm from bidding shortlists
reduced morale of company employees
possible criminal charges

The Next Step

The results indicate that greater attention should be given to the indirect costs of injuries. The indirect costs of medical-case injuries nearly match the direct costs. Although the field indirect costs of lost-workday injuries average little more than 20% of the direct costs, the total cost tends to be more than double the direct costs when liability claims are taken into account. Even if liability costs are not considered, the actual monetary amounts can still accumulate into large sums when there are many injuries.

Better safety performance will be realized when greater attention is given to the true costs of injuries. Supervisors commonly presume that they face a choice between worker safety and greater productivity. Such a presumption is particularly likely when the attitude in the firm is that insurance premiums are sunk costs (past costs that are unrecoverable and not relevant to an economic analysis). That mind-set assumes that any costs attributed to injuries can be ignored. That attitude must change. Safety and productivity should not be considered to be in conflict. When the true costs of injuries are computed, they generally make clear that compromising safety results in increased costs and decreased profits.

Sensitizing supervisory personnel to the true costs of injuries will improve safety. Supervisors must be made aware that safety and productivity are not in conflict. When they realize that the true costs of injuries are actually greater than the direct costs, as determined in the CII study, they have greater incentive for addressing safety objectively.

The Cost of Safety

The question is often posed, "How much does your firm spend on safety?" Answers vary greatly. Typical estimates range from less than 1% of project costs to more than 10% of project costs. No definitive work has been done in this area. Why do the estimated percentages vary so greatly? The answer may not necessarily be in differing amounts spent on safety but rather in the items included in safety. For example, one contractor may include the costs of scaffolding in the safety cost category. Another contractor may feel that the scaffolding is the only way to accomplish the work and may not consider it a safety expenditure. Numerous similar gray areas exist. Are hard hats, gloves, goggles, and other standard gear to be regarded as safety expenses, or are they, like hammers and drills, essential to accomplish the work? Would a welder consider doing any arc welding without a welding helmet? Would any prudent worker consider grinding metal without proper eye protection? Would a worker consider handling wire rope without gloves? Definitive costs are difficult to quantify.

Workers Compensation Fraud

The foregoing sections of this chapter have discussed the various costs associated with construction worker injuries. Most of that discussion has focused on the indirect costs of injuries. The direct costs are primarily those covered by workers' compensation insurance. The assumptions have been made that the injuries are legitimate and that they are truly work related. Therefore, the direct costs have not been questioned. Unfortunately, a large number of fraudulent workers' compensation claims are filed each year. Although the actual number of fraudulent claims is not known, some experts on the subject estimate that the number of such claims and their associated costs are staggering. Because of the temporary employment that is associated with many construction firms, the construction industry is a particular target for fraudulent claims.

Workers' compensation fraud was investigated extensively in the state of Florida. In a survey of Florida contractors, it was disclosed that 63.5% of all contractors surveyed had experienced what they believed to be fraudulent workers' compensation claims (Coble 1994). One very large firm reported a suspected 4,000 fraudulent claims per year.

The concern about workers' compensation fraud is obviously quite high. Many employers have taken positive steps to curb the filing of fraudulent claims. One method of reducing the filing of such claims has been the preselection of physicians to handle the workers' compensation claims for a construction project. Insurance companies can assist in this process, as they keep track of the numbers of compensation claims associated with specific doctors or clinics or occurring within specific geographical areas. Many contractors also require drug testing by a preselected physician for all workers involved in accidents. Contractors also try to educate their physicians about the type of work that is being performed so that modified work programs can be implemented. Most contractors who preselect physicians have reported that the practice is effective. Despite the success reported with the preselection of physicians, it is important to note that this is permitted in only 21 states. The study of the firms with annual volumes of business exceeding $200 million showed that 96% preselect physicians if they are permitted by law to do so. Among smaller firms (annual volumes less than $100 million), 46% preselect physicians when permitted.

Another means of curbing fraudulent claims is to expose the fraud. Fraud has been exposed in a number of cases through the use of private investigators. Of the larger contractors, 92% stated that they had hired private investigators in the past; among the smaller contractors, the number dropped to 42%. Back injuries are a type of injury for which fraud may be suspected. Suppose an "injured worker" reports having a serious back injury and misses several weeks of work during the convalescence period. If a private investigator then photographs or videotapes that same worker performing strenuous activities, perhaps as an employee of another firm, the case for a fraud accusation becomes more compelling. All contractors who had hired private investigators stated that the practice was beneficial. It was also reported that, when private investigators were not hired by the contractors, the insurance carriers frequently employed them on suspected fraud cases.

To help reduce fraudulent claims, some companies have formal training programs to educate their field supervisors to recognize suspicious activities or circumstances surrounding job-site accidents. Although fewer than half the large firms and only a few of the small firms have such formal programs, many of the other firms do communicate the signals of fraudulent claims to their employees. They do so through company newsletters, at weekly toolbox meetings, in paycheck inserts, and at company-sponsored events.

What are the signs of workers' compensation fraud? Obviously, this is a delicate question, and any one signal may not necessarily be compelling proof of fraud. However, if several signs indicate that fraud may be a factor, further investigation may be warranted. The Florida Office of the Treasurer and Insurance Commissioner has published a booklet concerning various types of insurance fraud (1994). For workers' compensation fraud alone, more than 100 hints are given. They include such signs as the following:

- Claimant has a history of reporting subjective injuries.
- The circumstances of the injury incident are suspicious (there were no witnesses, accident occurred late Friday afternoon or early Monday morning, worker was not at assigned work location when the accident occurred, etc.).
- Others report seeing the claimant employed elsewhere, or rumors indicate that the claim might be fraudulent.
- Claimant is never home when company personnel check on convalescence.
- Claimant demands a quick settlement.
- Claimant is unusually knowledgeable about all aspects of claims-handling procedures.
- Claimant's attorney or physician is known for handling suspicious claims.

Workers' compensation insurance was established to help injured workers; it is unfortunate that the costs are inflated by fraudulent claims. Also, the discussion here has been focused on fraud by claimants. It should be noted that the range of fraudulent activities is much broader, including employer fraud (underestimating payroll, producing incomplete payroll records, manipulating job classification codes, etc.), agent fraud (pocketing premiums, conspiring with employers, etc.), attorney fraud (filing fraudulent claims for workers), and medical provider fraud (supporting fraudulent claims within the medical profession). Successful results in prosecuting those involved in the filing of fraudulent claims will undoubtedly reduce the costs associated with workers' compensation insurance.

It is only in recent years that efforts to curb such fraudulent behavior have been initiated by state legislation. Florida and California have been particularly active in enacting legislation to reduce workers' compensation fraud. Although several successful prosecutions have been noted, the potential savings have not been determined.

Final Comments

The true costs of worker injuries are often not fully appreciated. The insurance premiums become a routine expenditure, and the indirect costs of injuries are generally absorbed in other line items in the budget. That is not a wise accounting approach, especially if those costs are not known. Closer examination of the total costs of injuries reveals that they are often quite high. Managers of construction should become fully aware of the magnitude of those costs. Managers who have examined such costs in greater detail have generally responded by placing greater emphasis on the safety aspects of construction work. To ignore the costs of injuries is not wise or financially expedient. The costs of injuries are high, even when they do not include the pain and suffering of the workers and their families. Once managers fully understand the magnitude of the true costs of injuries, it is easier for them to adopt a zero-accidents philosophy.

Review Questions

1. From the injury statistics presented in the Introduction to this book, develop a rough estimate of the annual cost of accidents in the construction industry. (Assume that medical case injuries are incurred at a rate of one per year per 5 construction workers.)

2. A large building project was completed with a safety record that included 19 medical-case injuries and 5 restricted-activity or lost-workday cases. Estimate the total costs of the injuries.

3. Several months after a highway project was completed, the insurance company reported that the project had had a total of 51 injuries, which resulted in a total direct cost of $79,000 to the insurance company. Estimate the total costs (direct and indirect) of the injuries.

4. A welder noticed a small amount of slag that needed to be cleaned off a piece of metal he had just welded. Since it was a small amount, he chipped at the slag without eye protection. He stopped suddenly when a small piece of slag got caught in his eye. A fellow worker took him to the doctor for treatment. In 2½ hours the welder and the helper were back on the job. The injured worker's eye was slightly inflamed but not seriously damaged. After three days, the injured worker returned to the doctor for a final checkup, which took 2 hours. He was released with a clean bill of health. Estimate the true cost of the injury.

5. A carpenter was working on the second-floor balcony of a townhouse project when she stepped off the edge of the building (guardrails were not in place at all locations). In the ensuing fall, the carpenter fell onto a stack of bricks on the ground level. She sustained several severe cuts, and it was apparent that her arm had been broken. The carpenter missed 6 hours of work on the day of the injury. The foreman who accompanied her in the ambulance returned to work near quitting time and began a thorough investigation of the accident. The superintendent also assisted in the investigation. They each spent 6 hours evaluating the accident. Estimate the true cost of the injury.

6. Describe three types of indirect accident costs that do not involve the injured worker or any other workers.

7. Describe the different types of indirect costs that may be incurred by injured workers.

8. Describe the different types of indirect accident costs that involve other workers on the construction site.

9. Describe how a construction firm might use information about the true costs of construction worker injuries. Consider either a generalized approach or a detailed approach to using the information.

10. Discuss the difference between the experience modification rate and the loss ratio as a measure of the safety performance of a firm.

References

Bird, F., and R. Loftus. 1976. *Loss Control Management.* Loganville, Ga.: Institute Press.

Blake, R. 1946. *Industrial Safety.* New York: Prentice-Hall.

Brown, D. 1988. "A Historical Examination of Accidents within the U.S. Army Corps of Engineers." Master of Science research report, University of Washington.

Business Roundtable. *Improving Construction Safety Performance.* 1982. Report A-3. New York: Business Roundtable.

Chaney, P. 1991. "The Hidden Costs of Jobsite Accidents." *Constructor* 73, no. 4, 40–41.

Chappell, K. 1991. "Boss, I Feel Lousy. Where's My Check?" *U.S. News & World Report,* July 29, 25–26.

Coble, R. 1994. *A Study of Fraudulent Workers' Compensation Claims.* Building Construction Industry Advisory Committee (BCIAC), Technical Publication no. 92. Gainesville: University of Florida.

Coble, R., and B. Elliott. 1995a. "Fraudulent Workers' Compensation Claims in the Construction Industry." In *Proceedings of the 31st Annual Conference, Associated Schools of Construction, Arizona State University, Tempe, Arizona, April 6–8, 1995,* edited by D. Koehler.

Coble, R., and B. Elliott. 1995b. "Fraudulent Workers' Compensation Claims As They Affect Contractors," *The American Professional Constructor* 19, no. 3, 2–7.

Florida Office of the Treasurer & Insurance Commissioner. 1994. *Fraud Detection Hints.* Tallahassee: Office of the Treasurer & Insurance Commissioner.

Heinrich, H. 1941. *Industrial Accident Prevention.* 2d ed. New York: McGraw-Hill.

Hinze, J. 1990a. "The Full Implications of Injuries." *National Utility Contractor* 14, no. 6, 24–26.

———. 1990b. "A New Study of Construction Injury Costs." *EXCEL, A Quarterly Newsletter of the Center for Excellence in Construction Safety* 4, no. 1, 1–4.

———. 1991a. "The Painful Cost of Construction Injuries." *Builder and Contractor* 39, no. 4, 19–21.

————. 1991b. "The True Costs of Injuries." Paper presented at Construction Industry Institute Annual Conference, August 14, in Monterey, California.

————. 1992. "Indirect Costs Are a Major Portion of Jobsite Injury Costs." *Concrete Construction* 37, no. 3, 229.

Hinze, J., and L. Appelgate. 1991. "Costs of Construction Injuries." *Journal of Construction Engineering and Management* 117, no. 3, 537–50.

Leopold, E., and S. Leonard. 1987. "Costs of Construction Accidents to Employers." *Journal of Occupational Accidents* 8, 273–94.

Levitt, R., and N. Samelson. 1993. *Construction Safety Management.* 2d ed. New York: John Wiley.

McCormick, J. 1995. "Litigation Down by Half Since Workers' Comp System Overhauled in Florida," *Florida Workers' Comp Advisor* 5, no. 7.

Naquin, A. 1975. "The Hidden Costs of Accidents." *Professional Safety* 20, no. 12, 36–39.

National Safety Council. 1985. *Supervisors Safety Manual.* 6th ed. Chicago: National Safety Council.

————. 1994. *Accident Facts.* Chicago: National Safety Council.

NCCI. 1994. *Getting to the Bottom of Workers' Compensation Fraud—Joining the Experts.* Boca Raton, Fl.: NCCI.

Perez, H. 1970. "Accidents: Money down the Drain." Editorial. *Construction Methods and Equipment* 52, no. 9, 69.

Robinson, M. 1979. *Accident Cost Accounting as a Means of Improving Construction Safety.* Technical Report no. 242 (August), Construction Institute. Stanford, Calif.: Stanford University.

"Safety: A Profitable Priority." 1983. *Builder and Contractor* 31, no. 10, 8–11.

Solomon, B., and J. Smith. 1992. "Premium Fraud: Part 1." *Safety Resources,* August.

Sheriff, R. 1980. "Loss Control Comes of Age." *Professional Safety,* September, 15–18.

Simpson, C. 1990. "Safety Pays on Contractors." *Construction Equipment* 82, no. 2, 50–51.

"What Does a Work Accident Really Cost?" 1987. *Northwest Builder* 1, no. 5, 3.

OSHA

Safety is more than an ideal; it is the law.

Congress passed the Occupational Safety and Health Act (also called the Williams-Steiger Act) on December 29, 1970. The act (hereafter called the OSH Act) was passed after several years of lobbying for a safer workplace for American workers. Ralph Nader was a key figure in the lobbying effort. Various labor groups also played instrumental roles in the passage of the law.

Key OSH Act Provisions

The essence of the OSH Act is that workers should have and be able to expect a safe place in which to work. It should be understood that the regulations apply specifically to employers; self-employed persons are exempt. The general duty clause of the law imposes an obligation on employers, as follows:

Sec. 5. Duties

(a) Each employer-
  (1) shall furnish to each of his employees employment and a place of employment which are free from recognized hazards that are causing or are likely to cause death or serious physical harm to his employees;

      (2)   shall comply with occupational safety and health standards promulgated under this chapter.

    (b) Each employee shall comply with occupational safety and health standards and all rules, regulations, and orders issued pursuant to this chapter which are applicable to his own actions and conduct. (29 USC 654)

The general duty clause states that it is not sufficient for an employer to comply with safety regulations. If a work condition exists that the employer knows is a health or safety threat, even if there is no specific standard addressing the condition, the employer has a duty to protect the employees from the threat.

OSH Act Agencies

When the OSH Act was passed, it established three different agencies: the Occupational Safety and Health Administration (OSHA), the National Institute for Occupational Safety and Health (NIOSH), and the Occupational Safety and Health Review Commission (OSHRC). Of these, OSHA is the most visible. OSHA is responsible for promulgating new regulations and for enforcing the regulations in the places of work. OSHA regulations are enforced through inspections of employer sites by OSHA compliance officers. OSHA is also charged with gathering statistics on injuries and job-related illnesses.

NIOSH, as the research arm of OSHA, conducts a variety of studies on safety and health problems, provides technical assistance to OSHA, and makes recommendations to OSHA concerning new safety and health regulations. NIOSH is also involved in some training activities. Although NIOSH has done extensive work in the areas of safety and health, the emphasis has clearly shifted to health hazards. During the early 1980s considerable emphasis was placed on such building materials as asbestos. In the late 1980s and early 1990s, the emphasis shifted to lead and other materials. Although NIOSH recommends new regulations to OSHA, there is no obligation on the part of OSHA to enact NIOSH-recommended standards.

The OSHRC performs a judiciary role, hearing cases in which employers disagree with OSHA's determination that its regulations have been violated. The amount of a fine or the length of the abatement period may also be contested. The OSHRC consists of a three-member board that is appointed by the President.

OSHA Standards

The standards that OSHA has promulgated have different focus areas—namely, general industry, maritime, agriculture, and construction. In general, the greatest emphasis is placed on the general industry standards, described in part 1910 of Title 29 of the Code of Federal Regulations, commonly referred to as 29 CFR 1910. The regulations that pertain specifically to the construction industry are described in 29 CFR 1926. Employers in the construction industry must comply with both sets of regulations. They must also comply with the numerous consensus standards, such as those adopted by the National Fire Protection Association (NFPA), the American Society of Agricultural Engineers

(ASAE), the American National Standards Institute (ANSI), American Standards for Testing and Materials (ASTM), and the American Society of Mechanical Engineers (ASME). The consensus standards are part of the OSHA regulations through reference.

Efforts to comply with OSHA regulations require an understanding of those regulations. A good beginning is to have a copy of the current regulations. They are available from the U.S. government at the following address:

Superintendent of Documents
U.S. Government Printing Office
Washington, DC 20402
(202) 783-3238

Most of the OSHA regulations provide direct guidance for maintaining safe physical conditions in the workplace. Some minor exceptions include regulations that focus on management's responsibility to assist in maintaining project safety and in training the workers. One such regulation is as follows:

§ 1926.20 General safety and health provisions.

(a) *Contractor requirements.* . . . [I]t shall be a condition of each contract . . . for construction, alteration, and/or repair, including painting and decorating, that no contractor or subcontractor for any part of the contract work shall require any laborer or mechanic employed in the performance of the contract to work in surroundings or under working conditions which are unsanitary, hazardous, or dangerous to his health or safety.

The foregoing provision implies that the term *construction* is to be interpreted in a broad manner. Not restricted to new construction, it may be interpreted as including maintenance work (as reflected in the inclusion of the word *repair*).

The focus of the standards is clearly split, with a focus on both safety and health. The trend since the late 1970s has been to place a greater emphasis on health. Of course, in construction the major cause of death is falls, followed by other causes that can be classified as safety-related. It is difficult to track the health statistics because many ailments have long latency periods, which make it difficult to establish a positive link between an exposure and a particular ailment.

Although the OSHA regulations focused largely on maintaining safe conditions, some requirements relate to helping employees prepare for job-site conditions. Those standards are relatively general. They address worker competency and employer inspection of the work premises, but they do not provide specific guidance. Their wording, which may appear vague, does permit them to apply to a wide range of employment settings.

§ 1926.20 General safety and health provisions.

. . .

(b) *Accident prevention responsibilities.*

(1) It shall be the responsibility of the employer to initiate and maintain such programs as may be necessary to comply with this part.

(2) Such programs shall provide for frequent and regular inspections of the job sites, materials, and equipment to be made by competent persons designated by the employers.

(3) The use of any machinery, tool, material, or equipment which is not in compliance with any applicable requirement of this part is prohibited. Such machine, tool, material, or equipment shall either be identified as unsafe by tagging or locking the controls to render them inoperable or shall be physically removed from its place of operation.

(4) The employer shall permit only those employees qualified by training or experience to operate equipment and machinery.

The regulations specifically address training. Again, however, they do not clearly define the details of training that is adequate to satisfy the regulations.

§ 1926.21 Safety training and education.

(a) *General requirements.* The Secretary shall, pursuant to section 107(F) of the Act, establish and supervise programs for the education and training of employers and employees in the recognition, avoidance and prevention of unsafe conditions in employments covered by the act.

(b) *Employer responsibility.*

(1) The employer should avail himself of the safety and health training programs the Secretary provides.

(2) The employer shall instruct each employee in the recognition and avoidance of unsafe conditions and the regulations applicable to his work environment to control or eliminate any hazards or other exposure to illness or injury.

(3) Employees required to handle or use poisons, caustics, and other harmful substances shall be instructed regarding the safe handling and use, and be made aware of the potential hazards, personal hygiene, and personal protective measures required.

(4) In job site areas where harmful plants or animals are present, employees who may be exposed shall be instructed regarding the potential hazards, and how to avoid injury, and the first aid procedures to be used in the event of injury.

(5) Employees required to handle or use flammable liquids, gases, or toxic materials shall be instructed in the safe handling and use of these materials and made aware of the specific requirements contained in subparts D, F, and other applicable subparts of this part.

(6) (i) All employees required to enter into confined or enclosed spaces shall be instructed as to the nature of the hazards involved, the necessary precautions to be taken, and in the use of protective and emergency equipment required. The employer shall comply with any specific regulations that apply to work in dangerous or potentially dangerous areas.

(ii) For purposes of paragraph (b)(6)(i) of this section, "confined or enclosed space" means any space having a limited means of egress, which is subject to the accumulation of toxic or flammable contaminants or has an oxygen deficient atmosphere. Confined or enclosed spaces include, but are not limited to, storage tanks, process vessels, bins, boilers, ventilation or exhaust ducts, sewers, underground utility vaults, tunnels, pipelines, and open top spaces more than 4 feet in depth such as pits, tubs, vaults, and vessels.

The OSHA regulations pertaining specifically to construction are contained in a single booklet. Although that booklet by itself is still a formidable document to many employers, the inclusion by reference of other standards makes the regulations even more formidable. That inclusion is accomplished in the following regulation:

§ 1926.31 Incorporation by reference.

(a) The specifications, standards and codes of agencies of the U.S. Government and organizations which are not agencies of the U.S. Government, to the extent they are legally incorporated by reference in this part, have the same force and effect as other standards in this part.

The section goes on to list the locations where the specifications, standards, and codes referred to may be examined.

Numerous terms are defined in the definitions section of the regulations. Some of the definitions of particular interest to employers are the following:

§ 1926.32 Definitions.

. . .

(d) "Authorized person" means a person approved or assigned by the employer to perform a specific type of duty or duties or to be at a specific location at the jobsite. . . .

(f) "Competent person" means one who is capable of identifying existing and predictable hazards in the surroundings or working conditions which are unsanitary, hazardous, or dangerous to employees, and who has authorization to take prompt corrective measures to eliminate them. . . .

(j) "Employee" means every laborer or mechanic under the Act regardless of the contractual relationship which may be alleged to exist between the laborer and mechanic and the contractor or subcontractor who engaged him. "Laborer and mechanic" are not defined in the Act, but the identical terms are used in the Davis-Bacon Act (40 U.S.C. 276a), which provides for minimum wage protection on Federal and federally assisted construction contracts. . . . "Laborer" generally means one who performs manual labor or who labors at an occupation requiring physical strength; "mechanic" generally means a worker skilled with tools. See 18 Comp. Gen. 341.

(k) "Employer" means contractor or subcontractor within the meaning of the Act and of this part. . . .

(m) "Qualified" means one who, by possession of a recognized degree, certificate, or professional standing, or who by extensive knowledge, training, and experience, has successfully demonstrated his ability to solve or resolve problems relating to the subject matter, the work, or the project.

Since the mid-1980s, a major emphasis has been on the hazardous materials to which workers on construction projects may be exposed. The regulations concerning hazardous materials are referred to as *hazard communication,* or "haz com." As the term implies, the education of the work force is at the very foundation of the regulations. Such education is a complex task for general contractors, who may have many employees on a single project for only a short while. A formal approach seems almost essential to ensure that every employee is fully informed about identified hazards in the workplace.

§ 1926.59 Hazard Communication.

(a) *Purpose.*

(1) The purpose of this section is to ensure that the hazards of all chemicals produced or imported are evaluated, and that information concerning their hazards is transmitted to employers and employees. This transmittal of information

is to be accomplished by means of comprehensive hazard communication programs, which are to include container labeling and other forms of warning, material safety data sheets and employee training.

The standards that have been quoted here may be considered to address management issues. That is, they address safety from a general perspective in which management is held accountable. More management-related requirements may be addressed in the OSHA regulations, but they tend to be specifically associated with particular safety requirements.

Promulgation of New Standards

As more information is gathered on specific topics of safety and health, OSHA sometimes elects to issue new standards. Before formally implementing new standards, OSHA publicizes its intentions in a "Notice of Proposed Rulemaking," which appears in the Federal Register. The notice is to solicit from interested parties information that will be used in drafting the final standards. Arguments, accompanied by supporting evidence, can be made in writing. Arguments can also be made at public hearings, which can be requested if they have not been scheduled. Before any new standard becomes final, OSHA publishes the new standard in its entirety, along with any justification or supporting information, in the Federal Register.

Under some conditions, OSHA may issue standards without first obtaining public input. Those are emergency temporary standards that OSHA wants to become effective immediately. The intent is for those standards to be subsequently replaced by permanent standards. Once a temporary standard has been published in the Federal Register, in anticipation of its becoming a permanent standard, the public is permitted to comment, to offer support or to voice objections, at a public hearing. A more extreme way of objecting to an emergency temporary standard is to file a challenge in the U.S. Court of Appeals.

Variances

As may well be imagined, the OSHA regulations cannot and do not cover every conceivable work condition or situation. There are situations in which the OSHA regulations offer little in the way of guidance. When such situations arise, the employer must simply be ingenious and devise a means by which worker safety and health can be preserved. A more perplexing problem arises when an employer has a solution that provides for the safety and health of workers when a specific safety and health standard already exists. An employer may find it virtually impossible to comply with a particular standard. Can such an employer simply use another means of providing for the safety and health of the workers, even though the method violates the existing standard? The answer is, "Probably not without a variance."

What is a variance? It is a means by which an employer can obtain the blessing of OSHA to deviate from the standard OSHA requirements. To obtain a variance, the employer must show that the proposed method is comparable to the existing standard in providing for the safety and health of the workers. Although the specific statistics are not published, historically the requests for variances have been relatively few, and the number of variances granted tends to be even smaller. Many variances are rejected simply because the employer has not shown that the safety and health of the workers would be as secure as if the OSHA regulations were followed. In some cases, variances have been rejected because OSHA considered the proposed procedures to be in compliance with the existing standards.

One type of variance that may be granted is the temporary variance. A temporary variance permits an employer to deviate from the standards until the employer can achieve full compliance with the standards. Full compliance must take place within a period established by OSHA. That period will not exceed one year. A temporary variance can be renewed up to two times for periods of six months each. Employees must be informed about the differences from OSHA standards that the temporary variance permits.

A permanent variance may also be granted. Under a permanent variance, an employer is allowed to continue to deviate from a specific standard when the employer has proven that the conditions, practices, means, methods, operations, or processes provide a safe and healthful workplace as effectively as would compliance with the established OSHA standard. Employees must be informed about any details concerning a permanent variance, and they can request a hearing.

Informing Employees

It is the responsibility of the employer to keep all employees informed about OSHA standards and any proposed or implemented changes. The information the employer must provide includes the following:

> a Job Safety and Health Protection workplace poster (OSHA 2203 or state equivalent)
> upon request, OSHA standards for employee inspection
> information on attempts to obtain variances from the standards
> copies of all OSHA citations and fines
> the Summary of Occupational Injuries and Illnesses (must be posted each year no
> later than February 1 and must remain in place until March 1)

Employees must also be informed about any construction materials or substances that are thought to pose some type of health threat. The employer must offer guidance in the proper handling of such materials. That guidance must include material safety data sheets, training programs, and labels attached to containers.

Compliance Inspections

Every employer's establishment is subject to inspection by OSHA. Compliance with OSHA regulations is monitored by OSHA compliance officers. An inspection can be initiated for any of the following reasons:

- prior knowledge, with reasonable certainty, of imminent danger (a situation that can be expected to cause death or serious bodily harm)
- the random selection of a work site

- a complaint (presumably by a worker on site) of an alleged violation of the OSHA standards
- the occurrence of a fatality or an incident that results in the hospitalization of five or more workers
- programmed, or scheduled, inspections of high-hazard industries, occupations (roofing, trenching, etc.), or substances
- follow-up inspections to verify that violations noted in prior inspections have been abated

When a compliance inspection does occur, the compliance officer is to introduce himself or herself, display his or her credentials, and ask to meet with an appropriate employer representative. There is no advance notice of such an inspection. The inspection may occur at any time during the normal working hours of the establishment.

The inspection begins with an opening conference, in which the compliance officer first explains how the site was selected for inspection. Then he or she explains the purpose of the inspection, the scope of the inspection, and the OSHA standards that apply to the site. At that time the compliance officer gives the employer a copy of the applicable standards. If a complaint of a violation was made, the officer also gives the employer a copy of the complaint (protecting the anonymity of the person filing the complaint if that person has requested anonymity).

The employer is asked to select a representative to accompany the compliance officer on the inspection. If the project has union representation, the union is also permitted to designate an employee to accompany the compliance officer. If there is a safety committee on site, the employee members of that committee are asked to designate a member to accompany the compliance officer. If no such group exists, the compliance officer may select an employee he or she deems suitable to represent the interests of the other employees. Note that the employer is not to select this employee. It is not required that an employee accompany the compliance officer. If no employee does accompany the compliance officer, the compliance officer may consult privately with selected employees during the site visit.

May an employer deny access to a compliance officer? According to a 1978 Supreme Court decision (*Marshall v. Barlow's, Inc.*, 436 U.S. 307), warrantless OSHA inspections cannot take place without the employer's permission. Actually, denying access is an option that can be exercised by the employer. Unless the compliance officer has a search warrant, he or she must obtain the employer's permission before making a formal job-site inspection. Of course, one must be wary of opting to deny access, as the compliance officer will probably be able to acquire the search warrant within a short time (he or she must show administrative probable cause for a search, or evidence of a violation). One can also anticipate that the compliance officer may be a bit more meticulous in the job-site inspection if the employer initially refused entry.

Compliance officers often begin by checking that injury records (OSHA No. 200) are current and that the required OSHA workplace poster (OSHA 2203) is properly displayed. Those examinations are followed by a general tour of the site. The route taken and the duration of the inspection are decided by the compliance officer. It is often advisable to take notes on the tour, just as the compliance officer does. The compliance officer may also ask questions of workers on the premises as a means of getting a full picture of the safety conditions on site. The compliance officer takes notes on conversations, makes sketches of conditions, takes measurements, takes photographs, and makes other efforts to fully document the conditions on the site. In general, the compliance officer tries to minimize disruption of the work. Even if the inspection is in response to a complaint or a fatality, the inspection may include the entire work site; however, the inspection may cover only a portion of the site.

As the compliance officer observes violations and unsafe conditions, he or she points them out to the employer's representative. The officer suggests possible corrective measures if the employer expresses an interest in such information. Some conditions that are obvious violations can be corrected immediately. The compliance officer notes any actions taken to correct unsafe conditions at the time of observance, and that information helps to document the employer's good faith in trying to comply. Even conditions that are immediately corrected, however, may become the basis for a citation, a penalty, or both.

Typically, at the conclusion of the inspection, the compliance officer summarizes the inspection results with the employer or the employer's representative in a closing conference. The closing conference tends to be an informal meeting with open discussion. The employer or the employer's representative should feel free to ask questions during the conference. All violations for which a citation may be issued or recommended are discussed. If any serious violations were identified, the compliance officer asks the employer to correct the conditions promptly. The officer usually specifies the abatement period; however, the period may be negotiated. If workers' lives are threatened by certain conditions, the compliance officer may very well elect to stop work on that portion of the project. The officer explains the appeals procedure if the employer has any interest in the information. Note that the compliance officer does not discuss the penalties, as they are determined by the area director after the full report has been reviewed. The compliance officer may also discuss the various services (guest speakers, handout packages, training and technical materials on the subject of safety and health, etc.) offered by OSHA.

If violations are identified in the OSHA inspection, citations will be issued and fines may be levied against the employer. The length of the abatement period will be stated. The citations and the notice of imposed penalties are sent to the employer by certified mail. The employer must post a copy of each citation near the location where the violation occurred, for three days or until the condition is abated, whichever is longer.

Penalties vary with the severity of the infraction. Table 4.1 is a brief summary of the types of violations and the penalties that may be proposed. Harsh penalties may

Table 4.1

Breakdown of Penalties for Different Types of OSHA Violations

Type of Violation	Penalty per Violation
Less than serious	up to $7,000
Serious	mandatory, up to $7,000
Willful	$5,000 to $70,000
Repeat	up to $70,000
Failure to correct a prior violation	up to $7,000 per day

also be levied for falsifying records, violating the posting requirements, or assaulting a compliance officer. Some of those penalties may include jail time in addition to fines. The amount of any penalty may be reduced according to the size of the firm and the firm's history of OSHA violations. Credits for good faith may also reduce the fines, but such credits are not granted on willful violations. If the total assessment is less than $50, when adjusted, no penalty is imposed.

Note that compliance officers do not cite workers. That is true even if the workers flagrantly violate OSHA regulations or if they continue certain unsafe practices after they have been told specifically to avoid them.

The employer is free to challenge the citation, the penalty, or the abatement period. To do so formally, the employer must submit a written objection to OSHA within 15 working days of receiving the citation. The area director then forwards the case to the OSHRC. The OSHRC, an independent agency not associated with OSHA, assigns the case to an administrative law judge. After the administrative law judge has ruled, any party to the case may request a further review by the OSHRC.

The employer may completely bypass the formal appeal procedure and may instead request an informal hearing with the area director. Even if the area director finds the violation justified, as noted earlier, he or she may decide to reduce the fine if the employer has a good past OSHA record, if the firm qualifies as a small employer, or if prompt action was taken to correct any identified hazards.

OSHA State-Plan States

Part of the OSH Act permits the enforcement of the OSHA regulations to be delegated to the states. The states that have elected to assume the enforcement role are called state-plan states. State-plan programs receive up to 50% of their funding from OSHA. To ensure that the spirit of the federal legislation is properly administered, OSHA monitors the state efforts through its regional offices. There are 10 such regional offices.

The state-plan states also have the power to promulgate their own safety regulations, provided that the state regulations are at least as stringent as the federal regulations. Although some state-plan states have adopted the OSHA regulations with virtually no significant changes, others have initiated considerable numbers of new safety regulations. Some of the changes adopted by state-plan states have subsequently been adopted in federal standards.

There are currently 21 state-plan states: Alaska, Hawaii, Arizona, New Mexico, California, Nevada, Utah, Oregon, Washington, Wyoming, Minnesota, Iowa, Michigan, Indiana, Kentucky, Tennessee, Virginia, North Carolina, South Carolina, Maryland, and Vermont. New York and Connecticut have state plans only for public-sector employees. The state-plan states do receive some funding from OSHA, but at least half the cost is borne by the individual states that develop their own state plans.

OSHA Consultation Services

The task of providing for the safety and health of workers need not be done without assistance. Some assistance may come from state government employees assigned to the consulting branch of OSHA. The federal government provides a considerable portion of the funds to support the consulting effort in each state. Thus, the consultants are truly independent of the compliance officers, who—except in the state-plan states—are federal employees. Consulting consists of advice and suggestions that construction firms can solicit without placing themselves at risk. Consultants can be contacted for advice on immediate problems and also for suggestions to help maintain effective protection for workers. Consultants can help to identify and correct specific hazards. They can also suggest ways of establishing, sustaining, and improving an effective safety and health program. They also offer training and education for contractors and their employees. Consultation services are available at no cost.

Consultations can occur by different means. One way is to obtain advice over the telephone. Questions posed over the telephone should ideally be of a generic nature, as the consultant cannot be expected to fully appreciate the environment or surroundings of any specific conditions. The most effective consultations are those in which the OSHA consultant is asked to physically examine the site and to offer suggestions. There is no overt risk involved in obtaining the assistance of an OSHA consultant. Consultants do not issue citations, and they do not propose penalties as a result of their consultations. In addition, the consulting service is completely confidential. A consultant does not routinely report the name of the firm or any information about the place of work to the OSHA inspection staff. Consultants are state employees with no powers of enforcement. The consultants work completely independent of the compliance officers; however, it is doubtful that a life-threatening condition would be treated lightly. Employers are well-advised to respond to the consultant's suggestions. After all, why call in a consultant and not heed his advice?

Consultants who are invited to a construction site will not become inspectors on a subsequent visit. Some contractors are reluctant to call OSHA for advice, but OSHA is the very agency that employers should consult when they are unsure of some safety aspect of a project. A consultant on a project visit may insist that blatantly unsafe conditions be corrected, but the consultant is not to make a detailed investigation with the intent of having a compliance officer make a follow-up visit. Consultants must be contacted if their advice is desired, as consultations do not occur without a request.

Other OSHA Programs

Voluntary protection programs represent an effort by OSHA to encourage worker protection that exceeds the minimum required by OSHA standards. There are three types of voluntary protection programs: the star program, the merit program, and the demonstration program. The programs are designed to recognize outstanding achievement by firms that have successfully incorporated comprehensive safety and health programs into their total management style, to motivate others to achieve excellent safety and health results in the same outstanding way, and to establish relationships between employers, employees, and OSHA that are based on cooperation rather than on coercion. The star program is the premier program. It is open to any employer who has managed a comprehensive safety and health program to reduce injury rates below the national average for the industry. Management commitment and employee participation are key ingredients of a star program. Other elements include a high-quality work-site analysis program, hazard prevention and control programs, and comprehensive safety and health training for all employees. All those programs must be fully operating and effective for the employer to be eligible for the star program. The demonstration and merit programs are lower-level progams that are stepping-stones to the star program.

In the fall of 1994, OSHA implemented focused inspections. Focused inspections are very specific in their scope. On a focused inspection, the OSHA compliance officer makes a quick inspection of certain conditions on the job site. If the compliance officer finds those conditions acceptable, OSHA does not conduct an in-depth inspection. For example, it is widely known and well documented through OSHA records that nearly half of all fatalities in construction are caused by electric shocks and falls. Thus, the compliance officers focus their inspections of construction sites on such life-threatening conditions as those likely to cause falls and electric shock. If no life-threatening conditions are found, no full-blown inspection is made. If conditions are not found to be satisfactory, a detailed inspection follows.

A more recent trend in OSHA is to consider targeted inspections. Although the specifics of the program have not been fully formulated, the intent of targeting is to direct OSHA inspections to the construction projects of firms that have not demonstrated adequate compliance with OSHA regulations in the past. Firms whose safety performance has historically been poor are considered more likely to have OSHA violations. With targeted inspections, compliance officers would not waste the time of contractors that have exemplary safety records.

Final Comments

The OSHA standards have been in force for more than 25 years. In that period, the standards have gone through many modifications. Most of the revisions have been driven by the need to address specific hazards more effectively. Although violations of the OSHA standards can result in severe penalties, contractors should not view OSHA as an adversary. Through its consulting services, OSHA can contribute greatly to safety by helping employers establish appropriate methods for accomplishing specific tasks. Even though the penalties for OSHA violations may appear high in some instances, they tend to be dwarfed by the costs incurred if the conditions are not checked and a serious injury results. By making a concerted effort to stay in compliance with the OSHA standards, an employer takes positive steps to avoid accidents. OSHA is here to stay, so the healthy approach is for employers to utilize the services it offers.

Review Questions

1. What are the different means by which an OSHA inspection site can be selected?
2. Why was the OSH Act passed?
3. What is the function of NIOSH?
4. What is a state-plan state?
5. How is an OSHA citation appealed if the employer does not agree with the assessment?

6. When might a variance be sought by an employer?
7. Even if an OSHA citation is justified, how can the penalty be reduced?
8. What is the cost to an employer who utilizes OSHA consultation services?
9. Compare or contrast the roles of OSHA and NIOSH in the promulgation of new safety standards.
10. Must OSHA compliance officers receive the permission of employers before making job-site inspections?

References

Hinze, J. 1993. *Construction Contracts.* New York: McGraw-Hill.

U.S. Department of Labor. Occupational Safety and Health Administration. 1990. *Analysis of Construction Fatalities—The OSHA Data Base 1985–1989.* November. Washington, D.C.

———. 1992. *All about OSHA.* OSHA 2056. Washington, D.C.

———. 1994a. *Construction Industry Digest.* OSHA 2202. Washington, D.C.

———. 1994b. *29 CFR 1926/1910; Construction Industry—OSHA Safety and Health Standards.* OSHA 2207. Revised July 1. Washington, D.C.

Problem Areas in Construction Safety

No worker expects to be injured.

One can learn much about safety by reviewing data about past safety violations and injuries. Several studies have been conducted in the past few years that provide considerable insight into this pervasive problem. As noted in the introduction, the construction industry is among the leaders in frequency of injuries and fatalities. The incidence of injuries and fatalities has declined significantly over the past decades, but the current levels are still unacceptable. One way of improving safety performance in the construction industry is to focus on the root causes of many of the injuries that do occur.

Problem Areas

In 1990, OSHA published a report on an analysis of fatalities that occurred in 1985 through 1989. That report clearly pointed out the primary areas of concern, or root causes of death, in the construction industry. The results are summarized in Figure 5.1.

As is clearly evident from the figure, construction safety efforts must strongly emphasize fall prevention. A clear secondary area of concern is that of electrical shocks. In the OSHA study it was found that, of all the fatalities, 11% were the result of contacts with overhead power lines.

Figure 5.1
Distribution of Construction
Fatalities (1985–89)

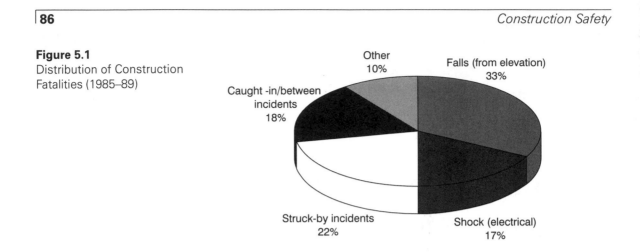

Problem Regulations

An analysis of the results of OSHA inspections conducted in 1980, 1985, and 1990 provides some interesting insights about the OSHA standards that warrant particular attention in the construction industry (Hinze and Russell 1995). The most often cited standards are presented in Table 5.1.

Although the standards mentioned in the most citations are of interest, of even greater interest may be the standards associated with the heaviest penalties. The analysis included a determination of the standards for which employers received the highest-penalty citations, those that exceeded $5,000. The standards for which the greatest numbers of those high penalties were imposed in the combined years of 1980, 1985, and 1990 were in the following order. Note that as the standards are expanded and modified over the years, the specific section titles may change:

- 1926.652 Requirements for protective systems (excavations)
- 5A.001 General duty clause of the OSH Act
- 1926.21 Safety training and education
- 1926.651 Specific excavation requirements
- 1926.550 Cranes and derricks
- 1926.451 Scaffolding
- 1926.105 Safety nets
- 1926.500 Floor openings
- 1926.28 Personal protective equipment
- 1926.950 General requirements (power transmission and distribution)

Each of those standards had more than 5 high-penalty citations for the three years combined. Of the 169 high-penalty citations given in those three years, 116, or nearly 69%, are attributable to the standards in the preceding list.

There were 39 high-penalty violations in 1980, 19 high-penalty violations in 1985, and 111 high-penalty violations in 1990. The sharp increase in the number of high-penalty citations in 1990 shows a trend that continued in the 1990s; that is, the amount of OSHA fines increased. There have been suggestions that OSHA has become too heavy-handed in its approach. Although that is debatable, politics may prevail, leading

OSHA once again to change its stance. The change would be for OSHA to act as a partner to the construction community, and not as a police agency. After-the-fact data will tell us if that approach is better for job-site safety.

Willful violations are also of interest. They are violations by employers who are presumably aware of the standards but blatantly ignore them. There were 222 willful-violation citations in the three years combined (36 in 1980, 64 in 1985, and 122 in 1990). It is readily apparent that the number of citations for willful violations has risen dramatically. In the three years combined, the standards associated with more than 5 willful citations were, in ranked order, as follows:

- 1926.652 Requirements for protective systems (excavations)[1]
- 5A.001 General duty clause of the OSH Act[1]
- 1926.552 Material hoists, personnel hoists, and elevators
- 1926.21 Safety training and education[1]
- 1926.651 Specific excavation requirements[1]
- 1926.500 Floor openings[1]
- 1926.451 Scaffolding[1]
- 1926.550 Cranes and derricks[1]
- 1926.105 Safety nets[1]
- 1926.28 Personal protective equipment[1]
- 1926.20 General safety and health provisions

---

[1]This standard was also among those for which employers received the greatest numbers of high penalties.

Table 5.1
Ranking of OSHA Paragraphs with the Largest Number of Violations

Standard		1980	1985	1990
1926.59	Hazard communication*	–	–	1
1926.21	Safety training and education**	4	3	2
1926.550	Cranes and derricks**	6	1	3
1926.451	Scaffolding—Design**	1	2	4
1926.20	General safety and health provisions	–	–	5
1926.500	Guarding of floor openings and platforms**	7	4	6
1926.651	Excavations—Access/egress	–	9	7
1926.451(a)	Scaffolding—General requirements**	9	8	8
1926.404	Wiring design and protection	–	–	9
1926.652	Excavations—Protection from cave-ins**	8	7	10
1926.400	Electrical—General	5	5	–
1926.28(a)	Personal protective equipment	–	6	–
1926.552	Material hoists, personnel hoists and elevators	–	10	–
5(a)(1)	General duty clause of the OSHAct	2	–	–
1926.28	Personal protective equipment	3	–	–
1926.50	Medical services and first aid	10	–	–

* The hazard communication standard was not in effect in 1980 or 1985.

** This standard paragraph ranked in the top 10 in number of violations in each of the three years.

The standards associated with willful violations are often also related to high-penalty citations. Note that 29 CFR § 1926.950 (general requirements for power transmission and distribution) is the only standard that was listed among the high-penalty violations but not among the standards with willful violations. Conversely, 29 CFR § 1926.552 (material hoists, personnel hoists, and elevators) and 29 CFR § 1926.20 (general safety and health provisions) were the only standards listed among the willful violations but not among the high-penalty violations. The conclusion is obvious: willful violations generally result in high penalties.

The same study included an examination of construction fatalities and their causes during the same three years. Worker fatalities are recorded in the OSHA database known as the Integrated Management Information System (IMIS). The causes of most construction accidents are classified into five broad event types. The event types, shown in Figure 5.1, are (1) falls, (2) struck-by incidents, (3) caught-in/between incidents, (4) electrical shock, and (5) other. The percentage of construction fatalities of each of the six event types for the three years studied is shown in Table 5.2. For comparison, the results of the OSHA study on construction fatalities in 1985–89 are also shown (Department of Labor 1990). Note that the results of the two studies are consistent.

It was noted that the frequency of fatalities due to falls increased with time. Interestingly, the number of citations for violations of the scaffolding design standards decreased during the same period. From that information it might be inferred that more stringent enforcement of certain OSHA standards results in fewer fatalities in those areas. The struck-by causes appear to have increased, and the caught-in/between causes to have decreased. Since those categories are the least well defined of the various causes, their apparent trends provide little insight and are not assumed to be significant.

Confirming what was already common knowledge in the industry, the study indicated that falls are the most common source of construction worker fatalities. An evaluation of the specific causes of the 508 falls reported in the database disclosed that the most common falls were as follows:

- off roof
- in scaffolding collapse
- off scaffolding

Table 5.2
Frequency of Occurrence of Different Causes of Fatalities.

Event Type	Frequency of Occurrence (%)			
	1980	1985	1990	1985–89 OSHA Study
Falls	34.8	36.6	39.6	33
Struck by	18.8	27.9	29.5	22
Struck against	2.5	0	0	0
Caught in/between	16.0	13.3	9.3	18
Electrical shock	19.7	17.1	16.9	17
Other	8.2	5.1	4.7	10

- in structure collapse
- through floor opening
- off ladder
- off structure
- through roof opening
- off edge of open floor
- off beam support

Many of the falls resulting in fatalities occur during work performed on roofs and on scaffolding. Of the types of falls in the preceding list, the first 5 accounted for 45% of all fall-related fatalities. The 10 types of falls listed accounted for 68% of all fall-related fatalities. Falls caused by external forces, as opposed to those in which workers simply lose their balance, constituted the majority of the fatalities. Examples of external forces are the collapse of a support system, a blow from an object, and a fall through an unknown or unprotected opening.

The height of fatal falls was also examined. The average fall height was 46.8 feet. The average fall height did not vary appreciably among the three years examined. The shortest fall was from a height of 5 feet and was described as follows: "Employee fell approximately 5 feet from the bed of a ¾ ton pickup truck landing directly on the back of his head, killing him. The truck was traveling at 8–10 mph." When information on low-level falls was examined, it was noted that head wounds were the most common cause of death of the workers.

After falls, the most common cause of fatalities was being struck. The specific circumstances of the struck-by incidents can be ranked as follows:

- worker struck by falling object
- worker run over by heavy equipment
- worker struck by crane, boom, or load
- worker run over by private vehicle
- worker struck in trench cave-in

The circumstances just listed constituted 70% of the struck-by fatalities. There was an increase in struck-by fatalities from 1980 to 1985 and 1990. The increase can be attributed largely to an increase in the number of workers run over by heavy equipment or struck by a crane, its boom, or its load. There was a decline in the later years in the number of fatalities caused by falling objects.

Incidents in which a worker was caught in or between objects were the third most common cause of construction worker fatalities. The specific circumstances of such incidents are ranked as follows:

- trench cave-in
- worker caught between pieces of heavy equipment
- overturning of heavy equipment or machinery
- worker caught in moving part of heavy equipment

The four listed causes of caught-in/between fatalities accounted for 62% of such fatalities. Cave-ins are a major source of such fatalities, accounting for 32%. Examination of the specific circumstances of caught-in/between fatalities revealed that several are very similar to those of the struck-by fatalities. Heavy equipment was involved in many of the fatalities.

The study included a closer examination of the trench cave-in fatalities, since they accounted for a significant number of the caught-in/between fatalities. The trench depths were of particular interest in that evaluation. Many of the trenching fatalities occurred in seemingly shallow trenches: 60% occurred in trenches that were no more than 10 feet deep. Those fatalities generally occurred when the worker was knocked to the ground by a trench wall collapse and subsequently buried by another collapse. Recovery efforts in such cases are generally futile. Although asphyxiation may be the cause of death in some trench cave-ins, in many cases the worker is seriously injured or killed by being struck by the trench wall. The number of trench cave-in fatalities decreased between 1985 and 1990. The decline might have resulted from the efforts of OSHA to emphasize the need for safety in trenching operations. The OSHA emphasis on trench safety received national attention in the late 1980s.

Electrical shock was the fourth most common cause of fatalities. The specific causes of construction worker electrocutions were examined, and the most prevalent causes were ranked as follows:

- direct contact with live wire
- contact of crane boom with power line
- contact of materials with power line
- contact of ladder with power line

The causes listed constituted 45% of electrocution fatalities. Direct contact (workers touching power lines) accounted for 20% of the fatalities. Electrocutions resulting when the booms of cranes came in contact with overhead power lines accounted for 14% of the fatalities. Fatalities that occurred with considerable frequency were those caused by the contact of other types of equipment (aerial lifts, forklifts, dump trucks, backhoes, concrete pump trucks, etc.) with overhead power lines. Fatalities caused by overhead power line contact by backhoes, concrete pump booms, and forklifts accounted for 6% of the electrocutions. The causes of many fatalities could not be accurately analyzed, since 35% of the causes were listed as unknown. In several electrocution cases, no witnesses were present to describe the incident. In some cases, more than one worker was killed in the same incident.

The fifth category into which causes of accidents are grouped is "other." It is simply a catch-all category that is not descriptive of the cause of any fatality. The most common causes of fatalities included in this category were as follows:

- toxic gas or lack of oxygen
- poor personal health
- fire
- drowning

Those causes accounted for 73% of the "other" fatalities. In general, the causes appear to have little in common.

In the preceding paragraphs the key areas in which fatalities can occur have been summarized. Employers should note the major causes of fatalities associated with the types of work performed by their crews. They should then take effective preventive measures to ensure the safety of their workers.

Problems with Injury Coding

Although some changes or trends may be surmised (a rise in falls, a rise in struck-by incidents, a decline in caught-in/between incidents, etc.), they do not appear to be significant trends. To some extent, the deductions that might be drawn about trends may be ill-founded. That statement is based on the observation that the coding of the event types appeared to be inconsistent. Several examples will illustrate this point.

The following are brief descriptions of the circumstances of various fatalities. Note that, although the first three cases should clearly be categorized as electrical shock cases, the coding by the OSHA personnel varied. Some coding seems to focus on elements of the activity taking place at the time of the incident, without focusing on the igniting cause.

A laborer was laying pipe in a trench when he was struck by an overhead energized line when the elbow of a back hoe made contact and caused the line to fall. The energized line struck the employee diagonally across the chest and hip. The employee then fell across the line in the trench causing the electrocution. [*Accident code: struck-by incident.*]

An employee operating a hydraulic crane came in contact with an electrical utility line and was electrocuted. [*Accident code: struck-against incident.*]

At approximately 10:15 A.M., an employee was preparing a steel pipe bridge for connection between two buildings. A crane was being used to lift the bridge into place. During the lift, the crane boom came within near proximity of a 138,000 volt electrical transmission line. An arc occurred and the employee received severe electrical shock and burns and later died at the hospital. [*Accident code: other incident.*]

There were three roofers engaged in roofing a residence. One worker was on the ground getting shingles, and the other two roofers were on the roof at the front of the house installing shingles. One of the roofers fell backwards off of the roof approximately 17 feet to the concrete sidewalk below. He was fatally injured. [*Accident code: struck-against incident.* (Coding this incident as a fall would appear to have been more appropriate.)]

An employee engaged in the scraping of an underground gasoline storage tank applied his oxy-acetylene torch to the tank and ignited the vapor given off by its residual contents. The tank had not been filled with water, purged, or inerted. Only an emulsifier of insufficient quantity had been added three days prior. This did not effectively blanket or break down the remaining product. In addition, the tank was moved after adding the emulsifier, allowing for increased liberation of flammable vapor. [*Accident code: struck-by incident.* (Although the worker was hit by material propelled by the explosion, it would seem more appropriate to code the incident as "other" or to add a new classification for explosions. In a different fatality case, an explosion was coded as "other.")]

At approximately 10 A.M. worker no. 1 went into an unprotected trench to remove mud from around the pipe. He entered the 8 to 10 feet deep trench several times while keeping the bucket of the track hoe over him. Part of the vertical wall of the trench on the street side collapsed and buried the worker. No protective system was used to protect the worker in the trench. The trench was adjacent to previously disturbed soil and water was in the trench. The employee's neck was broken and he died of asphyxiation.

[*Accident code: struck-by incident.* (The use of "other" or the addition of a new classification for trench collapse would appear more appropriate.)]

Many abstracts that were examined showed similar inconsistencies. One fatality resulting from injuries sustained when equipment rolled over the operator was coded as struck-by, whereas another fatality under similar circumstances was coded as "other." In one fatality case, a worker was struck by the boom of a crane, and the event was classified as a caught-in/between incident rather than as the usual struck-by incident. Although six categories for the causes of accidents would seem to be a small enough number to minimize overlap, there seem to be significant cases in which OSHA personnel do not use common definitions for the categories.

The Focus of OSHA Inspections

The sources or causes of fatalities and serious injuries should be understood by employers. Employers should be committed to avoiding circumstances that place their workers at risk. Employers may also be concerned about maintaining compliance with the OSHA regulations, as compliance serves the common goal of safety. Although avoiding injuries should be the primary objective of employers, there should also be some concern about the need to avoid OSHA citations and fines. Since the consequences of violations can often be quite severe, an understanding of the standards most frequently violated should be valuable information to employers.

What issues or standards are of particular interest to OSHA compliance officers in their inspections? A relatively good idea can be obtained by a review of the OSHA standards cited most frequently on OSHA inspections. That information has been gleaned (Hinze and Bren 1996) from OSHA's Integrated Management Information System (IMIS).

The OSHA database IMIS contains information on OSHA inspections that includes the identity of the firm cited, the location, the specific OSHA paragraphs violated, the amounts of any fines, and myriad other details related to the inspection. The intent of examining those data was to identify the unsafe work conditions warranting the greatest attention in the construction industry. The data examined were gathered during the period 1985–94.

Of particular interest is the number of citations issued for each of the 141 sections noted in the OSHA regulations during that period. The sections associated with the largest number of citations are summarized in Table 5.3. From that summary, it is clear that the hazard communication standard (with 59,183 citations) is associated with the greatest number of violations. In the entire sample, the analysis identified 68 sections with more than 100 citations, 56 sections with more than 250 citations, and 34 sections with more than 1,000 citations. Of the 141 sections, 31 were cited fewer than ten times.

The total number of citations issued for each of the OSHA sections is of particular interest; however, additional information may prove even more enlightening. Further analysis focused on identifying the sections with the largest numbers of citations for *serious violations*. A serious-violation citation is issued when OSHA determines that worker safety is in great jeopardy or that a worker's life is at risk. The sections with the largest numbers of citations for serious violations are summarized in Table 5.4. A comparison of Tables 5.3 and 5.4 reveals that the sections with the largest numbers of serious citations

Table 5.3
OSHA Regulations with the Highest Numbers of Violations

CFR Paragraph Number	Description of the OSHA Standard	Number of OSHA Violations
1926.59	Hazard communication (Subpart D—Occupational Health and Environmental Controls)	59,183
1926.404	Wiring design and protection (Subpart K—Electrical)	17,785
1926.451	Scaffolding (Subpart L—Scaffolding)	16,198
1926.405	Wiring methods, components, and equipment for general use (Subpart K—Electrical)	14,625
1926.500	Guardrails, handrails, and covers (Subpart M—Floor and Wall Openings)	13,512
1926.652	Requirements for protective systems (Subpart P—Excavations)	10,914
1926.651	General requirements (Subpart P—Excavations)	9458
1926.20	General safety and health provisions (Subpart C—General Safety and Health Provisions)	8137
1926.1052	Stairways (Subpart X—Stairways and Ladders)	7011
1926.21	Safety training and education (Subpart C—General Safety and Health Provisions)	6744
1926.152	Flammable and combustible liquids (Subpart F—Fire Protection and Prevention)	6587
1926.1053	Ladders (Subpart X—Stairways and Ladders)	6457
1926.50	Medical services and first aid (Subpart D—Occupational Health and Environmental Controls)	6037
1926.550	Cranes and derricks (Subpart N—Cranes, Derricks, Hoists, Elevators, and Conveyors)	5871
1926.100	Head protection (Subpart E—Personal Protective and Life Saving Equipment)	5813
1926.150	Fire protection (Subpart F—Fire Protection and Prevention)	5059

Source: Hinze and Bren 1996

are not necessarily the same as those with the largest numbers of violations. Of the 141 sections, 36 were cited for serious violations fewer than ten times, 7 were cited only once for serious violations, and 3 were never cited for serious violations.

Serious violations were not distributed in the same fashion as the total number of violations. When that difference was recognized, a ratio was developed to express the relationship between the number of serious violations and the total number of viola-

Table 5.4
OSHA Regulations with the Highest Numbers of Serious Violations

CFR Paragraph Number	Description of the OSHA Standard	Number of OSHA Serious Violations
1926.59	Hazard communication (Subpart D—Occupational Health and Environmental Controls)	29,138
1926.451	Scaffolding (Subpart L—Scaffolding)	13,096
1926.500	Guardrails, handrails, and covers (Subpart M—Floor and Wall Openings)	10,643
1926.404	Wiring design and protection (Subpart K—Electrical)	10,119
1926.652	Requirements for protective systems (Subpart P—Excavations)	8648
1926.651	General requirements (Subpart P—Excavations)	7554
1926.405	Wiring methods, components, and equipment for general use (Subpart K—Electrical)	6558
1926.20	General safety and health provisions (Subpart C—General Safety and Health Provisions)	5567
1926.21	Safety training and education (Subpart C—General Safety and Health Prov.)	5198
1926.100	Head protection (Subpart E—Personal Protective and Life Saving Equipment)	4500
1926.1053	Ladders (Subpart X—Stairways and Ladders)	4405
1926.550	Cranes and derricks (Subpart N—Cranes, Derricks, Hoists, Elevators, and Conveyors)	3647
1926.1052	Stairways (Subpart X—Stairways and Ladders)	3593
1926.28	Personal protective equipment (Subpart C—General Safety and Health Prov.)	3041
1926.152	Flammable and combustible liquids (Subpart F—Fire Protection and Prevention)	2563
1926.350	Gas welding and cutting (Subpart J—Welding and Cutting)	2427
1926.403	General requirements (Subpart K—Electrical)	2348

Source: Hinze and Bren 1996

Table 5.5
OSHA Regulations with the Highest Proportion of Serious Violations

CFR Paragraph Number	Description of the OSHA Standard	Ratio of Serious Violations to Total Violations
1926.556	Aerial lifts (Subpart N—Cranes, Derricks, Hoists, Elevators, and Conveyors)	0.866
1926.701	General requirements (Subpart Q—Concrete and Masonry Construction.)	0.846
1926.300	General requirements (Subpart I—Tools—Hand and Power)	0.837
1926.304	Woodworking tools (Subpart I—Tools—Hand and Power)	0.831
1926.451	Scaffolding (Subpart L—Scaffolding)	0.808
1926.651	General requirements (Subpart P—Excavations)	0.799
1926.652	Requirements for protective systems (Subpart P—Excavations)	0.792
1926.500	Guardrails, handrails, and covers (Subpart M—Floor and Wall Openings)	0.788
1926.102	Eye and face protection (Subpart E—Personal Protective and Life Saving Equipment)	0.775
1926.100	Head protection (Subpart E—Personal Protective and Life Saving Equipment)	0.774
1926.21	Safety training and education (Subpart C—General Safety and Health Provisions)	0.771
1926.28	Personal protective equipment (Subpart C—General Safety and Health Provisions)	0.763
1926.20	General safety and health provisions (Subpart C—General Safety and Health Provisions)	0.684
1926.1053	Ladders (Subpart X—Stairways and Ladders)	0.682
1926.550	Cranes and derricks (Subpart N—Cranes, Derricks, Hoists, Elevators, and Conveyors)	0.622
1926.1051	General requirements (Subpart X—Stairways and Ladders)	0.582
1926.251	Rigging equipment for material handling (Subpart H—Materials Handling, Storage, Use, and Disposal)	0.579
1926.404	Wiring design and protection (Subpart K—Electrical)	0.569
1926.59	Hazard communication (Subpart D—Occupational Health and Environmental Controls)	0.565
1926.1060	Training requirements (Subpart X—Stairways and Ladders)	0.561

tions for each section. That information is presented in Table 5.5. To maintain the focus on the paragraphs of greatest general interest, the table contains ratios only for sections for which at least 1,000 citations were issued. The sections with the highest ratios are those for which violations are most often serious ones. They represent the areas in which compliance is most often deficient. If compliance inspections are to be focused on life-threatening situations, the specific sections with the highest ratios are the areas in need of the greatest attention. Low ratios, on the other hand, may indicate excessive attention by compliance officers. For example, although more than 6,000 citations were issued for § 1926.50 (medical services and first aid), only 18% were for serious violations. The hazard communication standard (§ 1926.59), with 59,183 violations, was cited for serious violations in 49% of the citations.

Of the 141 sections, 104, or 74%, were cited for serious violations more than 50% of the times they were cited. However, 18 of those were cited for fewer than 10 serious violations altogether.

Some sections are frequently cited but seldom for serious violations. For example, the standard concerning access to employee exposure and medical records (§ 1926.33) was cited for 518 violations, but only 8 of those were considered serious. No serious violations were recorded for the standards concerning compressed air (§ 1926.803), underground transportation of explosives (§ 1926.903), or formaldehyde (§ 1926.1148).

Final Comments

Detailed analysis of data recorded by OSHA can provide meaningful information about the sources of citations and the causes of fatalities. In recent years, hazard communication is the OSHA standard for which employers have received the largest number of citations. Other standards for which numerous citations are issued are associated with safety training and education; cranes, hoists, and elevators; and scaffold design. Those are clearly areas in which employers have been deficient, at least from the perspective of OSHA compliance officers. This information will be helpful to employers who wish to avoid OSHA citations and who want to improve safety performances on their job sites.

Falls are the single most common cause of fatalities, according to the IMIS data. They are followed by struck-by incidents, caught-in/between cases, and electrocutions. Falls are most frequently associated with roofs or scaffolding. Fatal fall heights ranged from less than 10 feet to more than 100 feet, so fall protection appears to be delinquent on work tasks performed at all heights. Many struck-by fatalities resulted from trench cave-ins. The depths of trenches in which fatalities occurred ranged from less than 4 feet to more than 20 feet. Most trenching fatalities occurred in relatively shallow trenches, less than 10 feet deep.

Review Questions

1. If fatalities and serious injuries are to be avoided, where should a construction firm place its greatest emphasis?
2. If electrocutions are to be avoided, what conditions should be given particular attention?

3. What is the most common OSHA citation? What reasons might there be for its being the most common?
4. What are the conditions surrounding most falls?
5. What is meant when the OSHA database is criticized for coding problems?
6. Explain why the areas associated with the most construction worker fatalities may not be the same as those associated with the most OSHA violations.
7. What are the five common categories by which OSHA codes the causes of most construction worker fatalities?
8. What are willful violations?
9. Give examples of causes of fatalities that might be included in the category "other."
10. Suppose that a worker was working on the 10th floor of a steel-frame structure. While the worker's attention was focused on welding a connection, a load of steel decking was being hoisted to the floor by crane. The load, which was hoisted without proper signaling, struck the worker from behind and caused him to fall. He fell two floors and landed on a scaffold that was being erected. The scaffold collapsed and struck a power line, electrocuting the worker. Describe the different codes that might be applied. What would be the proper code to describe the cause of the fatality if the code is to isolate the initiating cause of the accident?

References

Hinze, J., and K. Bren. 1996. "OSHA Paragraphs of Particular Interest." *Journal of Construction Engineering and Management* 122, no. 1, 98–100.

Hinze, J., and D. Russell. 1995. "Analysis of Fatalities Recorded by OSHA." *Journal of Construction Engineering and Management* 121, no. 2, 209–14.

U.S. Department of Labor. Occupational Safety and Health Administration. 1990. *Analysis of Construction Fatalities—The OSHA Data Base 1985–1989*. November. Washington, D.C.

———. 1993. *The 100 Most Frequently Cited OSHA Construction Standards in 1991: A Guide for the Abatement of the Top 25 Associated Physical Hazards*. February. Washington, D.C.

Elements of an Effective Safety Program

> Safety is for life.

The actions of foremen, middle managers, and top managers that affect safety performance must have a foundation. In most large companies, a company safety program provides that foundation. The company can clearly delineate its goals through the preparation of an effective safety program. For a program to be effective, it must be clear in its intent, and it must be uniformly applied to all company projects and personnel. This chapter is a discussion of the components that might be included in a safety program.

The formulation of a safety program is not a matter of dusting off the safety program of another company and trying to adapt it to the circumstances of one's own company. In fact, although an effective safety program must be in writing, the true essence of a program is in the company philosophy and the commitment that top management has to safety. It is not sufficient to have carefully crafted words in a manual if actions at the job site do not make the project safer for the workers.

Some aspects of a company safety program will be applicable to every project. Some components of the safety program must be specifically oriented to the unique needs of individual projects. The basic components of the company safety program should form the basis for any project-specific safety program. The elements of safety programs described in this chapter have been identified in various contract documents I have examined.

Establishing Your Company's Safety Philosophy

Injuries are the result of a combination of unsafe physical conditions and unsafe actions. The unsafe actions may be the outgrowth of a number of causes, including lack of proper training, lack of attention to the work, carelessness, macho behavior, and inadequate instruction. Unsafe actions may include actions taken by managers or the failure of managers to act to make the job safe. The mental environment prompts many unsafe actions. Unsafe actions by workers may also be influenced by management. Note that unsafe actions occur even though most workers would prefer not to sustain any injuries.

Very early in the establishment of a safety program, top management must decide on the primary safety objective of the firm. It might be one of the following:

to minimize or avoid OSHA citations
to minimize or avoid litigation
to minimize or avoid injuries

The recommended objective is to avoid injuries. By focusing on avoiding OSHA citations, management directs its attention to the physical work conditions, particularly those that are expected to come under the closest scrutiny of OSHA inspectors. Remote sites are less likely to be inspected, and management might be inclined to place less emphasis on compliance with the OSHA regulations at such sites. By focusing on avoiding litigation, management gears its efforts toward trying to shift blame, often through indemnification and hold-harmless contract provisions. The objective of avoiding litigation can quickly become misguided, creating an atmosphere in which no one wants to feel responsible for job-site safety. That attitude will be reflected in each person's actions, which treat safety as the responsibility of "other parties." The best objective is to avoid injuries. Efforts to minimize injuries will probably automatically address the secondary objective of avoiding OSHA citations and may also be the best way to avoid litigation.

Once the company managers have established a clear safety philosophy (preferably to minimize injuries), diligent efforts can then be expended to draft an effective safety program. The safety philosophy is very important, as it is at the core of the safety program. Without the true commitment of top management to the safety program, the safety performance of company workers is jeopardized. Remember, workers do not want to be injured.

Statement of Policy or Mission

It is advisable to begin the development of a safety program with a mission statement. A safety mission statement is a general, yet powerful, statement of the company's view of worker safety. It is more than a few carefully crafted words; it is the driving force behind the safety program. The following is an example of a mission statement:

We are fully committed to safety, and we integrate safety into all of our activities. Safety is our top priority. We will not compromise our safety philosophy to meet budgets, deadlines, or scope-of-work objectives or to achieve any other project goals. Our commitment to safety means we are committed to performing all our tasks in a safe manner. That commitment to safe performance is mandated for all those employed by our firm.

Such a mission statement can be reinforced by adding that all personnel "are to give an overriding priority to the prevention of personal-injury and property-damage accidents during all construction projects." The commitment can be justified by expressing recognition that worker injuries constitute an "appalling waste of human life." The policy encompasses all personnel associated with a project. The safety commitment is the responsibility of every party on the project.

If management views every accident as avoidable and, furthermore, feels that management can have a major influence on the avoidance of future accidents, safety performance will improve. That is not to imply that management necessarily causes specific accidents to occur but simply that management should recognize that it can take certain steps that minimize the chance of the occurrence of accidents.

The Scope of the Safety Program

The standards and provisions set forth in the safety program are to be considered applicable to all on-site construction activities. Work procedures are to be consistent with the health and safety standards prevalent in the industry and those promulgated under the Occupational Safety and Health Act of 1970. The purpose of the written safety program is to promote working conditions and work practices that will assure all employees of a safe and healthful work environment for all construction activities.

It is important that the company make diligent efforts to establish a clear and positive "safety culture" on each construction site. That safety culture should be based on the conviction that no worker should ever be placed in a situation in which an injury has a high probability of occurring. Thus, safety is not a concept to be thought of as additional to the work itself; safety is to be considered an integral part of the work.

Accident prevention should not be confined to the hours of working on the project, but should be practiced in the off-hours as well. Cooperation in safety programs is the mutual obligation of all employees. Each employee should endeavor to

work safely on or off the job;
have regard at all times for the safety of others;
use knowledge and influence to prevent accidents;
call attention to unsafe conditions;
contribute ideas and suggestions for the improvement of safety conditions;
be courteous, and realize individual actions may cause injury to others.

The Responsibility of the Company

The firm shall at all times conduct the work safely and ensure a safe work site. It bears the overall responsibility for the safety of its employees, agents, and subcontractors. The firm is responsible for the adequacy and safety of all construction methods and procedures and the safe prosecution of the work. It is responsible for conducting the work and keeping the work site in compliance with all safety laws, including, but not limited to, OSHA requirements.

The Safety Director

To provide assurance to workers that the workplace is safe, the company should designate a safety director for each project before the start of construction. The safety director position may be full time or part time, depending on the nature and size of the project. The safety director should have the full power needed to carry out the duties of the position. It is not a symbolic position.

Preconstruction Meeting or Conference

It is customary before the start of construction for representatives of the contractor to meet with the owner's representatives to review their respective safety requirements and to discuss implementation of all health and safety provisions pertinent to the work under contract. The contractor should be prepared to discuss, in detail, the measures to be taken to control the hazards associated with the major phases of the work under contract and to comply with contractual obligations. The meeting is devoted to discussing the manner in which the firm intends to administer the health and safety program and to delegate the responsibilities for implementing the program. It is a good time to resolve questions before construction begins.

Preconstruction Checklist

Checklists are a good way of making sure that all details are covered. Some safety-related matters should receive special attention. The following matters should be taken care of before the start of work:

> preconstruction meeting
> posting of emergency telephone numbers
> medical arrangements for contingencies
> OSHA posting
> completion of the safety program for the project
> noting of critical hazards (and institution of preventive measures)

The Project Safety Program

The project safety program is a comprehensive written accident prevention program covering all aspects of on-site construction operations and activities associated with a particular contract. Many owners now require contractors to submit project-specific safety programs for approval (to be discussed at the preconstruction conference). Until the project safety program is approved, it is common for such an owner to refuse to process progress payments. Some job-specific items to include in the safety program submitted for approval are as follows:

job number
> The job or project designation according to the standard numbering system used by the firm.

job-site safety representative
> A competent person at the job site, designated by the contractor to serve as the safety representative, who will be responsible for implementing the safety program. The safety representative must have sufficient authority to change or stop performance of the work if he or she deems the work practices or conditions unsafe. In addition to being knowledgeable about the job-site safety requirements and the applicable safety regulations, the safety representative should be trained and sufficiently experienced to recognize safety and health hazards.
>
> The owner may require the contractor to submit a résumé of the qualifications of the competent person, including such information as experience, education, special safety and first-aid courses completed, safety conferences attended, any certifications or registrations, and familiarity with standards and regulations.
>
> The safety representative may be the superintendent.

OSHA standards applicable to the work
> A job hazard analysis may be the primary resource used in compiling the list of specific OSHA standards applicable to the work to be performed. The listing is to be as comprehensive as possible.

description of safety orientation and training for all employees
> Safety orientation and training should include explanations of standards of conduct, safety rules, the emergency plan, and the use and location of safety equipment and fire-protection equipment on the job site. Each employee should be trained in the recognition and avoidance of unsafe conditions and in the regulations applicable to the work environment. Each worker that begins work or a new work activity on the project shall attend a basic safety orientation and sign in.

days and times of regular weekly and monthly safety meetings

first-aid facilities and procedures

outline of each phase of the work, the hazards associated with each major phase, and the methods proposed to ensure property protection and the safety of the public and the employees
> Identify the work included in each phase by reference to specification section or division number.

emergency plans
> Plans for coping with possible emergency situations (floods, fires, cave-ins, explosions, power outages, wind storms, etc.).

written hazard communication program

schedule of regular job-site safety inspections

requirement of frequent safety inspections

A statement that frequent safety inspections will be conducted of all operations, including subcontractor operations.
recording and reporting of all injuries and illnesses
investigation of all injuries and illnesses
safety bulletin board
safety committee
maintenance of Material Safety Data Sheet (MSDS) information
signs for public safety
barricades
warning devices
subcontractor compliance

Requirements of the safety program may vary, depending on the nature of the project. For example, an owner may stipulate specific safety program criteria that have to be met if the project is a building that "is either 15 or more stories, 200 feet or more in height, or 100,000 square feet or more of lot coverage regardless of height."

Training

Training should be at the core of every safety program. It is important, first, to identify the areas in which training is required. Firm policies might be established on minimum training requirements. For example, a realistic goal may be to have every employee in a supervisory role trained in first aid. Some training may apply to all employees. For example, all employees should be trained in hazard communication so that every worker is fully knowledgeable about the labeling of all chemicals likely to be on site. Other training may include training on OSHA reporting requirements, electrical lockout, confined-space entry, trenching, asbestos abatement, lead abatement, back-injury prevention, fall protection, blasting, fire protection, substance abuse, traffic control, crane safety and rigging, equipment safety, and other safety concerns.

Although it is not always regarded as training, perhaps the most important training that can take place is the orientation of new hires. All new hires should complete a thorough orientation session. Even the most skilled workers and experienced foremen need to become familiar with the job-site layout, the project management personnel, company policies, and a variety of other subjects related to an unfamiliar project.

Safety Standards and Regulations on Owner's Premises

On some projects, the contractor will be asked to comply, not only with applicable federal, state, and local laws governing safety, health, and sanitation, but also with the owner's own safety guidelines. On such a project, care must be exercised to educate everyone concerning the added requirements. Some of the owner's requirements may simply echo provisions already contained in the company safety program. Requirements that might be imposed by the owner include the following:

Hard hats are required.

Eye protection is required.

Hearing protection is required.

Safety shoes are recommended for all workers.

First-aid supplies must be available in all work areas.

Workers who have had first-aid training should be known by all job-site personnel.

No visitors are permitted on premises without authorization.

All visitors must comply with applicable safety regulations.

The job site will be kept clean and free of debris.

Temporary chain-link fencing, or an approved equal, shall be furnished by the contractor and installed around the construction areas.

Persons under the influence of alcohol or drugs shall not be permitted on the premises.

Thorough equipment safety checks must be conducted regularly.

No smoking is permitted on the premises.

Everyone must comply with posted speed limits on the site.

Other topics that the owner's requirements may address include cutting and welding permits, welding tanks, electrical lockout, confined-space entry, worker lift procedures, asbestos removal, firearms, fire prevention, chemicals, radiation, heat, cold, explosives, excavations, fall protection, hoisting, traffic control, sketches of temporary power distribution, and safe clearance procedures.

OSHA Regulations

After many additions and modifications over the years, the federal regulations containing the OSHA standards for construction consist of over 200 sections and more than 1000 subsections, ranging from short paragraphs to several pages. The sections are grouped into 26 subparts (A through Z). Some sections may be of particular interest for specific jobs or projects. The following list is of some of the sections that commonly apply on most projects:

1. housekeeping (Section 25, Subpart C)
2. first aid, medical services, and sanitation (Sections 50–51, Subpart D)
3. personal protection (hard hats, eye and face masks, safety nets, safety lines, etc.) (Sections 100, 102, 104, 105, Subpart E)
4. traffic control (Sections 200–202, Subpart G)
5. hand tools (Sections 300–305, Subpart I)
6. ladders and scaffolds (Sections 451–452, Subpart L)
7. cranes, derricks, etc. (Section 550, Subpart N)
8. earth-moving equipment (Sections 600, 602–604, Subpart O)
9. excavation and trenching (Sections 651–652, Subpart P)
10. concrete and concrete forms (Sections 701–703, SubpartQ)
11. structural steel (Sections 751–752, Subpart R)

12. cofferdams (Section 802, Subpart S)
13. explosives (Sections 900–911, Subpart U)

Hazard Analysis

Although management should be concerned about avoiding all types of injuries, particular attention should be devoted to avoiding the more serious ones. Thus, before any construction work takes place, management should assess job-site conditions to identify potential areas of serious injuries. Many serious injuries are attributed to worker falls (from scaffolding, from ladders, off roofs, through floor openings, due to improper or missing guardrails, or due to failure to use safety belts); collapse (of scaffolding or other structures); being struck by vehicles (heavy equipment or private vehicles); being struck by cranes (the boom or the load); trench cave-ins; and electrical lines. The areas of potential serious injuries should be carefully assessed before construction work begins. In many cases, precautions can be exercised to minimize the potential for injury.

Before the beginning of each major phase of work, an activity hazard analysis (phase plan) should be prepared. Activity hazard analyses must be prepared for every contract activity and operation in each major phase of work. The analysis should address the sequence of work, the hazards of each activity performed in that phase, and the control measures, procedures, and safeguards necessary to eliminate the hazards or reduce the risk to an acceptable level. A phase is defined as an operation involving a type of work presenting hazards not experienced in previous operations or an operation in which a new subcontractor or work crew is to perform work. Where applicable, similar analyses should be required of subcontractors.

Safety Meetings

Safety meetings tend to be a strong component of many safety programs. At a minimum, a weekly 15-minute "toolbox" safety meeting with all personnel should be conducted. Toolbox meetings should be held early in the day. The meetings can be conducted by project management personnel (a practice that demonstrates management's commitment to safety), field supervisors, or foremen. All construction personnel should be required to attend toolbox meetings, or the contractor may require subcontractors to hold their own safety meetings with their personnel. If a separate meeting is held by each crew, project managers should expend the effort to attend at least some of them. Weekly safety meeting topics can include safety rules, hazards, corrective actions, accident prevention, and reviews of accidents and near accidents. Document the date of the meeting, the length of the meeting, the meeting chairperson, the topics discussed, the names of all personnel who attended, and the names of persons who were absent. Records should be maintained of each safety meeting.

Monthly safety meetings should be held for all levels of supervision. Those meetings are used to review the effectiveness of the project safety efforts, to resolve current health and safety problems, to provide a forum for planning safe construction activities, to plan ahead for new or changed operations, and to update the accident prevention program.

Safety Committees

The use of a safety committee—made up of supervisors, workers, and representatives of key subcontractors—can be very effective in assuring a safe job. The committee can serve several functions. It meets regularly (probably weekly) to review accidents and near misses and to discuss a variety of other safety matters. The committee, or a subgroup of the committee, is also responsible for making a weekly project-safety inspection tour. Safety committees on company projects bear testimony to the company's commitment to safety. If the membership of the committees constantly rotates, many of the workers on the project can learn more about safety. Those workers will then begin to identify and correct problems wherever they work.

Safety Budgets

The safety budget is another way that management can demonstrate its commitment to safety. Safety need not be expensive. Safety glasses are not expensive when compared with the value of the sight of an eye. The cost of a safety belt is insignificant if the use of the belt saves a life.

Thought should be given to the way the company establishes safety budgets. Some safety experts argue that safety items should be charged, not directly to the project, but to the home office or to general overhead (Levitt 1975). That accounting practice reflects a philosophy of charging jobs for injuries but not for safety. If the costs of safety items are not paid from project budgets, project managers may be less reluctant to require the use of certain safety items. For example, safety belts can be a job cost or a company overhead cost. If the cost of safety belts is charged directly to the job, the project personnel may be reluctant to purchase the belts. If the project personnel can obtain the belts by submitting a request to the home office, without affecting cost accounting on the job, they will be more inclined to acquire all the safety belts needed.

Such budget decisions must be made by the contractor, as they are generally outside the scope of the owner's power.

Substance Abuse Programs

Substance abuse in the workplace is often quite prevalent. For all areas of employment, estimates have been made that about 7% of the employees are substance abusers. Estimates of substance abuse among construction workers are even higher, about 17% (Duston 1996). From a safety standpoint, substance abusers pose a constant and serious threat. Thus, contractors are encouraged to consider the implementation of a substance abuse program. Many companies that have substance abuse programs have reported improvements in their overall safety performance. Naturally, the incidence of substance abuse declines in firms that have such programs.

Substance abuse programs can be formulated in a variety of ways, but testing is invariably a crucial element. Testing for cause and preemployment screening are the most common forms of testing. Consideration must also be given to blanket testing

(testing of everyone) and the more controversial issue of random testing. The consequences of failing a drug test must be carefully thought through. Possibly, the failure of a test will mandate a second test, for validation. The first time an employee fails a test, it is common for the company to order rehabilitation at the employee's expense. Repeated failure of drug tests typically results in termination.

Besides instituting testing, the company should adopt a policy that an employee whose ability or alertness is impaired by drugs, fatigue, illness, intoxication, or any other condition is not to be allowed to work.

Subcontractor Compliance

All subcontractors must be required to meet the safety requirements established for the project. Of course, subcontractor safety really has its beginning in the selection of the subcontractors. Only subcontractors with demonstrated abilities to perform work safely should be considered. Once a subcontractor is selected, and before the subcontract is actually awarded, outline for the subcontractor the safety requirements of the project. Mandate the subcontractor's acceptance of those terms throughout the project.

Inspection of the Work Site by Regulatory Personnel

In general, the chance of being inspected by OSHA compliance officers is relatively small. Construction projects tend to attract the interest of OSHA, however, and long-duration projects have a much higher probability of being inspected. The issue of OSHA inspections can be addressed in the safety program. The following two provisions from construction contracts demonstrate differing philosophies:

> If an OSHA Compliance Officer wishes to conduct a safety inspection of the Contractor's personnel and equipment or any of its subcontractors' personnel and equipment, the Contractor shall immediately request the approval of the Owner before permitting the inspection to begin.

> The Contractor shall admit, without delay and without the presentation of an inspection warrant, any inspection of the Occupational Safety and Health Administration upon presentation of proper credentials.

In the first provision, the owner wants to be fully involved in the process, to the point of being the party to grant permission for the OSHA inspection. In the second, the contractor is simply obligated to admit the OSHA compliance officer without delay. A contractor may wish to establish its own stance on this subject and include the appropriate wording in its safety program.

Safety Performance Evaluations

It is important to establish a means of evaluating safety performance. That will make it possible to assess the effect of a specific change that the company may wish to make. To evaluate safety, it is important to have a reliable measure. The rate of occurrence of

OSHA-recordable injuries may be one such measure. Others may also be used, such as the insurance experience modification rate, the insurance loss ratio, the incidence of medical-case injuries, or even measures of compliance with the safety standards.

The company should evaluate the safety performance of various levels of management, the first-line supervisors (foremen), and the subcontractors. Those performance evaluations should have meaning. That is, good performance should be associated with some type of recognition or award, and inferior performance should carry sanctions, or negative consequences.

Some owners want to monitor safety performance during construction. They may stipulate the type of reporting required. The following is an example of such a provision:

> The Contractor shall submit a monthly safety report to the Owner. The report shall cover the Contractor's employees and the employees of all subcontractors. The report shall include (1) the number of worker hours worked, (2) the number of OSHA-recordable accidents, and (3) the number of lost-time accidents.

Emergency Plans

No matter how safe an operation appears to be, it would be foolish to ignore the possibility of a serious accident. It is best to anticipate any major problems that might arise and to prepare for them. A homeowner does not normally expect the home to be burned to the ground, but it would be foolish to have children in a home and never develop a contingency plan with them. The consequences of not planning for emergencies may be the difference between an unfortunate incident and a catastrophic event. The following provision, prepared by an owner, sets out the elements of an emergency plan:

> The Contractor shall set forth a contingency plan for the safe and effective response to emergencies. The Contractor shall provide all medical services for its personnel and its subcontractors' personnel. The Contractor's medical services shall include first-aid treatment (including all necessary first-aid supplies), ambulance service (or other standing arrangement for the immediate transport of injured workers to medical treatment facilities), clinic or hospital emergency room treatment, hospitalization, and physician's services. The Contractor shall establish, publish, and make known to all employees procedures for ensuring the immediate removal to a hospital or a doctor's care of persons, including employees, who may have been injured on the project. Anyone acting in a supervisory capacity shall have the authority to order an emergency response. The Contractor shall prominently post the names, addresses, and telephone numbers of the following personnel on the Job Site: (1) the Contractor's and subcontractors' personnel to be notified in case of emergency and (2) the Contractor's medical services personnel and institutions.

Accident Reporting

Many owners now want to be apprised of safety performance on their projects. They do not want surprises. To keep informed, they may mandate minimum standards for reporting. The following are examples that have been used by different owners:

The key to improving safety activities lies in improving the information that the Contractor supplies to the Owner concerning where accidents occur, why, and when.

The Contractor shall report all personnel-injury accidents, property-damage accidents, fires, spills, and near misses to the Owner within 24 hours of their occurrence. All accidents causing death or serious injuries or damages shall be reported immediately to the Owner. Each injury report shall include the accident data and location. Each shall present a concise, thorough description of the accident, its cause, the injuries sustained, and procedures implemented or proposed to prevent recurrence. A complete description is to be provided of all property-damage accidents, including the estimate of the impact, if any, of the accident on the schedule of the Work. The Contractor shall report orally on all incidents that could have resulted in personnel injury or property damage. Each month the Contractor shall submit a standard summary report showing the number of injuries incurred to date, the number of injuries incurred in the previous month, and other related information. Supplementary written reports may be required at the Owner's discretion.

Except for rescue and emergency measures, the scene of a serious accident or incident shall not be disturbed or the operation resumed until authorized by the Owner. The Contractor shall conduct a complete investigation of each major accident or incident and shall submit a comprehensive report of findings and a recommendation to the Owner. The Contractor shall be responsible for any independent investigation that the Owner might authorize.

It is important not to forget the injured worker after taking the worker to receive medical treatment. Someone in the company, preferably the immediate supervisor and someone in upper management, should keep in touch with an injured worker during his or her convalescence. Whenever possible and appropriate, the company should find work that the injured worker can perform. Although there may be a stigma in being the "walking wounded" or in doing make-work, rehiring may be justified if meaningful work can be found. Rehiring not only utilizes the services of a person who has made a sacrifice for the company, but it also helps to rebuild the self-esteem of the injured worker. Naturally, no rehiring should occur if the work might jeopardize the worker's rehabilitation.

Investigation of Accidents and Incidents

Although there is a legal requirement to report accidents, there should also be a moral obligation to investigate accidents and other incidents (near misses, etc.). The intent of such investigations is to determine the cause of the accident or incident so that management can devise means of preventing reoccurrence.

Avoiding Liability

Although it is clearly not within the normal definition of a safety program to address liability, it is important to note that many owners would rather leave all safety matters to the contractors. Consequently, liability is a constant concern, and it might very well creep into a company's safety program.

Some obligations of contractors in regard to project control are fairly uniform. An owner's safety program may state them succinctly. For example, it may state that all construction contractors must provide safety controls for the protection of the lives and health of their employees and other persons involved in the work on the job. It may further recognize the owner's responsibility for enforcing the provisions of the contract, with the stipulation that provisions and regulations that, by law, are the fundamental responsibility of other agencies should not be monitored by the owner. The safety program may add the following statements:

> For such provisions and regulations, the Owner will cooperate fully with the responsible agency and will use such sanctions as are consistent with the contract terms to assist the responsible agency in enforcing laws, rules, and regulations. The Contractor has responsibility for complying with the federal construction safety standards. . . . It is not intended that the Owner's personnel perform detailed, in-depth safety inspections of the Contractor's operations, since such inspections are the responsibility of OSHA.

Provisions may go further, with the intent of limiting the owner's role to those aspects of the project that specifically exclude safety. For example:

> The Contractor shall be solely and completely responsible for the conditions of the Project Site, including the safety of all persons and property in the performance of the work. This requirement shall apply continuously and shall not be limited to normal working hours. The required or implied duty of the Owner's representative to conduct construction reviews of the Contractor's performance does not, and shall not, be intended to include review of the adequacy of the Contractor's safety measures in, on, or near the Project Site.

Some broad form provisions have been used to make the contractor solely responsible for all safety matters. The following provision has the clear intent of freeing the owner of any obligation for safety on the project:

> The Contractor shall be solely responsible for safety on the project. Nothing in these specifications shall be construed to reduce in any way that responsibility of the Contractor or to create any duty or responsibility on the part of the Owner to provide or enforce safety requirements for the Contractor. The duty, responsibility, and liability for safety shall remain with the Contractor. Any failure of the Owner to suspend work or to detect violations of any regulatory standards shall in no case relieve the Contractor of the Contractor's safety responsibilities.

The following is another example of an attempt to have the contractor bear the entire burden of project safety:

> To the full extent permitted by law, the Contractor shall indemnify and hold harmless the Owner and the Owner's agents and employees from and against all claims, damages, losses, and expenses, including, but not limited to, attorney's fees arising out of or resulting from the performance of the work, provided that any such claim, damage, loss, or expense is attributable to bodily injury . . . and is caused in whole or in part by the negligent act or omission of the Contractor or any subcontractor, . . . regardless of whether or not it is caused in part by a party indemnified.

Although such broad hold-harmless provisions are fairly common, the certainty of their intended effect is often questionable. Some states do not allow such provisions. In other states, courts have often failed to enforce such provisions as being too onerous.

Selection of an Insurance Carrier

Insurance should not be purchased without a great deal of thought. Purchasing insurance is not simply a matter of finding the lowest premium rate. The fine print of every policy must be fully evaluated. Besides reading the policy, it is prudent to ask the insurance carrier about the specific services that will be provided. How often will reports of claims be provided to the firm? Will the insurance carrier have a representative visit construction projects while they are under way? If so, how often will such visits be made? Will a report be made as a result of each visit? Is the insurance carrier willing to review contract documents to assess the appropriateness of the coverage specified? Having that "second pair of eyes" can be very helpful to the contractor. The insurance carrier should be a player on your team, looking out for your best interests.

The philosophy of the insurance carrier should be consistent with that of the contractor. Although an insurance company may be expected to aggressively fight or challenge questionable or fraudulent claims, it may be equally important to have an insurance company that will help in avoiding injury accidents. That is where on-site project inspections of insurance representatives can be quite helpful. A contractor may fail to see a hazard that develops over a period of time, whereas an inspector, new to the project, may identify it immediately as a problem. It is advisable that the inspections by insurance representatives result in formal reports. The original report should be given to someone at the project, preferably someone who accompanied the inspector on the project-safety inspection tour. A copy of the report should be sent to the designated safety officer in the main office. Personnel in the main office can then follow up on the report to ensure that it is given serious consideration. An insurance carrier that has a standard practice of providing such a service may prove to be a valued ally.

It is also helpful to know that the insurance carrier is willing to perform some basic analyses of the experiences of the company. Some injury records may point in the direction of a unique hazard that is responsible for many injuries. That information could be valuable to a company. Some education of company personnel on insurance matters may also be worthwhile. It may be helpful for all key personnel to be knowledgeable concerning such insurance matters as experience modification ratings, loss ratios, and reserves. In fact, it may be helpful to have someone from the insurance carrier simply go over the insurance reports to clarify exactly the type of information they contain. Once the company personnel are educated in the fundamentals, project safety may noticeably improve. The company should seek an insurance carrier that will help in such educational matters.

Other Elements

It may seem farfetched to suggest that part of the safety program lies in the company's efforts to help workers feel good about their employment with the company. In truth, those efforts are a crucial component of the safety program and may do more than any other component to minimize worker injuries. Employees work more safely when they like the firm and have developed a loyalty to it. Remember that many accidents occur as a result of a poor mental or psychological climate in the workplace. Workers who are not as dedicated to the company tend to be more easily distracted during the workday.

It is important to try to foster the types of feelings between workers and management that make for a closer working relationship. That will help in a number of ways, not just in safety performance. To foster such feelings, it is best to try to keep crews together from job to job if at all possible. The foremen should try to develop the talents of the workers by encouraging them to offer their ideas for approaching unique situations that arise on the job. The foremen should always be sensitive to the workers' feelings. Workers should be shown the respect they deserve.

A cohesive spirit between management and workers can be enhanced by better communication. Communication can take many forms. A good start is a company newsletter. A newsletter can be used to inform workers about the activities occurring on all the company jobs, and it can describe projects soon to be undertaken. Company dinners, company picnics, organized sports, and company retreats can also be used as effective mechanisms for educating the employees and increasing their team spirit.

Company managers can make excellent use of their time by making regular visits to the job sites and by showing a genuine concern for the welfare of the workers. Such actions require little effort but can generate big dividends.

Many accidents occur as a direct result of inadequate planning. Thus, planning the various tasks on a project can be part of the safety program. If project activities are carefully planned, uncertainty and risk are minimized. A carefully thought-out master schedule and the diligent preparation of short-interval schedules pay dividends in safety performance as well as profit. A poorly planned project, on the other hand, is typified by a series of "brush fires" to be put out and by unexpected deadlines, all of which are detrimental to project safety. For a schedule to be realistic, it should take account of the constraints of subcontractors. A closer working relationship can be assured if the subcontractors are afforded the opportunity of participating in the schedule development.

Companies may want to consider implementing a "flex and stretch" plan, in which workers start the day by doing warm-up exercises together. In some cases the philosophy of such a plan can be adopted by having workers park a given distance from the work site. Walking to the site will help to warm up muscles before workers begin their work tasks.

Whatever the company does, care should be taken to document all safety efforts. The safety documents, to have meaning in the firm, must be reviewed by someone in authority. Reviewing safety reports should be considered every bit as important as reviewing a cost report.

Final Comments

Planning is one way to avoid unplanned events. Since accidents are unplanned events, an effective safety program can help avoid job injuries. A safety program must be thorough, and it must be applicable to all aspects of the job, from the estimating phase of the project until the last worker has left the premises at the completion of the project. All parties to a construction project must be included in some way in the safety program. Each program must be specific to a particular project.

Review Questions

1. What is the purpose of the mission statement?
2. How can budgets be set up so that they do not discourage expenditures for safety?
3. What should be the role of the project safety director?
4. What kinds of safety issues might be discussed at the preconstruction meeting or conference?
5. Describe some matters related to safety that should be taken care of before the actual start of construction activities.
6. What kinds of training components might logically be included in a safety program?
7. Why might an owner wish to establish safety standards that differ from the mandated OSHA standards?
8. How might a company safety program differ from a project-specific safety program?
9. In what ways can a general contractor address or influence subcontractor safety?
10. What services should an insurance carrier provide?

References

Duston, D. 1996. "Drug-Abuse Rates Vary by Profession." *The Seattle Times,* April 12, page A15.

Hinze, J., and C. Harrison. 1981. "Safety Programs in Large Construction Firms." *Journal of the Construction Division, ASCE* 107, no. 3.

Levitt, R. 1975. "The Effect of Top Management on Safety in Construction." *Department of Civil Engineering Technical Report,* no. 196, Stanford Construction Institute, Stanford, CA.

Job-Site Safety Assessment

*If you don't make a concerted effort to find project hazards,
you may find them by accident.*

Job Hazard Analysis

Injuries occur as a consequence of unsafe physical conditions, unsafe work practices, or—most often—a combination of the two. Eliminating an unsafe physical condition directly reduces the likelihood of injury. Training workers to recognize unsafe physical conditions and to employ proper and safe work methods also aids in the achievement of good safety performance.

Project safety begins well before the construction activities actually begin. Before any work is performed on site, the work activities should be planned. The planned activities should then be examined to identify those that warrant special attention to ensure that they will be performed in a safe manner. Some hazards will be readily apparent from an understanding of the general nature of the project to be undertaken. Others may be identified only after consideration has been given to the specific methods to be employed in accomplishing the work. A schedule of activities that accurately reflects the activities to be undertaken can serve as a good resource for this analysis. A checklist is also helpful; however, full reliance can never be placed on a checklist that is used for all types and sizes of projects.

To accomplish good safety performance, it is important to examine work procedures before they are used. That is, hazards and dangerous work methods must be anticipated. Only then can positive steps be taken to enhance the safety environment. That is where job hazard analysis comes in. Job hazard analysis consists of considering the various components of a project and looking for any existing or potential job hazards. It is appropriate to conduct a job hazard analysis on every construction project undertaken, regardless of the project size. A project cannot be too small to warrant a job safety analysis.

It is ideal to conduct job hazard analyses on projects that are to be constructed. It is possible, often advisable, to conduct a subsequent job hazard analysis on a project that is well under way. Projects warranting such attention are those in which the work to be performed is of an unusual or untried nature. Projects that have reported an unacceptable number of injuries or illnesses should also be targeted for job hazard analysis.

Assessment of General-Conditions Hazards

A good starting point for conducting a job hazard analysis is with information from past projects. The OSHA logs for the immediate past years might be reviewed to determine if any patterns of injuries or illnesses exist for projects of a given type, size, location, or other characteristic. If reviewed carefully, the OSHA log can provide useful insights. Other valuable resources include safety violation reports and notes from past safety meetings. It might be quite a good idea to develop a list of general-conditions hazards to consider when conducting virtually every job hazard analysis. The list can grow as additional typical hazards are encountered. The following sample questions can provide guidance in starting a job hazard analysis:

- Do existing site utilities, especially power lines, pose a hazard to workers?
- Can access to the job site with cranes and other equipment be safely accomplished?
- Is neighborhood traffic a concern?
- Can dust be maintained at acceptable levels?
- Will construction noise hinder communication?
- Will construction noise pose a threat to hearing loss?
- Is fire protection equipment readily available?
- Is lighting adequate?
- Is ventilation adequate?
- Are workers trained properly (in equipment use, fire protection, hazard communication, etc.)?
- Are all employees wearing the appropriate personal protective equipment?
- Does the job-site topography pose any safety concerns?
- Are any known chemicals of obvious concern?
- Are job roads safely marked?
- Are major pieces of equipment (e.g., cranes) of particular concern?
- Can trenches and excavations be safely dug and safeguarded?
- Is wind a particular safety concern?
- Will materials in the storage area be accessed safely?
- Will rain create any unique safety concerns?

- Will temperature extremes (hot or cold) compromise safety?
- Will any explosives be used on site?
- Have all power tools and hand tools been examined for required repairs?
- Is all heavy equipment in proper running order (including brakes, rollover protection, back-up signals, horns, etc.)?
- Are all emergency exits clearly marked?
- Are there any confined spaces on site?
- Have tests been made for oxygen deficiency and toxic fumes?

Assessment of Hazards of Specific Operations

After the general-conditions issues have been addressed, the focus of the job hazard analysis turns to specific operations to be conducted on site. Some of the job-specific issues may have been addressed, to a limited degree, in the assessment of the general conditions. This assessment is a more focused and more detailed analysis of the work operations. Whereas the general-conditions assessment is a look at the overall job site, this assessment is an examination of the various components of the project.

The proper approach to use is a matter of choice. For example, one might examine the various provisions in the technical specifications to evaluate any unique hazards. Another means of directing the focus of the hazard assessment is to examine the schedule of values. Those may be effective strategies; however, they tend to focus on project components. One must then consider the operations that are entailed in getting the components installed. The project schedule may be the best source of information on the different operations involved in the project. A time-focused schedule consists primarily of the operations required to install the various components. In the job hazard analysis, the operations are of primary interest and of major concern. For example, the schedule of values may indicate the value attached to the construction of a particular slab. The network schedule, on the other hand, will identify the work, or operations, required to erect the falsework, erect the formwork, add the reinforcing steel, place the concrete, and—finally—remove the forms and the falsework. The analysis might identify areas of concern associated with the falsework, especially if the site conditions or loading conditions are unusual. Even the concrete placement operation might be found to impose its own hazards if, for example, a crane is used to hoist and swing concrete buckets over other work areas or near overhead power lines. The operations entailed in the construction of a slab can be more readily visualized if the source of information used clearly sets forth the various operations.

It is appropriate to examine each operation to identify the operations that pose the greatest threat to worker safety and health. For each operation, a unique set of questions must be asked. The following general questions may help bring to mind questions more specific to the operation:

- How might the worker or workers performing the operation be endangered (by falling, by being struck from above, by being struck by a moving component, by being caught in or between components, by electrical shock, etc.)?
- Is there a safer way of performing the operation?
- Must the operation be performed at all?

- Are safeguards available that can ensure worker safety?
- Are workers trained adequately to perform the operation safely?
- Does proximity to other operations pose a hazard?
- Are there any special hazards due to heavy equipment?
- Are there any special environmental hazards (dust, chemicals, welding fumes, noise, etc.)?

The process is repeated for each of the major operations identified for the project. Thus, it is readily apparent that considerable time is entailed in conducting a thorough job hazard analysis for a construction project.

Documenting the Hazards

When conducting a job hazard analysis, one must take care to document all the hazards that are identified. Once the hazards have been identified, attention can begin to focus on the source or cause of each hazard. The cause of the hazard may or may not be inherent in the operation. For example, constructing a steel frame may pose a variety of fall hazards. The cause is not inherent in the construction of a steel frame, but rather it is a function of the means employed to erect the steel frame. If the steel frame is modular, with much of the structure prefabricated on the ground, the fall hazard is much less than if the steel frame is constructed in place one piece at a time. Thus, it is a valuable step in the analysis to examine the actual cause of each hazard. Understanding the cause of each hazard will provide a quicker means of devising corrective measures for resolving problems resulting from the hazards.

One way to think of the cause of the hazard is to think of the events that must take place in order for a worker to be injured in an accident. That analysis may uncover a series of events that would contribute to the accident. With the series of events identified, it may be possible to develop several means by which the risks associated with some hazards can be greatly reduced.

Corrective Measures

Once the causes of hazards are identified, attention can then be focused on the necessary corrective measures. Determining the measures to be taken is no small task. If the causes of the hazards have been clearly delineated, however, the task is much less arduous. Of course, it is not enough to simply determine what an appropriate response would be for a given hazard. Some positive action is required. It is one matter to identify a hazard, and it is another matter to do something about the hazard.

Suggestions for solutions may be offered by a number of persons. The workers on the job site may prove particularly resourceful in coming up with ingenious suggestions. Asking the workers for such suggestions will help them understand the purpose of a job hazard analysis, and it will help educate them on the importance of this task. It may also be appropriate to designate a person to be responsible for correcting the problem or implementing the proper preventive measures.

In considering solutions, it is best to think first of means by which the cause, and the hazard, can be eliminated. That may be a simple task or it may a be very difficult one. In some cases, it may be possible only to devise a backup, or secondary, plan to reduce the hazard of a particular cause. In other instances, it may be possible to make slight modifications in the work operation to completely eliminate some hazards. In still other situations, it may be possible only to reduce the frequency with which workers are exposed to the potential hazard.

Obviously, all other things being equal, priority should be given to measures that eliminate the hazards. Hazards may be eliminated by changing the operation, using different equipment, changing the number of workers required for a task, changing the task itself, or other means. Hazards may typically be reduced by such means as the use of personal protective equipment, increased training of workers, or a slowing of the work pace.

Some sort of follow-up may be required, particularly if the responsibilities for different corrective measures are allocated to different persons. It is important that no hazard be overlooked simply because everyone thought that someone else was going to take care of it. At the very least, some form of monitoring or feedback procedure should be implemented to create a historical record of the tasks that have been performed and the issues that are yet to be fully addressed. The documentation of the job hazard analysis may take several forms. The form shown in Figure 7.1 is an example.

Job Hazard Analysis Form

Project No.: _____   Date of Analysis: _____

Project Location: _____   Prepared by: _____

Task/Operation/Area	Hazard	Cause of Hazard	Preventive Measure
1.			
2.			
3.			
4.			
5.			
6.			
7.			
8.			
9.			
10.			
11.			
12.			
13.			
14.			
15.			

Figure 7.1
Example of a Job Hazard Analysis Form

Being Ever Vigilant

Although a job hazard analysis is performed before the start of construction, the analysis must not stop at that point. Even as work is proceeding, it is important to be constantly on the lookout for new or previously unnoticed hazards. Workers can be a valuable resource for identifying such hazards. The information can be brought up at the regularly held safety meetings. Again, a person must be designated to be responsible for carrying out the preventive measures.

The occurrence of an injury or a near miss is a flag to the safety analyst, indicating that the job hazards should be reexamined. Perhaps the job operations have been altered in such a way as to introduce new hazards to the work environment. Possibly some hazards were overlooked during the initial job hazard analysis. If the job hazard analysis is thorough, the incidence of accidents should be minimal.

If workers are properly indoctrinated in the purpose of the job hazard analysis, and if they fully appreciate the commitment of top management to safety, they are generally an excellent resource for identifying job hazards during construction. It is important that job supervisors be sensitive to the concerns about safety hazards that workers bring to their attention. Remember, if the supervisor is not sensitive to safety concerns brought up by workers, the workers may resort to other means to ensure the safety of the workplace. The actions workers may take if the supervisor is not attentive to safety concerns include the following:

Submit complaints directly to upper management concerning job safety conditions.
File formal complaints with government agencies, such as OSHA or state safety and health agencies. Anonymity can be protected if requested.
Participate in union committees or other similar committees concerning safety and health.
Participate in project safety inspections.
File complaints with other agencies.
Resort to other legal avenues.

OSHA Consulting

As mentioned in Chapter 4, OSHA compliance officers have their educational counterparts in the OSHA consultants. An employer may call the OSHA office on the telephone and, if time permits, can obtain a considerable amount of useful information. It would be inappropriate for OSHA to provide information through its consultants and then later to have a compliance officer issue a citation for work being done in accordance with the consultants' suggestions. Although such problems might arise, no such conflicts have been publicized.

In every state, free on-site consultation services are available to help employers identify job safety and health hazards. The consultations may also include suggestions for corrective measures. Information about the consultations is considered confidential, so compliance officers cannot generally acquire information about particular employers from the OSHA consultants. It might be suspected that consultants might inform compliance officers about specific job-site conditions if they observe an imminent danger or serious violations of the OSHA standards and if the employer failed to correct the problem within the period recommended by the consultant. This is speculative and would not take place through any formal channels.

An OSHA consultation by telephone is appropriate when a specific situation or set of circumstances arises. The employer may have a single question to ask, and the consultant may quickly help the employer address the problem in an appropriate manner. Consultations may also occur at the place of employment. For example, suppose a contractor is about to undertake a particular project. The contractor may wish to have an OSHA consultant make a site visit to discuss appropriate safety measures in greater detail and on a greater variety of topics than would be possible in a telephone call. Such prejob consultations are advisable. In some cases, a contractor may realize after a construction project has begun that additional advice is warranted. That is another good time to ask for consultation services. The consultant can serve as a second pair of eyes and may even be able to identify problems that the contractor had not envisioned.

Whenever an OSHA consultation takes place, it is important to respond favorably to the consultant's suggestions. Although the suggested measures may not always be the most economical, the employer must be conscientious about addressing all recognized hazards. Once the hazards have been identified, the employer has a duty to address them.

Safety Committees

Even with constant vigilance, it is not likely that all safety problems on a project will be identified. Therefore, it is helpful for the project manager to get input from other sources. One such resource is the safety committee. The objective of the safety committee is to serve as a second pair of eyes for management in identifying areas of safety that warrant attention. The safety committee performs most of its work by conducting periodic (typically weekly) job-site inspections.

Safety committees can be structured in a variety of ways. The safety committee is typically made up of several workers, each representing a different craft. Thus, the members of the committee bring different perspectives to the group. A valuable benefit of working with different crafts in the committee is that the members broaden their knowledge of other crafts and, specifically, of other areas of safety. Some companies set up their safety committees in such a manner that the makeup of the committee is constantly changing. For example, the committee may be made up of five workers. Each worker participates in the committee for a period of 10 weeks. Every second week, one of the workers is dropped from the committee and a new member is added. The rotation of membership also has some benefit. The new members of the committee are trained to be more sensitive to a variety of safety issues. Meanwhile, the members that have left the committee continue to look for hazards in the workplace. In a way, the members that have officially been dropped from the committee are functionally an extension of the committee. All they need is a forum for pointing out the hazards to someone in authority. Of course, any member of the safety committee can serve as a conduit of such information. It should be the objective of project management to identify all safety infractions and correct all those that are brought to its attention.

Job-Site Safety Inspections

Worker injuries are the result of unsafe physical conditions, unsafe worker actions, or a combination of the two. Safety meetings can address those causes to some extent, but it is safer to make additional efforts to reduce unsafe physical conditions. One such effort is to conduct job-site inspections. The inspections are generally conducted by the job superintendent or the project manager and are separate from inspections conducted by the safety committee. The active involvement of high-level project personnel in this activity communicates clearly that safety is an important component of the project.

The purpose of job-site safety inspections is to identify all conditions that can effectively be corrected. The inspection tour should cover the entire project, with particular attention given to the work being performed by subcontractors. The workers of subcontractors should receive the same message about the importance of safety as the workers employed by the general contractor.

Job-site safety inspections do not occur on all projects. Such inspections should, however, be an integral part of every safety program. A job-site safety inspection is not to be confused with a project manager's observation of unsafe conditions while he or she is involved in other job activities. Although it is exemplary for project managers and job superintendents to be constantly looking for unsafe conditions, job-site safety inspections are formalized activities. That is, a job-site safety inspection is the sole focus of the person conducting the inspection.

Job-site safety inspections should generally be conducted weekly. Depending on the size of the project, the job superintendent or the project manager should set aside one or two hours during which he or she will perform no tasks other than trying to identify unsafe conditions and unsafe work activities. It may be ideal for the inspection tours to be scheduled at a random time each week. Random scheduling gives the workers no forewarning of the inspections. Just as the timing of the inspections should be random, so, too, the tour path should not be the same each week. The inspection might even be performed as a simulated OSHA inspection.

When corrective actions are warranted, they are to be implemented promptly. The information obtained through job-site safety inspections can be a source of subject material for the following week's safety meeting.

The inspection results should be well documented. Preprinted checklists can simplify the record keeping. They may also help ensure that a predetermined set of job-site conditions are examined in each inspection. If the same type of report is used consistently over a period of time, a baseline measure can be established. From that, management can quickly ascertain whether the safety conditions on a project are below par for the firm's projects.

The checklists in Figures 7.2 to 7.9, at the end of this chapter, provide some basic guidance on the nature of the key issues to be observed. Note that the sample checklists include assessments both of physical conditions and of worker behavior as it relates to a variety of issues. The checklists should be customized for the types of projects typically undertaken by a firm. Some of the checklists may be sufficiently generic to need little or no modification from one project to another. For example, the checklist for sanitation and the checklist for personal protective and lifesaving equipment may have such general utility. Other checklists may vary considerably between projects.

Mock OSHA Inspections

Some companies conduct simulated OSHA job-site inspections. The intent is to give a project an extra-thorough inspection once in a while. It is one way to avoid getting too lax in maintaining job safety. Although little has been written on the protocol to follow in such an inspection, presumably a mock OSHA inspection is more involved than the routine weekly inspections that might be conducted by the project manager, the job superintendent, or the job-site safety committee. In some companies a poor showing on it may carry greater consequences for the project. Certainly, a poor report on such an inspection foretells problems in the event of an actual regulatory inspection. The inspection can assist in the recognition of potential hazards. Once the hazards are identified, steps can be formulated to eliminate them, and in the end the procedure helps to prevent the occurrence of accidents.

Mock OSHA inspections may best be performed by personnel not already assigned to the project. One key objective of such inspections is to obtain a second opinion about the conditions on a project without the consequences that would accompany the identification of hazards by regulatory personnel. The inspection is different from typical inspections in that the focus is not exclusively on hazards, but also on regulatory requirements. For example, the "inspectors" should check that the firm has satisfied all posting requirements, maintains documentation of safety meetings, has the required written programs in place, and conducts regular inspections of the job site.

Insurance Carrier Job Inspections

Some insurance carriers conduct regular job-site safety inspections on the construction projects of their contractor clients. Those inspections vary in degrees of thoroughness. In fact, some insurance carriers do not provide such services on a regular basis. For companies in the market for insurance, one service to consider would be whether the firm provides job-site safety inspections.

Some argue that insurance job-site safety inspections tend to be superficial. They contend that the inspections are deliberately superficial because insurance carriers do not want to tell their clients that they are doing poorly on a project. That has not been my experience. In fact, I have found that the insurance safety inspection reports can be effective tools in getting top management to change certain field practices pointed out in the reports. Insurance inspectors occasionally see problems that have been completely overlooked by those who are on the project daily.

In some companies little attention is paid to the job-site safety inspection reports prepared by insurance representatives. That may be true especially when the reports are vague or generic. If the reports provide virtually no guidance, the information is of little value. The insurance company may be reluctant to exercise any clout (e.g., to threaten to cancel an insurance policy) when the construction firm has a good performance history. The insurance company may fear that if it gives the client too many reports of poor safety practices, the client will eventually seek a new insurance carrier. If that is the fear of the insurance company, the inspection services will be of diminished value.

Some construction firms take the stance that an insurance carrier should provide job-site safety inspection reports regularly, perhaps monthly, as a fundamental service.

The insurance inspector can look at the construction project with fresh eyes and may look at the project in a manner similar to that of an OSHA compliance officer. Any insights offered by the insurance inspector should be carefully heeded.

Final Comments

If hazards can be identified, they can be avoided or eliminated. In many cases, the hazards are created by undertaking a particular task in a given manner. Changing the method of accomplishing the task may be all that is required to avoid the hazard. Employers should use all available resources to identify project hazards. Those resources include the project personnel: the workers, the supervisory personnel, the safety personnel, the subcontractors, and all others associated with the project. They should be included in the task of hazard identification and assessment, as they too have a stake in safety by being present on the job.

Review Questions

1. When is the best time in a project to conduct a job hazard analysis?
2. Explain how safety committees can be considered part of a firm's safety training program.
3. Should an employer have any reluctance to call an OSHA consultant, especially when a known hazard exists on a project? Explain.
4. Describe a protocol that might be appropriate for conducting job-site safety inspections.
5. Who might be assigned the task of conducting a mock OSHA inspection?
6. In what formal ways might workers be utilized in hazard analysis? In what informal ways might workers be utilized?
7. Use information from one of the OSHA standards to develop a job-site safety checklist.
8. How might information from past projects help in conducting a job hazard analysis of an upcoming construction project?
9. Why might job inspections by insurance representatives be particularly beneficial to a contractor?

References

U.S. Department of Labor. Occupational Safety and Health Administration (OSHA). 1990. *The Occupational Safety and Health Act of 1970, PL 91-956.* OSHA no. 2001. Washington, D.C.
————. 1991. *Consultation Services for the Employer.* Rev. ed. OSHA no. 3047. Washington, D.C.
————. 1992. *All about OSHA.* Rev. ed. OSHA no. 2056. Washington, D.C.
————. 1992. *Job Hazard Analysis.* Revised. OSHA no. 3071. Washington, D.C.
————. 1995. *Training Requirements of OSHA Standards and Training Guidelines.* OSHA no. 2254. Washington, D.C.

Checklist

Sanitation (CFR 1926.51)			

	OK	Not OK	Condition or Practice
Drinking water	☐	☐	Adequate supply
	☐	☐	Containers tightly closed and marked "For Drinking Only"
	☐	☐	Containers equipped with a tap
	☐	☐	Single-service cups provided
	☐	☐	Trash receptacles provided
Washing water	☐	☐	Temperature at 70–100°F
	☐	☐	Individual hand towels provided
	☐	☐	Trash receptacle provided
	☐	☐	Hand cleaner or soap provided
	☐	☐	No slip hazard at wash location
	☐	☐	Facilities near location of work involving harmful contaminants
Nonpotable water	☐	☐	Clearly marked "Unsafe for Drinking"
	☐	☐	Water system not crossed with potable water system
Sanitary facilities	☐	☐	Adequate number provided: 20 or fewer workers (1 toilet required) 20 or more (1 toilet seat and 1 urinal per 40) 200 plus (1 toilet seat and 1 urinal per 50)
	☐	☐	Facilities available every 3rd floor
	☐	☐	Facilities available within 200' horizontal distance
	☐	☐	Facilities cleaned regularly
	☐	☐	

Figure 7.2
Checklist for Sanitation

Checklist

Personal Protective and Lifesaving Equipment			
	OK	**Not OK**	**Condition or Practice**
Head protection (CFR 1926.100, 1926.951(a)(2))	☐	☐	Hard hat available nearby for each worker
	☐	☐	No metal on headgear near electrical work
	☐	☐	Hard hats worn by all workers
Hearing protection (CFR 1926.101)	☐	☐	Hearing protection in place near noise
	☐	☐	
Eye and face protection (CFR 1926.102, 1926.353(d)(2), 1926.303(c)(9))	☐	☐	Protection from flying objects
	☐	☐	Protection from welding
	☐	☐	Eye protection free of defects
	☐	☐	
Worker clothing (CFR 1926.201(a)(4))	☐	☐	Bright vests worn near moving vehicles
	☐	☐	Short-sleeved shirts, long pants, and shoes are minimum requirements
	☐	☐	Clothes not loose-fitting
	☐	☐	
Foot protection (CFR 1926.96)	☐	☐	Leather shoes with nonslip soles
	☐	☐	Athletic-style shoes with leather uppers permitted only if danger is minimal
	☐	☐	No open-toed shoes, sandals, dress shoes, or canvas shoes allowed
	☐	☐	
Work near moving equipment or parts (CFR 1926.551(e))	☐	☐	Caps, hair nets, or other head protection worn by workers near hair-catching or fire hazards
	☐	☐	Clothes snug-fitting
	☐	☐	Short-sleeved shirts worn
	☐	☐	No jewelry
	☐	☐	

Figure 7.3
Checklist for Personal Protective and Lifesaving Equipment

Checklist

	OK	Not OK	Condition or Practice
Motor Vehicles (CFR 1926.600 and 1926.601)			
Proper setup	☐	☐	Brakes in operational condition
	☐	☐	Headlights and taillights working
	☐	☐	Horn working
	☐	☐	Automatic reverse alarm audible from 15'
	☐	☐	Glass and mirrors not cracked or broken
	☐	☐	Defrost system working
	☐	☐	Tools and material secured
	☐	☐	Seat belt and seat for each employee to be carried
	☐	☐	Operating levers guarded against accidental operation
	☐	☐	Fenders in place on all rubber-tired equipment
	☐	☐	
Roadways	☐	☐	Roadways well maintained
	☐	☐	Dust kept to a minimum
	☐	☐	Adequate turning radius on roadways
	☐	☐	Safe and secure parking location
	☐	☐	Adequate signs on all roadways
	☐	☐	
	☐	☐	

Figure 7.4
Checklist for Motor Vehicles

Checklist

	OK	Not OK	Condition or Practice
Material Storage [CFR 1926.250, 1926.953(c), 1926.957(f)]			
	☐	☐	Materials secured against sliding, falling, or collapse
	☐	☐	Load limits posted in storage areas
	☐	☐	Aisles and passageways kept clear
	☐	☐	Grading, ramps, blocking, etc., provided for changes in work elevations
	☐	☐	6' clear space from hoistways
	☐	☐	Noncompatible materials segregated in storage
	☐	☐	Cement and lime bags stacked less than 10' high
	☐	☐	Bricks stacked less than 7' high
	☐	☐	Lumber stacked less than 20' high (no nails in the lumber)
	☐	☐	Structural steel kept in low piles
	☐	☐	Corrugated and flat iron stacked in flat piles less than 4' high
	☐	☐	Rigging equipment inspected before each shift
	☐	☐	No storage permitted on scaffolds or runways

Figure 7.5
Checklist for Material Storage

Checklist

	OK	Not OK	Condition or Practice
Scaffolding (CFR 1926.451)			
Proper setup	☐	☐	Solid, sound footing or anchorage
	☐	☐	Guardrails and toeboards on all open sides if higher than 10'
	☐	☐	Guardrails and toeboards on all open sides if 4–10' high if a horizontal dimension < 45"
	☐	☐	Capable of supporting 4 × intended load
	☐	☐	Damaged components replaced or repaired
	☐	☐	Planking level, with 12" min. overlap, or secured from movement
	☐	☐	Planking extending 6–12" over end supports
	☐	☐	Uprights plumb and rigidly braced
	☐	☐	Access ladder provided
	☐	☐	Platforms: at least two 2 × 10s, or 18" min. width
Miscellaneous	☐	☐	Scaffold towers: height < 4 × smallest base width
	☐	☐	Screen cover from toeboard to guardrail if workers are exposed below
	☐	☐	Overhead protection if workers are exposed to overhead hazards
	☐	☐	Wire or rope for suspended scaffolds capable of supporting 6 × the rated load
	☐	☐	
Work practices	☐	☐	Materials hoisted onto scaffold only with tag line
	☐	☐	No more than two workers per 8' of scaffold
	☐	☐	No excess accumulation of tools or materials
	☐	☐	No work permitted during high winds
	☐	☐	

Figure 7.6
Checklist for Scaffolding

	OK	Not OK	Condition or Practice
Steel Erection (CFR 1926.750–752)			
Flooring requirements	☐	☐	Permanent floors installed as steel erection progresses
	☐	☐	No more than 4 floors of unfinished bolting or welding
	☐	☐	Erection floor decked over its whole surface except for access openings
	☐	☐	Erection floor no higher than 8 stories above highest completed permanent floor
	☐	☐	Safety nets in place to prevent fall from temporary floor structures
	☐	☐	Standard railings in place at peripheries of temporary metal-decked floors during steel assembly
	☐	☐	A tightly planked floor maintained within 2 stories or 25' of steel erection work
	☐	☐	Gathering and stacking always done on temporary planked floors
	☐	☐	Steel structure of building with rough double-wood flooring erected as building progresses
	☐	☐	Single-wood floor or other flooring systems planked where floor joists are installed
	☐	☐	
Structural steel assembly	☐	☐	When final solid-web members are placed, load not released from hoist line until members are stable
	☐	☐	Open-web steel joists not put on structural steel framework unless it is safety bolted
	☐	☐	Bar joists bolted at columns to give lateral stability in steel framing construction
	☐	☐	Center row of bolted bridging installed for lateral stability on longspan joists or trusses (>40')
	☐	☐	Tag lines used to control loads
	☐	☐	Work performed under experienced supervisor
	☐	☐	Workers not allowed to ride on steel being hoisted
	☐	☐	If no planking or scaffolding, safety nets used
	☐	☐	
	☐	☐	

Figure 7.7
Checklist for Steel Erection

Checklist

Hand and Power Tools (CFR 1926.300–307)			

	OK	Not OK	Condition or Practice
Tools	☐	☐	Guards in place on all tools
	☐	☐	Tools well maintained
	☐	☐	Belts, gears, and shafts covered
	☐	☐	Switches in good working condition
	☐	☐	On/off switch clearly marked
	☐	☐	Lock-on control capable of being disengaged by a single motion
	☐	☐	Hand tools in good condition (e.g., no worn jaws on wrenches)
	☐	☐	Wooden handles free of splinters and cracks
	☐	☐	Electric tools double-insulated
	☐	☐	Compressed air <30 psi when used for cleaning
	☐	☐	Air hoses used only at recommended pressures
	☐	☐	
Operation of tools	☐	☐	Eye protection provided and used
	☐	☐	Hearing protection provided and used
	☐	☐	Masks provided and used when recommended
	☐	☐	
	☐	☐	

Figure 7.8
Checklist for Hand and Power Tools

Checklist

Tower Crane (CFR1926.550)			
	OK	**Not OK**	**Condition or Practice**
Proper setup	☐	☐	Foundation certified by a professional engineer
	☐	☐	Crane able to swing 360° without striking any obstructions
			Crane tested with design-rated load:
	☐	☐	Hoisting and lowering
	☐	☐	Trolley travel
	☐	☐	Swing travel
	☐	☐	Limit, locking, and safety devices
	☐	☐	Crane travel (when applicable)
	☐	☐	Foundation and erection
	☐	☐	Safe access to cab
	☐	☐	Operator protected from the weather
Work practices	☐	☐	Tag lines used on all freely swinging loads
	☐	☐	Loads not swung over workers
	☐	☐	Workers not riding with the hook
	☐	☐	
	☐	☐	

Figure 7.9
Checklist for Tower Cranes

Safety Meetings

> *If you look for hazards, you will find them; if you don't look for hazards, they will find you.*

Construction site safety meetings have two broad purposes: to educate and to persuade. The educational component is to enlighten those in attendance about the proper procedures to use for specific tasks or in certain environments. The persuasive component of the safety meetings is to capture the attention of those in attendance and provide them with information so compelling that it coaxes them to accept it and to willingly follow the directives. Thus, the meetings consist of content that imparts knowledge and encouragement that induces behavior that responds to the knowledge acquired.

A safety meeting may be a mass gathering of all personnel on a construction site, or it may be a discussion between a supervisor and one or two workers. Both fit the description in the preceding paragraph. Some safety meetings are formal and others are informal. The purpose of conducting such meetings must always be kept in mind.

When the topic of safety meetings is mentioned on many construction projects, it commonly conjures up images of traditional toolbox meetings. Although those are certainly safety meetings, they are by no means the only type of safety meeting to be held on a construction site. Safety sessions may be conducted for various levels of supervision. Most of the comments in this chapter, however, will refer to the toolbox or tailgate sessions oriented to workers.

Safety meetings are invariably an integral component of safety programs. For some firms, safety programs consist almost entirely of safety meetings. Although safety meetings are important, they should never be considered sufficient to obviate other safety measures.

Although the OSHA regulations focus almost exclusively on matters related to specific physical conditions, one exception is the requirement that employers conduct regular safety meetings for their workers. The standard is as follows:

29 CFR § 1926.21 Safety training and education.

(b) *Employer responsibility.* . . .

   (2)   The employer shall instruct each employee in the recognition and avoidance of unsafe conditions and the regulations applicable to his work environment to control or eliminate any hazards or other exposure to illness or injury.

   (3)   Employees required to handle or use poisons, caustics, and other harmful substances shall be instructed regarding the safe handling and use, and be made aware of the potential hazards, personal hygiene, and personal protective measures required.

   (4)   In job site areas where harmful plants or animals are present, employees who may be exposed shall be instructed regarding the potential hazards, and how to avoid injury, and the first aid procedures to be used in the event of injury.

   (5)   Employees required to handle or use flammable liquids, gases, or toxic materials shall be instructed in the safe handling and use of these materials and made aware of the specific requirements contained in subparts D, F, and other applicable subparts of this part.

   (6)   (i) All employees required to enter into confined or enclosed spaces shall be instructed as to the nature of the hazards involved. . . .

There is a less-than-flattering stereotype of safety meetings. It is that safety meetings are the meetings held during the first 15 minutes of the workday on Monday mornings. Some sarcastically refer to such meetings as "Monday morning quarterback sessions." Others regard them as a last effort to get all workers sobered up after a wild weekend. Despite those impressions, safety meetings can be vital to the safety performance of construction workers. Care must be exercised so that the sarcastic impressions are not applicable.

Although safety meetings may be held during the first 15 minutes on Monday mornings, scheduling is by no means the only issue to be resolved about safety meetings. In planning safety meetings, the following questions should be carefully addressed:

- When should the meetings be held?
- Who will be required to attend the meetings?
- Who will conduct the meetings?
- What topics will be discussed at the meetings?
- What kind of preparations will be required for the meetings?
- What kind of records will be kept of the meetings?

From the beginning, company managers must convey the importance of safety meetings to all the employees. One way to relay the appropriate message is to refer to the meetings as training sessions. That establishes a genuine purpose for the meetings, a purpose other than simply complying with the OSHA regulations. Calling them training sessions, instead of meetings, may appear to be a matter of semantics, but it can convey the company philosophy about the importance of the sessions.

When Should the Safety Training Sessions Be Held?

Injury data generally show that, as a rule, the largest numbers of injuries occur on Mondays. The numbers of injuries tend to diminish toward the end of the week, with Fridays being associated with the smallest number of injuries. Even before that distribution of injuries was substantiated through the evaluation of several large databases, the higher incidence of injuries on Mondays was almost universally known, largely through intuition. Construction contractors have responded to that fact by conducting many of their safety meetings on Monday mornings.

Some thought should be given to the scheduling of safety meetings. Monday morning is a common choice for the meetings. It is the best time to review the activities that will be taking place in the workdays to follow. If the meeting is conducted in a serious manner, having it first thing Monday also conveys to the workers that safety has a high priority on the project.

Some contend that holding a meeting rigidly each Monday morning may not always be appropriate. For example, the nature of the work may change dramatically between Wednesday and Thursday. On such a project, it might be more prudent to hold the safety meeting on Thursday morning. Perhaps it would be appropriate to hold the Thursday morning meeting as a second safety meeting for the week. A second safety meeting in some weeks may pay real dividends if it helps workers avoid accidents. It might also be argued that holding the safety meetings on different days each week helps to avoid making the meetings too routine and boring.

On one project I visited, the superintendent did not conduct weekly safety meetings. The project employed about 40 to 50 workers. In describing his job meetings, the superintendent did not even use the term *safety meeting.* He called his meetings "gang meetings." He held gang meetings whenever the nature of the work changed. The meetings concerned the approach that the workers were to take in accomplishing the work. The superintendent stated that safety was never a special topic of discussion in the meetings, but rather was an integral part of each discussion. Thus, the superintendent had safety ingrained in all the work discussions. The workers never felt that safety was being discussed to satisfy a regulatory requirement mandating that safety meetings be held. Because the meetings occurred as changes in the work required them, they were not necessarily held on a regular schedule. In fact, such meetings might be held on four days in one week, on two the next, and so forth. The meetings were not timed, either; they ranged in duration from a few minutes to more than a half hour. The subject to be discussed dictated the time needed for the meetings. It bears mentioning that the superintendent could justly be proud of the outstanding safety record on that project.

The type of meeting just described is what the National Safety Council calls a "production huddle" or a "tailboard conference." It is essentially a gathering in which the work is discussed, the discussion of safety being built in. Such meetings, when conducted in the proper setting, have been referred to as "the best kind of safety meeting" (National Safety Council 1985).

Who Should Attend the Safety Training Sessions?

Literally all workers on the construction site should be required to attend a safety session each week. The issue to be resolved by project managers is whether all workers are to attend one such session held for the entire project or whether separate sessions are to be held for different trades or for workers assigned to different areas on the project. The decision may be driven in part by the size of the work force. Naturally, a large number of workers attending a single session may present unique challenges for those conducting the sessions. For example, it may be more difficult to get every worker's attention, it may be difficult for all attendees to hear the topic being discussed, and it may be difficult to get all attendees to feel free to contribute to the discussion.

Who Should Conduct the Safety Training Sessions?

Who should conduct the safety meetings? The answer depends to some degree on the type and size of the project. If meetings are held at the crew level, the foreman or one of the workers, who has been carefully selected, should conduct the meetings. If the project is small and all workers are required to attend the same safety meeting, it may be deemed appropriate for the project manager or the job superintendent to conduct the safety meetings. At the very least, the top company representatives at the project level should attend the meetings. If they do not conduct the meetings, they should certainly contribute to the discussion to indicate management's support of safety.

Anyone selected to conduct the meetings should be able to speak clearly, should have a voice that projects well, and should be able to organize his or her thoughts so as to impart a coherent message in an interesting way. If voice projection is a problem, some type of sound amplification should be considered.

It is very important for those conducting the meetings to solicit input from those in attendance. Comments from workers in attendance should be taken seriously. If they are, workers will be more likely to offer their suggestions at all safety meetings.

What Topics Should Be Addressed?

The topics to be discussed at safety meetings must provide information that contributes to the training of the workers. One practice of some firms is for the company safety officer to notify each project of the safety topics to be discussed at each meeting. The purpose of that practice is to give those conducting the meetings a focus for the meetings. It is a good intention; however, the prescribed topics may not always be germane to the actual work to be performed on a project. Thus, it is desirable to grant some latitude to those conducting the meetings to develop their own meeting topics.

How might the topics for a meeting be established? One way is to examine the construction schedule to determine which activities will take place during a given week. The safety meetings are an excellent and appropriate time to convey that information. Information from the past week's activities can also be of value at safety meetings. For example, the person conducting the meetings could review the overall project with a job safety inspection. He or she should keep notes on all safety infractions observed, be they unsafe actions of workers or unsafe physical conditions. Naturally, any such infractions should be corrected at the time they are observed, but the entire work force can benefit from having the information shared.

For best results, the topics discussed at safety meetings should be well focused. A discussion of many different issues might result in a cursory treatment of each subject. Attendees will not benefit from a meeting that touches on many topics in a cursory fashion. A discussion on a limited number of topics is advised. The topics might relate to a recent accident or near miss, the functioning of a new piece of equipment on the project, or a specific hazard that has been identified on site. Time should always be allotted for comments and questions that are germane to project safety.

Preparation for Safety Training Sessions

Deciding on the appropriate topic, or topics, to be presented and discussed at the safety training session is the most important aspect of preparing for an effective meeting. If the topic is selected by the person who will conduct the meeting, there should be considerable comfort in presenting the subject matter. If the topics that have been suggested by the main office are appropriate for the project, the person who will conduct the meeting should carefully study the material before the meeting.

Regardless of the topic selected for the safety meeting, careful attention should be given to the way the material is to be presented. It is a serious mistake to "wing it" at the time of the meeting by reading the information. The person conducting the meeting should be able to deliver the information in his or her own words. That will ensure that the delivery is more interesting. If the material is not interesting and if it is not presented in an interesting manner, the value of having a meeting is greatly diminished.

When preparing for the meeting, consider using props, as that is an effective way to drive home major points. Also, devise some key questions that relate to the topic. The answers given by those in attendance will provide a quick assessment of how well the workers understand the material. A simple quiz prepared beforehand can also be an effective teaching device, even if the exams are not turned in or graded. For some topics, it will be beneficial to enlist the assistance of others on the project who have a better understanding of the subject.

The manner in which the material is presented will depend on the subject matter and the expertise of those in attendance. Thus, the preparation required will change from time to time.

Documentation of Safety Training Sessions

Just as in any other activity that takes place on a construction site, an effort should be made to carefully document the information shared at the safety meetings. The record should indicate the time of the meeting, the person conducting the meeting, the names of the attendees (often recorded with their own signatures), the topics discussed, and any actions that are to be taken as a result of the meeting. A sample form for such a record appears in Figure 8.1.

```
┌─────────────────────────────────────────────────────────────────┐
│                    Weekly Safety Meeting                          │
│                                                                   │
│  Project: _____    Date: _____    │
│  Presided by: _____                               │
│                                                                   │
│  Attendees (signatures):                                          │
│                                                                   │
│  _____    _____    _____         │
│  _____    _____    _____         │
│  _____    _____    _____         │
│  _____    _____    _____         │
│  _____    _____    _____         │
│  _____    _____    _____         │
│  _____                                                 │
│                                                                   │
│  Topics Presented:                                                │
│                                                                   │
│  _____      │
│  _____      │
│  _____      │
│  _____      │
│  _____      │
│  _____      │
│  _____      │
│  _____      │
│  _____      │
│  _____      │
│  _____      │
│  _____      │
│  _____      │
│                                                                   │
│  Comments:                                                        │
│                                                                   │
│  _____      │
│  _____      │
│  _____      │
│  _____      │
│  _____      │
│  _____      │
│  _____      │
│  _____      │
│  _____      │
│  _____      │
│  _____      │
│  _____      │
│                                                                   │
│  Supervisor's Signature: _____       │
└─────────────────────────────────────────────────────────────────┘
```

Figure 8.1
Example of Form for Recording Weekly Safety Meeting Information

Supervisory Safety Meetings

The emphasis of most safety meetings is on the workers. That is, the subject material of the meetings tends to be addressed to the workers, because the workers face the daily job-site conditions that might injure them. Occasionally it may be appropriate for safety meetings to address the job-site supervisors. Those supervisory safety meetings are attended by the various supervisors on the job site. In most instances it is appropriate to include all foremen on the jobsite, including the foremen of subcontractors.

Since the supervisory meetings are attended by the supervisors and not the workers, the meetings might logically be conducted in a different manner. The meetings are conducted by the project manager or the job-site safety director, but he or she should encourage input from all those in attendance. Some selected parties might be asked to give presentations on specific topics.

Typically, supervisory safety meetings are held about once a month. The topics of discussion may be focused on general issues. A starting point might be an overview of job-site safety performance to date. The trends should be discussed, whether the trends are good or bad. If safety performance is good, the supervisors must be told that management recognizes that achievement. If the news is bad, the trends should be discussed so that positive steps can be taken to improve the safety performance record. Different tactics might be suggested and implemented. If they are implemented, the results of those efforts can again be discussed at the following supervisory safety meeting.

There is no regulatory model to follow for the supervisory meetings. Thus, it is difficult to describe the meetings held by an "average" firm. Some firms have no separate safety meetings for supervisors. They include safety issues in regular supervisory meetings. Some have even gone to the extreme of giving safety awards at the regular supervisory meetings, rather than at a special company meeting, as described in the following section. The intent is to convey that safety is not a separate issue but an integral component of whatever the company does. That is one possible approach that will help make a statement. The important point is that safety must not be treated in such a fashion that, when compared with achievements based on profits or project delivery, it appears to be of minor importance.

Company Safety Meetings (Dinners)

Some companies hold annual or semiannual safety meetings or dinners. Those meetings are not generally regarded as instructional sessions. In fact, they are rarely meetings in the typical sense of the term. Such "meetings" or dinners are generally held to recognize the appropriate personnel in the company for their contributions to construction safety. The supervisors, especially, are the center of attention at the safety dinner. The highlight of the dinner tends to be the awards that are given to those who have performed particularly well. Although the company president or, possibly, a local celebrity may give a keynote presentation, the theme is safety. The intent is to make the supervisors realize that the company is serious about safety and that it will reward those who strive to be safe.

All supervisors may be asked to attend, but recognition is only for those who have excelled in their safety efforts. Although foremen are often included in the recognition awards, particular emphasis is placed on the awards for those in higher supervisory positions, including general foremen, job superintendents, general superintendents, project managers, and safety personnel.

Safety dinners frequently involve the family members of the company employees. Including families in the event helps convey the company philosophy about safety to the family members and helps to bring the philosophy into the home.

Final Comments

Safety meetings might properly be referred to as reminder sessions or awareness sessions. For many in attendance at the weekly safety meetings, perhaps little information is actually new. Even if the information is "old hat" to some, the safety talk may harbor a significant message. If one worker works in a slightly safer manner because of the safety meeting, or if one worker dons safety gear that would otherwise have been left in the shed, the cost of the meeting is justified. Along with the direct message presented during the safety meeting, the company also sends a message about its commitment to safety. If the company requires all workers to attend the safety meetings, but no company personnel above the foreman level ever attend, the company is sending an unfortunate message to the workers. Management can communicate the company commitment to safety very effectively through the safety meetings. Make sure the workers get the message the company wants to send.

Review Questions

1. How might one choose the topic or topics to discuss at a toolbox safety meeting?
2. What message is conveyed by the position held by the person who conducts a toolbox safety meeting?
3. How should the scheduling of toolbox safety meetings be determined?
4. What are the OSHA regulations concerning toolbox safety meetings?
5. How do toolbox safety meetings compare with supervisory safety meetings?
6. How might a company decide whether safety meetings are to be held at the crew level or the project level?

References

Bush, V. 1975. *Safety in the Construction Industry: OSHA.* Reston, Va.: Reston Publishing.

Fullman, J. 1984. *Construction Safety, Security, and Loss Prevention.* New York: John Wiley.

Goldsmith, D. 1987. *Safety Management in Construction and Industry.* New York: McGraw-Hill.

Hinze, J. 1978. "Effective Safety Meetings." *National Utility Contractor* 2, no. 8, 26–27.

Levitt, R., and N. Samelson. 1993. *Construction Safety Management.* 2d ed. New York: John Wiley.

MacCollum, D. 1995. *Construction Safety Planning.* New York: Van Nostrand Reinhold.

National Safety Council. 1985. *Supervisors Safety Manual.* 6th ed. Chicago: National Safety Council.

Petersen, D. 1988. *Safety Management.* Goshen, N.Y.: Aloray.

Peyton, R., and T. Rubio. 1991. *Construction Safety Practices and Principles.* New York: Van Nostrand Reinhold.

Safety Incentives

Safety is not an after-the-fact Band-Aid; safety consists of all the preventive measures to ensure an entire healthy body.

When the topic of safety programs is brought up, many people immediately think of safety awards or safety incentives. Such people have a very narrow view of safety programs. Many effective safety programs have no aspects of the traditional safety incentive or safety award programs. Conversely, some firms contend that their excellent safety records are almost solely due to their incentive or award programs.

Clearly, safety programs can be successful without the implementation of a traditional safety incentive program. In fact, safety research results have provided only limited support for the value of safety incentives. At best, research findings tend to support the notion that safety incentives may contribute to improved safety performance, but their contribution is not paramount to the success of a safety program.

If a safety incentive program is to be used, what types of incentives will contribute most to good safety performance? Some basic understanding of the role of incentives must be kept in mind. On the surface, incentives are designed to reward good performance. But that view is too narrow. An appropriate incentive will actually cause workers to alter their behavior in such a way that performance is improved. If an incentive does not (1) reinforce good behavior patterns and (2) alter poor behavior patterns, it is not appropriate. The test of the value of an incentive is whether workers are cognizant of the incentive and, as a direct response to that incentive, behave in a desired manner. In a study of 49 of the top 100 construction firms, it was shown that safety incentives for workers generally have a benefit (Hinze and Harrison 1981). The results of that study are shown in Figure 9.1. Although the differences in injury frequencies between the firms with worker incentives and the firms without worker incentives seem dramatic, it should be noted that, from a statistical point of view, the differences are not significant. Nonetheless, the evidence does appear to support the use of worker safety incentives.

The key to an effective incentive is for it to remain alive in the minds of the workers. That may mandate that the incentive be particularly interesting, so that it captures the minds of the workers. An incentive that becomes stale in the minds of the workers can be a problem. Thus, an incentive that is effective in the first year of implementation may not be effective in the second. Change may be inevitable.

Several issues must be considered when an incentive program is established on a project. Whose performance is to be rewarded? How frequently will the awards be given? What kind of performance will be required to earn a reward? What will be the value of the award? How often must the award be changed?

Most incentive programs are set up to reward workers for good safety performance. Even with that decided, some consideration must be given to the nature of the performance to be rewarded. For example, will each individual worker be rewarded for performing safely, or will each member of a crew be rewarded when the entire crew performs safely? It is generally considered better for a reward to be earned by workers only if the entire crew performs safely. Under such a program, every worker is encouraged to work safely, and every worker is also encouraged to look out for the safety of fellow workers.

The frequency with which rewards are given is also important. Ideally, the frequency should be such that workers feel they have a stake in the reward. For example, if the rewards are given annually, the reward may seem too remote. Furthermore, if any injury occurs in a crew in the first month of the year, the reward offers no incentive for safe performance for the remainder of the year, as no reward will be earned. It is more realistic to have the rewards given on a biweekly, monthly, or bimonthly basis. Then, if a worker is denied a reward in one incentive period, the worker is still encouraged to work safely in the next period.

What kind of behavior is to be rewarded? It is generally not considered appropriate to issue rewards to a crew for having no lost-time injuries. That is because lost-time

Figure 9.1
Safety Performance and Worker Incentives

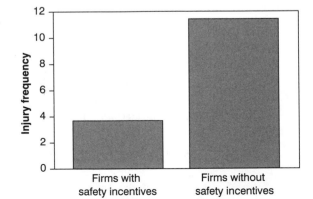

injuries are, statistically speaking, rare events. Most crews will not sustain a lost-time injury in a two-week period. Thus, a reward system based on lost-time injuries will probably not alter behavior, as the rewards will probably be earned regardless of behavior. A more realistic measure is first-aid injuries or OSHA recordable injuries. They are more frequent events. Additionally, rewards should be denied when a crew has a near miss or a safety violation by any member of the crew.

The value of the incentive is generally not very great when the reward is geared toward workers. Interest, rather than value, is the important attribute of the rewards. In some cases, the reward may even be of a progressive nature, one in which points are earned during each incentive period. The points can then be cashed in at any time for an appropriate reward. A reward for having no injuries and no safety violations in a month might give a worker the option of receiving a coffee mug with the company logo on it. If several months without injury are recorded and the points are allowed to accumulate, the worker may become entitled to a larger gift, such as a baseball cap, an ice chest, or a windbreaker.

One company claimed that it had great success using trading stamps as the incentive. Every second week, the workers who had earned rewards were given trading stamps, similar to those that were once very popular with some supermarkets. The company felt that the success of the incentive was that it tended to get the family involved in the incentive program. The worker would bring home the trading stamps, and the worker and the spouse would begin to plan on certain gifts to acquire when a given number of stamps had been earned. Although trading stamps are not used as widely as they were in the past, some companies continue to use the same principle by specifying the numbers of points required to obtain gifts that are listed in a specially prepared company gift catalog.

Sometimes a company will accidentally hit on a reward that has genuine appeal to the workers. On one job, the company gave specially ordered belt buckles as its primary reward. Although other rewards were available, some workers repeatedly asked for the belt buckles when they earned them. The rumors on the project were that the belt buckles, which cost the company about $3, had a "black market" value of about $30. That project had its own unique logo, and the belt buckle with the project logo was therefore unique to the job.

Safety rewards can seem to be gimmicks. If the gimmick works, it will pay real dividends. The trick is, first, to find out what gimmicks work. Second, it is important to recognize when a gimmick has run its course. It is commonly felt that most gimmicks run their course in about six months. After six months every worker has at least two of whatever reward has been given for safe work performance. It is best to change the reward before the workers tire of the old reward. Choosing the time to change the reward is not an easy task. It may require a particular understanding of the work force at the time of the construction project. It may also depend on the logo (if there is one) that goes with the reward.

If may be difficult to determine what type of award or gimmick will capture the imagination of the workers. Of course, if the company catalog is carefully planned, a significant number of awards might be available, virtually ensuring that each worker will always want at least one of the items listed. With the work force in construction changing to include more women and different ethnic groups, greater diversity in the types of awards is important.

On one project, the contractor set aside $1 per worker for every week of work performed on the project. If 40 workers were on the project over a two-week period, $80 would be allocated for the safety award. Recognizing that $2 was not an impressive award for an individual worker, the contractor set up a type of lottery. The lottery was essentially a game of chance in which a number between 1 and 100 was drawn. The drawing was held on payday. The winner was the worker with the payroll check in which the last two numbers of the check sequence number came closest to the drawn number without exceeding it. Ties were split between the winners. Workers on crews that had had an injury in the past two weeks were not eligible to participate. Although a $2 award may not have been a sufficient inducement to be safe, the chance of winning a larger sum created quite a bit of excitement on the project. The workers had fun with the lottery, and it was for a good cause.

In a recent study of the use of motivational techniques by large contractors, the significance of incentives became apparent (Indradjaja 1995). The study consisted of a survey of the top 400 construction companies in the U.S. A total of 32 companies responded. Of the respondents, 6 reported that their 1994 safety record included no lost-time injuries. Of those 6 companies, 4 reported that they employed some form of incentive program.

A further comment about the value of the gimmick or reward: The reward should never be so high that a worker will avoid reporting an injury in order to remain eligible for the reward. That result is counter to the purpose of any incentive program. It can happen if the reward is too high. Any tendency to conceal safety problems must be controlled. The purpose of the incentive program should not be clouded by high stakes. Safety should always remain the foundation on which the program is based, and the workers should never be enticed to think of it any other way.

Disincentives for Unsafe Behavior

Although positive reinforcement has value in virtually any setting, one must always remember that unsafe work practices simply are not to be tolerated. If a worker does not follow specific safety guidelines or exercises poor judgment in the execution of the work, some mechanism should be formally established and consistently implemented to prevent further occurrences of such practices. The need for such a mechanism brings to bear the issue of negative reinforcement. Although negative reinforcement or disincentives may not be the ideal management approach for job satisfaction for a worker, there is not always an acceptable alternative where safety is concerned.

To ensure consistency in the execution of a safety program, some degree of formalization of the policies and practices is essentially required. It will also add assurance that the policies are carried out without prejudice. If a given unsafe behavior is certain to result in some type of sanction for a worker, that worker will quickly alter work practices, especially if the sanctions are such that an undesirable result is in store for the worker. For example, a worker who violates a work practice protocol might be given a reprimand for a safety violation. The reprimand should be delivered both orally and in writing. A face-to-face confrontation can help to convey the seriousness of the matter, and it affords an opportunity for some type of dialogue. The written reprimand is also important, primarily as a historical record.

The safety violation report in Figure 9.2 is an example of a form for tracking unsafe behavior. An important aspect of the report is that it includes information about the

Safety Violation Report

Project: _____   Date: _____

                                                Time: _____

Job task description: _____
_____

Description of violation: _____
_____
_____
_____
_____

Persons involved: _____   ☐ Witness   ☐ Party to incident
                  _____   ☐ Witness   ☐ Party to incident
                  _____   ☐ Witness   ☐ Party to incident
                  _____   ☐ Witness   ☐ Party to incident

Responsible supervisor: _____

Signature of party briefed: _____

Corrective action taken: _____
_____

Remedial measures taken: _____
_____

Follow-up inspection warranted?   ☐ yes   ☐ no   If yes, when? _____

Inspector: _____

Follow-up Report

Description:
_____
_____
_____
_____

Reinspected by: _____   Date: _____

Figure 9.2
An Example of a Safety Violation Report Form

need for follow-up inspections. The person filling out the report must assess the merits of or the need for such follow-up.

It is not sufficient simply to document unsafe worker behavior. The important point is to prevent recurrence of the behavior. Thus, it is important to stress the magnitude of the importance of compliance with proper safety procedures. That might be accomplished with some type of formal system of consequences. For example, a reprimand may be sufficient where an unsafe behavior is not life-threatening. More severe measures may very well be warranted if a violation is repeated or if the infraction is serious. Severe measures may begin with dismissal from work without pay for a stipulated number of days. In some cases, job termination may be thought necessary. Note that if one unsafe worker is permitted to get by the system without any sanctions, the system quickly loses its credibility. Firmness and consistency are of paramount importance.

If a worker safety incentive program is established on site, it seems appropriate to link safety violations to that program. Although reprimands and termination may still be appropriate for the violators, it seems logical to remove the violators from the pool of individuals eligible to receive safety awards in a given period.

Incentives for First-Line Supervisors

First-line supervisors, or foremen, are generally recognized as playing a key role in the success with which work gets done on a project. It is also the foremen that dictate the degree of success that is attained in accomplishing the work with a minimum of injuries. It stands to reason that they should be given due consideration when any thought is given to offering safety incentives on a project. As mentioned earlier, the research findings about the value of safety incentives is equivocal; however, no study has shown safety incentives to be associated with higher frequencies of injuries. One study of the practices of 49 of the top 100 construction firms indicates that safety incentives for foremen may pay dividends (Hinze and Harrison 1981). The effect of such incentives is depicted in Figure 9.3.

Figure 9.3
Safety Performance and Foreman Incentives

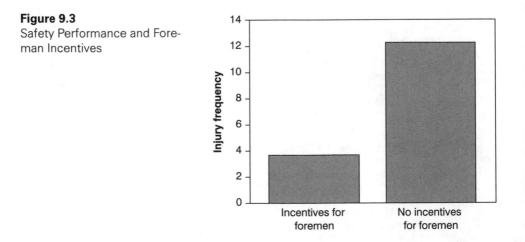

As with worker incentives, the incentive for foremen must be carefully examined before the program is implemented. Incentives for foremen generally have greater value than do those for individual workers; however, greater emphasis is often placed on the prestige and recognition that accompany the award than on the magnitude of the award itself.

Incentives for Superintendents

Incentives for superintendents generally cover longer periods than those for workers, and their value tends to be significantly higher. A reward may consist of a gold watch, a shotgun, a paid vacation, a cash bonus, or one of any number of items that are assumed to be valued.

Incentives for superintendents generally need not be changed as frequently as those for workers. In many instances, the rewards are progressive in that one reward may be given when 100,000 worker hours have been worked without a lost-time injury, another reward when the total number of hours reaches 250,000, and so on. Note that the incentives for superintendents are often based on the less frequent lost-time injuries, which are particularly costly to a firm.

Incentive programs should not generally be restricted to the job superintendents. It must be remembered that a superintendent incentive program has as its goal influencing one individual. Worker incentives have the goal of influencing every worker on the site. Thus, if the superintendent does not buy into the incentive program, all is lost if only superintendent incentives exist. It is better to try to influence the masses rather than one individual (Peyton and Rubio 1991).

It is to costly incentives for superintendents that the caution given earlier is particularly germane. Will the superintendent feel that there is a benefit in, or even encouragement of, not reporting a injury, merely to keep a safety record intact? There are commonly allegations that superintendents who are close to receiving a safety reward keep seriously injured workers on the payroll, putting them to work behind a desk or having them "count nuts and bolts." Is the work valuable? Is the work actually performed?

There are different philosophies about the appropriate way to handle such injured workers. Workers who are employed at different tasks to avoid being listed as lost-time injuries have been referred to by some as the "walking wounded." Although the practice of finding other work for such workers may appear somewhat fraudulent, it may not be. Naturally, the work to which an injured worker is assigned cannot be such that the worker's well-being is in any way jeopardized. In addition, returning to work is ultimately a decision that must be made by the worker. Of course, most workers enjoy their work, and they are pleased when they are allowed to continue working, albeit at a vastly different task, and to continue drawing the same pay. The benefits accrue to both the injured workers and the company. Such reemployed workers are assumed to have a greater sense of pride in themselves, and they also develop a greater sense of loyalty to their employer. Some company managers admit that they would rather avoid having an idle worker sitting at home with nothing to do but think such thoughts as "Does the company really care what happens to me? Should I call a lawyer? I wonder if I would have a chance to win in a lawsuit?"

Figure 9.4
Type of Incentive Program
Implemented

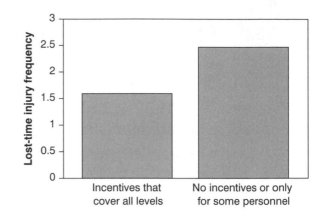

One might ask whether incentives are best focused on workers, on foremen, or on superintendents. The issue has not been examined in any great detail. In his study of San Francisco Bay–area contractors, Levitt (1975) examined it to a degree. Instead of identifying the area in which incentives are ideally focused, he found that incentives are most effective when applied broadly. That is, the safer firms were those that had established incentives for all levels, rather than those that employed no incentives or those that applied incentives only to specific levels on a project (see Figure 9.4). Although Levitt examined a sample of contractors that was small, the results provide some interesting information.

Project Safety Incentives

Incentives for safety can also be set up for entire projects. Such incentives differ from those set up for workers and supervisors in that they are contractually established and they accrue to the benefit of the contractor. Whether the contractor shares the benefits with site personnel is generally entirely up to the contractor.

Project safety incentives can provide substantial rewards for good safety performance. Naturally, the magnitude of the benefit is established by the project owner. There is no established protocol for determining the amount. Some baseline of performance should be considered. A beginning point could be the injury frequency average for the industry. From that it would be possible to estimate the numbers of OSHA recordable injuries and lost-workday injuries that could be expected on the project. By assigning a stipulated value to each expected injury, possibly based on the costs discussed in Chapter 3, the owner can set a total amount.

The total amount of the award might be paid to the contractor if the project injury frequency is below some prescribed value. The amount of the award might be apportioned in some manner. For example, if the injury frequency is half the industry average, the contractor might receive half the award amount. Various schemes can be developed for compensating the contractor for good safety performance.

An Example

A small Florida construction company specialized in highways and other heavy projects. The owner and president of the firm, Walter Travis (not his real name), kept close tabs on the firm's jobs in the state. It was common for Mr. Travis to personally visit every company project at least twice a month. For many years he paid little attention to safety performance; profits were the primary goal and focus of all operations.

Through the years Mr. Travis had been quite successful, even though an increase in the incidence of injuries remained unchecked. One day the severity of the situation became painfully real to Mr. Travis. He realized that through the years the workers' compensation experience modification rating (EMR) of the firm had more than crept up. It had moved progressively from 0.98 to 1.12 to 1.19. The next year, Mr. Travis was informed, the EMR would be 1.43. It only took some simple computations for Mr. Travis to realize that he could not be competitive under such an insurance burden. Perhaps he considered folding up the business and starting a new firm with an EMR of 1.0, but that was not a strategy he wished to pursue. He presumed that the high EMR was due to a neglect of safety and that the neglect would have to end for the company to succeed.

As noted, the company operations had previously focused on profits. For example, the company bonuses earned by project managers and project superintendents had been based solely on the profits realized on their respective projects. That system had apparently worked in the past, but it was not to continue. Mr. Travis immediately devised a means of measuring safety performance. He even accepted that additional money might have to be allocated to projects to encourage changes in the way work was performed.

Once the process had been thought through, Mr. Travis carefully drafted the means by which future bonuses would be awarded. Safety was the mainstay of the bonus system. When Mr. Travis made his regular tour of the company projects during the next two weeks, he carefully went over the details of the new bonus plan in person with each project manager and each project superintendent.

Although it took several years to vacate the bad injury years from the computation of the EMR, the safety efforts did pay off. Within five years, the EMR of the company was 0.45. The EMR of 0.45 now gave Mr. Travis a competitive edge against other contractors. The company continues to be quite successful, and no one in the firm even suggests that safety is a cost. The EMR of Mr. Travis's firm was once a disadvantage, but it became a bargaining chip.

The typical bonus of a project manager or a project superintendent was not trivial. The bonus was generally equivalent to 4–6 months' salary. Thus, the bonus or incentive was of such an amount that top management's commitment to safety was obvious. Earlier it was suggested that a safety incentive with too high a value might have a negative effect. Note that in this case the incentive had been based solely on profits and then became based almost solely on safety performance. The change sent a clear message.

Final Comments

The use and effectiveness of incentives to improve safety performance gives clear testimony to the importance of the mental aspects of safety. Incentives do not impart new information to workers that makes them work more safely. Incentives do not mandate that specific procedures be followed in the workplace. The function of incentives is to keep workers thinking about the very thing they want to think about: being safe. Along with the incentive comes the message that there is a company commitment to safety. Incentives are effective when they truly influence the way workers perform their jobs. In some cases, they merely reinforce the safe behavior of workers. For an incentive to be successful, the incentive must be acceptable to and desired by the workers.

Review Questions

1. Describe how the amounts or the nature of safety incentives often vary, depending on whether the incentive is for workers, foremen, or superintendents.
2. Describe how the timing of safety awards often varies, depending on whether the incentive is for workers, foremen, or superintendents.
3. Describe features that should be avoided in worker incentive programs.
4. Outline the basic elements of a safety incentive program that could be applied to a construction project.
5. Why does it often appear that the nature of worker safety incentives must be changed from time to time?
6. Discuss the relative merits of setting up a safety incentive for workers and setting up one for supervisors. What are the key considerations?
7. Discuss the implications of basing a worker safety incentive program on lost-time injuries instead of on OSHA recordable injuries.
8. Describe features of worker safety incentive programs that have been shown to be effective for longer periods of time. That is, what types of programs need to be changed less frequently?
9. In its most basic form, what must an effective safety incentive program do?
10. Discuss different approaches that can be used to discourage unsafe behavior on a project.

References

Hinze, J., and C. Harrison. 1981. "Safety Programs in Large Construction Firms." *Journal of the Construction Division,* ASCE 107, no. 3, 455–67.

Indradjaja, R. 1995. "Techniques of Motivation for Construction Workers." Master's thesis, University of Washington.

Levitt, R. 1975. *The Effect of Top Management on Safety in Construction.* Technical Report no. 196 (July), Construction Institute. Stanford, Calif.: Stanford University.

Levitt, R., and N. Samelson. 1993. *Construction Safety Management.* 2d ed. New York: John Wiley.

Peyton, R., and T. Rubio. 1991. *Construction Safety Practices and Principles.* New York: Van Nostrand Reinhold.

Safety in Construction Contracts

If you don't run a safe job, you may ruin a good one.

Construction safety has received increased attention in the past decade. The increased attention has stemmed from the combined effects of increasing costs of workers' compensation, increased litigation associated with liability suits, changes in OSHA's focus on construction safety, initiation of new safety legislation, and an increased awareness of the adverse impacts of construction injuries on overall construction costs.

The costs of injuries are ultimately borne by the facility owner. That fact has resulted in increased concern by owners for safety performance on their construction projects. This concern may be reflected in the construction contract documents. The concern may be expressed in indemnification provisions, which essentially represent an attempt by the owner to have the contractor bear the full costs of any injuries incurred during the construction phase. Other attempts by owners to avoid injury costs may be addressed more toward prevention—for example, clearly spelling out contractor safety requirements in the contract documents.

Construction contract documents may be written with no mention of safety. If they are, the contractor still has an obligation to comply with existing laws and regulations. That obligation cannot be waived by the owner. In some instances, safety requirements are included in a contract to ensure that the contractor does comply with the safety regulations. In other instances, the contract requirements may obligate the contractor to take added steps in the area of safety.

By addressing safety specifically in their contracts, owners send the message that safety is important to them. They also show that compliance with the safety regulations is not their sole safety objective. The objective might well be to preserve worker safety. A proactive stance on safety is widely regarded as an effective means of improving job safety. If worker safety is, then, the objective, what proactive measures should an owner take? More specifically, what measures are taken in construction contracts to improve safety? Although the magnitude of the effect of specific safety provisions may not be easily evaluated, the intent is obvious.

Since the costs of injuries become part of the cost of construction, it is natural for owners to be interested in curbing those costs if the costs are regarded as substantial. Perhaps the most obvious means of curbing the costs is through a concerted effort to reduce injury occurrence. What role do owners play in reducing worker injuries? The most obvious answer lies in the stance that owners take on safety. An owner's position on safety may be evidenced in the contract documents. A review of the extent to which an owner is involved in construction worker safety may be disclosed by the contract language.

I conducted a review of more than 200 construction contract documents to provide answers to questions about the manner in which safety is addressed in contracts. The objective of the review was to obtain specific information about owner practices and policies concerning construction safety by assessing the means used to address safety in construction contracts. I conducted an extensive review of the construction contract documents used by many different owners. The contract documents I examined included those used by 4 federal agencies, all 50 state highway authorities, 101 large municipalities (identified through the 1990 roster of the American Public Works Association), and 60 large private owners. The private owners included in the survey mailing consisted of 35 members of the Business Roundtable and 25 owner-members of the Northwest Construction Consumer Council. Those owners represent a reasonably broad cross section of federal, state, municipal, and private owners.

I examined the general conditions and the technical specifications employed in construction contracts by many different owners. The general conditions generally contain the most information related to the safety requirements on a particular project. The technical specifications may address safety in the discussion of the requirements related to the traffic control plan, the work-site traffic supervisor, the traffic maintenance setup, and so on. Regardless of their location, provisions addressing construction worker safety are present in many construction contract documents.

Some of the topics mentioned in the contract documents have already been discussed in prior chapters; others relate to material that will be discussed in subsequent chapters. Consequently, some information will be presented without much discussion. Other chapters deal with some topic materials in greater detail.

Compliance with Existing Laws and Regulations on Safety

Perhaps the most widely used provisions are those that relate to the requirement that the construction contractor abide by the applicable safety laws and regulations, whether at the federal, state, county, or municipal level. Different versions of these all-encompassing safety provisions are used by different owners. The provisions are typically located in paragraphs entitled "Laws to Be Observed." The following provision of a public agency focuses attention on the need for the contractor to comply with existing laws.

> The Contractor shall observe all federal, state, and local laws and regulations. Attention is directed to the regulations of federal and state agencies. . . .

Such provisions do not expand on the requirement of complying with the existing laws and regulations. Do they cast any additional responsibility on the contractor? A contractor has an obligation to comply with the laws and regulations, even absent such a provision. The inclusion of such provisions does stress the importance of safety in the execution of the contract. Even without an OSHA inspection, the owner could find the contractor in default of the contract for failure to provide adequately for the safety of the workers. The responsibility for safety is clearly placed on the contractor with such provisions. Although the contractor is already obligated to comply with the safety regulations, the inclusion of such provisions in the contract may have both a psychological and a contractual benefit for the owner.

The provision quoted is vague in that it does not specify the contractor's obligation to provide for the safety of workers, for it does not mention safety or employees. Variations of the provision are used in some documents. Those provisions are slightly more detailed, making some reference to safety and either to employees of the contractor or to construction workers. The following provision is typical of many such clauses:

> It is a condition of this contract, and shall be made a condition of each subcontract entered into pursuant to this contract, that the Contractor and any subcontractor *shall not require any laborer or mechanic employed in performance of the contract* to work in surroundings or under working conditions which are unsanitary, hazardous, or dangerous to his health or safety, as determined under construction safety and health standards and regulations (Title 29, Code of Federal Regulations, Part 1926, formerly Part 1518, as revised from time to time) promulgated by the United States Secretary of Labor. . . . (italics added)

The foregoing provision states in general terms that workers must not be asked to work in unsafe environments. It is questionable whether the addition of the phrase "laborer or mechanic" actually broadens the scope of the provision.

Another variation of the previous provision occurred in some documents. In addition to mandating compliance with existing laws and specifically mentioning workers, these provisions include specific statements related to safety. For example, the following provision explicitly assigns responsibility for worker safety to the contractor:

> The Contractor shall keep fully informed of all federal and state laws, local bylaws, ordinances, and regulations, including any orders and decrees . . . *which affect those engaged or employed on the work or which in any way affect the conduct of the work. . . . The Contractor shall provide for the safety of his employees* and the public along with protection of property. . . . (italics added)

With regard to worker safety, this provision stands out in comparison with the previously discussed clauses, as it expressly gives the contractor responsibility for construction worker safety. Other similar provisions expand the contractor's responsibility for worker safety. For example, the following document outlines specific requirements:

(a) The Contractor shall keep fully informed of all federal and state laws, all local. . . .
(b) The Contractor shall comply with all federal, state, and local laws governing safety, health, and sanitation. *The Contractor shall provide safeguards, safety devices, and protective equipment and take any other action necessary to protect the life and health of employees on the job. . . . Attention is directed to federal, state, and local laws, rules, and regulations concerning construction safety and health standards. The Contractor shall not require workers to work in surroundings or under conditions that are unsanitary or dangerous to their health or safety.* (italics added)

This provision addresses safeguards, safety devices, and protective equipment and outlines the contractor's responsibility for protecting the life and health of the employees. Another provision included specific requirements by adding the following:

> The Contractor shall construct or erect all safety devices or appurtenances required by federal or state laws for contractor's employee safety prior to the performance by the Owner's personnel of required survey work, inspection, or testing in an affected area.

This provision details clearly that safety devices must be in place before the owner's personnel do any work on the project.

Another document anticipated the possibility of an OSHA inspection and stated, "Any inspector of the Occupational Safety and Health Administration or other legally responsible agency shall be admitted at any time."

Safety requirements are often included in the provisions related to health and sanitation. Although the sanitary provisions address hazardous conditions in general, they also accent the contractor's responsibility in relation to enforcement of safety standards. Note that the following provision extends the contractor's responsibility by stating that a worker shall not be required to work in an unsafe condition, even if all specific laws are followed. The provision may be regarded as analogous to a general duty clause for work safety.

> It is a condition of this contract, and shall be made a condition of each subcontract entered into pursuant to the Contract, *that the Contractor and any subcontractor shall not require any laborer or mechanic employed in performance of the Contract to work in surroundings or under working conditions which are unsanitary, hazardous, or dangerous to his health or safety, as determined under construction safety and health standards and regulations.* . . . The Contractor and each subcontractor shall permit inspection without delay and at any reasonable time on any premises where the work is being performed. (italics added)

The general intent of this provision is typical of many documents. However, there is much variation in the specific requirements.

Many documents include additional detailed worker safety instructions, but others *make no further mention* of safety. Although safety provisions commonly appear in the safety, health, and sanitation section, similar provisions appear in other parts of some documents. In short, there is a trend toward including safety provisions with those addressing sanitation, but the variability of the actual wording is considerable.

The last-quoted provision shows the detail that is sometimes incorporated into safety provisions. The provision specifically extends safety responsibilities to the subcontractors. It states that subcontractors must be aware of safety requirements. The inclusion of subcontractors adds an additional party to those responsible for the maintenance of a safe work site and working conditions.

The following provision adds detail that addresses accident prevention responsibilities:

> The Contractor shall at all times take necessary precautions to protect the life and health of all persons employed on the project. He shall familiarize himself with the latest accepted accident prevention methods and provide necessary safety devices and safeguards in accordance therewith. The Owner will refuse to provide inspection service at plants or work sites where adequate safety measures are not provided and maintained.

This provision imposes the added responsibility of understanding the "latest accepted accident prevention methods." In addition, the contractor is told that inspections, and therefore progress of work, will not occur if unsafe conditions exist.

Statement of Policy or Mission

It is common for some owners to start a written contract with a mission statement. The intent of such statements is varied. They can serve to alert the contractor that safety is to be taken seriously on the project. They are also a means by which the owner can state the philosophy to be applied to the project. One such statement is as follows:

> We are committed to safety and integrate safety into all of our activities. Our commitment to safety is a priority item, and we do not compromise our safety philosophy to meet cost, timing, or scope-of-work objectives.

"Our commitment to safety" means "we are committed to doing things right." That commitment is reinforced by stating that all personnel

> are to give an overriding priority to the prevention of personal injury and property damage accidents during both the design and the construction of projects. This policy encompasses the personnel of both the Owner and the Contractor. In addition, the Contractor shall have a safety program that is consistent with the programs of the Owner, and the Contractor shall adhere to the Owner's programs. The safety commitment is the responsibility of each person.

Scope

Contract provisions can be used to define the scope of responsibility for safety. Some owners promulgate their own standards of safety performance, invariably as an extension of the OSHA standards. For example:

> The standards and provisions set forth herein are applicable to all on-site construction-type activities, whether performed by the Owner, Contractor, Subcontractor, or Supplier forces. . . . These standards are consistent with the health and safety standards prevalent in the industry and those promulgated under the Occupational Safety and Health Act of 1970. . . . The purpose of this manual is to promote working conditions and work practices which will ensure all employees a safe and healthful work environment in all construction-type activities. . . . [E]xemptions to provisions of this manual require specific approval. . . .

Another owner included statements designed to broaden the scope of safety. This owner recognized the "appalling waste of human life, the suffering, and the tremendous economic loss by our citizens." Specifics of site safety were addressed:

> Accident prevention should be confined not only to the hours of working on the project, but to the off hours as well. Cooperation in safety programs is the mutual obligation of every employee. Each employee should endeavor to:
>
> Work safely on or off the job.
> Have regard at all times for the safety of others.
> Use knowledge and influence to prevent accidents.
> Call attention to unsafe conditions.
> Contribute ideas and suggestions for the improvement of safety conditions.
> Be courteous and realize individual actions may cause injury to others.

Another owner extended safety to the design of the facilities.

> The *Owner will continue to study and improve work site safety* for the eventual project users and *the Contractor's employees*. . . . The Owner will work to *improve in-house awareness of work safety issues in the design stages* of projects. (italics added)

Responsibility of the Contractor

Once the scope of safety is defined for the owner, it is logical to outline the scope of safety responsibilities for the contractor. That may be done with a provision such as the following:

> The Contractor shall at all times conduct the work safely and ensure a safe work site. The *Contractor shall be responsible for the safety of the Contractor's employees, agents, and subcontractors.* The Contractor shall be responsible for the adequacy and safety of all construction methods and procedures and the safe prosecution of the work. The Contractor shall be responsible at all times for conducting the work and keeping the work site in compliance with all safety laws, including but not limited to OSHA requirements. (italics added)

Preconstruction Checklist

Safety planning may be directly addressed in the contract provisions. That is another means by which the owner can be assured that the contractor will put some forethought into addressing worker safety in the construction project activities. Note that the safety planning requirements also carry with them the need for the contractor to discuss the implementation of the safety provisions with the owner before commencing work.

> Representatives of the Contractor shall *meet with the Owner's Representatives prior to the start of construction* for the purpose of reviewing the respective safety requirements and discussing implementation of all health and safety provisions pertinent to the work under contract. The Contractor shall be prepared to discuss, in detail, the measures intended to be taken to control the hazards incident to the major phases of the work under contract and to comply with contractual obligations. This meeting will be devoted to discussing the manner in which the Contractor intends to administer the health and safety program and delegate the responsibilities for implementing the program. (italics added)

The requirements to be prepared to discuss the details of measures for implementing hazard controls might be interpreted as requiring the contractor to submit an accident prevention plan and as requiring that prior to the start of work, not prior to the acceptance of the bid. Thus, the selection of the contractor is not based on the accident prevention plan that is submitted. It is therefore important that the requirements of an accident prevention plan be clearly stated. The requirements typically include such items as the following:

- contractor attendance at a preconstruction safety meeting
- posting of emergency telephone numbers
- medical arrangements
- OSHA posting
- the contractual obligation of the contractor to comply with OSHA regulations
- written contractor safety program, which is on file and includes
    1. contractor's management support of the safety program
    2. designation of the contractor's project safety officer and staff
    3. designation of the contractor's company safety officer
    4. contractor's commitment to make frequent safety inspections on the project
    5. a description of the plan for training employees to recognize and avoid unsafe conditions
    6. contractor's commitment to investigate and report on all injuries and illnesses
    7. contractor's commitment to conduct regular safety meetings
    8. contractor's commitment to remain current on OSHA regulations
    9. assurance of subcontractor compliance with the program
- noting of critical hazards and description of preventive measures put in place

Contractor's Safety Program

The preceding list of requirements includes an outline of items to include in a safety program. Some provisions are very explicit about the various elements to be included in the safety program. The following is such an example:

> Before on-site work begins, the Contractor shall *submit for approval a comprehensive written accident prevention program* covering all aspects of on-site construction operations and activities associated with each respective contract. The Owner will review the proposed program for compliance with OSHA and project requirements. If the program requires any revisions or corrections, the Contractor shall resubmit the program. *No progress payments will be processed until the program is approved.* Unless adequately covered in the original plan, a supplementary detailed plan will be submitted prior to the start of each major phase of work or when requested by the Owner. The Contractor acknowledges *that costs of the accident prevention program are included in the bid* that was accepted by the Owner.
>
> The Contractor shall submit the written construction safety program at the preconstruction conference. The Contractor shall enforce the requirements of the safety program on all employees, including the subcontractors' personnel. The safety program shall contain the following at a minimum:

1. job number
2. designation of a competent person to serve as the Job Site Safety Representative, who will be responsible for implementing the program. The Safety Representative shall have sufficient authority to change or stop performance of the work if the work practices or conditions are deemed unsafe. In addition to being knowledgeable about the Job Site safety requirements and the applicable safety regulations, the Safety Representative should be trained and sufficiently experienced to recognize safety and health hazards. A resume of the qualifications of the competent person must be submitted to the Owner, including such information as experience, education, special safety and first aid courses completed, safety conferences attended, familiarity with standards and regulations, and certification or registrations. The Safety Representative shall be the Contractor's superintendent unless otherwise designated in writing by the Contractor.
3. OSHA standards applicable to the work (by listing or by reference)
4. contractor's program description of safety orientation and training for all employees. Safety orientation and training shall identify standards of conduct, explain safety rules, ensure communication of the Owner's safety information and safety requirements, explain the Contractor's emergency plan, and identify the use and location of safety equipment and fire protection equipment on the Job Site. Each employee should be trained in the recognition and avoidance of unsafe conditions and the regulations applicable to the work environment. Each worker that begins work, or begins a new work activity on this project, shall attend a basic safety orientation and sign in.
5. regular weekly and monthly safety meetings
6. first aid procedures
7. outline of each phase of the work, the hazards associated with each major phase, the methods proposed to ensure property protection and the safety of the public and Contractor's employees. Identify the work included under each phase by reference to specification section or division numbers.
8. plans for possible emergency situations (floods, fires, cave-ins, explosions, power outages, windstorms, etc.)
9. a written hazard communication program
10. regular job-site safety inspections
11. subcontractor compliance

The Contractor shall not be allowed to begin work on the project until the Contractor's safety program has been received and reviewed for content by the Owner's representative. Acceptance of the initial and supplementary safety programs only signifies that the submittals generally conform to the requirements contained and referenced herein. It does not relieve the Contractor of the responsibility of providing employees with a safe and healthful work environment, or of complying fully with all aforementioned requirements and applicable specification paragraphs.

Following the preconstruction meetings, a second meeting shall be held for the purpose of reviewing the Contractor's written safety program. The Contractor's principal on-site representative, the general superintendent, and the Job Site Safety Representative shall attend this meeting. (italics added)

Requirements of the safety program may vary depending on the nature of the project. For example, one owner stipulated that specific safety program criteria would have to be met if the project is a building that "is either 15 or more stories, 200 feet or more in height, or 100,000 square feet or more of lot coverage regardless of height."

Construction Checklist

Some documents include provisions that essentially constitute construction safety checklists. They stipulate specific administrative tasks that must be carried out as part of the contractual agreement. Some include the following:

- frequent safety inspections (including inspections of subcontractor operations)
- recording and reporting of all injuries and illnesses
- investigation of all injuries and illnesses
- maintenance of safety bulletin board
- maintenance of safety committee
- holding of regular safety meetings
- maintenance of material safety data sheets (MSDS)

Requirement to Follow Safety Standards and Regulations on Owner's Premises

Provisions may go well beyond the requirement that the contractor abide by the safety regulations. The owner may reiterate specifically some of the provisions that should be of particular importance to the contractor when carrying out the construction work. The contractor may even be required to comply with the owner's safety and house-keeping rules, which may be more strict than the federal or local regulations. Such rules are intended to emphasize and serve as a reminder of some of the more important requirements. Requirements that may be stressed include the following:

- Hard hats are required.
- Eye protection is required.
- Hearing protection is required.
- Safety shoes are recommended for all workers. Appropriate work shoes are required.
- First-aid equipment is available in all work areas.
- Workers who have had first-aid training should be known by all job-site personnel.
- No visitors are permitted on the premises without authorization.
- All visitors must comply with applicable safety regulations (e.g., wearing of hard hats).
- The job site will be kept clean and free of debris.
- Temporary chain-link fencing, or an approved equal, shall be furnished and installed around the construction areas.
- Persons under the influence of alcohol or drugs shall not come onto the premises.

Other requirements may include those related to other personal protective equipment, smoking restrictions, site speed limits, cutting and welding permits, welding tanks, electrical lockout, confined space entry, worker lift procedures, asbestos removal, firearms, fire prevention, chemicals, radiation, heat, cold, explosives, excavations, fall protection, hoisting, traffic control, a sketch of temporary power distribution, and safe clearance procedures.

One provision made specific reference to the OSHA regulations that warranted special attention. That owner's safety program stated:

> The federal regulations containing the OSHA regulations for construction contain over 200 sections and 1000 subsections ranging from short paragraphs to several pages in length. These sections are grouped into 26 subparts (A through Z). Of these, 43 sections (in 13 subparts) are of particular concern on our projects. These are:
>
> 1. Housekeeping (Section 25, Subpart C)
> 2. First aid, medical services, and sanitation (Sections 50–51, Subpart D)
> 3. Personal protection (hard hats, eye and face masks, safety nets, safety lines, etc.) (Sections 100, 102, 104, 105, Subpart E)
> 4. Traffic control (Sections 200–202, Subpart G)
> 5. Hand tools (Sections 300–305, Subpart I)
> 6. Ladders and scaffolds (Sections 450, 451, Subpart L)
> 7. Cranes, derricks, etc. (Section 550, Subpart N)
> 8. Earth-moving equipment (Sections 600, 602–604, Subpart O)
> 9. Excavation and trenching (Sections 651–652, Subpart P)
> 10. Concrete and concrete forms (Sections 700–701, Subpart Q)
> 11. Structural steel (Sections 751–752, Subpart R)
> 12. Cofferdams (Section 802, Subpart S)
> 13. Explosives (Sections 900–911, Subpart U)

The owner that provides this listing, a state highway authority, enumerates these standards as helpful guidance to contractors. The owner does state that the contractor must be aware of other provisions. The provisions continue with an admonishment to the contractor that

> this does NOT mean that hazards which are not covered in these areas may be ignored. WHEN A HAZARDOUS CONDITION OR SITUATION IS OBSERVED, SOME TYPE OF ACTION MUST BE TAKEN, regardless of whether the hazard is covered by these—or any other—rules or regulations. . . . The Owner's personnel will not tell the Contractor what action to take to eliminate the hazard, although they may make suggestions. However, the Contractor must make the final determination of the actions to take.

Hazard Analysis

Some provisions require the contractor to conduct a hazard analysis. This requirement is an extension of the requirements that have been addressed in the provisions of other sections. The hazard analysis forces the contractor to focus on safety problems and to try to minimize or eliminate them. One such provision states the following:

> Prior to beginning each major phase of work, an *activity hazard analysis (phase plan) shall be prepared* by the Contractor. Activity hazard analyses must be prepared for every contract activity and operation in each major phase of work. The analysis *will*

address the sequence of work, hazards for each activity performed in that phase, and the control measures, procedures, and safeguards necessary to eliminate the hazards or reduce the risk to an acceptable level. A phase is defined as an operation involving a type of work presenting hazards not experienced in previous operations or where a new subcontractor or work crew is to perform work. The analysis will be discussed by the Contractor and the Owner's Representative. A formal report shall be submitted to the Owner. (italics added)

Safety Meetings

Safety meetings tend to be a strong component of many safety programs. The following is a typical requirement:

As a minimum, the Contractor shall conduct weekly 15-minute "toolbox" safety meetings with all its personnel. Toolbox meetings should be held early in the day. These meetings shall be conducted by field supervisors or foremen and attended by all construction personnel, or the Contractor may require all subcontractors to hold their own safety meetings with their personnel. Weekly safety meeting topics shall include safety rules, hazards, corrective actions, accident prevention, and reviews of accidents and near accidents. The Contractor shall document the date of the meeting, the length of the meeting, the meeting chairperson, the topics discussed, the names of all personnel attending each meeting, and the names of persons who were absent. . . . The Contractor shall submit a report of each safety meeting.

On one cost-reimbursable contract, the owner allocated $20 per hour for each worker for the duration of the project. The duration of the meetings was assumed to be 30 minutes. Thus, the number of worker hours anticipated for the project could be used as a means of determining the appropriate amount to budget for safety meetings. The owner noted that this was considered to yield a quite conservative budget amount.

The following is another safety meeting provision:

The Contractor shall conduct monthly safety meetings for all levels of supervision. The Owner should be given advance notification of each such meeting for possible attendance. These meetings will be used to review the effectiveness of the Contractor's safety effort, to resolve current health and safety problems, to provide a forum for planning safe construction activities, to plan ahead for new or changed operations, and to update the accident prevention program. An outline report of each meeting shall be submitted to the Owner.

Some provisions include the involvement of the owner in the safety meetings. Those provisions convey a very strong message that the owner is concerned about safety and that the owner will oversee or review the contractor's work. An example is as follows:

The Contractor shall be represented at safety meetings held by the Owner. The Owner reserves the right to hold safety meetings on both regular and extraordinary schedules. The Owner's safety meeting agendas will include a discussion of the effectiveness of the Contractor's safety effort, a discussion of observed safety hazards, resolution of health and safety problems related to current operations, a forum for planning safe future construction activities, and a review of accidents and near accidents.

Substance Abuse Programs

Many injuries are directly linked to substance abuse. Thus, it is understandable that some owners address the issue. Note that it is a sensitive issue and that owners are often reluctant to address it. Even the following provision might be regarded as "soft" on total owner involvement in the process:

> The Contractor is *encouraged to have a substance abuse program,* preemployment drug testing, and testing for cause. Employees whose ability or alertness is impaired because of drugs, fatigue, illness, intoxication, or other conditions shall not be allowed to work. (italics added)

Subcontractor Compliance

Although the requirement that the subcontractors must abide by the safety regulations may be addressed in a variety of locations in the different safety provisions, some contracts include a specific clause that makes it clear that the subcontractors are duty-bound to comply with the established safety rules. For example:

> The Contractor shall ensure that all subcontractors meet the same safety requirements as the Contractor.

Inspection of the Work Site by the Contractor

A few provisions place the responsibility for inspecting the job site for safety hazards on the contractor. To ensure that the inspection is done properly, it is common for the owner to have some form of review responsibilities. The following is an example of a contractor inspection provision:

> The Contractor shall utilize *competent personnel to perform frequent and regular formal safety inspections of work operations* and work areas, materials, and equipment on the project. The Contractor shall immediately correct safety hazards involving employees of the Contractor or Subcontractors. A monthly report shall be submitted, indicating the deficiencies observed and the corrective measures taken. (italics added)

Inspection of the Work Site by the Owner

The owner often reserves the right to conduct periodic reviews of the job-site safety conditions to determine the level and effectiveness of the contractor's safety program. The involvement of the owner helps to emphasize the importance of safety. An example of such a provision is as follows:

> The Owner may conduct inspections to assist the Contractor in providing a safe work environment as required by the Occupational Safety and Health Administration. The dates and times of these inspections may or may not be coordinated with you in advance, depending on the number of ongoing projects at any given time. In either case, the Owner's inspectors shall have authority to enter and inspect the job site.

Findings of all inspections will be discussed with on-site Contractor personnel and submitted in a written report to the Owner. These inspections in no way relieve the Contractor of any other required inspections or of any responsibility for employee safety.

Inspection of the Work Site by Regulatory Personnel

Owners recognize that an OSHA inspection is always a possibility. Some provisions, as noted earlier, may be drafted specifically to address this issue. One provision stipulates that the owner's permission is to be sought before any compliance officers are admitted.

If an OSHA Compliance Officer wishes to conduct a safety inspection of the Contractor's personnel and equipment or any of its subcontractors' personnel and equipment, the Contractor shall immediately request the approval of the Owner before permitting the inspection to begin.

A different philosophy is evidenced by the following provision. It states essentially that the admission of compliance officers is not to be delayed in any way.

The Contractor shall admit, without delay and without the presentation of an inspection warrant, any inspector of the Occupational Safety and Health Administration upon presentation of proper credentials.

Contractor Failure to Comply with Safety Standards or Regulations

There is always a possibility that the contractor will fail to comply with the safety regulations. Is it sufficient for the owner simply to require and expect the contractor to abide by these regulations? Some apparently feel that it is.

The Contractor shall be notified in writing of any violations of safety orders and conditions or practices which may endanger the public or any personnel on the project.

That provision states no specific sanctions for such violations.

Some owners feel it is not sufficient to include the requirements in the contract; they impose consequences on the contractor for failure to comply.

Should the Contractor fail to follow OSHA regulations, the Owner's Representative may suspend the work by written notice until compliance has been achieved. Any such failure to comply with OSHA regulations shall constitute waiver of any right to claim for such suspended work. If regulations are in conflict, the more strict regulation will apply.

If the owner's representative determines that a condition constitutes a serious violation or imminent danger, the representative is often given authority to "shut down that particular phase of the work." One provision stated that a serious violation exists "where there is substantial probability that death or serious physical harm could result" and that an imminent danger exists "where there is reasonable certainty that a hazard exists that can be expected to cause death or serious physical harm."

The following is another provision imposing consequences for the contractor's failure to comply with safety requirements:

The Contractor's failure to construct or erect the safety devices or appurtenances for use by Owner personnel will be cause for considering this work as the current controlling operation, and working days will be assessed against the contract time allowance during the period that this work is not complete. Delays incurred as a result of the Contractor's failure to provide the required safety devices or appurtenances will not be considered for extending the contract time allowance.

Safety Performance Reports to the Owner

The contractor may be required to provide feedback to the owner on project safety performance. The feedback may be provided through specific reports that indicate the level of safety performance on the project.

The Contractor shall submit a monthly safety report to the Owner. The report shall cover the Contractor's employees and the employees of all subcontractors. The report shall include (1) the number of worker hours worked, (2) the number of OSHA recordable accidents, and (3) the number of lost-time accidents.

Another provision is more explicit in the various requirements:

The key to improving safety activities lies in improving the information that the Contractor supplies to the Owner concerning where accidents occur, why, and when.

The Contractor shall report all personal injury accidents, property damage accidents, fires, spills, and near misses to the Owner within twenty-four hours of their occurrence. All accidents causing death or serious injuries or damages shall be reported immediately to the Owner. Each injury report shall include the accident date and location. Each shall present a concise, thorough description of the accident, its cause, injuries sustained, and procedures implemented or proposed to prevent recurrences. A complete description is to be provided on all property damage accidents, including the estimate of the impact, if any, of the accident on the schedule of the Work. The Contractor shall report orally on all incidents which could have resulted in personal injury or property damage. Each month the Contractor shall submit a standard summary report showing the number of injuries incurred to date, the number of injuries incurred in the previous month, and other related information. Supplementary written reports may be required at the Owner's discretion.

Emergency Plans

The contractor may be required to develop plans of action to follow when certain types of accidents occur. The immediate care of the injured worker or workers must be planned so that the actions can be carried out smoothly. Training and education are key ingredients of such provisions.

The Contractor shall set forth a contingency plan for the safe and effective response to emergencies. The Contractor shall provide all medical services for its personnel and its subcontractors' personnel. The Contractor's medical services shall include first-aid treatment (including all necessary first-aid supplies), ambulance service (or other standing arrangement for the immediate transport of injured workers to medical treatment facilities), clinic or hospital emergency room treatment, hospitalization, and physicians services. The Contractor shall establish, publish, and make known to all employees procedures for ensuring immediate removal to a hospital or a doctor's care of persons, including employees, who may have been injured on the project. Anyone acting in a supervisory capacity shall have the authority to order an emergency response. The Contractor shall prominently post the names, addresses, and telephone numbers of the following personnel on the Job Site: (1) The Contractor's and subcontractors' personnel to be notified in case of emergency, (2) The Contractor's medical services personnel and institutions.

Accident Reporting

The following is an example of a provision regarding accident reporting:

> Except for rescue and emergency measures, the scene of a serious accident/incident shall not be disturbed or the operation resumed until authorized by the Owner. The Contractor shall conduct a complete investigation of each major accident/incident and submit a comprehensive report of findings and recommendations to the Owner. The Contractor shall be responsible for any independent investigation that the Owner might authorize.

Safety Officer

One commonly accepted prerequisite for administering a successful safety program is the designation of a safety officer at the project level. It is a standard practice on many large projects to require a safety officer. The following are examples of provisions requiring a safety officer:

> *The Contractor shall assign or designate a competent representative* with authority to act in cooperation with the Owner's representative in the promotion and enforcement of safety provisions and safe practices on or related to the project for the duration of construction. (italics added)

> A safety inspection will be required at the beginning of each major phase of the operation. Repeated inspections may be necessary for phases of long duration. All safety inspections shall be made and *reported by the Contractor's safety officer,* even though the phase of the operation may be subcontracted. . . .
>
> The contractor shall make adequate provisions satisfactory to the Engineer for safety of inspectors, particularly at sampling locations. (italics added)
>
> . . . Prior to commencement of construction activities on the project, the Contractor shall comply with the following provisions:
>
> 1. Safety Supervisor—The Contractor shall designate a person with authority and responsibility to administer the accident and fire prevention program on the work to be performed under the contract, who will be known as the Safety Supervisor. An Alternate Safety Supervisor shall be named, who shall perform these functions in the absence of the Safety Supervisor. The person designated as Safety Supervisor, or alternate, shall be able to devote as much time as is necessary for this responsibility.

Accident Prevention Plan

A proactive stance on safety is demonstrated when job-site conditions have been examined before construction and all major anticipated hazards have been identified. Those hazards are then eliminated, minimized, or specifically addressed in safety training and hazard communication. The project is organized so that an ongoing review is made of conditions on the site, to ensure worker safety. Those elements constitute the essence of an accident prevention plan.

A few documents were noted to require contractors to submit detailed accident prevention plans. The plans, although varying in length and complexity, have a common objective. They provide a framework in which worker safety (and public safety) will be maintained on the job site. Generally, the plans are completed and agreed on by the engineer and the contractor before construction is allowed to begin. The benefits of such arrangements can be numerous. If the project is organized with safety in mind, worker injuries should be reduced. Since accident prevention plans vary in detail, as warranted by changes in the project type and scope, specificity in the general conditions is understandably lacking. The following provision enumerates several requirements related to the accident prevention plan:

> In order to protect the life and health of employees in the performance of this contract, the Contractor shall. . . .
>
> The Contractor shall submit five copies of the accident prevention plan to the Engineer. The plan shall outline the safety program the Contractor intends to enforce as part of the Contract. The Engineer may furnish a guide for preparing the accident prevention plan. The plan will be reviewed by the Engineer and the Contractor to determine adequate coverage of the project work.
>
> The Contractor has full responsibility for implementing the accident prevention plan before start of project work and further commits to indemnify the Department from any liability related thereto.
>
> Nothing in the Contract shall relieve the Contractor of responsibility for safety, federal requirements, or state and local laws and ordinances.
>
> The Contractor shall maintain an accurate record of and shall report to the Engineer and the state insurance fund on specified forms all cases of death and accidents arising out of or in the course of employment on work under this contract. These forms may be obtained from the Engineer.
>
> The Engineer will notify the Contractor in writing of any noncompliance with the foregoing provisions and the Contractor shall, after receipt of such notice, immediately correct the conditions to which attention has been directed.
>
> If the contractor fails or refuses to correct unsafe conditions, the Engineer may issue an order stopping all or any part of the work. Such stoppage of work will not relieve the Contractor of finishing the project within the specified contract completion time. When satisfactory corrective action is taken, a start order will be issued.

Detailed Safety Requirements

Detailed safety requirements are addressed by some documents, which include specific detail to clarify the general intent of the overall safety plans. Commonly included items are requirements for workers to wear hard hats and flagger vests. Their inclusion appears to be the result of a need to address the lack of specificity in the general safety provisions. Often there is overlap between the detailed safety requirements and the accident prevention plans. The following paragraphs show how this is addressed in one document:

> Comply at all times with applicable federal [and] state . . . [regulations]. . . . Take any other needed action, or proceed as directed, to protect the life, health, and general occupational welfare of personnel employed on the project. When, in the Engineer's opinion, employees are exposed to extraordinary conditions which could or do constitute a hazard, modify such equipment, devices, and job procedures to ensure protection against the hazard or to reduce the risk to employees engaged in the work.
>
> All areas of a project will be hard hat areas. Require all persons within the project limits to wear protective headgear, including . . .
>
> At the preconstruction conference, submit a written project safety program for Department review. . . . Give special emphasis to providing safeguards for any specially or unusually hazardous operations and health hazards. Include initial indoctrination and continuing instruction for all employees to enable them to perform work in a safe manner. Include in the instruction project safety practices, manner of reporting accidents, availability of medical facilities, and explanation of individual responsibility for accident-free operations.
>
> Immediately take corrective action, upon notification by the Engineer of any noncompliance with the provisions of this section. . . . Require all persons to wear orange vests, shirts, or jackets while in work zones adjacent to traffic.

There are numerous documents with this level of detail. Such provisions add clarity to the goals of the owner concerning safety.

Specific Items

Some documents list in detail specific requirements, such as confined space provisions and hazardous material provisions, to give specific guidelines to the contractor on the need to specifically address such situations. One document addressed these issues by requiring

> . . . practices as will safeguard the Contractor's employees against inhalation of toxic vapors and ingestion of or prolonged bodily contact with hazardous materials. Workers shall be required to employ good industrial hygienic practices, as would preclude or counteract the effects of prolonged skin exposure to toxic pigments, and to use such protective devices as respirators approved by the U.S. Bureau of Mines, when the above described operations are being performed.
>
> The Contractor shall be responsible for the "Right to Know" training of his employees according to the OSHA Standards.

Confined Spaces

The Contractor shall be responsible for gas detection in and ventilation of confined spaces. When procedures require workers to enter confined spaces such as steel or concrete box section type superstructures, the Contractor shall be cognizant of the potential health hazards, particularly when the interior is closed off at both ends.

It shall be the Contractor's responsibility to adhere to all applicable MOSHA regulations. The Contractor shall have available approved detecting devices and shall conduct tests for oxygen content and presence of gases, such as combustible gas, carbon dioxide, methane, [and] carbon monoxide. . . . The Contractor shall apply mechanical ventilation continuously to the confined space during occupancy to maintain the proper oxygen content. The Contractor shall conduct air tests periodically during the occupancy.

Traffic Supervisor

Traffic supervisors are often required on contracts involving the traveling public. Such persons, although not exclusively safety supervisors, are responsible for maintaining a safe flow of vehicles through the project and therefore indirectly affect the safety of the workers. The traffic supervisors often hold meetings with owners, similarly to the safety supervisor; however, their main function is to inform subcontractors and the contractor's foremen of the traffic plan. For example:

> The Contractor shall provide a Worksite Traffic Supervisor, who shall be responsible for the Contractor's maintenance of traffic operations on a 24-hour basis. . . . Duties include . . . [h]old[ing] traffic *safety meetings with the superintendents and foremen of the Contractor and subcontractors prior to beginning construction, and periodically thereafter as necessary or as directed by the Engineer. The Engineer shall be provided the opportunity to attend these meetings.* . . . (italics added)

Traffic Plan

A few owners require a traffic control plan, which merely outlines the movement of traffic under different scenarios and at different phases throughout the project.

> A traffic control plan (TCP) is a drawing or drawings indicating the method or scheme for safely and efficiently routing traffic during construction. If a TCP is not included, the Contractor must submit one for approval.

Engineer's Authority

Most documents have a standard provision giving the engineer the final authority in relation to safety violations. It is not clear if the authority is given to the Engineer to make up for any deficiency in a safety program, or if it is merely to augment the safety program. Overall, however, this provision is imperative, as it places the final decision-making power with a designated individual. Such a designation is important for providing quick decisions when necessary. The following is a typical provision:

> The Engineer shall have the authority to withhold further payment or to suspend the work, wholly or in part, due to the failure of the Contractor: (1) to correct conditions unsafe for workers or the general public. . . .

This type of provision appears in many documents. With the authority it gives, the Engineer can make decisions on the gray areas of worker safety. However, if very poor safety provisions exist in the document, the engineer will be very busy policing safety on the work site.

Indemnification

Many contract documents include a statement that the owner's representative has no charge of the methods, means, techniques, sequences, and procedures. Such a provision is written to insulate the designer or the owner's representative from the field operations. More recent versions reduce the ambiguity even further. In fact, a version found in some recent contracts is even more clear on this point. It states that the owner's representative has no charge of the methods, means, techniques, sequences, procedures, *and safety precautions.*

Owners often include provisions, much like the provisions requiring compliance with all laws, that are designed to ensure that the contractors are held responsible for essentially all activities occurring on the construction sites. Besides using the provision discussed in the preceding paragraph, they incorporate indemnification provisions into the documents. Typically, indemnification provisions are physically located adjacent to paragraphs that address contractor compliance with safety regulations. The indemnification provisions are designed to protect the owner, while the regulatory compliance provisions are to provide protection to the workers. Indemnification clauses are to reduce or eliminate for owners the liability that could arise from on-site injuries. Although the intent of the indemnification provisions appears straightforward, the actual wording in the different documents varies. Some provisions might be regarded by contractors as more onerous than others. Examples of indemnification provisions read as follows:

> The Contractor shall protect and indemnify the Owner and its representatives against any claim or liability arising from or based on the violation of any such law, ordinance, regulation, order, or decree, whether by the Contractor or by any of his subcontractors or suppliers or by any of their employees.

> All Contractors doing work for the Owner must provide safety controls for the protection of the lives and health of the Contractor's employees and other persons involved in the work on the job. The Owner has the responsibility for enforcing the provisions of the contract; however, provisions and regulations which, by law, are the fundamental responsibility of other agencies should not be monitored by the Owner. For such provisions and regulations, the Owner will cooperate fully with the responsible agency and utilize such sanctions as are consistent with the contract terms in assisting the responsible agency in enforcing laws, rules, and regulations. The Contractor has the responsibility for complying with the federal construction safety standards. . . . It is not intended that the Owner's personnel perform detailed, in-depth safety inspections of the Contractor's operations, since such inspections are the responsibility of OSHA. . . .

> The Contractor shall be solely and completely responsible for the conditions of the Project Site, including safety of all persons and property in performance of the work. This requirement shall apply continuously and not be limited to normal working hours. The required or implied duty of the Owner's representative to conduct construction review of the Contractor's performance does not and shall not be intended to include review and adequacy of the Contractor's safety measures in, on, or near the Project Site.

> The Contractor shall be solely responsible for safety on the project. Nothing in these specifications shall be construed to reduce in any way that responsibility of the Contractor or to create any duty or responsibility on the part of the Owner to provide or enforce safety requirements for the Contractor. The duty, responsibility, and liability for

safety shall remain with the Contractor. Any failure of the Owner to suspend work or detect violations of any regulatory standards shall in no case relieve the Contractor of the Contractor's safety responsibilities.

To the fullest extent permitted by law, the Contractor shall indemnify and hold harmless the Owner and the Owner's agents and employees from and against all claims, damages, losses, and expenses, including but not limited to attorney's fees, arising out of or resulting from the performance of the work, provided that any such claim, damage, loss, or expense is attributable to bodily injury . . . caused in whole or in part by the negligent act or omission of the Contractor, [or] any subcontractor, . . . regardless of whether or not it is caused in part by a party indemnified.

Incentives for Safety

As discussed earlier, most contracts that include provisions related to the contractor's obligation for construction worker safety have one of two aims: requiring the contractor to follow the regulations that must be followed anyway or having the contractor indemnify the owner for any worker injuries. The intent of such provisions is not active promotion of safety. Requirements to follow OSHA and other regulations are redundant, and indemnification provisions have as their essential intent, not reducing injuries, but only assuring that the owner is not held responsible for injuries. Indemnification provisions often lack the clout that the drafting parties intended.

A proactive stance on safety by the owner can be demonstrated in a number of ways. It can begin to be demonstrated with contractor prequalification criteria that include an emphasis on safety. It can be further demonstrated by the active involvement of the owner in the ongoing safety performance of the project. The intent of such efforts is to reduce injuries. Owners have begun to recognize that they are potentially liable for almost any injury that occurs. Thus, it makes sense to try to minimize the number of injuries. Perhaps trying to minimize injuries is not a common practice now, but it is anticipated that in the future a greater number of contracts, especially those in the private sector (where there is greater susceptibility to lawsuits), will include provisions designed to improve construction safety performance. One provision found in a recent large construction contract reads essentially as follows:

Construction Safety Incentive/Disincentive

The Owner has developed an incentive/disincentive program for this Contract that has two objectives: to promote construction safety awareness during the construction phase of the Contract and to reduce the number of claims against Workers' Compensation insurance, and thereby reduce or eliminate increased insurance premiums charged to the Owner.

The maximum incentive to be earned by, or disincentive to be assessed to, the Contractor is $100,000.00. This incentive/disincentive program is based on a formula that is to be used on the contract. The Owner shall use the Contractor's cumulative incident rate (CIR) for lost-workday cases/lost-time incidents, as determined by the Bureau of Labor Statistics formula shown below:

$$CIR = LTI \cdot 200,000 \div WH$$

$$LTI = \text{number of lost-time incidents}$$

$$WH = \text{total hours worked by all Contract site employees}$$

For computational purposes, each fatality will equal 5 LTIs.

Incentive: The maximum incentive shall be paid to the Contractor if the actual CIR for the Contract is 3.8 or less. No incentive shall be paid if the CIR for the Contract is 5.8 or above. If the CIR is between 3.8 and 5.8, the incentive will be prorated and paid to the Contractor.

Disincentive: The maximum disincentive shall be assessed to the Contractor if the actual CIR for the Contract is 7.8 or greater. No disincentive shall be paid if the CIR for the Contract is 5.8 or less. If the CIR is between 5.8 and 7.8, the disincentive will be prorated and assessed to the Contractor.

Computation: Computation for determining the CIR for the Contract will be accomplished as of the date of Substantial Completion for the Contract.

Payment:

A. If the computation results in a disincentive to be assessed to the Contractor, the Owner will retain such disincentive amount from the final payment in accordance with the "Final Payment" provisions.

B. If the computation results in an incentive to be paid to the Contractor, such payment will be made from the allowance established therefor and will be included in the final payment in accordance with the "Final Payment" provisions.

The foregoing incentive/disincentive provision is novel. It puts the contractor at risk if poor safety performance is realized. At the same time, the owner asserts the importance of safety by setting aside a considerable sum of money that will be paid if safety performance is particularly good.

Final Comments

The analysis of the contract documents indicates that considerable variability exists among the documents of different owners. Although some standard provisions, such as laws to be observed, were in wide use among owners, not one provision was consistent for all.

Specific provisions for worker safety in the documents varied widely. General requirements, however, were similar. Mandates that the contractors not require a worker to perform in unsafe conditions and that basic safety procedures established by OSHA be followed appeared in most documents.

The review of the various safety provisions contained in the general conditions of contract documents shows that there is considerable variability among different documents. There are some outstanding exceptions, which utilize concise and clear language to provide meaningful direction to ensure worker safety. Most provisions tend to address safety in bland terms. Nevertheless, the provisions clearly contain requirements and expectations for the safety of workers on the jobs.

Specific provisions may address the size of a trench that can be dug safely, the amount of oxygen that should be pumped into a confined working space, and various other specific requirements. Such provisions clearly communicate the safety expectations to the contractor (even though the requirements may already be mandated by law). Other provisions address safety in general terms and give the engineer sole responsibility for determining what is safe and what is not. Such general provisions often fail, whether by neglect or by a deliberate intent not to elaborate on specific safety expectations. Their failure puts the weight of "safety patrol" on the engineer's shoulders, with little guidance provided to the contractor.

Most documents contain provisions that address safety programs, but they also tend to include language whereby the contractor agrees to indemnify the owner for liability resulting from worker injuries. Granted, some safety considerations are written with good intentions; yet the real emphasis often appears to be on protecting the owner from lawsuit. However, it should be noted that, regardless of the reason for their creation, there are many excellent provisions. Several provisions, showcased in this chapter, are models for other owners to follow or to improve. Owners are advised to examine those sample provisions and also to explore safety provisions that other agencies and companies have devised.

In addition, all owners should attempt to index their safety provisions so that the provisions can be readily located in the contract documents. A thorough index will ensure easy access to this important information. For example, the majority of publications included safety in their indexes, but safety statements and issues could be found nested in other provisions throughout the documents. Such unlisted provisions are time-consuming to find if proper indexing is not provided. If the owner expects contractors to comply fully with the safety provisions and if safety is regarded as particularly important, that attitude can be conveyed more effectively by having the safety provisions referenced appropriately.

Review Questions

1. What is the most widely used safety-related provision found in construction contracts, and what are the implications of its inclusion in construction contracts?
2. What kind of assurances do owners have that the safety program submittals will be made by the contractors?
3. Devise a contract provision that outlines a safety incentive program.
4. What might the owner do to help ensure that the contractor will comply with the safety standards outlined in the contract?
5. What kinds of safety reports might an owner expect to receive from a contractor?
6. As far as the owner is concerned, what is the primary role of the contractor's safety officer?
7. What is the purpose of an indemnification provision?
8. Describe a specific accident prevention plan that may be required because of unique conditions on a construction site.
9. What types of safety-related tasks might be required to be performed before construction work begins?
10. Describe circumstances in which the owner may require the contractor to address safety issues according to specifications that far exceed the OSHA requirements.

Substance Abuse

> *A little safety never hurt anyone.*

The subject of substance abuse conjures up many different images in different people. For those using a narrow definition of substance abuse, the substances in question constitute such illegal drugs as heroin, cocaine, marijuana, crack, and LSD. However, substance abuse is more properly given a much broader definition. Other substances that could very well be abused include alcohol, over-the-counter drugs, and prescription drugs. Although the legality of the use of a particular substance may be of some concern, where worker safety is concerned, the misuse of any substance that will make a worker less safe is to be avoided. Just as the goal of zero accidents may exist in a firm, so, too, the goal may be to have a drug-free workplace or no substance abuse.

The Incidence of Substance Abuse

It has been estimated that in the industrial work force approximately 10% of the workers are substance abusers. One study estimated that 29% of employed Americans between the ages of 20 and 40 had used illicit drugs at least once during the previous year (National Institute on Drug Abuse 1990). Another study found that 24% of workers had personally observed or had heard of illicit drug use by fellow workers (Gallup Organization 1990). The type of substance abuse appears to be age-related. For example, one study found that more substance abusers were over 35 years of age and that alcohol was the leader among the drugs used. For those under 35, the leader was also alcohol, but there was an increased use of marijuana. Over the years, the use of illicit drugs among those over 35 has been declining. In general, substance abuse is more prevalent among men than women (Gust and Walsh 1990). Numerous experts have estimated that in the construction industry the incidence of substance abuse may be over 20%.

The primary concern with regard to substance abuse is that the mental state of a worker will be altered by the use or excessive use of a substance. Such an altered mental state generally results in impaired judgment, which increases the chance of an injury, whether to the substance-abusing worker or to fellow workers. A 1988 study headed by Senator Dan Quayle (1988) showed that 5–10% of workers suffer from substance abuse and that 3–7% use some form of illicit drugs. Furthermore, the study concluded that 40% of all industrial fatalities and 47% of industrial injuries could be traced to substance abuse. Although substance abuse among workers appears to be widespread, it should not be tolerated in the place of work.

Safety is not the only problem of employers where substance abuse is concerned. Increased crime is commonly associated with substance abuse. On construction sites increased crime can have serious adverse ramifications through jobsite theft. Productivity losses can also be substantial. Another consequence is that, through peer pressure, the substance abusers may entice other workers to use drugs. Thus, the problem may grow, even if turnover is minimal. Various estimates have been made of the costs the construction industry suffers as a result of substance abuse. The total cost to the industry is in the billions of dollars.

One of the problems with substance abuse is that the abuse or misuse of the substance may actually occur off site. It is the lingering effect of such abuse that poses the safety threat. This situation presents a unique problem to the construction firm. Should the company have a means of determining if a worker has indeed abused a mind-altering substance, or should there be an effective means of assessing worker behavior to determine the fitness of the workers? Of course, basing decisions on behavior may result in the occurrence of unfortunate events (injury accidents) before anyone ever suspects that a worker is not fit to work on a particular day.

In the construction industry, experts generally assume that the incidence of substance abuse is high. Reducing substance abuse in construction is a major task. One obstacle is that many construction contractors fail to see the consequences of substance abuse on their job sites or that they do not perceive themselves as being in a position to reduce the substance abuse. Some firms simply do not recognize substance abuse as a problem on their projects. The failure to recognize the problem is complicated by the general forbearance that employers seem to have toward alcohol use, even when the use is excessive.

Drug Testing

The topic of substance abuse and how to begin to address it leads naturally to the most controversial issue related to substance abuse: drug testing. Organized labor has been a vocal opponent of drug testing; however, labor opposition is not universal, and it is clearly diminishing. A Gallup poll on the attitudes of construction workers toward drug testing showed that 81% favored or supported drug testing (Gallup Organization 1990).

It has been stated that drug testing should not be an area of dispute between labor and management. It has also been suggested that it is the labor leaders who are opposed to drug testing and that they may not be representing the true sentiments of the union members (de Bernardo 1990). It should be remembered that *no* employer is to "require any laborer or mechanic employed in the performance of the contract to work in surroundings or under working conditions which are unsanitary, hazardous, or dangerous to his health or safety" (29 CFR § 1926.20). Could it be concluded that, if an employer knowingly permits employees to work in areas where another employee is under the influence of a drug, the OSHA standards are being violated? Certainly a tort lawyer would make it a key or central issue if it could be proven that the substance abuser was the root cause of a serious injury or fatality and that the employer could have known or should have known that the abuser was unfit for work. Drug testing may be the solution that reduces injuries and liability claims.

Some organized labor groups have become proponents of drug testing. In many instances, it is the type of drug testing that is at issue. The types of drug testing are pre-employment screening, postaccident testing, periodic testing, random testing, testing for reasonable cause, and follow-up testing. Postaccident testing is a specific type of testing that might otherwise be included in the category of testing for reasonable cause.

Preemployment screening, when implemented by a company, is drug testing that is mandatory for all new hires. Failure to pass such a test will end consideration of the applicant for employment. Although a second test may be taken by those testing positive for drugs, the second test is generally given only after a considerable amount of time (typically six months) has elapsed.

Postaccident drug testing is self-explanatory to a large degree. Nevertheless, firms implementing postaccident drug testing should formally establish the policies and procedures. Although it may be clear when such drug testing is to occur (immediately after an accident), without protocol it may not be clear who is to be tested. If an accident results in an injury, it may have been caused by one or more injured workers or by fellow workers. Thus, it may be appropriate to test all workers who were closely involved with the task or tasks being performed at the time of the accident. Additionally, the term *accident* must be clearly defined to clarify whether near misses and no-injury incidents qualify for testing.

Periodic testing may simply be a blanket testing of all workers that occurs at some specific interval, or the timing of the tests may be variable. Several construction contractors have elected to employ blanket random screening. When periodic tests are conducted, all workers are tested. The testing should also include superintendents, project engineers, and project managers. Some programs extend this testing to personnel in the main or home office, as such broad application of the test reduces the reluctance of workers to be tested.

Random testing, the most controversial type of drug testing, is testing that is applied with an element of chance. Such testing can be implemented whether or not a screening test is done. The principle behind random testing is that if a worker has a reasonable probability of being tested, the worker will be discouraged from substance abuse. Blanket testing, testing every worker on site, makes testing a certainty, but it is costly. The cost of each test may range from $30 to $50 or more. The primary reason that random testing has been so controversial is that the determination of who is to be tested may not be truly random. Although that problem is averted with blanket testing, the cost is higher. Many firms have reported that the incidence of substance abuse dropped after random testing was implemented.

Testing for reasonable cause is warranted when the behavior of a worker suggests an assessment is needed of that individual's body content of certain substances. The most common reason to test for reasonable cause is an accident, so some programs include postaccident testing in the category of testing for reasonable cause. The inclusion of postaccident testing in the reasonable-cause category is not recommended. There are philosophical reasons for this recommendation. Testing for reasonable cause should ideally occur in an attempt to maintain a drug-free workplace. Although postaccident testing may reveal that an accident may have been caused or contributed to by a worker who was under the influence of a drug, it does not avert the accident. Testing for reasonable cause may be triggered by near misses or unusual behavior, such as slurred speech, disorientation, lack of attentiveness, drowsiness, irritability, and moodiness. Job records may also identify drug abusers through such behavior traits as increased sick leave, high absenteeism, tardiness, excessive breaks, increased reprimands, missing tools and equipment, high injury rates, and low-quality work. Physical features that may signal substance abuse include bloodshot or watery eyes, a runny nose, sudden weight loss, excessive perspiration, and a poor complexion.

Follow-up testing is associated with the other forms of drug testing. It may occur for a number of reasons, although it is generally focused on workers who have gone through a rehabilitation program. Follow-up tests are then conducted to maintain assurance that the rehabilitated workers remain drug-free. There may be a single follow-up test, conducted at a randomly selected time, or a battery of such randomly administered tests. Although not as commonly, follow-up testing may also be used for employees who were absent on days when periodic testing was performed. In addition, if a worker's test indicates a trace of a substance of interest, but the amount is below the established positive level, a follow-up test might be conducted.

A study of drug testing was conducted among 26 of the Northwest's largest construction contractors (Creasy 1995). Of those contractors, 20 (76.9%) conduct some form of substance abuse testing. Among the firms that conduct testing, the study revealed the extent to which the different types of testing methods are employed: preemployment, 90%; postaccident, 90%; annual, 25%; random, 25%; and for-cause, 80%. This study did not assess the extent of blanket testing. Because of the large size of the participating contractors and the recentness of the study, it may be no surprise that some of these percentages are considerably higher than those reported in earlier studies on drug testing. In the study conducted by Maloney in the mid-1980s, only 18.4% of the participating construction firms conducted drug tests.

How common or widespread is drug testing in the construction industry? A study of this topic was conducted by Richard Coble (1992) with the members of the Associated Builders and Contractors in Florida. The study showed that drug testing was very much influenced by company size. That is, very few small companies (those with fewer than 10 employees) have drug testing programs, whereas most large companies (those with more than 100 employees) do have drug testing programs (see Figure 11.1).

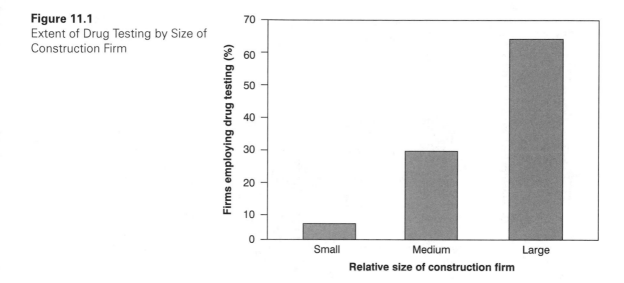

Figure 11.1
Extent of Drug Testing by Size of Construction Firm

Coble's findings about the use of drug testing in construction are similar to the findings of a government study that showed that 43% of the nation's largest companies (those with more than 1,000 employees) had drug testing programs whereas only 2% of the small firms (those with fewer than 50 employees) had drug testing programs (U.S. Department of Labor 1989). From a 1992 survey, to which 52% of the firms contacted responded, the Associated Builders and Contractors reported that 80% of the firms tested for cause, 78% did preemployment screening, 54% used random testing, and 30% tested all employees.

In a study involving 152 construction contractors in Florida, information was obtained on the types of drug testing conducted (Hill 1993). The findings are summarized in Figure 11.2. That study disclosed that most of the contractors employing drug testing had begun doing so in 1992.

The reasons for setting up drug testing protocols were examined in the Florida study. It was noted that Florida legislation established a workers' compensation discount as an incentive for firms to test for drugs. The various reasons given by the 83 respondents for setting up drug testing are as follows (some gave multiple responses):

safety on the job	47
workers' compensation discount or reduction in insurance cost	27
better quality of employees	19
contract requirement	18
financial savings or improved efficiency	13
help in controlling liability	7
improvement of company image or public relations	7

Some respondents gave as many as four or five reasons for setting up a drug testing program. A few of those stating that contract requirements mandated drug testing also stated that the requirement was only on a single contract.

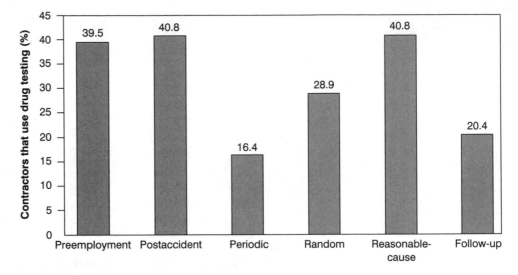

Figure 11.2
Types of Drug Testing Employed by Florida Contractors
Source: Hill 1993

The contractors were also asked about the effect of drug testing on worker morale. Although 5% of the contractors did not have a sense of the effect of drug testing, 82% stated that it improved worker morale or that workers were supportive of the practice. In general, it appears that workers have come to accept drug testing and to recognize its contribution to safety in the workplace. Many workers are supportive of and appreciate companies that have drug testing programs. Although cost is often a concern, most contractors felt that drug testing saved the company money overall.

The Florida study asked the contractors that did not employ drug testing why they did not. The most common reason given was that they knew their employees well and they did not feel that drug testing was necessary. Several of the 69 contractors not doing drug testing stated that they were small firms (some with one or two employees) and they knew their employees were not drug abusers. Some of the small firms employed only relatives. Although some firms did not test for drugs because they knew their long-time employees well (i.e., they had low turnover), others said they did not test because of the high turnover in their business. A few indicated that, although they had not tested in the past, they were considering the establishment of a drug testing program, but they did not elaborate on why they had not tested in the past or why they would test in the future. Others commented that drug testing was not done because "I would not have any employees" or the workers would "feel it is an invasion of privacy." The various reasons for not employing drug testing are summarized in the following list:

We know our employees well.	27
Drug testing is unnecessary.	22
Drug testing is too expensive.	15
We have high turnover of employees.	8

We do not know how to test.   5

Drug testing is a violation of privacy.   2

Of course, it would be inaccurate to suggest that the controversy over drug testing is restricted to random testing. The accuracy of drug tests has been much debated. Most of the controversy regarding the accuracy of drug testing is based on the chain of custody. That is, when a urine sample is taken and sent to a laboratory, where hundreds or even thousands of samples are analyzed in a short period of time, what is the certainty that the results of a particular test will be properly matched to a specific individual? Can a sample that proved positive be retested with assurance that it is in fact the same sample and that it came from the individual to whom it is matched? The reasons for those concerns are not without merit. In fact, during the early 1980s there were some notable cases in which positive drug test results were improperly matched with the wrong individuals. However, because of the seriousness of the matter, proper control mechanisms have been instituted by most drug testing firms so that chain of custody is no longer a serious problem.

With serious consequences often resulting from positive drug tests, errors in the test results must be eliminated. Another issue that has generated some debate is that of false positives, positive test results when no drugs have been taken. It has been alleged that some legal substances may be metabolized in the body in such a way as to create positive results. Those claims are largely unsubstantiated, but the debate is serious and continuing. Some persons who know they will be tested for drugs purposely avoid eating poppy-seed rolls or muffins, fearing they will generate positive test results. Although it is not debated that the analysis may detect the poppy seed as a drug, it is generally felt that the level of the drug in the body will be well below the positive threshold level. Some other products (cough medicines, etc.) have also been linked with positive drug test results.

One last comment about chain of custody is warranted. The chain of custody begins at the point of taking the sample, and it ends after the sample results have been recorded. Is the sample taken really the urine specimen of the person ostensibly being tested? There have been various schemes in which persons being tested would smuggle in "clean" urine samples and deposit them in the specimen vials. Such schemes are easily avoided by having an observer present when the sample is taken, thereby raising the issue of the right to privacy.

Consequences of Testing Positive for Drugs

The Department of Labor (1990a) has published a guide to help employers implement substance abuse programs. The three essential components include (1) informing employees about assistance or services that are available to them concerning their drug problems, (2) informing employees about the adverse effects substance abuse has on company productivity, product quality, absenteeism, health care costs, and the incidence of accidents, and (3) explaining the company's substance abuse program and policies, especially those related to drug testing.

Regardless of whether a drug test is a preemployment screening, a random test, or a test for reasonable cause, serious consideration must be given by the company to the consequences of a positive result. It is common for positive results on a preemployment drug test to exclude the person tested from further immediate consideration for employment. Some company policies state that positive results on a preemployment test will bar an applicant from being considered for employment for at least six months and that, after six months, negative test results must be noted.

What should be the consequences of positive results on a random test or a test for reasonable cause? That question again will require the serious consideration of company management. It may be an immediate reaction to dismiss any worker who fails (tests positive on) a drug test, but dismissal may do nothing to solve the problem. If such a worker is dismissed, he or she will most likely seek employment with another construction firm. Thus, the problem is not reduced; it is simply spread around a bit. That is not the long-range goal of any substance abuse program.

Substance abusers must be viewed as workers with illnesses, diseases that can be cured if treated effectively. Unlike most diseases, however, the sick person (being a substance abuser) is reluctant to admit that anything is wrong. That is where management can play a major role. Drugs have destroyed many lives in this country. Proper treatment might have reduced the actual numbers considerably. Management might elect to institute a policy whereby rehabilitation treatment is offered to substance abusers. If the company is willing to bear some of the costs of rehabilitation, the worker will often see that the mental health of the workers is important to the firm.

Companies viewing substance abuse as a disease may want to consider the establishment of a Employee Assistance Program (EAP). Such programs are set up to help workers in a number of ways. An EAP typically includes employee assessment, counseling, and possible referral to an alcohol and drug rehabilitation program. Employees are evaluated or tested, and those having positive results are offered treatment programs. Those refusing treatment are generally terminated as employees. Those accepting treatment are generally offered their original jobs when they return from treatment. Workers who have had treatment are given periodic follow-up tests to ensure that rehabilitation has been effective. To date, full EAPs are uncommon and can generally be found only in the larger construction firms.

What if a worker has a positive result on a drug test, accepts rehabilitation training, and subsequently has a positive result on a follow-up drug test? Many company policies are such that there is no tolerance for two-time offenders. In other words, positive test results for a worker who has gone through drug rehabilitation often result in the immediate dismissal of the worker. Some companies may be more lenient and may give the worker a second chance at being rehabilitated.

It has been suggested that companies should keep lists of workers who have been dismissed for having positive drug test results and that the lists should be consolidated with those maintained by other firms. By sharing the lists, companies would have greater certainty that they are hiring "drug-free" workers, or at least that they are not hiring known substance abusers. Although the idea may appeal to some employers, the procedure is illegal and need not be given further consideration.

Where substance abuse is concerned, the overall objective of every construction firm should be to have a drug-free workplace. The Department of Labor (1990b) has recommended some basic steps by which employers might achieve that goal. They are essentially as follows:

1. Take a firm stance against substance abuse in the workplace, and communicate that stance to all workers.
2. Acquire information on how drugs and alcohol affect workplaces and individual workers, and communicate that information to all workers.
3. Note all signs and symptoms that suggest substance abuse in the workplace, as detecting substance abuse may be vital to the overall well-being and safety of the workers and the general public.
4. Provide the assistance necessary to help employees with substance abuse problems.

Effect of Substance Abuse Programs on Safety Performance

There have been no noteworthy results of construction studies that have examined substance abuse programs and the resultant effect on safety performance. That may be because substance abuse programs began to be implemented by many firms in the 1980s, just as they were beefing up their safety efforts through enhanced safety programs. Therefore, it is difficult to determine whether improvements in safety performance reflect the effect of the substance abuse programs or of the safety programs. The most successful results are those reported by individual firms.

Several firms have reported astounding improvements in safety performance, which they attributed to their substance abuse programs. One large construction company in the Northwest reported that, within one year of the implementation of mandatory preemployment drug testing, its incidence of injuries was cut in half. That result may give some insight into the magnitude of the injuries that may actually be caused or contributed to by substance abusers. It must also be recognized that substance abusers are often health deficient because of the drug abuse. As workers, they tend to miss more days of work, they tend to be tardy more often, and they typically are weaker job performers. Since substance abusers are often not as healthy as the average worker, they tend to be a particular heavy burden on the health care programs that firms may have set up for their workers.

Information about firms that have drug testing programs spreads among construction workers. When one firm in Texas began preemployment drug testing, 30% of the job applicants had positive results. Two years after the firm started the drug testing, the number of job applicants with positive results was below 1%. Another phenomenon, reported by Tropicana Products, was that job applications declined 52% when it implemented preemployment drug testing (Checket-Hanks 1991). The mere threat of drug testing apparently dissuades those who anticipate test results that would cause them to be rejected.

In a Construction Industry Institute study on substance abuse, 59% of the 250 contractors involved in the study reported that substance abuse is a serious or extremely serious problem in the construction industry, and 21% felt it was a serious or extremely serious problem in their firms (Maloney 1988). From the contractors' responses, it was estimated that approximately 10% of construction workers are substance abusers. The problem drugs in the firms (with the estimated percentages of respondents reporting them) were alcohol (84%), marijuana (54%), cocaine or crack (29%), amphetamines/speed (8%), Valium (4%), barbiturates (3%), and lesser used drugs (2%). It was estimated in the study that construction costs have risen substantially because of drug abuse in the workplace. The increases have been in design and construction costs (an increase of more than 8%), health care costs (more than 16%), workers' compensation costs (more than 17%), and other insurance costs (more than 14%). Similar percentages (generally more than 15%) were estimated for increases in absenteeism, late starts, early quits, safety incidents, accidents, injuries, and turnover.

One study on construction safety examined the relationship between safety performance and implementation of substance abuse programs (Altayeb 1990). That study was not able to state conclusively that there was a significant association between reduction in injury incidence rates and the implementation of substance abuse testing. Although the results lacked statistical validity, the average injury incidence rates of firms that had implemented drug testing were 19% below those of firms without testing programs. That study did not reveal any differences in the experiences of firms of different sizes.

In a study in which questionnaires were sent to the 400 largest U.S. contractors, of which 32 firms responded, it was discovered that firms conducting drug testing had lower injury frequencies than those that did not test (Indradjaja 1995). Those specifically mentioning that they did drug testing had an OSHA recordable injury rate of 6.17 and a lost-time injury rate of 1.35 per 100 employees. Firms not conducting drug tests reported 8.85 OSHA recordable injuries per 100 employees and a lost-time injury rate of 1.73.

A survey of 152 construction contractors in Florida showed that there may be a sizable monetary incentive for establishing a drug-free workplace program (Hill 1993). Firms with drug-free workplace programs reported average claims costs that were about 50% lower than the average claims costs experienced by firms without drug-free workplace programs. For example, in 1993 the average claim cost for firms with drug-free workplace programs was $4,759, and for firms without such programs the average was $9,489. The difference was noted in each region of the state that was examined, and it was also noted to be true for 1992 data. Assuming that firms without drug-free workplace programs employ more substance abusers, it can be concluded that, when substance abusers are injured, their injuries are more severe.

Final Comments

Drug testing in the workplace is becoming a less controversial issue, and so it should be. Drug testing should not be viewed as an issue addressing constitutional rights, but rather as one addressing the right of every worker to work in a safe environment. Substance abusers pose a potential threat to job safety, so it is reasonable to keep them off the job by not hiring them. To avoid hiring substance abusers, it is imperative to identify them. Such identification can come primarily through drug testing. Fewer substance abusers in the work force will result in higher productivity, fewer absences, better safety performance, improved quality, and other benefits. Whereas drug testing focuses on persons who are already drug users, employers should also consider ways in which they can educate their employees so that they will not be easily tempted by drugs.

Review Questions

1. What does the term *chain of custody* refer to?
2. Describe the different types of substance abuse.

3. What is the stance of organized labor on the subject of drug testing?
4. What have research studies shown about the relationship between safety performance and the implementation of substance abuse programs in construction firms?
5. Describe the different types of drug testing.
6. What type of drug testing is probably most effective at ensuring a drug-free workplace?
7. Other than job-site injuries, what are possible negative consequences of substance abuse in the workplace?
8. Do the OSHA regulations address substance abuse in any way?
9. Under what types of circumstances might an employer be justified in requiring a drug test for reasonable cause?
10. How prevalent is drug testing in the construction industry?

References

Altayeb, S. 1990. "Drug Testing and Its Impact on the Incident Rate in the Construction Industry." Ph.D. dissertation, Clemson University, Clemson, S.C.

Associated Builders and Contractors. 1992. "Drug Testing Programs Increase." *Construction Issues* 4, no. 4, 2.

Checket-Hanks, B. 1991. "Drug-free Contractor Group Seeks to Reassure Consumers." *Air Conditioning, Heating, and Refrigeration News*, October 14, 1–2.

Coble, R. 1992. "An Empirical Investigation of Factors Related to the Drug-Free Workplace." Ph.D. diss., University of Florida.

Creasy, D. 1995. "Northwest Construction Contractors' Substance Abuse Policies and Practices." Master's research report, University of Washington.

de Bernardo, M. 1990. *What Every Employee Should Know about Abuse: Answers to 20 Good Questions.* Washington, D.C.: Institute for a Drug-Free Workplace.

Gallup Organization. 1990. *Institute for a Drug-Free Workplace, Washington, DC: Florida Statewide Study.* Lincoln, Neb.: Association Research Group.

Gust, S., and J. Walsh, eds. 1990. *Drugs in the Workplace: Research and Evaluation Data.* NIDA Research Monograph 91. Rockville, Md.: National Institute on Drug Abuse.

Hill, S. 1993. "Drug-Free Workplace Policies and Their Acceptance in the Construction Industry." Master's thesis, University of Florida.

Hinze, J. 1986. "Your Firm Needs a Substance-Abuse Policy." *Pacific Builder and Engineer* 92, no. 23, 20.

Indradjaja, R. 1995. "Techniques of Motivation for Construction Workers." Master's thesis, University of Washington.

Levitt, R., and N. Samelson. 1993. *Construction Safety Management.* 2d ed. New York: John Wiley.

Maloney, W. 1988. "Substance Abuse in Construction." *ASCE Journal of Construction Engineering and Management* 114, no. 4, 614–30.

National Institute on Drug Abuse. 1990. *Research on Drugs and the Workplace.* NIDA Capsules. Rockville, Md.: Press Office, National Institute on Drug Abuse.

Petersen, D. 1988. *Safety Management.* Goshen, N.Y.: Aloray.

Peyton, R., and T. Rubio. 1991. *Construction Safety Practices and Principles.* New York: Van Nostrand Reinhold.

Quayle, D. 1988. *American Productivity: The Devastating Effect of Alcoholism and Drug Abuse.* Employee Assistance Programs. Chicago: Charles C. Thomas.

U.S. Department of Labor. 1989. *Survey of Employer Anti-drug Programs.* Report no. 760. Washington, D.C.: National Clearinghouse for Alcohol and Drug Information.

———. 1990a. *An Employer's Guide to Dealing with Substance Abuse.* Washington, D.C.: National Clearinghouse for Alcohol and Drug Information.

———. 1990b. *What Works: Workplaces without Drugs.* Washington, D.C.: National Clearinghouse for Alcohol and Drug Information.

Safety Record Keeping

Hazards are not a way of life.

Safety records prepared and maintained must be consistent with those mandated by OSHA. Additional record keeping is generally advisable from a management point of view. One of the goals of the OSHA record-keeping requirements is that the information be useful to OSHA as it seeks direction in its mission. The injury data compiled from employers in the various states can be used to develop statistical information on which actions may or may not be warranted. For example, after information was compiled on the number of trenching fatalities that occurred in the early 1970s, OSHA devoted considerable funds to evaluating trenching practices so that a new trenching standard could be developed.

Aside from being valuable to OSHA, injury data collected by an employer can be very helpful in identifying the major sources or causes of injuries and illnesses in the workplace. Although employers may elect to keep additional records that help monitor safety performance, it is important that the mandated record-keeping requirements be known and followed. Which construction employers must keep injury records? The requirement has been defined to apply to all construction employers (Standard Industrial Classification [SIC] codes 15–17) with 11 or more employees at any one time in the previous calendar year. Employers are exempt from the record-keeping requirements if they had no more than 10 full-time or part-time employees at any one time in the previous calendar year. Because there is inherent value in the information contained in safety records, smaller firms are well advised to keep some type of records for their own use.

A contractor is not responsible for keeping records on employees of other firms. Thus, on a single construction site with many subcontractors, each employer is responsible for maintaining the records of injuries sustained by their own employees. Independent contractors are not considered employees.

It is in the area of independent contractors that there is increasing concern. For example, a contractor may enter into an agreement with an individual for that individual to install ceramic tile in a rest room in a new building under construction. Similar agreements are made with two other individuals, who will install ceramic tile in additional rest rooms. The pay for the work is computed on a piece-rate basis, but since the total area can be easily determined, the individuals know exactly how much they will be paid for their labor. If the contractor does not supervise the details, means, methods, and process by which the work is accomplished, each tile setter may be regarded as an independent contractor. Some allegations have been made that contractors use this type of practice to avoid paying workers' compensation insurance on the workers. Supposedly, the practice is more widespread in some areas; however, little information is available to substantiate or refute the allegations.

Despite the waiver of the record-keeping requirements for small employers, all employers must comply with the OSHA standards, display the OSHA poster, and report to OSHA within 48 hours after any accident that results in one or more fatalities or the hospitalization of five or more employees. All employers, including those normally exempt from record keeping, should be fully familiar with other safety or recordkeeping requirements that may exist in their area. For example, employers in OSHA state-plan states may find that the exemptions do not apply or that they are enforced differently.

Compliance with the record-keeping requirements consists of the use of two OSHA forms: the Log of Occupational Injuries and Illnesses (OSHA No. 200) and the Supplementary Record of Occupational Injuries and Illnesses (OSHA No. 101).

Log of Occupational Injuries and Illnesses (OSHA No. 200)

The OSHA No. 200 form, commonly referred to as "the log" or "the "OSHA log," consists of a listing of injuries and illnesses. The log provides abbreviated information on all the injuries that are recorded during the year (see Figure 12.1). Thus, one can scan the OSHA log and quickly determine the number of injuries that have occurred during the year, and a little more study of the log reveals the types of injuries that have occurred. The OSHA log must be made available for inspection and copying by employees, former employees, and their representatives.

Injuries are classified as fatalities, lost-workday cases, cases not resulting in death or lost workdays, and first-aid (not recordable) cases. The recordable injuries are to be noted on the OSHA log.

The OSHA log shows the following information about each recorded injury or illness:

- the time of occurrence of the injury or illness
- the name of the affected worker

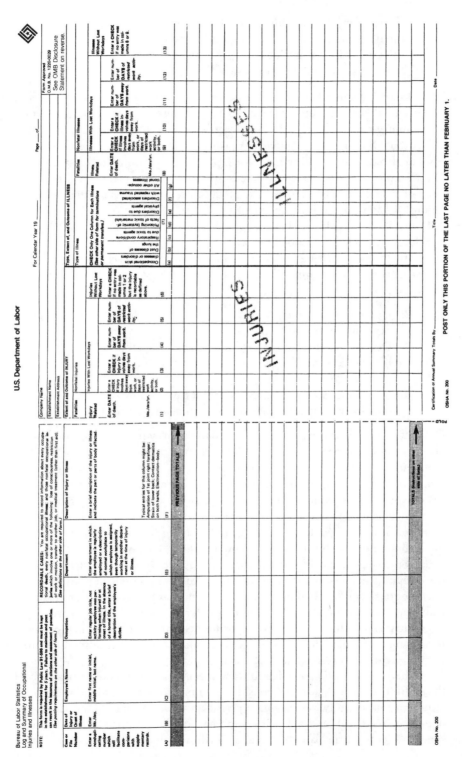

Figure 12.1
Form for Log of Occupational Injuries and Illnesses (OSHA No. 200)

187

- the regular job of the injured or ill worker
- the department in which the injured worker was employed
- the kind of injury or illness
- the amount of time lost because of the injury or illness

The OSHA log consists of three parts: a descriptive section identifying the employee and briefly describing the nature of the injury or illness, a section describing the extent of the injury recorded, and a section describing the extent of the illness recorded.

Although OSHA has standard forms to use in completing the OSHA log, employers can also develop their own versions, provided they contain the same level of detail. If an employer elects to do this, it is advisable to have the form evaluated by the Bureau of Labor Statistics to ascertain that full compliance is maintained with the regulations. Some firms find it convenient to generate the logs on the computer. The printout must be as readable and as comprehensive as the OSHA No. 200. Most employers use the standard log developed by OSHA.

Which cases must be included in the OSHA log? OSHA (1986) has outlined the following steps to determine which cases are to be logged:

1. Verify that a death, an illness, or an injury has occurred.
2. Determine that the occurrence was work related, resulting from an event or exposure in the work environment.
3. Determine whether the case is an illness or an injury.
4. If the case is an illness, record the information and check the appropriate illness category in the log.
5. If the case is an injury, record it if it involved medical treatment, loss of consciousness, restriction of work or motion, or transfer to another job.

Cases that are not recordable include situations in which workers are hospitalized for observation but receive neither medical treatment nor diagnosis of an illness. To be recordable, a case must first be established as a work-related illness or a work-related injury requiring medical treatment, an incident involving loss of consciousness, or a case involving restriction of work or motion, or transfer to another job. The recurrence of a previous case is not recordable. If a worker trips on the job and hurts a knee that was previously injured, the incident would be recordable as a new case, as the need for medical attention is the result of a new incident. The symptoms of illness may wane and then reappear. Such reappearances are generally not recordable cases; however, the previous entries of the case may need to be updated. Suppose a carpenter has become sensitized to wood dust and the ailment has previously been recorded. If medical treatment is required when the carpenter is again exposed to wood dust, a new case entry is warranted, as a new exposure occurred. Note that first-aid cases are not recordable. Note also that workers' compensation claims may apply to injuries that are not necessarily recordable.

What are first-aid cases? For OSHA, specific parameters have been established for this definition. OSHA does not consider it a first-aid case if first aid is administered as a temporary measure before having a physician treat an injury. First aid consists of any one-time treatment, and any follow-up visit for the purpose of observation, of minor scratches, cuts, burns, splinters, and so forth, which do not ordinarily require medical care. Such one-time treatment and follow-up visit for observation are considered first aid even though provided by a physician or registered professional personnel. For example, a company may have a policy in which an eye injury requires the attention of a physician. Suppose a worker has a dust particle lodged in his eye and that considerable eye irritation occurs. The dust particle is successfully removed by another worker on site, but the injured worker is asked to see a physician. The physician merely examines the worker's eye and determines that the eye is clear of dust and that only superficial irritation has occurred. The worker resumes work at the preinjury task. That is not a recordable case.

If a worker becomes unconscious as the result of an injury, the case is recordable regardless of the type of treatment. If work is restricted, the case is recordable. The restriction may be that the worker cannot return to work on the following workday as a result of the injury or that the worker has to be reassigned to a different type of work because of inability to perform the preinjury work. Even if a worker is reassigned to another type of work, the injury is considered a lost-workday case. Whenever an injury is such that a worker cannot perform the normal job duties over a normal work shift, the injury is considered a lost-workday case. In other words, a lost-workday case is one in which the injury adversely affects the worker beyond the day of the injury.

Most injuries and illnesses that occur on the employer's premises and are treated by a physician are regarded as recordable. If an injury occurs in the employer's parking lot, it is generally not regarded as recordable. Exceptions apply. For example, suppose a worker, Beth, is sent to a local hardware store to purchase some materials for the company project. Beth is asked to use her personal vehicle, a pickup truck. Upon returning to the construction site, the truck is parked in the designated lot. Josh is asked to help unload the materials. While unloading some of the materials, Josh is injured when he stumbles on a pneumatic hose, one of the items Beth just purchased. The injury, a cut, requires three stitches. Since the injury is work-related, it is recordable. If Beth had been similarly injured while loading the truck at the hardware store, she, too, would have sustained a recordable injury.

Supplementary Record of Occupational Injuries and Illnesses (OSHA No. 101)

Whenever injuries occur, some type of record keeping must be done. OSHA requires that a Supplementary Record of Occupational Injuries and Illnesses, which is known as OSHA No. 101 (see Figure 12.2), be filed for each injury or illness. It may be submitted in the format established by OSHA, or it may be submitted in some other form that presents the same basic information. Some contractors elect to use forms developed by their workers' compensation insurance carriers. Such forms are generally acceptable as substitutes for the OSHA No. 101 as long as they present the required information. Insurance companies often want additional information that is not requested on the OSHA No. 101. Thus, they develop their own forms and include all of the items requested on OSHA No. 101 so that both the OSHA requirements and the insurance requirements are satisfied on the same form.

The forms developed by workers' compensation carriers are commonly known as the Employer's First Report of Injury, or the E-1. The completed supplementary

Bureau of Labor Statistics
Supplementary Record of
Occupational Injuries and Illnesses

U.S. Department of Labor

This form is required by Public Law 91-596 and must be kept in the establishment for *5 years.* Failure to maintain can result in the issuance of citations and assessment of penalties.	Case or File No.	Form Approved O.M.B. No. 1220-0029

Employer

1. Name

See OMB Disclosure Statement on reverse.

2. Mail address *(No. and street, city or town, State, and zip code)*

3. Location, if different from mail address

Injured or Ill Employee

4. Name *(First, middle, and last)*   Social Security No.

5. Home address *(No. and street, city or town, State, and zip code)*

6. Age   7. Sex: *(Check one)*   Male ☐   Female ☐

8. Occupation *(Enter regular job title, not the specific activity he was performing at time of injury.)*

9. Department *(Enter name of department or division in which the injured person is regularly employed, even though he may have been temporarily working in another department at the time of injury.)*

The Accident or Exposure to Occupational Illness

If accident or exposure occurred on employer's premises, give address of plant or establishment in which it occurred. Do not indicate department or division within the plant or establishment. If accident occurred outside employer's premises at an identifiable address, give that address. If it occurred on a public highway or at any other place which cannot be identified by number and street, please provide place references locating the place of injury as accurately as possible.

10. Place of accident or exposure *(No. and street, city or town, State, and zip code)*

11. Was place of accident or exposure on employer's premises?   Yes ☐   No ☐

12. What was the employee doing when injured? *(Be specific. If he was using tools or equipment or handling material, name them and tell what he was doing with them.)*

13. How did the accident occur? *(Describe fully the events which resulted in the injury or occupational illness. Tell what happened and how it happened. Name any objects or substances involved and tell how they were involved. Give full details on all factors which led or contributed to the accident. Use separate sheet for additional space.)*

Occupational Injury or Occupational Illness

14. Describe the injury or illness in detail and indicate the part of body affected. *(E.g., amputation of right index finger at second joint; fracture of ribs; lead poisoning; dermatitis of left hand, etc.)*

15. Name the object or substance which directly injured the employee. *(For example, the machine or thing he struck against or which struck him; the vapor or poison he inhaled or swallowed; the chemical or radiation which irritated his skin; or in cases of strains, hernias, etc., the thing he was lifting, pulling, etc.)*

16. Date of injury or initial diagnosis of occupational illness   17. Did employee die? *(Check one)*   Yes ☐   No ☐

Other

18. Name and address of physician

19. If hospitalized, name and address of hospital

Date of report	Prepared by	Official position

OSHA No. 101 (Feb. 1981)

Figure 12.2

Form for Supplementary Record of Occupational Injuries and Illnesses (OSHA No. 101) record, or No. 101, must be present in the place of work within six workdays after the employer receives information that an injury or illness has occurred.

A supplementary record entry should be made on OSHA No. 101 for every injury or illness that is recorded in the OSHA log. The information to document in the supplementary record includes a description of how the accident or illness exposure occurred, a listing of the objects or substances involved, and an indication of the nature of the injury or illness and the part or parts of the body affected (refer to Figure 12.2).

Maintenance of OSHA Records

The log and the supplementary records are to be kept at each work establishment. In some cases that means that an employer must keep additional or duplicate records when two establishments exist. For small construction firms where the workers are dispatched out of a primary home office, the records should be kept where the workers report each day. If records for a construction firm are maintained at the home office, the address and telephone number of the place where records are kept must be available at the construction site, and there must be someone at the home office during normal business hours that can provide information from the records.

The log and the supplementary records are to be kept by the employer for a period of five years after the end of the year to which they pertain. During the five-year period that the records are kept, updating is required for the log. That is, if information changes or if additional information becomes available about a particular injury or illness that occurred in a prior year, the log must be updated. For example, a worker who is injured near the end of the year may not have returned to work by the time the next year begins. When the worker returns to work, the number of lost workdays must be updated in the log.

Annual OSHA Summary Report

Every employer required to keep records must also prepare an annual summary for each establishment. The summary is prepared by totaling the column entries on the log. The log must also be dated and signed.

Incident Reports

It is advisable to examine every incident in which a worker could have been injured or in which material or equipment could have been damaged. Such near misses can serve as wake-up calls for management to change work practices before a serious accident actually occurs. Thus, it is prudent for management to evaluate every such incident and to posit a new approach to accomplishing the work. It is suggested that the incidents be investigated by the crew supervisor or even the job superintendent. Someone more removed from the crew activities than the immediate supervisor may be able to make a better assessment of the nature of the problem and to devise new strategies for doing the tasks. This information can also be useful for developing discussion topics for inclusion in the weekly safety meetings. The report may be a simple one, in which bare essentials are captured. If the form of the report is simple, there may be less reluctance to write up many incidents. Figure 12.3 is an example of a simple report form, in the format of a notepad that can easily fit in one's pocket.

The sample form is simple by design. If it is a constant companion of a supervisor, daily entries may be made on some projects. The philosophy should be that there can always be improvements to existing practices. Where equipment is concerned, it is important always to question the work setting: Is the equipment being used appropriate for the task? Should another piece of equipment be used? Where should the equipment be located relative to the task? How should the equipment be used? Is the equipment properly maintained? And so on. Similar questions should be asked about the material: Is the selection appropriate? Is the material properly placed? Is the material handled properly? Is the process appropriate? Finally, questions should focus on the worker: Has the worker been properly selected? Is the worker properly trained? Is the worker properly positioned? Is the worker properly supervised? More global questions might also be asked as to the merits of performing a particular task in a particular manner.

Documenting the various incidents on a construction site can be the beginning of a very effective feedback mechanism. That mechanism develops when the firm utilizes the information to actually implement changes in the work. The changes may relate directly to the crew that is performing a particular task. The value of the tool is more widespread, however, if the information is also shared with the other workers in the weekly safety meetings. The meetings can help other workers see how tasks can be

Figure 12.3
Example of a Supervisor's Incident Report

Supervisor's Incident Report

Employer: _____

Injury?   ☐ yes   ☐ no *(Also complete an accident report for injuries.)*

Name of worker involved: _____

Craft of worker: _____ Age: _____

Description of work: _____

Date of incident: _____ Time: _____

What happened?_____

_____

_____

_____

Why did it happen?_____

_____

_____

_____

What should be done?_____

_____

_____

_____

performed more safely. In fact, the workers may be helpful as a resource for generating suggestions for performing different tasks more safely.

The full value of the use of incident reports is not realized if there is no attempt to evaluate the merits of implementing the suggested changes. Thus, it is important to conduct follow-up inspections of certain tasks to see if the suggested changes were made and to assess the improvement (if any) in the new approach to performing a task.

Accident Investigation Reports

The form OSHA No. 101 is for recording information that is largely focused on the nature of the injury. It does request information on the work being performed at the time of the injury, but it does not request detailed information. When additional information is desired, an accident report might be more appropriate. More detailed information can be recorded on such forms, as shown in Figure 12.4. Such forms are in wide use by large construction firms that maintain their injury information in databases. The statistical information can then be examined in a variety of ways to identify trends or simply to find out the root causes of most of the injuries sustained by company employees.

It is advisable to investigate every accident, even those in which no injury occurs. The use of an incident report may be considered sufficient for most near misses. If the potential exists for a serious injury to occur, a more detailed investigation may be deemed appropriate. Some firms may include near misses in the category of accidents requiring an investigation. The investigation of all accidents is done primarily to identify the root causes of the incidents. For injury accidents, there may be an additional objective of carefully documenting the particulars of the incident in the event that litigation evolves out of the injury.

Accident investigations should be undertaken with the intent of finding out the facts. The objective is not necessarily to find out on whom to place the blame. If the facts are known, the causes of the accident can generally be identified. Once the causes are identified, they can be eliminated so that further injuries can be averted.

When an accident is investigated, it should be done with full concentration on the facts surrounding the events leading up to the accident. To get those facts, it is important not to allow the scene of the accident to be disturbed before the investigation is complete. Before the scene is disturbed, it would be wise to capture the information on film. A series of photographs may be very helpful in the future. Sketches of the scene, along with detailed measurements, may prove worthwhile. Obviously, the nature of the incident itself will dictate the extent of detail warranted in this area.

An additional source of information is any witnesses to the accident. Because memories tend to quickly forget details of events as time passes, it is important to obtain full statements from all witnesses soon after the accident. It may be most helpful to get witnesses to write down their observations in addition to interviewing them and recording the essence of their comments.

Companies can gain a great deal of information from accident investigation reports. Remember, the objective is to find out why an accident occurred. The information can then be effectively used to prevent future accidents. To be sure that the investigations are conducted in the proper detail and thoroughness, companies should establish

CE & M CONSTRUCTORS, INC. – ACCIDENT INVESTIGATION

1 INJURED'S NAME

2 ACCIDENT DATE:

3 HOME ADDRESS | S S NUMBER | JOB NAME | JOB NUMBER

IMMEDIATE SUPERVISOR | JOB OFFICE ADDRESS

INJURED'S JOB TITLE | COMPANY SERVICE (MOS.- YRS.) | AGE | ACCIDENT INVESTIGATED BY WHOM: | TITLE

4 NAMES AND ADDRESSES OF WITNESSES OR PERSONS WHO CAME UPON THE SCENE IMMEDIATELY FOLLOWING OCCURRENCE OR OTHERS HAVING KNOWLEDGE OF INCIDENT

DESCRIPTION OF ACCIDENT - (THE INJURED WAS (DOING WHAT?), WHEN (WHAT HAPPENED?), HOW & WHY?

INJURED PERSON'S DESCRIPTION OF ACCIDENT

5 INJURY SOURCE (OBJECT OR SOURCE DIRECTLY INFLICTING INJURY) (CIRCLE ONE)

- A FOREIGN BODY
- B GRINDER WHEEL
- C GROUND/FLOOR
- D HAND TOOL
- E MATERIALS
- F SAW BLADE
- G WELDING ARC
- H OTHER (WRITE IN)

8 PERSONAL FACTORS CONTRIBUTING TO THE ACCIDENT INJURY (CIRCLE ONE)

- A ATTITUDE
- B INATTENTIVE
- C LACK OF JOB SKILL OR KNOWLEDGE
- D NOT USING ADEQUATE PROTECTIVE EQUIPMENT
- E PHYSICAL DEFECTS OR CONDITIONS
- F OTHER (WRITE IN)

9 TIME LOST

10 IMMEDIATE TREATMENT AFTER INJURY

FROM ___ TO ___
TOTAL TIME LOST ___ DAYS
HOSPITALIZED
WHERE? | PHYSICIAN'S NAME | HOW LONG?

PLEASE CIRCLE THE APPROPRIATE DESCRIPTIONS

11 BODY PART INJURED	12 TYPE OF INJURY	13 TYPE OF ACCIDENT	14 INJURED'S ACTIVITY (AT THE TIME OF THE ACCIDENT)	15 ACCIDENT SOURCE (OBJECT, SUBSTANCE OR CONDITION THAT CAUSED OR INITIATED THE INCIDENCE IN WHICH THE INJURY OCCURED)
1 ABDOMEN	1 ABRASION	1 STRUCK AGAINST	1 CARRYING (OBJECT)	1 HAND TOOL (NOT POWERED)
2 ANKLE	2 AMPUTATION	2 STRUCK BY	2 CLIMBING	2 HAND TOOL (POWERED)
3 ARM	3 ARC-PIT	3 CAUGHT IN OR BETWEEN	3 DE-BENCHING	3 MATERIAL
4 BACK	4 BURN-CHEMICAL	4 FALL-SAME LEVEL	4 DRIVING	4 MECHANICAL EQUIPMENT
5 BODY (GEN'L)	5 BURN-HEAT	5 FALL-DIFFERENT LEVEL	5 HANDLING MATERIAL	5 STRUCTURE
6 BUTTOCKS	6 CONTUSION/BRUISE	6 SLIP-NOT FALL	6 HOE/DISPLAY	6 LADDER
7 CHEEK	7 DISLOCATION	7 OVER EXERTION	7 LIFTING	7 SCAFFOLD
8 CHEST	8 DERMATITIS	8 STRAIN	8 OPERATING MACHINERY	8 CHEMICAL
9 EAR	9 FRACTURE	9 SPRAIN	9 PULLING	9 CONCRETE
10 ELBOW	10 FOREIGN BODY (EYE)	10 TEMP-EXTREME	10 PUSHING	10 STAIRS
11 EYE	11 HERNIA/RUPTURE	11 ELECTRIC CURRENT	11 RIDING	11 STEPS
12 FACE	12 CUT	12 INHALATION	12 RUNNING	12 PLATFORM
13 FINGER	13 IRRITATION	13 ABSORPTION	13 USING HAND TOOLS	13 FLOOR OR GROUND
14 FOOT	14 LACERATION	14 INGESTION	14 WALKING	14 OTHER
15 FOREHEAD	15 PENETRA-PUNCT	15 ARC-RAY EXPOSURE	15 WELDING/BURNING	
16 GENITALS	16 POISONING	16 TRAFFIC	16 ROUTINE WORK ASSIGNMENT	
17 GROIN	17 SPRAIN-STRAIN	17 IRRITATION		
18 HAND	18 TOE	18 WIND BLOWN OBJECT		
19 HEAD	19 WRIST	19 VEHICLE		
20 HIP	20 OTHER	20 OTHER		
21 KNEE	MULTIPLE			
22 LEG				
23 LUNGS				
24 MOUTH				
25 NECK				
26 NOSE				
27 RIBS				
28 SCALP				
29 SHIN				
30 SHOULDER				
31 SKULL				
32 SPINE				
33 TEETH				
34 THIGH				
35 THROAT				
36 THUMB				

Acc Inv

Figure 12.4
Sample Accident Report Form

PLEASE CIRCLE THE APPROPRIATE UNSAFE ACTION AND/OR CONDITIONS INVOLVED.

16	A — UNSAFE PRACTICES OR ACTS			B — UNSAFE CONDITIONS		19 — RESPONSIBILITY

A — UNSAFE PRACTICES OR ACTS

1	FAILURE TO USE SAFE ATTIRE OR PERSONAL PROTECTIVE EQUIPMENT	20	FAILURE TO USE OR SECURE LADDER	25	UNNECESSARY CLIMBING OR JUMPING
2	USE OF DEFECTIVE TOOLS OR EQUIPMENT	21	INSECURE OR WRONG TYPE HITCH	26	RIDING EQUIPMENT
3	USING HANDS INSTEAD OF TOOLS	22	HANDS BETWEEN SLING AND LOAD	27	FAILURE TO SECURE
4	OPERATING WITHOUT AUTHORITY	23	FAILURE TO OBSERVE KNOWN SAFETY PRECAUTION	28	OTHER (Write In)
5	FAILURE TO SECURE	24	FAILURE TO WARN OR SIGNAL		
6	MAKING SAFETY DEVICES INOPERATIVE	EXPLAIN:			
7	WORKING ON MOVING OR DANGEROUS EQUIPMENT				
8	TAKING UNSAFE POSITION OR POSTURE				
9	OPERATING OR WORKING AT UNSAFE SPEED				
10	UNSAFE LOADING PLACING OR MIXING				

B — UNSAFE CONDITIONS

1	IMPROPER ARRANGEMENT	11	CONGESTION
2	PROCEDURE ETC	12	PROTECTIVE EQUIPMENT NOT PROVIDED OR UNAVAILABLE
3	IMPROPER DRESS OR APPAREL	13	PHYSICAL DEFICIENCY
4	IMPROPERLY GUARDED	14	METHOD OR PROCESS
5	UNGUARDED	15	IMPROPER, INADEQUATE OR NO INSTRUCTIONS
6	DEFECTIVE TOOLS OR EQUIPMENT	16	INHERENT CHARACTERISTICS OF JOB
7	IMPROPERLY MAINTAINED	17	SUPERVISORY FAILURE
8	POOR HOUSEKEEPING	18	RECOGNIZED HAZARD NOT CORRECTED
9	DESIGN OR CONSTRUCTION	19	KNOWN SAFETY RULE NOT ENFORCED
10	SAFETY DEVICE MISSING OR NOT PROVIDED	20	OTHER (Write In)

19 — RESPONSIBILITY

CIRCLE ONE WHICH IS MOST RESPONSIBLE FOR ACCIDENT

1	INJURED EMPLOYEE
2	INHERENT HAZARD OF JOB
3	BAD PRACTICE
4	SUPT. MGMT.
5	OTHER (Write In)

11	HORSEPLAY
12	PLACING TOOLS MATERIALS ETC TO CLOSE TO EDGE
13	STRIKING OR DRIVING TOOLS, MATERIALS OF SAME HARDNESS
14	TOOL REST LOOSE
15	TOOLS TOO FAR FROM WHEEL
16	PLACING HANDS IN UNSAFE POSITION
17	IMPROPER GRIPPING ETC
18	IMPROPER LIFTING AND/OR PLACING ETC
19	FAILURE TO OBSERVE SURROUNDINGS

17 — PREVENTIVE MEASURES

TO PREVENT A REOCCURRENCE OF THIS KIND OF ACCIDENT WHAT HAS BEEN, WILL BE OR SHOULD BE DONE?

| 18 | DATE | SIGNATURE OF INJURED'S IMMEDIATE SUPERVISOR | TITLE |

20 — **ADMINISTRATIVE REVIEW   TO BE FILLED OUT BY JOB SUPERINTENDENT**

DOES THE INJURED PERSON HAVE A HISTORY OF REPEATED ACCIDENTS?   ☐ YES ☐ NO   EXPLAIN

IN YOUR OPINION, COULD THIS ACCIDENT HAVE BEEN PREVENTED BY FOLLOWING KNOWN SAFETY PRACTICES OR PROCEDURES?

WHAT HAS BEEN THE SAFETY PERFORMANCE OF THE INJURED PERSON'S IMMEDIATE SUPERVISOR?   ☐ ABOVE AVERAGE ☐ AVERAGE ☐ BELOW AVERAGE   HAS THIS ACCIDENT BEEN SATISFACTORILY INVESTIGATED?

COMMENTS:

SIGNATURE OF JOB SUPERINTENDENT

EQUIPMENT MATERIAL DAMAGE	MEDICAL COMP COSTS				EXTENT OF INJURED'S RECOVERY FROM DISABLING INJURY
ITEM DAMAGE DESC LOSS	DATE	AMOUNT	DATE	AMOUNT	
1					TEMPORARY DISABILITY
	$				PERMANENT (PARTIAL)
					PERMANENT (TOTAL)
2				TOTAL	FATAL

LEGAL ACTION: GIVE DATE, LOCATION + SETTLEMENT

	$	
3		ATTORNEYS:
	$	COMMENTS:
0 OTHER	$	
T TOTAL (1+2+3+0)	$	DATE CLOSED	SIGNATURE

Acc Inv II

Figure 12.4
Sample Accident Report Form

clearly stated policies regarding the proper procedures. Some training may be appropriate to maximize the effectiveness of the investigations. Most important, the company must act on the information that is gleaned from the investigation reports.

The Level of Reporting in Safety Reports

Safety performance, especially at the project level, can be measured in many ways. The most common measure is injury frequency, which may also be classified according to severity. Thus, the reporting may isolate medical-case injuries from the restricted-work or lost-workday injuries. The use of lost-time injuries as the sole measure of safety performance may be ill-advised. Statistically speaking, lost-time injuries are rare events; at least they should be rare on projects that have a concerted safety program in place. Is a job successful if there are no lost-time injuries? At one time such a job may have been deemed a successful project. Can all the other injuries be ignored? If a project had 90 recordable medical-case injuries and no lost-time injuries, one might be inclined to suspect that perhaps divine intervention kept the project from sustaining a lost-time injury.

Heinrich (1931), one of the earlier researchers on safety, postulated that, for every major injury, there were 29 minor injuries and 300 no-injury accidents. If near misses are related in some way to the minor and serious injuries, it is most prudent for project managers and supervisors to pay attention to the no-injury accidents. It is the minor or no-injury accidents that provide the low-cost warnings of a possible impending injury. If the warnings are taken seriously, the causes of the no-injury accidents can be eliminated before they cause an injury (National Safety Council 1985).

In a construction safety study, deStwolinski (1969) found that operating engineers reported 5 minor accidents for each lost-time accident. For the members of Operating Engineers Local Union No. 3, the participants in the study, the lost-time injury rate was 4.6 injuries per 100 workers or 200,000 hours. Additionally, he found that near misses were encountered by the operating engineers (more than 800 respondents) with the following frequencies:

at least 1 each month	75%
at least 1 each week	20%
at least 1 each day	13%

Because of the large percentage (13%) of operating engineers who reported daily near misses, the total number of near misses that would be encountered each year by the entire responding group is significant. With some very rough calculations, it can be estimated that there are about 1,000 near misses for each lost-time injury. In this study the number of near misses per lost-time injury is greater than that postulated by Heinrich. Nonetheless, the estimates are generally of similar magnitude.

It must be recognized that the number of near misses will probably depend on the type of work being done and the work environment itself. For example, assume two operators are on different projects but both are operating the same type of vibratory compactor. One is compacting fill in a parking lot for a new supermarket under construction. The other is compacting fill on a road-widening project. The operator on the parking lot project may experience no near misses, while the operator on the road-widening project may have several close calls with poor drivers. Even differences in the dust conditions on the compaction projects could make a significant difference in the numbers of near misses experienced.

If the no-injury accidents are carefully tracked, management has a much better opportunity to minimize injuries at the project level. Thus, it is appropriate to focus attention on the smaller events, including near misses and property-damage accidents, and to prepare response actions for such events. Safety performance must be measured carefully; that is, it must go beyond the more serious lost-time injuries or the proper responsibility will not be taken for accident prevention (National Safety Council 1985).

Some firms simply satisfy the OSHA recordkeeping requirements and do little more in terms of paperwork. Their limited record-keeping approach probably stems from the natural aversion that many construction personnel have to paperwork. Other companies may go to the other extreme in the area of safety record keeping. Companies may keep close track of all noncompliance or worker safety violation reports, reports of near misses, first-aid cases, workers' compensation costs per injury or per worker hour of exposure, safety committee tours, mock OSHA inspections, and more. Do the additional reports provide any true value to a firm? According to a study of top management practices, conducted by Levitt (1975), safety performance is directly affected by such record-keeping activities. Figure 12.5 contains the essence of that finding.

Although the differences in injury frequency may appear small, the results do indicate that safer performance is associated with the use of a greater variety of safety measurements. For those measurements to be taken, there must be a mechanism for obtaining the information. That mechanism is best achieved through a formal record-keeping system. The information can serve many purposes. For example, the incentive program may very well be based on measurements other than injury frequency or severity. In fact, different measurements may be appropriate for the incentives established for different personnel on site.

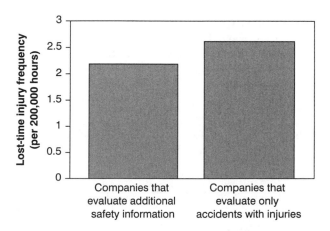

Figure 12.5
Effect of Evaluating Safety by Criteria Other Than the Frequency and Severity of Injuries (Source: Levitt 1975)

Levitt's study examined the level of reporting that was appropriate. He found that better safety performances existed in those firms in which the safety reporting isolated the safety performances of individual projects. Thus, it is not sufficient to know that the safety performance in the company is at an acceptable level, but it must be ascertainable that the safety performance on each company project is acceptable. If a project is found to have safety performance that is not on a par with the other company projects, a greater focus can be placed on that project to try to identify any problem areas. If the statistics from different projects are consolidated into a single report, isolated problem areas on one project may be masked by good performance on other projects.

Final Comments

Record keeping can be regarded as bureacratic drudgery or as a management tool. By law, the OSHA forms certainly must be maintained. It must be remembered that the basis for many management decisions is information. If records are kept of injuries, safety violations, job-site inspections, and other safety data, valuable information may be available with which management can make informed safety-related decisions. In addition to providing a means of documenting information for management decisions, records are also valuable as a means of providing a permanent record of various activities that have taken place. It is often difficult to speculate how a particular historical record might later be used. The ideal use occurs when a manager can make a task safer by having access to specific information.

Review Questions

1. A contractor has hired 30 workers during the past year. The most employed at any one time was 9 workers. Must the contractor comply with OSHA's record-keeping requirements?
2. A worker was stung on the forearm by an unidentified insect while stacking lumber on a project. The worker suffered from localized burning, and his wrist started to swell. The worker was sent to the doctor for fear that the sting might have been that of a poisonous spider. The worker was observed by the doctor, who applied an ointment to the skin to reduce the burning. By the time the worker returned to work, the swelling had subsided, and the stinging sensation was greatly reduced. The worker resumed work. Should the incident be logged as a recordable injury?
3. What are the three broad categories of injuries that are considered recordable?
4. What is a lost-workday case?
5. Are all workers' compensation cases also OSHA recordable cases?
6. What are some differences between the OSHA log and the OSHA No. 101?
7. Must the OSHA forms be utilized, or can an employer customize the forms?
8. When (in relation to the time of occurrence) must the OSHA No. 101 be completed with information concerning a particular injury?
9. How long must the log and the supplementary records be kept by the employer?
10. What is the primary purpose of conducting accident investigations? What is the ultimate measure of whether an accident investigation is successful?

References

de Stwolinski, L. 1969. *A Survey of the Safety Environment of the Construction Industry.* Technical Report no. 114 (October), Construction Institute. Stanford, Calif.: Stanford University.

Fullman, J. 1984. *Construction Safety, Security, and Loss Prevention.* New York: John Wiley.

Goldsmith, D. 1987. *Safety Management in Construction and Industry.* New York: McGraw-Hill.

Heinrich, H. 1931. *Industrial Accident Prevention: A Scientific Approach.* New York: McGraw-Hill.

Levitt, R. 1975. *The Effect of Top Management on Safety in Construction.* Technical Report no. 196 (July), Construction Institute. Stanford, Calif.: Stanford University.

Levitt, R., and N. Samelson. 1993. *Construction Safety Management.* 2d ed. New York: John Wiley.

MacCollum, D. 1995. *Construction Safety Planning.* New York: Van Nostrand Reinhold.

National Safety Council. 1985. *Supervisors Safety Manual.* 6th ed. Chicago: National Safety Council.

Petersen, D. 1988. *Safety Management.* Goshen, N.Y.: Aloray.

Peyton, R., and T. Rubio. 1991. *Construction Safety Practices and Principles.* New York: Van Nostrand Reinhold.

U.S. Department of Labor. Occupational Safety and Health Administration (OSHA). 1986. *A Brief Guide to Recordkeeping Requirements for Occupational Injuries and Illnesses.* OMB no. 1220-0029 (June).

Safety Culture

A   A   8   8   0
Working on a project without establishing a strong safety culture is like holding a "dead man's hand."

The key to a successful safety program is for it to be so broadly based and so universally adopted within a company that every worker on the company's construction projects realizes that all work activities are to be safe ones. The cliché in the industry, "Support for safety must begin at the top," is absolutely correct. That means that the president of the company must give more than lip service to the safety efforts of the company and must be committed to enhancing the company safety efforts whenever possible. The responsibility for safety can never be fully delegated to subordinates in the firm. Perhaps this commitment can occur only when top managers truly believe that good safety performance is not a random occurrence—that is, that safety on construction projects is the calculated result of specific management actions.

Management sets the tone for safety on a project. To a large extent, concern for safety is the natural outgrowth of genuine concern for the well-being of the company's construction workers. Although even a cold, calculating economist can be convinced that there is a financial payback in being safe, a holistic safety culture recognizes the humanitarian aspects of safety as an integral component.

The safety culture on a project is solid when safety is foremost in the minds of all project and company personnel, beginning at the worker level and proceeding all the way to the president and the owner. The safety culture begins at the top, and if it is pure, it will be felt at the level of the workers. Workers must be fully informed about the safety procedures followed within the company. Informing them entails orientation and training. Compliance with safe procedures must be demanded. No worker should be permitted to work in an unsafe manner. It should be every worker's duty to point out unsafe procedures being employed by any other workers on the site. In short, workers should have safety so ingrained in them that they think of only safe ways to perform tasks.

The idea of establishing a safety culture on a project may sound simple, but it may be difficult to implement if all parties are not fully committed to safety. That problem can occur if, for instance, compliance with safety regulations is regarded by cost control personnel as unduly costly or if compliance with safety is viewed as compromising progress on the project schedule. Under such conditions, safety will not be given the priority it deserves. Note that the scenarios pit costs against safety and time against safety. Under those interpretations, it is assumed that it is possible to have one or the other but not both. Establishing a safety culture effectively entails the amalgamation of safety with cost control, with scheduling, with quality control, and so on. In other words, safety is an integral component of every element of the project. Safety is not something that can be isolated from the elements of a project or from the elements of a managerial control strategy. Safety is an inherent element of everything that is done on a project.

In the chapter on safety meetings, a brief description was given of a superintendent who did not hold toolbox safety meetings. He held what he referred to as gang meetings, in which safety became an integral component of every task. There was no need, in that superintendent's eyes, for a separate safety meeting, as safety was incorporated directly and automatically into every planned task. That project is an example of one in which a safety culture is firmly rooted in the core of all project activities. Such a safety culture is worth emulating. The beauty of the program is that there were no safety gimmicks, nor were there any safety rallies; that is, safety was simply regarded as a natural part of getting the job done.

Much has been written about total quality management (TQM) in recent years. Safety is one topic that frequently crops up when TQM is discussed. Traditionally, a successful project was one in which the project was delivered within the budget, within the scheduled time, and with the requisite quality. That is, cost, time, and quality were the sole measures of the success of a project. That was a shortsighted view of success. Other elements can easily be added. Naturally, one would hope that disputes would be kept to a minimum. Communications between the various parties should be clear. Safety must also be a vital component. Although many might contend that a successful project will not have excess disputes or communication problems, they may not see those issues as central to the mission of the company. Safety must be viewed as a driving force in the mission of the company. No project on which a worker has been permanently disabled or killed can be considered a success. The quality must be *total*, and total quality includes the overall safety of every worker on the project.

Safety performance on a project is just as much a measure of the success of that project as are measures related to time, quality, and cost! The goal of having a safe project that is delivered on time, within budget, and with the requisite quality should not be viewed as presenting in any way a conflict of interest. All goals are concurrently achievable. It is indeed rare to find a project that was completed late, went over budget, and had many quality flaws but still received a safety award. Good safety performances are most frequently realized on projects that rate well on all of the noted criteria.

A corporate safety culture that is solid has no room for doubt. Top safety performance must be accepted as an achievable goal. The goals must be set at a high level. It is not sufficient for a company president to find comfort in the fact that the company's safety performance is slightly better than the norm for the industry. Much better performance is achievable, and steps must be taken to attain that goal. Remember, if you set your goals at a low level of performance, you will probably attain that goal. Is that kind of goal one to be proud of? Certainly not.

The commitment to safety must be fixed and unbending. A recent trend has been for companies to establish a safety goal of having zero accidents. Although such a goal was virtually unheard of a decade ago, many companies have now embraced it as their safety objective. Zero accidents is a goal worth pursuing. In setting such a goal, one must truly believe that the company can achieve it. If there is no belief in the goal's being attainable, it surely will not be attainable.

I recently heard of an interesting situation in which a large firm with a strong commitment to safety hired a highly touted safety director from a competitor. The new safety director started work on the very day that a corporate meeting was being held for the firm's project managers, who had flown to the meeting from various parts of the country. The new safety director was asked to address the assembly because the meeting provided such a rare opportunity to address so many company project managers at a single gathering. The speech began with the usual modesty about the credentials that had just been used to introduce the new safety director. He continued by discussing his mission in the company as it pertained to safety. At one point he stated something to this effect: "Well, surely we will have some injuries on our projects, and in some rare instances, possibly a fatality might occur, but with a concerted effort these can be kept to a minimum." Although such language may have been acceptable two or three decades ago, it does not reflect the current thinking about what is truly possible in safety. Such an attitude, when expressed by the company's new kingpin of safety, establishes the assumption that injuries will happen and that we should plan for them. Perhaps, if we plan for injuries, they will happen. Incidentally, the new safety director was looking for a job the next day. Zero injuries are achievable, and that should be every company's goal.

The zero-accident objective is a bold but important move for a construction firm. Adopting that goal constitutes "a significant safety paradigm shift that requires top down commitment for success" (Construction Industry Institute 1995). Success in establishing a zero-accident culture begins with the personal involvement and commitment of top management. Without the committed involvement of top management, the zero-accident goal will be handicapped. On the bright side, several large construction projects have been completed in the past few years with no recordable injuries. Zero accidents is not a nice platitude that is unachievable. Zero accidents is a goal that is achievable, and it is one to be pursued with rigor.

Safety Must Be a Sustained Effort on All Fronts

In the chapters that follow, it will become very apparent that safety is a "people thing." Workers are people who have concerns, desires, ideas, feelings, and a plethora of other emotional needs. Those needs play into the overall picture of safety just as much as do the safety regulations that tell us that boards with protruding nails should not be left strewn about the construction project. Considerable discussion of the roles played by the various parties, from the workers to the president, will provide strong evidence that every party on a construction project has a stake in determining the safety performance ultimately achieved at the project level.

Much of what will be discussed in subsequent chapters addresses issues that seem to relate to the mental well-being of the workers. Many of those issues, at first glance, may not appear to be safety related. Although they may not be safety related, they are injury related. That may appear to be paradox, but the following chapters will clarify the point.

So often we read that 90% of the injuries are caused by worker actions and that 10% are caused by unsafe conditions. Those numbers are not substantiated and really do not mean very much. With a little thought about the occurrence of accidents, it quickly becomes apparent that most accidents are really a combination of physical conditions and worker actions. If workers did absolutely nothing on a construction site, they probably would not get injured unless they happened to be standing or sitting in the path of a vehicle or another type of equipment. Conversely, if a worker were to perform a task without any tools or materials, the likelihood of an accident would also be quite small. Neither scenario makes any sense, as no work is accomplished if activities are not performed and if tools, equipment, or materials are not involved. In short, virtually every accident involves actions and physical conditions. Thus, safety must focus on physical conditions and on the worker who will be performing certain actions.

The focus on safety must address physical conditions and the mental environment provided or created for the worker. That environment can affect the mental acuity of the workers. If the worker is well focused on the work and the surroundings are relatively safe, the chance of an injury is greatly reduced. As will be seen in the following chapters, worker actions are influenced by the workers themselves, the immediate supervisors (foremen), the superintendents, the project managers, and even the top managers. The influence of facility owners and the project designers is also evidenced in project safety performance. Each plays a role in the delicate game of safety. For a project to be safe, each of the parties, from the worker level to the president, must be committed to providing a work environment that is conducive to good safety performance.

There are of course many ways that the safety culture can be established and sustained on a project. One shot in the arm that management can give to worker safety is to include messages about safety in the monthly newsletter. Notes might also be included with the paychecks. One company included the following message to its workers with the paychecks:

Jobsite Safety

Is safety important on our job sites? Are we going to talk safety again? Do we harp too much on safety? We feel that it is impossible to harp too much on safety. That goes for labor and management. We would be at fault if we did not constantly dwell on safety. Safety is part of the work we do. It is the only way we will do our work.

Without safety, we will have accidents and injuries. These are real issues and they can cost us plenty. That cost will be paid in part by you, the workers.

We all know that part of the cost of safety is paid in the form of workers' compensation insurance premiums. There are additional costs, which include safety equipment, lost productivity, additional paperwork, work delays, time-consuming inspections, and all sorts of other costs. Most workers will look at all those costs as being paid for by the employer. WRONG!!! If you doubt this, you should examine your pay stub. Look at the deductions. That is how much was required this week to pay for your share of the medical aid and supplemental pension funds. If you have a friend who works for one of our competitors in the construction industry, you might be very interested to see how your insurance deduction compares. Yours will probably be different. Why? Because the deduction is based on the safety experience and rating of the contractor. Not only do your work practices affect how much we have to pay for workers' compensation; what we have to pay will affect how much you have deducted from your paycheck. You do have control over how safely you work, and now you see that being safe will directly benefit you. So work safely for our mutual benefit.

The notice is brief, but it carries a strong message. The message focuses on the economic benefits of being safe and the way those benefits accrue to the workers and the employer. The message in a subsequent week might focus on safety from an entirely different point of view. Whatever the message, it is always about safety.

Final Comments

Some companies establish an industry reputation for their positive stance on safety. The development of such a reputation is the result of a concerted effort to provide a safe environment for the workers. Such a reputation pays dividends in that workers develop a greater sense of pride when working for a firm that cares about their well-being. That pride is associated with increased worker morale, which is evidenced in greater productivity. By standing for safety, a company benefits in several ways. There are no adverse consequences for taking a proactive approach to safety.

Review Questions

1. Considering top management involvement, explain how the establishment of a safety culture on a project might be influenced by the size of the firm.
2. Discuss how a company with a goal of zero accidents can maintain its safety culture if a serious injury occurs on one of its projects.
3. What makes the zero-accidents concept so unique, especially when compared with safety philosophies of two or three decades ago?
4. Describe ways that top managers can demonstrate their personal support for project safety.

References

Construction Industry Institute. 1995. "Design for Safety: The Zero Accident Culture." *CII News* 8, no. 3, 1.

Levitt, R., and N. Samelson. 1993. *Construction Safety Management.* 2d ed. New York: John Wiley.

Petersen, D. 1988. *Safety Management.* Goshen, N.Y.: Aloray.

Safe Workers

No worker wants to be injured.

For a safety program to be successful, it is important to recognize that every worker is capable of performing the work in a safe manner. Little can be done to screen workers to identify their propensity for being injured. The only exception is drug testing, which is designed to reduce the hiring of workers who may be substance abusers and may therefore work in an unsafe manner and endanger other workers. Other screening methods are just not practical. Although statistics may suggest that injury occurrence is associated with age or other demographic variables, such associations tend to be inconclusive. Other than drug testing, there is no viable mechanism by which unsafe workers can generally be screened. Besides, discrimination in hiring practices (other than for substance abusers) must be avoided.

All workers should be safe workers; they are every company's best resource. For many firms, the workers are the only resource and are worth protecting. All losses due to injuries are to be avoided. The human element plays a major role in safety. Although a company may have a wonderful written safety program and personnel fully versed in the OSHA regulations, the true success of the company's safety efforts is dictated, to a large degree, by how the workers are treated. It is therefore imperative that supervisors and managers recognize workers as individuals. As individuals, the workers have needs. Most of those needs can be satisfied with little difficulty. One must only be sensitive to be able to recognize when these needs are not being satisfied.

New Workers

One of the basic tenets of worker safety is that new workers pose a high safety risk. The term *new* warrants some discussion. The immediate reaction may be to assume that a new worker is one who has not worked previously in the construction industry or who has worked only a short while in a particular trade. That definition is much too narrow for the purposes of addressing worker safety. A new worker is any worker who is new to a particular project. That includes workers who have worked on other jobs undertaken by the same company, and it includes workers who have become very skilled at their craft through many years of service in the construction industry.

Why do new workers warrant so much attention? It must be realized that every worker has some concerns about how things are done on a particular project. Essentially, when a new worker is placed on a project, the worker is immediately faced with numerous unknowns. Those unknowns pose a threat to any worker's ability to stay focused on work tasks. In other words, the unknowns can be a source of stress, and that stress can make a worker more susceptible to being injured. That is why some companies regard new workers as "accidents waiting to happen." Thus, it is imperative, for safety reasons, to quickly dispel many of the sources of stress that the new workers may have in a new work setting. The new worker is especially vulnerable on the first day of work. Although the vulnerability diminishes with time, an increased injury risk is posed during the first few weeks on the job. The increased risk is posed primarily by the numerous distractions that a new worker faces on the first day of work. The distractions theory discussed in Chapter 1 can be used to explain this heightened chance of injury for new workers. It is depicted in Figure 14.1.

Figure 14.1
The Distractions Theory Applied
to a New Construction Worker

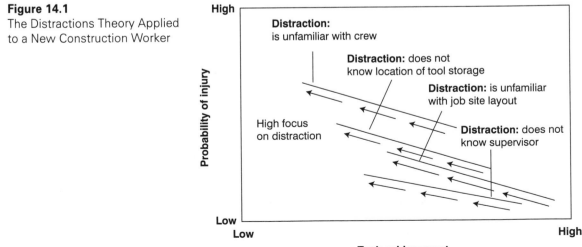

Through an examination of the potential distractions or sources of anxiety that a new worker might have on the first day of work, it quickly becomes apparent that these distractions do not have to exist. With a thorough orientation that includes a walk around the job and introductions to key personnel on the project, several sources of anxiety can be eliminated. The distractions can be further reduced by placing the new worker with a veteran worker. The veteran will then take the new worker under his or her wing and be very watchful of all work activities. As soon as the new worker is unsure how to properly perform any work, the veteran can immediately provide the proper training and instruction. The distractions will effectively be removed before they become a serious problem for the new worker. The aim is to preserve the safety of the new worker until the new worker becomes a more self-sufficient veteran worker.

Thus, the solution is to deal with the unknowns. If the unknowns can be reduced or eliminated, the stress associated with the job is also reduced or possibly eliminated. The unknowns can be addressed quite simply in many circumstances, through an orientation session or a brief training session. Keep in mind that the unknowns about the project are broad. They may relate to such topics as the location of tools and equipment, the identity of the management personnel on the project, and information concerning such matters as starting time, breaks, quitting time, cleanup, drinking water, parking arrangements, personal leave, overtime, car pools, and labor agreements.

The unknowns can be addressed easily in an orientation session. The orientation session should help the new worker become acquainted with all the different topics concerning the job. Of course, it is important also to stress the company position on project safety. Remember, though, that simply introducing a worker to the project manager, project superintendent, and other "company brass" may pay real dividends in worker safety. The main idea is to get the new worker to feel more at home, as that feeling will contribute to the worker's own safety. Some of the general topics to address in the orientation of new workers are the following:

- introduction of key company personnel
- description of general company policies that apply to the project
- description of general and specific safety policies for the project
- orientation to the overall project scope
- orientation to the project schedule in general terms
- orientation to the project layout
- notification of dangerous areas on the work site
- information about any known health hazards on the work site
- clear instructions concerning each work assignment
- introduction of the immediate supervisor

Note that the topics discussed in the orientation are much broader than the standard safety meeting subjects. Also, the orientation does not end after the initial orientation session. Continued training and indoctrination will be needed. As the worker becomes more familiar with the work and the work setting, the need for additional training will diminish, however, the training never fully ceases. As is typical of all construction projects, the physical conditions are in a constant state of change. The entire workforce on the project can be regularly informed on anticipated changes through the weekly safety meetings.

The discussion of safety during the orientation process has to be paramount. It is important that the worker understand the attire required on the project. The policy regarding tools must be explained. Basic rules of safety linked to the OSHA regulations must be carefully explained. Any unique rules that the company has should also be explained at this time. For example, a company may have a policy in which running on the project is forbidden. Workers may also be required to keep their hands on the rails when using stairs or ramps. A company may adopt a large number of such rules, which are designed to help workers to be more safety conscious on the job. The orientation session is an excellent forum and the appropriate time to enlighten the new workers. Workers who receive adequate instructions on safety policies and related matters are involved in fewer accidents.

Whatever is deemed necessary to be discussed with the new workers, it is important to formally establish a standard orientation process. Materials should be prepared to ensure that each and every worker receives all the information that every other worker receives. An informal treatment of such matters may be more appealing to some managers, but some assurance should be provided that every worker receives the same complete body of information.

On large projects the orientation may consist of having several new hires view a series of videos or read specially prepared company safety literature. Perhaps a better approach is to use several different modes of communication. For example, a slide show, a video, a written test, and a personal demonstration of knowledge may provide the variety needed to maintain the interest of the workers. The orientation session is to be regarded as a session at which vital information is imparted to new workers. Thus, it is important that it be presented in an interesting manner.

It would be so simple if an orientation of every new worker were the only thing required to ensure a safe job. There must be some follow-through. What should happen after the worker has been oriented? Can the worker then be treated as a veteran? Such treatment is not advisable, nor is it ever prudent. The worker may very well be assigned to work alongside one of the company's better workers. The role of the companion worker is to continue the on-the-job orientation and to be an immediate contact for the new worker. Others in management are well advised to check in occasionally with the new worker, especially during the first few days on the job. The effort to look out for the worker's well-being should never stop. In a study of more than 600 Navy Seabees, it was found that the Seabees with less than one year of experience in the Navy had nearly twice as many first-aid injuries (Van de Voorde 1991). Thus, the emphasis on new workers must be sustained.

Working with Friends

It is a well-established tenet in the area of productivity that greater performance is obtained when workers are assigned to tasks in which they work alongside their friends. Does the same apply to safety performance? According to a study of road crew workers in Missouri, there is a similar link between worker safety performance and working alongside other workers with whom a long-standing working relationship has been established (Banki 1979).

In Figure 14.2 the benefits of consistency in crew composition are readily apparent. As workers are associated with fellow workers for longer periods of time, they naturally become more familiar with each other. It is not uncommon in such long-standing crews for the members to become friends outside the work environment. In performing job tasks, such workers develop almost a sixth sense about what each of the crew members will be doing. That simplifies job planning and makes the work much safer.

In the road crew study, it was noted that the workers with better safety records were those who stated that their fellow workers got along well. They also felt that they themselves were liked by their fellow crew members. Camaraderie is very important to job satisfaction.

We have all heard of or observed workers with personal problems in work settings. Such workers tend not to be very productive, as they are constantly being distracted by the personal problems that haunt them. Some of their anxieties can be greatly diminished if they are able to discuss the problems. In the road crew study, it was found that workers with better safety records were those who felt they could discuss their personal problems with their fellow workers as opposed to keeping them to themselves.

Workers who work in crews that can be classified as cohesive have better safety records. That is, not only do workers like to work with their friends, but assigning them to work with friends pays dividends in improved safety performance; that is, workers work more safely when working with their friends. The same safe workers commented that the crew members got along well with each other. Familiarity with coworkers undoubtedly removes some of the anxiety that might otherwise exist when working on a project. A worker who works with a stranger will have greater uncertainty about the work procedures that will be employed. When working with a stranger, workers may feel that they have to "look out for their backsides." The added stress caused by the stranger may be reflected in an increase in injury frequency.

Many companies are sensitive to the preference of workers to work with their friends. Those firms make it standard procedure, as much as possible, to keep work teams together from project to project and to permit, as much as possible, the workers to have input concerning their own crew assignments. Many firms have such a policy

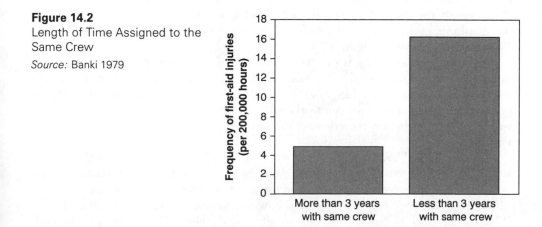

Figure 14.2
Length of Time Assigned to the Same Crew
Source: Banki 1979

for reasons of motivation. It is known that worker productivity is generally higher when workers are assigned to work alongside their own friends. Naturally, such assignments make the task more enjoyable, and the work also tends to be more rewarding. Improved safety is a natural by-product.

Job Satisfaction and Loyalty to the Company

In cold terms, the employee-employer relationship can be viewed as a contract. That is, the employee is expected to expend efforts to accomplish a task or a series of tasks. In return, the employer compensates the employee. If there is no warmth in that association, the relationship with the worker will be viewed as expendable by the employer. Conversely, the relationship with the employer will be viewed as expendable by the employee. If those views accurately reflect an employee-employer relationship, there is little substance to the relationship. In fact, the employee could easily become a part of another employee-employer relationship and vacate or withdraw from the former relationship. That can occur when there is no bond established between the parties.

The quality of the employee-employer relationship is determined to a large degree by the satisfaction that the employee gains from the work environment. That includes the satisfaction the employee derives from the work itself, including the experience of seeing a facility materializing out of the efforts of labor. That satisfaction is intrinsic in that the satisfaction comes from the physical work effort itself. A major component of the satisfaction equation includes the extrinsic satisfaction in the work environment, which is derived largely from the enjoyment received by working with fellow workers and supervisors. Since an eight-hour-a-day commitment to perform work is significant, it stands to reason that workers expect to derive value from the job experience that extends beyond the wages earned.

It is difficult to quantify job satisfaction. There are means by which a clearer sense can be established of the probable satisfaction that a job offers to a worker. One such measure is related to the loyalty that an employee has developed toward the employer. Presumably, a worker who has a stronger desire to stay with a particular employer has a greater loyalty than does a worker who is more willing to leave to pursue employment elsewhere. In the study of workers in road crews, questions were asked about loyalty to the employer, and the responses were compared to the workers' safety experiences. The results are shown in Figure 14.3.

Safer workers are those who have developed a loyalty to the company. Thus, job satisfaction is directly related to the safety performance of workers. The loyal and safe workers also indicated that they would remain with their present employers for longer periods of time than the less safe workers (Banki 1979). The same study showed that workers with better safety records were those who had been with their current employers longer.

The amount of loyalty that a worker has to an employer is associated with the length of time that satisfaction with the employer is sustained. Truly loyal workers are generally those who have been employed by the same company for a number of years. Those longtime workers understand well how the company functions at various levels. What can be done to ensure that such loyalty will develop? The answer may lie with

Figure 14.3
The Safety of Workers and Their Responses to Other Job Opportunities
Source: Banki 1979; Hinze 1981

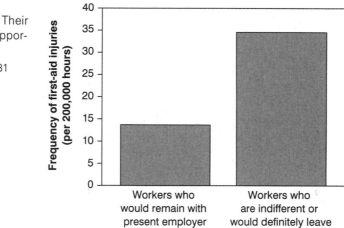

the many levels of management in the company, beginning with the craft foreman and continuing to the company president.

Loyalty of workers to a company may not be the stated mission of a firm. It may be the by-product of what a company does or how a company operates. If loyalty can be nurtured, it should be. Workers who feel a sense of loyalty to a company obviously have a sense of comfort in being employed by the firm. In other words, the loyal workers do not face all the unknowns that new workers must deal with.

Experience in the Industry

Experienced workers tend to have fewer injuries than do less experienced or new workers. Familiarity with a task is good for safety. The definition of experience is not simply the amount of time that a worker has spent developing skills in a trade. For example, it is not enough for a worker to be experienced in a particular craft, but particularly safe workers are those who not only have worked for the same firm for an extended period but also have transferred together from project to project under the same job superintendent or project manager.

The sad truth about the construction industry is that not every company always has a continuing need for every worker that is hired. It would be naive to suggest that, in the name of safety, every construction firm should retain all its employees regardless of the economic circumstances. Suffice it to say that transfers from project to project should be made with the intent of keeping work crews as intact as possible.

Worker Safety and Job Pressures

Construction contracts generally contain three elements associated with the delivery of the facility to be constructed, namely, cost, time, and quality. It is the areas of cost and time that potentially harbor the greatest sources of stress on the construction site. If job costs begin to overrun the budget, profits are lost. If the construction effort starts to get

Figure 14.4
How Often Crews Are Faced
with Deadlines

Source: Banki 1979; Hinze 1981

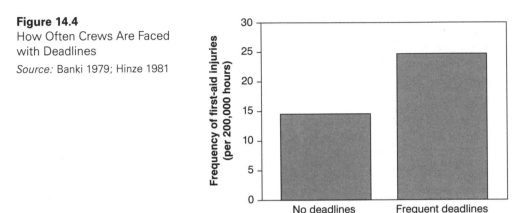

behind schedule, the consequences to the contractor generally include additional costs, which also mean profits are lost. Projects that overrun the budget or run behind schedule are all too common. What are the implications for safety performance when a project runs over budget or behind schedule? Not surprisingly, safety performance can be compromised if the job pressures are unduly harsh on the workers.

The study of road crews included an examination of the effect of job pressures on safety performance. One issue examined was that of deadlines (see Figure 14.4). Workers often do not perform safely when faced with deadlines. The deadlines are often ones over which management has some control. Simply pushing for production may not be beneficial to the company or the individual workers; the adverse effect on safety is readily apparent.

Pressure placed on workers becomes a job distraction, which may ultimately result in an injury. Note that pressures of all types have the same effect. Of primary interest is the reduction or elimination of pressures that are generated on the construction site. Pressures may be imposed on a crew by disclosure of the estimated or budgeted costs for performing certain work. The pressure is even greater when the workers are asked to meet budgets that have been specifically altered "for the field."

Figure 14.5
How Often Crews Compete
with Each Other

Source: Banki 1979; Hinze 1981

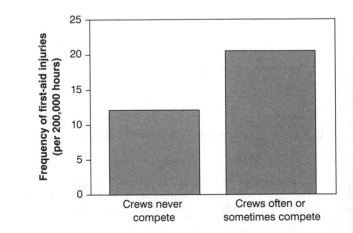

Competition between crews may also be a source of pressure. Sometimes management may even try to set tasks up so that crews are put into competition with each other. That practice, too, may have dire consequences (see Figure 14.5).

Treating Workers with Respect

Except for the type of work that they do, construction workers are essentially no different from any other people. They have egos, feelings, and personal needs like everyone else. It is important that this be remembered. As already stated, workers are to be viewed as a valuable resource. Workers provide a valuable service through their manual efforts, but their potential contribution to the job site goes well beyond manual labor. Construction work is often complex, and it is ever changing. Thus, it is important to continually reassess the methods of performing various tasks.

Job supervisors need not tackle project planning alone. The workers themselves can be a very valuable resource for new ideas. The workers, directly involved in the work, often see viable solutions to construction problems. Their ideas should be tapped. How do workers respond to having their ideas sought? Like anyone else, they obtain a greater sense of self-worth and self-esteem. Does the practice of considering workers' ideas have anything to do with safety? In the road crew study, it certainly did (see Figure 14.6).

Workers who had their ideas solicited and given serious consideration by supervisors and managers had better safety records. By giving thoughtful consideration to the ideas offered by workers, managers give workers the message that they are viewed as team members. That type of feedback is important in any job setting (Goldsmith 1987). It is particularly important in construction, where problems seem to constantly present themselves.

The issue of ego is an important one to people. Workers like to feel good about themselves. Workers know when they have done a good day's work. They derive satisfaction from seeing the results of their labor. It requires only a small effort for management to complement that satisfaction with specific laudatory comments. Positive rein-

Figure 14.6
How Often the Good Ideas of Workers Are Given Serious Consideration
Source: Banki 1979; Hinze 1981

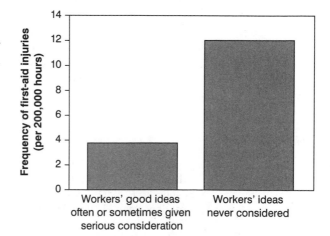

forcement is one of the central themes of many motivational programs. The best part about it is that it can be given at a minimal expenditure. A pat on the back can pay marvelous dividends in the goodwill it generates. If workers earn praise, they should receive it.

It is important that workers feel good about their work. If they do not, the consequences typically include reduced productivity. Reduced productivity is associated with a reduction in worker morale, which is not good for overall safety performance. In the Seabee study mentioned earlier, it was found that the Seabees with lower morale in their jobs also had 70% more injuries (Van de Voorde 1991).

Final Comments

Workers are the most important resource on construction projects. It is logical then to pay particular attention to their safety and welfare. Much of the research on worker safety suggests that worker safety can be improved simply by treating workers with respect. That means that workers are to be viewed as individuals. Each worker is unique, and each can contribute to a project in a special way. An effective supervisor or manager will utilize those singular traits.

Review Questions

1. Which workers are particularly vulnerable to injuries?
2. How can the association that a worker has with fellow crew members influence safety performance?
3. How can the leadership style of a supervisor influence safety performance?
4. What evidence suggests that worker satisfaction may be closely linked to safety performance?
5. Why is worker orientation so important, and why should worker orientation be standardized, at least to some extent?
6. What issues should be addressed in worker orientation? What kind of follow-up should take place after new workers have been oriented?
7. How can loyalty to an employer be encouraged?
8. What kind of pressures might be imposed on construction workers on the job?
9. Other than knowing that safety performance will probably be improved, why should supervisors use participative management and positive reinforcement?
10. Describe distractions that workers might encounter on the job site that are innate to the project.

References

Banki, M. 1979. "The Relationship between the Mental Environment of Workers and the Incidence of Injuries." Ph.D. diss., University of Missouri.

de Stwolinski, L. 1969. *A Survey of the Safety Environment of the Construction Industry*. Technical Report no. 114 (October), Construction Institute. Stanford, Calif.: Stanford University.

Goldsmith, D. 1987. *Safety Management in Construction and Industry.* New York: McGraw-Hill.

Hinze, J. 1978a. "Turnover, New Workers, and Safety." *Journal of the Construction Division, ASCE* 104, no. 4, 409–17.

———. 1978b. "Worker Turnover and Job Safety." *National Utility Contractor* 2, no. 1, 17.

———. 1981. "Human Aspects of Construction Safety." *Journal of the Construction Division, ASCE* 107, no. 1, 61–72.

———. 1990. "Addressing the Unique Needs of Newly Hired Workers." *EXCEL, A Quarterly Newsletter of the Center for Excellence in Construction Safety* 3, no. 3, 3–4.

Levitt, R., and N. Samelson. 1993. *Construction Safety Management.* 2d ed. New York: John Wiley.

Van de Voorde, J. 1991. "Work-Related Injury Frequency Rates in the Navy Seabees." Unpublished Master's research report, University of Washington.

Safety and First-Line Supervisors (Foremen)

If you think injuries are just a part of the job, they will be.

First-line supervisors in the construction industry, more commonly called foremen, play a very key role in the construction process. It is under the guidance of the foremen that facilities are transformed from construction drawings to physical facilities. The foremen, who often also work with their tools, are the primary link between management and the labor force.

Foremen play perhaps the most important role in establishing and maintaining worker safety on the job. It is the foremen who plan out the daily activities of their crews. It is the foremen who are initially contacted when something goes wrong. It is the foremen who must decide how to rearrange job assignments when required equipment for a task is not available or when unannounced worker absences occur. In short, the workday of most workers begins, continues, and ends with communications with the foreman. With such frequent contact, it is clear that the influence of the foreman on a worker is not trivial. Certainly the influence that foremen have on the safety performance of their crews is not trivial.

With the strong role played by foremen, it is clear why many companies have special training sessions set up for their foremen. The sessions are designed to streamline the learning process for foremen and to make them better leaders. The leadership style of foremen in particular is often crucial in setting the tone for safety in a crew.

Foremen and New Workers

The relationship between a foreman and a worker begins when the worker is first assigned to the foreman. That is also when the foreman's role in worker safety begins. Regardless of the amount of experience that the worker has, the worker is considered a new worker. Therefore, some orientation must be provided for the worker. If the worker is new to the company, the orientation may consist of a few hours of watching films, reading literature, attending lectures, and taking quizzes. If the worker is familiar with the company but is new to the foreman, the orientation is typically different. The primary emphasis of the orientation for such a worker is on acquainting the worker with the foreman, the crew, the tasks to be performed in the near future, the general layout of the project, any unique procedures or policies that apply to the work, and the job-site safety policies to be followed. Regardless of the type of new worker, the goal is to quickly make the worker feel comfortable in the new work setting.

There are differing approaches to the treatment of new workers. In a study of 30 pipefitter foremen on a nuclear construction project (McMeel 1979), it was found that differences in the treatment of new workers are often associated with differing safety performances (see Figure 15.1).

The results of the study concerning new workers were interesting. Since the study was conducted on a single project, the general nature of the orientation provided was very similar for the different foremen. Although the safety performances of the foremen's crews were affected by the orientation itself, what had the greatest impact on safety was what the foremen did with the new workers after the orientation.

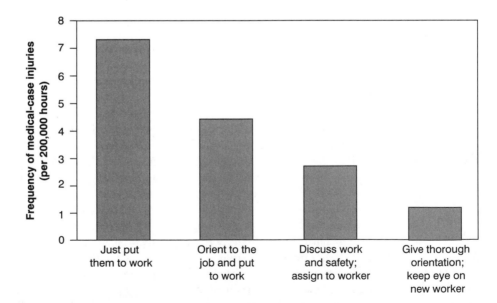

Figure 15.1
What Foremen Do with New Hires on Their First Day
Source: McMeel 1979

From the information in Figure 15.1, it is clear that it is not prudent to simply put the worker to work. The orientation procedure is important. The thoroughness of the orientation is reflected in the safety performance. It is also not sufficient to regard the orientation as adequate to bring the new worker up to speed. There must be some follow-through. One successful approach is to assign the new worker to an experienced worker. The experienced worker will, possibly without consciously knowing it, continue to provide valuable orientation information concerning the work being performed and the project in general. The foremen with the best safety records were those who personally continued to have a watchful eye on the new worker. They would be available to the new worker to answer questions and, in general, to be assured that the new worker was adjusting well to the job (McMeel 1979).

Other studies have also given some insights into the influence of the orientation process on safety performance. Safer records have been noted among foremen who take a personal interest in the new workers. A foreman can demonstrate that personal interest in a variety of ways, including asking the new workers about their experiences in the trade, their previous projects, and their personal lives (marital status, home location, number of children, hobbies, etc.). Some foremen make it a point not to treat safety as a separate issue. They integrate safety into the discussion of the work being done and do not isolate safety. As in the prior study, foremen should pay more attention to the new workers during their first few days on the job (Samelson 1977). The first few days that a worker is on a project are crucial to safety. The foreman plays a vital role in this area.

Considering Motivational Approaches

Construction workers with any experience have been on many different projects. Much learning accompanied the exposure that the workers had on those many projects. A foreman is wise to try to utilize the knowledge that the crew members have acquired through the years. Many situations arise in which a fixed answer does not exist. They require some ingenuity. The best way to maximize the opportunities for resolving the problem is to ask the crew members to offer suggestions. That practice pays off very nicely when the workers realize that their ideas and suggestions are given serious consideration and that some of the ideas are actually put to use. It boosts the self-esteem of the workers, and they feel like members of a team. Such an environment is conducive to good safety performance.

One of the most cost-effective and inexpensive management tools available to virtually any manager is positive reinforcement. A pat on the back or a "Way to go!" will go a long way toward job satisfaction. Research studies have also shown that recognition of workers for tasks well done is related to better safety performance. It is important for first-line supervisors to be familiar with the tasks being performed by the workers under their supervision. When those tasks are performed particularly well, it is important that the accomplishment be properly acknowledged. Workers feel better about themselves when they are praised for doing their jobs well, and they will try to meet or to surpass these accomplishments in the future.

Job Pressures

The relationship of job pressures to safety performance was introduced in Chapter 14. Supervisors are often accused of imposing pressure on workers by setting deadlines for them to meet. Instituting competition between crews can also be a source of pressure. Although many workers may never see the actual cost reports on the work they are performing, the first-line supervisors are in a position to convey the essential information to the workers. Some supervisors are tempted to modify the estimates to give workers a harder goal to pursue. Their intent is to make the workers feel that their performance levels are below average, and they hope that this realization will have a good motivating influence on the workers. If the adjusted goal is unduly harsh, the result may be a greater number of injuries as the workers are stressed and distracted by the imposed pressure. This effect is illustrated in Figure 15.2, which presents findings from a study of foremen in the roofing industry (Hymel 1993).

It might appear appropriate for foremen to share information about the time allocated for a particular activity. It would give the workers a goal to try to achieve. But what if the estimated time is in error? The workers will then be trying to accomplish the task in a time frame that is not realistic. That will frustrate the workers, as they, like all of us, want to achieve their objectives.

Stress can be generated by pressures imposed on workers, but the pressure may not always be generated on the job; that is, the pressure that causes stress for a worker may not be job related. For example, a worker may be worried about a personal or family problem that weighs heavily on his or her mind. Such a worker carries to the job considerable "mental baggage," which might impair work performance. Such pressures are the most difficult to deal with, as worker behavior must be quite noticeably affected before it becomes apparent to other workers or supervisors. If the behavior of a worker is of concern to the foreman, it is appropriate to have a meaningful discussion with the worker. Sometimes it is important for a person to be able to discuss a problem. Although the supervisor cannot be expected to provide a solution for the troubled

Figure 15.2
Foremen Provide Crews with
Scheduled Durations for Work
Tasks

Source: Hymel 1993

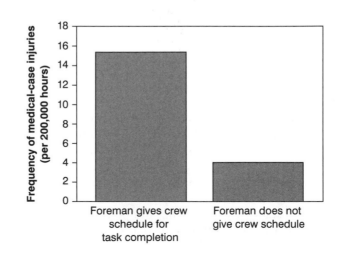

worker, being able to talk to someone about the problem may be a major step for the worker toward resolving it.

Managerial or Supervisory Style

Most foremen are workers who still work with their tools to some extent. On some types of work it may not be practical for the foreman to do so. However, even a foreman who does not work with the tools on a project has the skills to do so. Thus, most foremen have advanced to their supervisory status by demonstrating their skills in the trades. How do workers learn skills useful in becoming foremen? For most foremen, there is no formal training. In most cases, workers attempt to emulate the styles of leadership exhibited by foremen they have admired and with whom they have had a pleasant working association.

The primary function of a foreman is to provide guidance to workers. An effective foreman is one who carefully outlines tasks for a crew in such a manner that all workers in the crew have a clear idea of the scope of all the individual task assignments. At times, some workers undertake tasks that only they are expected to perform. At other times, two or more crew members are required to accomplish a single task. If the work is properly organized, no worker will ever be idle for any extended period for lack of something to do.

Do supervisory styles affect safety? There is a direct relationship in many instances between supervisory approaches and safety performance. A study of more than 600 Navy Seabees (Van de Voorde 1991) provided some interesting information on this subject (see Figure 15.3). Good supervisory skills entail a broad spectrum of traits. In the Seabee study they were defined to include such leadership traits as (1) setting a good example on and off the job, (2) praising workers when they have performed a job well, (3) helping workers who have personal problems, (4) showing respect for the workers, (5) considering the ideas offered by workers, and (6) possessing the skills required to motivate workers.

Figure 15.3

How Well the Foreman Exhibits Strong Leadership Skills

Source: Van de Voorde 1991

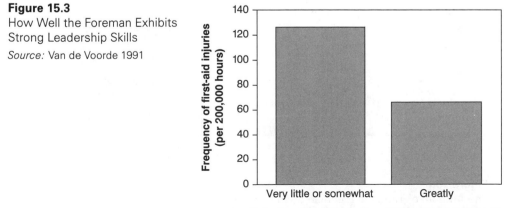

Being a good foremen often means being available. Workers may encounter an unusual situation, or they may become confused about a particular aspect of a task undertaken. A tool may malfunction, bringing the work suddenly to a halt. The construction materials to be installed may be found to be defective. The conditions at the job site may be different from those shown on the drawings. Without proper guidance or direction, the work may cease for an extended time. A good foreman is one who can quickly sense the need to intervene and then tries to assess the problem. Even if the problem cannot be resolved immediately, a good foreman will be able to quickly reassign workers so that they can be productive at some other task while the problem is being resolved.

To address the numerous situations that may arise during the course of a normal workday, it is important for the foreman to be accessible to the crew members on short notice. Accessibility essentially means that the foreman must be near the workers. As shown in Figure 15.4, the foreman's accessibility is associated with good safety performance. The sources of stress that accompany sudden changes in the work can cause distractions that make workers more susceptible to being injured. By being available to the workers, foremen can more quickly dispel the associated job anxieties (McMeel 1979; Hymel 1993).

As mentioned earlier, better safety performance is realized when undue job pressures are not imposed on the workers (see Figure 15.2). What if workers are assigned to perform a task and the work is not accomplished in the allotted time? What is the

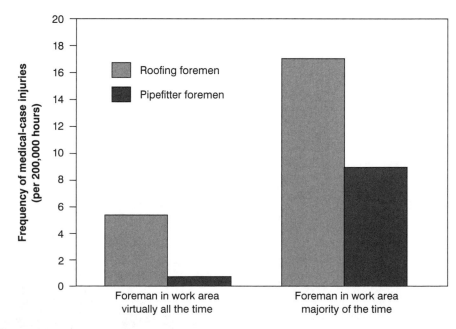

Figure 15.4
The Amount of Time the Foreman Spends in the Work Area
Source: Hymel 1993; McMeel 1979

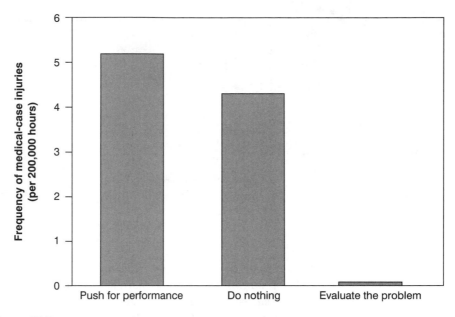

Figure 15.5
The Foreman's Response When the Schedule Is Not Met
Source: McMeel 1979

proper managerial approach? A hint is available from an examination of the information gleaned from the pipefitter study, as shown in Figure 15.5. Note from these results that doing nothing is only slightly better than confronting the workers with the poor performance and pushing for increased performance. The best approach is not to take it out on the workers but rather to be more analytical about the reasons for the failure to complete the task in the estimated time. That last approach does not involve the assumption that someone is at fault (McMeel 1979).

If performance does not meet expectations, it is best, from the standpoint of safety, to be introspective about the reasons for the shortcoming in performance. That approach does not put the workers and the foreman in an adversarial relationship. It serves little purpose to place blame on the workers. The fault may have been in the estimate of the time needed to perform the task. The instructions may not have been clear. At any rate, the foreman should try to find an answer. Ranting and raving about the problem will not help. In fact, a display of anger in front of the crew will demonstrate a lack of self-control, which may ultimately compromise the foreman's ability to properly lead the workers (Samelson 1977).

Safety and Project Constraints

There are some aspects of the project over which the foremen have little or no control. The type of work may directly affect safety performance. For example, from Figure 15.4 it is apparent that the roofers had a higher injury frequency than did the pipefitters.

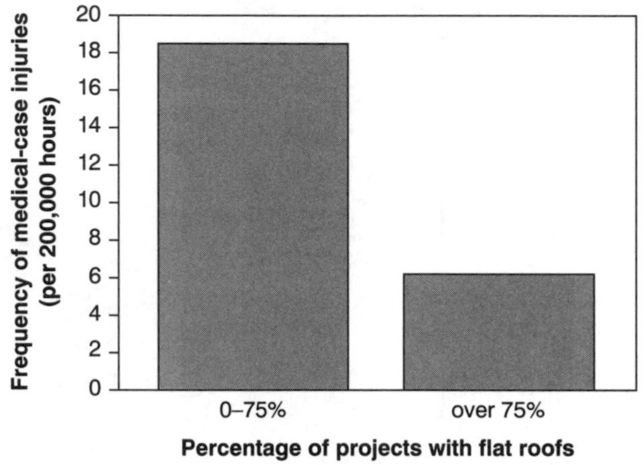

Figure 15.6
Percentage of Projects with Flat
Roofs
Source: Hymel 1993

Percentage of projects with flat roofs

Figure 15.6 is an illustration of the safety effects of a particular aspect of roofing work. Although roofing is known be one of the more hazardous types of work in the construction industry, the risk varies with the type of roof. From the results, it is readily apparent that flat roofs, which offer better footing for workers, are associated with fewer injuries than are pitched roofs.

Despite the difference between the frequencies of injuries sustained by crews on pitched roofs and those on flat roofs, the injury frequencies for both are still quite high. Foremen can do little to change the types of roofs on which they will work, but they can be cognizant of the unique dangers associated with each type of roof. As mentioned, pitched roofs offer the constant threat of a fall. This is an environment in which fall protection is especially important. On flat roofs, the fall protection is generally adequate if the perimeter of the building receiving the roofing is protected, as with guardrails or high parapets. On flat roofs, more injuries are likely to occur from the substances that are being applied. For example, built-up roofing is adhered to the roof with a hot asphalt compound. The material itself can be a hazard. In the summer months, the added heat from the roofing materials may contribute to heat exhaustion. Even roofing materials that are applied cold may emit vapors that can be harmful, or they may be caustic if they come into direct contact with the skin. Foremen on any type of roof must be aware of the potential inherent hazards.

Another concern over which a foreman may be able to exert little control is crew size. Some labor agreements establish the maximum crew size before another foreman must be hired. Does crew size have any implications for safety performance? Based on the road crew study, Figure 15.7 contains some interesting information in this regard (Banki 1979). Why should crew size have any influence on safety performance? The answer may lie in the leadership and managerial issues that have already been discussed. If foremen have larger crews, they cannot devote as much attention to each worker. Their influence is more diffused. Also, with more workers to organize, the foreman finds it more difficult to pay as much personal attention to each worker. In addition, the foreman does not get to know the workers as well as would be possible in a smaller crew.

Figure 15.7
The Typical Size of a Foreman's Crew

Source: Banki 1979

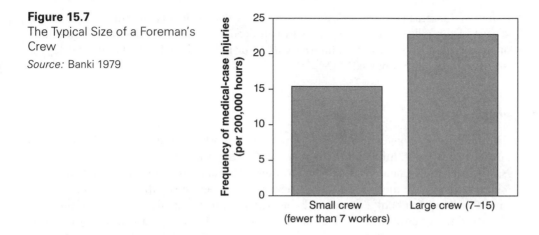

The issue of control has already been mentioned as a factor that may be conductive to safety. How effective can a supervisor be if many workers are to be organized? Control is obviously more difficult when crews get large. As crew size increases, safety performance may suffer. The information in Figure 15.8 shows that safety performance is considerably better or improved when the worker-supervisor ratio is less than 2.7. A supervisor with a small crew can more effectively keep tabs on every worker. If crews get too large (some as large as 15 were noted), the foreman can no longer give attention to the work of all workers in the crew. Some workers have to be self-starters. This situation is not good for safety.

A Good Attitude about Safety

Foremen must recognize that they do play a vital role in the area of safety. They must accept the responsibility that goes with that role. They must have a commitment to

Figure 15.8
Safety Performance and the Worker-Supervisor Ratio

Source: Reed and Hinze 1986

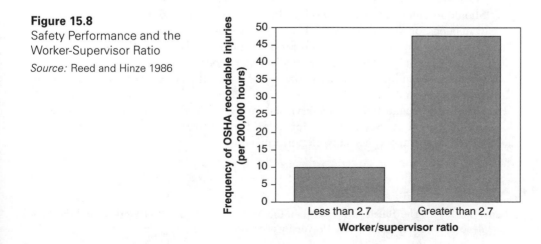

safety. If a foreman has the attitude or perception that accidents and injuries are simply a part of the job, accidents and injuries will occur in greater numbers. The safe foremen are those who realize that injuries will occur if they do not take the proper steps to prevent them (de Stwolinski 1969).

Final Comments

Foremen have an ongoing relationship with their workers, so it is reasonable that they are instrumental in influencing their safety. The foremen play a pivotal role in worker safety. A good foreman motivates the crew members and provides the necessary leadership to accomplish the work. Workers have a basic need to see their efforts materialize into the components of a completed construction project. Thus, the goals of the foremen and the goals of their workers are the same. The foremen must provide the necessary guidance to ensure that the work is delivered, with safety as the foremost objective. The task is not insurmountable, because the very forces that make for a safe work crew also make the efforts of a crew productive and profitable.

Review Questions

1. Describe an approach a foremen should consider when starting out a new worker in the crew.
2. What motivational techniques, traditionally associated with improved productivity, have also been noted to improve safety performance?
3. Describe different ways in which a foreman can actually be the cause of pressures on workers that result in personal stress.
4. Discuss the role the foreman can play in reducing anxieties that are created by the job environment.
5. What can a foreman do if a worker feels pressured by events that are not part of the project?
6. What kind of leadership qualities should a foreman possess?
7. Should foremen remove themselves from the work area so as not to be viewed as watchdogs, or should they stay close to the workers?
8. What is an appropriate approach for a foreman to take when the performance of the crew is not as high as was originally anticipated?
9. Describe the influence that crew size may have on the effectiveness of a foreman in productivity and safety.
10. It has been suggested that supervisors with good leadership skills facilitate work accomplishment. Such facilitation is said to motivate workers. Explain how it might also be good for safe work performance.

References

Banki, M. 1979. "The Relationship between the Mental Environment of Workers and the Incidence of Injuries." Ph.D. diss., University of Missouri.

de Stwolinski, L. 1969. *A Survey of the Safety Environment of the Construction Industry.* Technical Report no. 114 (October), Construction Institute. Stanford, Calif.: Stanford University.

Hinze, J. 1978a. "Turnover, New Workers, and Safety." *Journal of the Construction Division, ASCE* 104, no. 4, 409–17.

———. 1978b. "Worker Turnover and Job Safety." *National Utility Contractor* 2, no. 1, 17.

———. 1981. "Human Aspects of Construction Safety." *Journal of the Construction Division, ASCE* 107, no. 1, 61–72.

———. 1990. "Addressing the Unique Needs of Newly Hired Workers." *EXCEL, A Quarterly Newsletter of the Center for Excellence in Construction Safety* 3, no. 3, 3–4.

Hymel, R. 1993. "A Research Study on the Effects of Foremen on Safety in Construction." Unpublished Master's report, University of Washington.

Levitt, R., and N. Samelson. 1993. *Construction Safety Management.* 2d ed. New York: John Wiley.

McMeel, K. 1979. "The Effect of Foremen on Safety on Super Projects." Unpublished Master's report, University of Missouri.

Reed, D., and J. Hinze. 1986. "A Study of Construction Safety in Washington State, USA." Paper read at IABSE Symposium, Tokyo, September.

Samelson, N. 1977. *The Effect of Foremen on Safety in Construction.* Technical Report no. 219, Construction Institute. Stanford, Calif.: Stanford University.

Van de Voorde, J. 1991. "Work-Related Injury Frequency Rates in the Navy Seabees." Unpublished Master's research report, University of Washington.

Safety and Middle Managers (Superintendents)

If you cut enough corners, you may eventually have a hole to fall into.

The term *middle manager* should be defined, since the use of the term is not universal in the construction industry. The definition applied here is that middle managers are the top company personnel at the project level who are resident at the site of the construction project. In construction, the title of a person in such a position will rarely be "middle manager," and the role may change with the size or organization of the company or the project. For example, on a small building project, the middle manager is usually the job superintendent, with the project manager for the project working out of the home office and having responsibility for several projects. On a large highway project, middle management may include the project manager, the project engineer, and the project superintendent, positions held by individuals who are assigned to the project and are resident at the job site.

Despite the variability in the use of the term *middle manager,* in most instances it refers to the superintendent. Although middle management often includes several company employees at the project level, the term *superintendent* will be used for convenience in this discussion. Almost all projects have superintendents assigned to them, so this is a convenient way to use the term. It must be remembered that, on larger projects especially, the term includes several company employees at the project level.

Although the role of first-line supervisors is crucial in achieving safe performance at the crew level, superintendents play an equally important role in achieving safe performance at the project level. The foremen and the superintendent can assist each other.

It must be recognized that the size of the project has an influence on the best way for a superintendent to affect safety performance. In general, the small projects (those with fewer than 25 workers) are often safer when a family environment is established. On larger projects, it is important for the superintendent to address safety in a more formal fashion. Some of the characteristics of superintendents that have been found to influence safety performance will be discussed.

Superintendents and New Workers

Regardless of the level of management, the issue of new workers must be addressed for the manager to stay in control of safety. New workers constitute the group most likely to be involved in accidents. Superintendents who recognize new workers as having unique problems and needs can do much to keep their projects accident-free.

Perhaps the first step for superintendents to take is to try to keep the number of new workers at a minimum. Although all workers who are new to a project might legitimately be called "new," workers who have a familiarity with and have worked in the past with a particular superintendent have a reduced risk of being injured. That has been shown in past research studies in construction. The results of studies conducted on projects in the San Francisco Bay Area and on the Gulf Coast are shown in Figure 16.1.

Superintendents who are able to transfer more of their workers with them from project to project have a considerable advantage in maintaining a safer project (Hinze 1978a). Keeping the same workers from project to project results in safer performance. Such workers already "know the drill." With a large number of familiar workers on the project, the superintendent has less difficulty in establishing the safety culture on the job. With many veteran workers on the job, the number of new workers is also significantly reduced. Both factors are good for safety.

Of course, it is unrealistic to expect all workers to be transferred from project to project with a given superintendent. Some new hires will be required. How should the superintendent relate to the new workers? Past research results offer suggestions concerning the superintendent and new workers (see Figure 16.2). The superintendents with better safety records on their projects are those who take a personal interest in the new workers and are personally involved in their job orientation.

A superintendent's involvement with the new workers may consist of a simple introduction and an informal conversation. The objective is to humanize the project. It is accomplished when new workers are quickly assimilated into the project team. The superintendent is the leader of the project team. Personal contact with the superintendent helps new workers feel more comfortable in the new work setting. The superintendents with the better safety records also verify that the foremen on the project give the new workers a good orientation to safety and that they pay closer attention to the new workers during their first few days on the project. Once the project layout and the project staffing are understood by the new workers, they can begin to efficiently address the tasks to be performed. With the project unknowns reduced, in part through

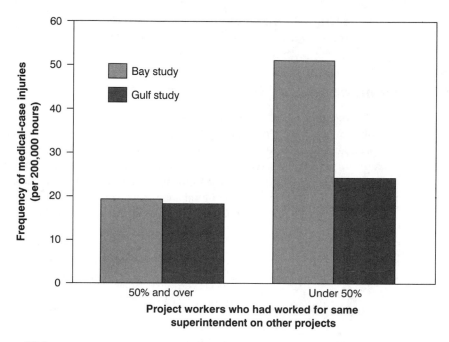

Figure 16.1
The Number of Project Workers Who Worked for the Superintendent on Other Projects
Source: Hinze 1976

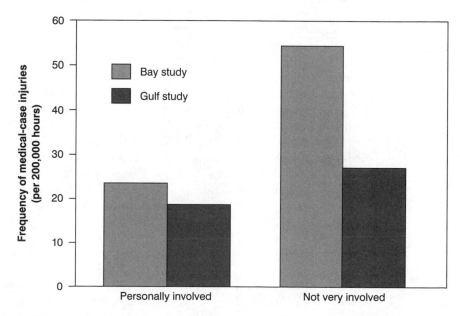

Figure 16.2
The Extent of the Superintendent's Involvement with New Workers
Source: Hinze 1976; Hinze 1978a

the efforts of the superintendent, the new workers are more comfortable in their work environment, and they work more safely (Hinze 1978a).

Safer Superintendents Are Good Managers

Among the characteristics that superintendents must possess to have good safety performance on their projects is being good managers. A good manager is a leader, a planner, an organizer, and a good role model for others. As such, a good manager is sensitive to the personal needs and feelings of workers. It is also incumbent on the superintendent to keep close contact with job-site activities so that a clear understanding is maintained about job progress. Good managers can quickly assess or identify problems before they become critical. They can also quickly relate to the problems that others may encounter on the project.

Poor managers, on the other hand, often have poorer safety records. They tend to be autocratic, dogmatic, insensitive, manipulative, and aloof. Because of their style of managing, or their failure to manage at all, such superintendents are sometimes typified by running around "like chickens with their heads cut off" or by being so busy "fighting fires" that they have no time to even plan any activities.

Quantifying the managerial characteristics of superintendents tends to be a subjective matter. It is the results of their efforts, rather than an assessment of their managerial styles, that can be quantified in objective terms. Despite this apparent problem, the managerial characteristics of superintendents were examined in one study (Hinze 1987). The method by which they were examined was quite simple.

First I interviewed 35 different superintendents. I then described each superintendent in general terms by writing down those characteristics of each superintendent that stood out in my mind. This was done without any knowledge about the past safety performance of the superintendents. Another researcher examined my descriptions and noted whether each characteristic or behavioral approach was indicative of a good manager or a poor manager. This procedure resulted in a tally of good and bad traits for the superintendents. For each good trait a positive point was recorded, and for each poor trait a negative point was recorded. This process resulted in scores ranging from –10 to +12.

After the scores had been calculated, information was obtained on the past safety performances of the superintendents. The sample was split essentially into two "halves" (one with 17 and one with 18). The group with the better safety records was referred to as the superintendents with the good safety records. The other group was referred to as the superintendents with the poor safety records. The designations *good* and *poor* are relative terms only and are applicable only to the extent just described. The results are shown in Figure 16.3.

From the figure, it is apparent that all superintendents with high or excellent ratings on managerial qualities had good safety performances. Not one superintendent with a poor safety record was evaluated as possessing excellent managerial qualities. In general, superintendents with excellent management skills do not have poor safety records, and superintendents with poor management skills rarely have good safety records. To a considerable extent, poor managers have higher injury frequencies on their projects than do good managers (Hinze 1987).

Personnel management is an important component of the responsibilities of superintendents. Superintendents must remember that every worker on a project has a personal life and that each worker has feelings, needs, and concerns that should not be ignored by management. Superintendents should be sensitive to such personal needs when dealing with the various project personnel (Hinze and Gordon 1979). The influence of that sensitivity on safety performance has been demonstrated through the results of construction safety studies (see Figure 16.4).

How can a superintendent demonstrate sensitivity or flexibility in addressing personnel problems? An example can help illustrate the use of these terms. Suppose a worker has worked on a few projects with the superintendent. The superintendent then promotes the worker to foreman on a particularly complicated task. The new foreman does not appear to be able to handle the task. What should the superintendent do? Some superintendents have said, "If I promote a worker to foreman, that decision becomes my responsibility. I have a stake in the decision and I must work it out." With that attitude, the superintendent will try to work with the new foreman and provide assistance until the task is under control. The superintendent might also decide to shift the foreman to another task, realizing that the initial assignment should not have been made on such complicated work. Another approach might be not to make the foreman fully responsible for the task until it is clearly under control.

What would constitute a less sensitive approach? Certainly an insensitive approach would be simply to dismiss the foreman. Another approach might be to demote the

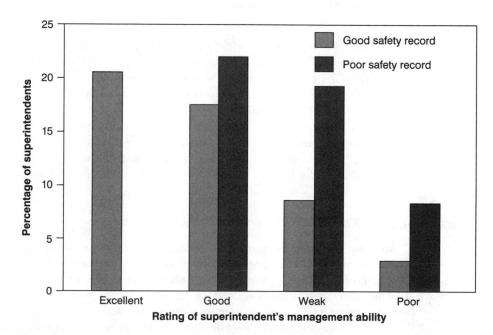

Figure 16.3

Distribution of Superintendents by Management Qualities and Safety Performance

Source: Hinze 1987

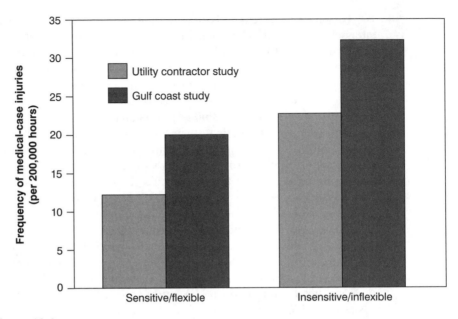

Figure 16.4
Safety Performance Related to a Superintendent's Sensitivity and Flexibility in Addressing Problems
Source: Hinze 1976; Hinze and Gordon 1979

foreman to worker. Some might even set up the promotion in such a manner that a demotion could be made with ease. Obviously, a demotion or, certainly, a dismissal would be a harsh measure for the new foreman to accept. It should be kept in mind that, although this approach may appear overly harsh, comments reflecting it have actually been offered by some superintendents.

The evidence is reasonably clear that good management skills and good safety performance go together. Although some management traits are personal, some characteristics can be developed through training. Firms should strive to hire individuals with the appropriate skills, or firms should endeavor to help superintendents develop those skills.

Superintendents Keep Job Pressures Down

In some cases, job pressures may be unavoidable. Are additional job pressures beneficial to project performance? There are some advocates of job pressure who contend that projects get completed through pressure and that pressure must be imposed in some instances to get the job done. In the previous two chapters, the effects of job pressure on safety performance were discussed. Knowing that pressures may have an adverse impact on safety, why do some managers and supervisors in construction persist in imposing the pressures? Perhaps the answer to this misguided practice is as simple as this: productivity and safety are viewed as being in conflict, and productivity is viewed as more important to success.

Are safety and productivity in conflict? With the strong emphasis that has been placed on safety in the past few years, many construction leaders now espouse disdain for the myth that safety and productivity are not mutually achievable. Nevertheless, there are still many doubts among others. It is a myth, however, and the sooner everyone in the industry recognizes that fact, the sooner we will see dramatic changes in the safety performance of the industry. Most advocates of the joint or mutual achievement of safety and productivity base their views on common sense.

I have made a few observations in the past few years about model construction projects. As a judge for a number of contractor association Project of the Year awards, I have noticed that the truly superb projects are completed on or ahead of schedule, within the budget, and with exemplary safety records. I have never seen a project that was truly successful in the areas of cost and schedule but had a dismal safety record. I truly feel that the criteria of a successful project must include safety and that, if safety performance fails, other measures of performance will also suffer.

In one study on construction safety (Hinze 1976; Hinze and Parker 1978), the relationship of safety and performance was examined. The procedure was simple. Construction superintendents were rated by their superiors on their abilities to meet budget and schedule goals. The results are shown in Figure 16.5. The findings are clear. Not only are safety and productivity (as measured by the meeting of budgets and schedules) not in conflict, but they appear to be dependent on each other. In most cases, it appears that excellent performance cannot be achieved in the absence of good safety performance (Hinze 1976; Hinze and Parker 1978).

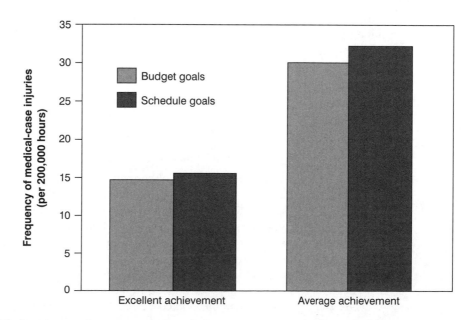

Figure 16.5
The Superintendent's Ability to Meet Corporate Goals
Source: Hinze 1976; Hinze and Parker 1978

Figure 16.6

The Superintendent's Philosophy about the Use of Cost Information

Source: Hinze 1976; Hinze and Parker 1978

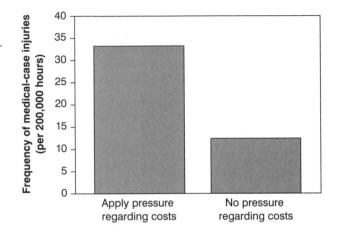

Safe superintendents know that their subordinates are motivated to do good jobs. It is not necessary to place extra pressure on them. Thus, the safe superintendents do not pressure their subordinates, primarily through the foremen, on issues of costs and schedules. Budgets must be met for profits to be realized. However, cost overruns on particular items (especially when many other items are below budget) must not result in excessive admonitions about the importance of keeping within the budget. Foremen realize the importance of delivering projects within the projected costs. If project items begin to overrun budget projections, foremen put pressure on themselves. Added pressure (as might be imposed by the superintendent) is unwarranted and unnecessary. The added pressure may, in fact, be the root cause of serious injuries. The problems associated with cost overruns and delays are readily apparent to those involved in the construction process; what is needed is a solution. Superintendents can help by examining the problem and offering suggestions for bringing the costs under control. In some instances, it must also be recognized that estimated cost figures can be made in error.

In one study of construction safety, superintendents were asked about their philosophy about sharing cost information with the foremen (Hinze 1976; Hinze and Parker 1978). The results are shown in Figure 16.6.

Cost information that is shared with foremen can be the source of pressure. The worst tactic is for a superintendent to deliberately deceive the foremen into accepting a cost projection that has been significantly reduced. For example, suppose the budget for forming a grade beam is based on a projection of 85 carpenter hours. To "motivate" the foreman, the superintendent tells the foreman that the budget has 60 hours allotted for this form work. The pressure on the foreman becomes quite high. The foreman wants to meet the goal and may very well share that desire with the carpenters assigned to the task. That situation is not healthy for safety.

Taking a less extreme approach, some superintendents tell the foremen whenever they are running over budget on a job cost item. This practice is particularly frustrating for foremen when they are never praised for delivering other cost items under budget. The communication is purely negative or punitive in form. Focusing only on cost overruns is an after-the-fact tactic that cannot change the past performance but can create adverse pressure that may compromise safety on the work to be done. Generally, performance is safer when superintendents do not use cost information to try to pressure foremen (Hinze and Parker 1978).

Running behind schedule does not please anyone. Again, it is not necessary for the superintendent to inform the foremen and other personnel that the schedule is slipping. Most construction personnel are sufficiently motivated that they keep track of their own production status. The schedule is thus a sufficient means of informing them about the status of their performance. A schedule should be viewed as a tool that helps performance on the project; it should not be used as a tool to put pressure on the people in the field. Pressure is more detrimental to safety performance than it is beneficial to construction progress. If work is behind schedule, the superintendent should examine the problem and offer assistance to remedy the situation. Admonitions about the importance of staying on schedule will not help resolve the problem.

Pressure may take various forms on construction projects. It may be evidenced in competition between crews. Competition is considered by many superintendents their favorite means of enhancing productivity. In some cases, competition may be healthy, but in others it can compromise safety. Examine the information in Figure 16.7. It shows that competition may or may not be healthy on a construction site.

Competition is an issue that must be carefully addressed. The issue is not so much whether competition exists in the workplace as what the source of the competition is. The findings suggest that competition that is initiated and encouraged by management may result in more injuries. On the other hand, competition that develops at the worker or crew level can be a source of inspiration for workers. Such competition can be healthy without compromising safety performance. Thus, superintendents may set up conditions in which competition can be a natural outgrowth of the circumstances, but superintendents should not formally instigate the competition.

Consider the following case of overt competition that was instigated by a superintendent: A project consisted of the construction of three identical 12-story buildings.

Figure 16.7

The Superintendent's Philosophy about Competition

Source: Hinze 1976; Hinze and Parker 1978

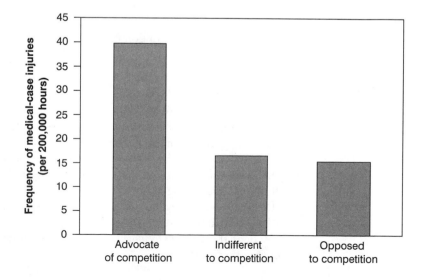

Two of the buildings were begun at the same time by two different crews. The superintendent announced that the crew that "topped out" first would be assigned the task of building the third structure. In other words, the reward for finishing ahead of the other crew was continued employment. With the local unemployment rate at 30%, it is not difficult to imagine the tremendous pressure that this placed on the workers. The OSHA recordable injury rate on this project was 124, one of the worst I have ever encountered.

If two crews are doing similar tasks, it is common and almost human nature for the crews to compare their progress. Many experts on productivity believe that this is an ideal situation because the workers work hard at their tasks (when they can compete with others), and they enjoy the work. The competition should never become too formal. For example, if the production can be accurately measured for comparison, the two crews may agree that the team with the lower production during the week will buy lunch from the lunch truck for the "winning" team on Friday. The stakes in such a competition are not sufficiently large to compromise judgment, so the competition may be acceptable. According to the results shown in Figure 16.7, it may even be good for safety. It is when the stakes get too high that workers may start to cut corners. One should never want a worker to go into an unshored trench to avoid 10 minutes of installing shoring. Even when superintendents are not the instigators of competition, they should be sufficiently observant to be sure that safe practices continue to be exercised.

Final Comments

As middle managers, superintendents and project managers are in key positions to set the tone for safety at the project level. They possess overall control of the project, and that control places a considerable responsibility on their shoulders. They must be ever mindful of the influence they have on the overall project. Company policies are viewed as being implemented by middle managers, and middle managers communicate project concerns to top management. Thus, they play a vital role in transmitting information from top management to the worker level and from the worker level to top management. To avoid any communication problems, middle managers must be careful to transmit accurate and clear information.

Review Questions

1. What should be the superintendent's role concerning newly hired workers?
2. What do some superintendents do that increases the pressures on the job site?
3. How does turnover among the workers affect safety performance?
4. Are all forms of competition between crews on the job site to be avoided?
5. What are some managerial traits that are associated with good safety performance?
6. What are some managerial traits that are associated with poor safety performance?
7. What might be a safe approach for a superintendent to take toward addressing cost estimates with the foremen?
8. Why does the term *new worker* apply to all workers who are new to a particular construction site?

9. How can a superintendent or project manager help establish the safety culture on a project?
10. What can a firm or a superintendent do to keep worker turnover at a low level?

References

Hinze, J. 1976. *The Effect of Middle Management on Safety in Construction.* Technical Report no. 209 (June), Construction Institute. Stanford, Calif.: Stanford University.

————. 1978a. "Turnover, New Workers, and Safety." *Journal of the Construction Division, ASCE* 104, no. 4, 409–17.

————. 1978b. "Worker Turnover and Job Safety." *National Utility Contractor* 2, no. 1, 17.

————. 1987. "Qualities of Safe Superintendents." *Journal of Construction Engineering and Management, ASCE* 113, no. 1, 169–71.

Hinze, J., and F. Gordon. 1979. "Supervisor-Worker Relationship Affects Injury Rate." *Journal of the Construction Division, ASCE* 105, no. 3, 253–62.

Hinze, J., and H. Parker. 1978. "Safety: Productivity and Job Pressures." *Journal of the Construction Division, ASCE* 104, no. 1, 27–34.

Levitt, R., and N. Samelson. 1993. *Construction Safety Management.* 2d ed. New York: John Wiley.

Peyton, R., and T. Rubio. 1991. *Construction Safety Practices and Principles.* New York: Van Nostrand Reinhold.

Top Management Practices, Company Activities, and Safety

Start work safe so that accidents won't stop work.

Top company managers have many different titles. In the discussion of safety, the titles of particular interest are owner, president, and chief executive officer. It is at the very top level of management that policies are set. If top management expresses support for certain issues, those issues will be promoted at the jobsite. That is true of virtually any topic. It is more than a cliché that the success of a safety program begins with the commitment of top management. If a safety program is implemented without the commitment of top management, there can be no surprise if the program fails.

The commitment of top management to safety can be shown in a number of ways. There is probably a big difference between the way the president of a large conglomerate shows a commitment to safety and the way the president of a small firm does. The president of a small firm has a greater number of opportunities to express the commitment to safety in a variety of ways. Also, the sincerity of the small company top executive is less likely to be questioned, since the commitment can be shown or expressed personally and in a variety of ways.

Company Size

Various features of companies can be used to classify them. It is interesting to note that some of those classifications are also helpful in giving an indication of the safety record a company might have. One common means of classifying firms is size. In 1994 the Bureau of Labor Statistics published an analysis of nonfatal injuries, in which it was reported that the general size of a firm is related to safety performance (see Figure 17.1). The results show that firms with 20–249 employees had the worst injury records.

In other research studies of small to medium-sized firms, it was disclosed that the smaller firms had better safety records than the medium-sized firms (Hinze and Pannullo 1978; Reed and Hinze 1986). There were few large firms in those studies. (See Figure 17.2.) Note that the findings are consistent with the BLS statistics. For the data shown in the general contractor study, half of the contractors had fewer than 20 employees. Thus, very few firms were in the "large" category, as defined by the BLS (Maxwell 1986).

Why Do Different-Sized Companies Have Different Safety Records?

Many findings of safety research show that size is a factor in safety performance. Although a company of any size can have a good or bad safety record, the common trend is depicted in Figure 17.1. The following case may help to show why.

Sam graduated from high school and then went to college part time while working for a utility contractor. While working for the utility contractor, Sam came to the realization that he wanted to make utility construction his career. After a little over a year, Sam no longer took college courses. He worked full-time for the utility contractor. He

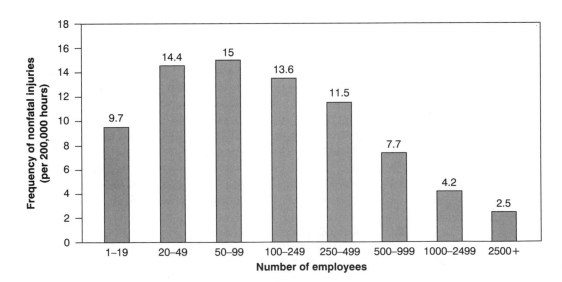

Figure 17.1
Injury Frequency in Relation to Company Size
Source: Bureau of Labor Statistics 1993

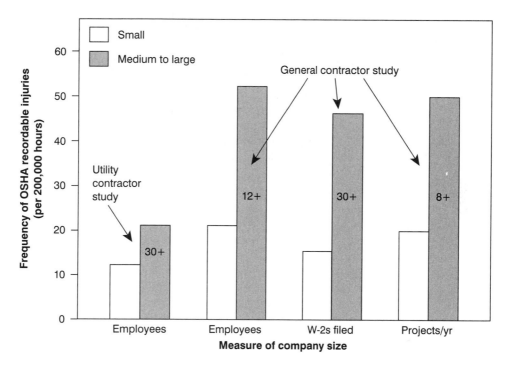

Figure 17.2
Various Measures of Size and Injury Frequency
Source: Hinze and Pannulo 1978; Reed and Hinze 1986

was occasionally asked to operate the hydraulic excavator and the front-end loader. He eventually moved up to the position of operator, and after only three years, he was considered the company's best operator. As operator, he had to make crucial decisions for the company. He was a valued employee and was never laid off in the 12 years he worked for the company. After 12 years Sam felt he knew the business, and he decided to start his own company.

Year 1 of Sam's Company   Sam successfully negotiated a utility contract on a subdivision that was being developed. To get the work done, Sam rented a hydraulic excavator and a front-end loader. He then called three friends who had worked with him on other jobs and hired them to help out on this first project. On that first project, Sam was the operator, and the other workers became his loyal crew. He kept the crew together from project to project. Sam was the owner of the company, but he was always on the job sites. Several similar jobs were completed with the same group of workers. In his first year, Sam had about $500,000 in contracts.

Year 3 of Sam's Company   Sam's company had been profitable, and it continued to grow. He ended up with two contracts that had to be undertaken at the same time. He continued to be the operator on one job. On the other job, he put Pat in charge. Pat had been the lead person in the crew since the company started. Sam would visit Pat's job early in the morning before starting up his own project, and he would swing by Pat's job at the end of the workday to make sure everything was running smoothly. His annual volume was now $2.5 million.

Year 5 of Sam's Company Sam's company continued to prosper, and Sam continued to be successful in acquiring work. He now had three projects under contract at the same time. He decided he could no longer run the company and be operator. He relinquished his hands-on duties on the projects and simply roved among the different projects. He now had three different crews. He still knew the names of the workers, but he was less familiar with their personal lives. His primary field contacts were with the foremen on the projects. He was finding it difficult to do all the estimating at night, but he didn't feel comfortable about sitting in the office during the day when field work was going on. The company's annual volume was now over $4 million.

Year 7 of Sam's Company Sam was finding it exceedingly difficult to manage his time—being the roving superintendent; keeping in touch with the lenders, equipment dealers, sureties, and insurance agents; and still pursuing new contracts. He decided to hire a roving superintendent so that he could devote his time to the administrative side of the business. He found that it was an area of the business in which he had reasonably strong skills. His company's annual volume of construction business now exceeded $8 million.

Year 10 of Sam's Company Sam's company had enjoyed continued success. He was now running 5 crews, had hired two office employees to help with the administrative tasks, and owned several pieces of equipment. Sam decided to hire an assistant, who functioned as a project manager and handled any major problems in the field. The roving superintendent reported directly to the project manager, but occasionally Sam wanted to receive reports. Sam rarely got out on the jobs anymore. The annual company volume had moved up to $12 million, and Sam was seeing growth as a very viable venture.

Year 15 of Sam's Company Sam now had several assistants. He was never able to visit any job sites. He knew only a few of the field workers, mostly those who had been with him when he started the company. His annual volume now exceeded $40 million. Some of the company projects were now in neighboring towns and communities. Sam relied heavily on several roving superintendents for feedback. The project manager had three assistants. Sam had his sights on getting contracts amounting to at least $50 million in the next year.

Some companies start out just as Sam's company did. Some company owners set the volume of business that they want to do and try to stay at that level. Other owners, like Sam, decide to let the company grow as long as contracts can be acquired. There are some firms that have grown at twice the rate of Sam's company. What are the implications for safety of the different stages that Sam's company went through? Note that when Sam's company started out, Sam was always on the project and he personally knew each of the workers. Once the company was doing $40 million of construction work a year, Sam was an infrequent field visitor, and his personal contacts with the workers were virtually gone. Sam no longer had the same degree of control of the projects. For a worker in Sam's firm, the sense of loyalty to the company would naturally be stronger in the smaller setting.

Sam made changes in the company as they seemed needed. When he could no longer handle some aspect of the work, he hired someone. The company grew in that manner. Sam made the changes in response to conditions. He never fully anticipated change until the need for change was presented. With each change, Sam entered a position of less direct control in the company. With the growth of the firm, the injury frequency rate probably also grew. Perhaps, in the next year or so, Sam would recognize the high cost of injuries and their impact on company profits. The change that his recognition of that condition would spawn was a more formal approach to safety. Such a change, as will be shown in the following sections, is what must take place if worker injuries are to be controlled. Keeping in mind the changes that take place as a company grows will help in developing an understanding of how company size and safety are related.

Small Company Operations

Since small companies were consistently safer than their larger counterparts, it appears that some type of group dynamics is taking place that enhances job safety. An examination of the operations of the smaller companies may show why they are often safer than the larger ones. One key feature of small firms, those with fewer than 20 employees, is that top management is typically closely involved in monitoring construction progress. That is true because the firms are so small that there are no other personnel who can monitor job progress. To make monitoring by top management possible, the home office must be located close to the projects. Many small firms undertake projects only in their immediate metropolitan areas. In fact, many restrict most of their operations to a 25-mile radius or a 50-mile radius. The firms that have most of their projects in close proximity to the home office have better safety records (see Figure 17.3).

One can imagine a number of reasons for the improvement in safety performance when more projects are located near the home office. Certainly, one reason is that top management is more accessible to the field personnel. That accessibility essentially makes it possible for the field superintendents to have backup. It may also be related to project control in that the home office personnel can lend more support to the field when they can be on the project within a matter of minutes or in less than an hour. For example, if a utility construction crew is forced to stop work suddenly because of a broken hydraulic hose on the excavator, a quick call to the home office can result in an immediate response. Such support can help the construction effort go more smoothly. Specific operations associated with small firms will be examined.

Project Control and Safety Performance

Project control can have many definitions. For our purposes here, project control has three components. The first component, the one most commonly implemented, is that of acquiring information or data about a facet of the project. Virtually all projects have some form of record keeping, whether it is of costs, schedule, quality, or some other

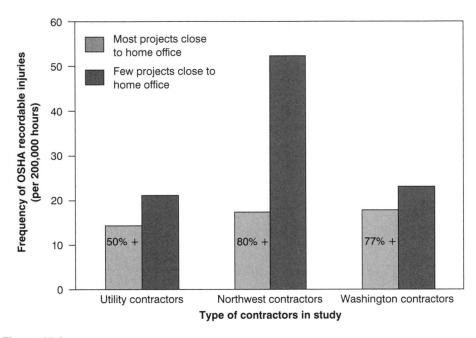

Figure 17.3
Safety Related to the Proportion of Projects Near the Home Office
Source: Hinze and Pannullo 1978; Reed and Hinze 1986; Piepho 1993

aspect. Information gathered need not be formally recorded to be effective. The second component of project control is that of analyzing the information in a rational manner and assessing the acceptability of the information. The third component is that of action. It consists of doing something about some facet of the project when the data indicate a detrimental impact.

As mentioned, one way to document information is to write it down. It is the prudent manner of recording information for historical purposes or for communicating it to those who are unable to observe the situation firsthand. On small projects, problems can be readily grasped upon a visual inspection. Thus, a site visit by top management may be appropriate. What are the implications for safety performance when such visits from the home office occur regularly and frequently? Figure 17.4 provides one possible answer.

The results show that safety performance is better when the president or owner of the construction firm visits the job sites with considerable frequency, in some cases daily. Through such visits the president or owner can personally observe the progress that is being made. He or she may also make suggestions to the superintendent or the project manager for addressing different situations. If a top management visit is viewed as one in which assistance can be provided, the visit can help make the construction work go more smoothly.

A personal visit by the company president or owner can help the project personnel in a variety of ways. One way is to offer advice or to suggest different methods of approaching certain tasks. Also, personal contact with the president or owner may be

Figure 17.4

The Frequency of Visits by the President or Owner to Most Job Sites

Source: Hinze and Pannullo 1978

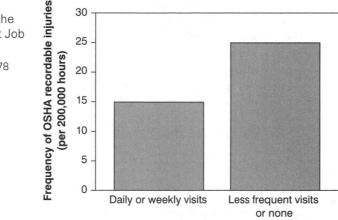

rewarding to field personnel. It tends to humanize the relationship between the field personnel and top management. Conversely, when the president or owner cannot visit the site, top management is viewed as more remote. In fact, when top managers do not visit the site, they may be ill informed on how to respond to questions.

Once a firm is too large for top management to be personally involved in field operations, field personnel may have no contact with top management. Top management is more remote in the larger firms, and the communications and policies are more bureaucratic. The extent to which a firm has become a bureaucracy can be measured by the number of levels of management in the firm (see Figure 17.5). The number of

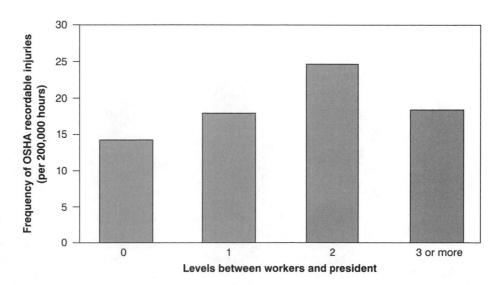

Figure 17.5

Safety Performance and Levels of Management

Source: Piepho 1993

levels of management is expressed as the number of levels between the president and the worker level. Safer firms are those in which there are no layers of management between the worker and the company owner or president. Fewer levels of management mean that more direct communication can be maintained between the different levels within the firm. More frequent contact also provides an avenue for greater control.

It is interesting to note that the injury frequency begins to show a noticeable improvement when three or more levels of management exist. This result may be echoing the same phenomenon that is shown in Figure 17.1. It implies that some benefit to safety occurs when the number of levels of management gets quite large. Large firms with several levels of management may be of such magnitude that they must deal with safety concerns in a more formal manner. This subject will be examined in greater detail later.

Company Turnover and Safety Performance

High turnover has been noted to be detrimental to safety performance (see Figure 17.6). This effect may occur, in part, because more workers must be hired and the new workers hired are more vulnerable to injury. The way to keep the number of new workers to a minimum is to employ the workers for extended periods. That means that management must expend the effort to retain personnel. Retention of personnel requires an investment in the workers to cause them to want to stay with the firm. The efforts to retain workers also help new workers adjust quickly to the work. With a more rapid

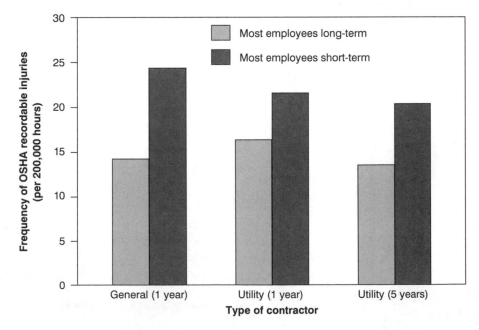

Figure 17.6
Safety Performance and Employment Duration
Source: Hinze 1978b; Piepho 1993

adjustment, new workers can get "on the learning curve" sooner and become as productive as the other workers.

Competitive Work Environment

In previous chapters, the subject of job pressures was examined at the crew and project levels. Job pressures are detrimental to construction safety. At the company level, the source of pressure is more closely related to the amount of potential profit that may exist on a project. If the profit margin is small, there is pressure on the field personnel to preserve that small margin as much as possible. If a larger profit is possible, the pressure is reduced in that some cushion of comfort exists on the project. The profit margin, to a large extent, is determined by the nature of the competitive environment in which the contract was awarded. On competitively bid projects, the environment is determined by the number of bidders. If many bidders are vying for a project, the profit margins in their bids, especially the lowest bids, are generally small. It is often said that if many bids are submitted, the winner is the bidder who made the biggest mistake.

The number of bidders was examined in one study (see Figure 17.7). The results indicate clearly that the number of bidders does have an influence on the safety performance of firms. Thus, firms that consistently pursue and acquire contracts for which four or fewer bidders vie have better safety records. The pressures felt by the small profit margins on projects with more bidders apparently channel into greater pressures on the work crews, and that pressure is not conducive to good safety performance.

Policies on Safety That Include Top Managers

The degree of top management commitment to safety can be shown in many ways. Although company policies can be attributed (to a large degree) to top management, it is in the area of nonpolicy issues that top management can make its strongest statement about its commitment to safety. For example, a strong point would be made by a company

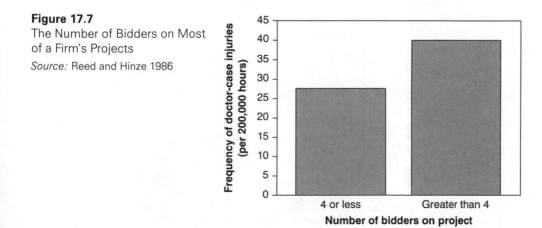

Figure 17.7
The Number of Bidders on Most of a Firm's Projects
Source: Reed and Hinze 1986

president who scheduled a project visit so that he or she could make personal appearances at several crew safety meetings, at the project safety meeting, or at the superintendents' safety meeting. A few prepared comments on safety at that time by the president would assure those in attendance that the timing of the visit had been planned.

When safety policies are established, the role of top management must be carefully integrated into the overall program. If company policies appear to insulate top management from matters related to safety, the commitment of top management is greatly diminished in the eyes of the company employees, be they field workers or supervisors. If safe practices, as outlined in company policies, are to be fully integrated into the work processes, top management must continue to participate in the implementation of the safety program. In other words, top management cannot simply mandate some new safety policy and then let the field personnel implement it. Top management must follow through with its commitment. The steps might be outlined as follows:

1. Policies for safe work practices are established by top management.
2. Top management announces the safety policies and expresses its support for them.
3. Top management actively participates in efforts to implement the safety policies.
4. Top management gives recognition to the employees implementing the policies.
5. Top managers continue to personally show their support for the safety policies.
6. All levels of management have responsibility for supporting the safety policies.

Company policies are next to meaningless without corporate support and commitment. This support comes the form of aggressive encouragement and also in the form of funds. If the commitment is sincere and convincing, other levels of management and field supervisory personnel will also support the policy. When the support of all levels of management is clear, the field workers will readily embrace the new policy.

New workers have repeatedly been mentioned as those warranting special attention, especially during their first few days on the project. In a larger company, what policy should exist concerning the new workers? The findings of one study on construction safety give a good indication (see Figure 17.8). Better safety performance is realized when the orientation of new workers is formal. When a training session is for-

Figure 17.8
Worker Orientation and Safety
Source: Hinze and Harrison 1981

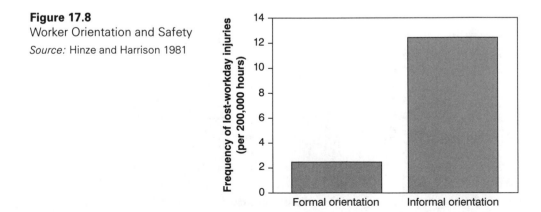

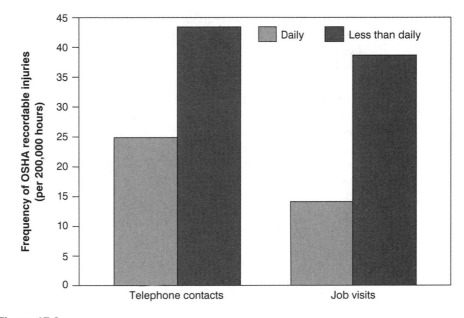

Figure 17.9
Top Management Contacts with Company Projects
Source: Hinze 1976

mal, especially in a larger company, there is greater assurance that the training will actually occur. A formal process ensures that the same thorough training is offered to every worker. Top managers can ensure that the formal training takes place by monitoring records that document the sessions. Although top managers may not be directly involved in the training, they are in a position to make sure that it occurs. Safety is a natural outgrowth of the process.

In smaller companies, it has been noted that the top manager—namely, the company owner or president—often makes daily visits to the project sites. Although daily visits may not be possible on all projects undertaken by large firms, frequent and regular contacts can still be made. Frequent contact also benefits safety. The results shown in Figure 17.9 indicate that the companies in which daily visits to the jobs occurred had better safety records. Although companies had good safety records when daily telephone contacts took place between top management and field personnel, their safety performances were not as good as when daily visits occurred. Daily contact, whether by telephone or in person, serves a good purpose for safety. It probably also helps the project run more smoothly. Field personnel have the necessary channels of communication by which problems can be quickly resolved. That situation reduces job anxiety and, in general, lets the field personnel focus more attention on project planning.

Pressure can be imposed on field personnel by the criteria on which they are evaluated. There are different measures that can be used to evaluate construction personnel. Note that on most construction contracts the contractor is obligated to deliver the project within a certain time period and that for this effort a stated sum of money will be paid to the contractor. These contractual obligations related to time and money can be the source of pressure on a construction site. Are similar measures also used to evaluate field supervisory personnel? If they are, the safety performance of the projects may suffer (see Figure 17.10).

Companies that evaluate their supervisors solely on their ability to meet time and cost goals have consistently poorer safety records. Companies that also use other criteria for evaluation criteria have better safety records. Other criteria include safety and also such subjective measures as quality, satisfied customers, and goodwill.

In the area of safety record keeping, top management should be made a part of the program. For example, imagine two types of reports being generated by the project personnel on a given day, namely, the job cost report and the safety report. To whom should those reports be routed? The safety study by Levitt (1975) offers some information on this topic. What are the implications if one type of report is reviewed by top management and the other is not? Obviously, the one reviewed by top management is the one deemed to be of greater importance. If cost reports are sent to top management, but safety reports are not, it is clear which performance criteria are of greater importance (see Figure 17.11).

If reports of safety performance stop short of the president's desk, the information is probably perceived as unimportant to the company. Perhaps top management views safety as one of those issues that top management must occasionally support but that is not of prime importance in the firm. This attitude will be echoed by those in the field. It is difficult to imagine a situation in which the president of a company did not want to review a job cost report. Should there be any difference where safety reports are concerned? If safety reports are sent to the president as a matter of routine, the clear signal is that a strong commitment to safety exists.

The concern for safety can also be emphasized in informal communications between top management and the field personnel. For example, if the president visits the job site and expresses a concern about safety, the field personnel will perceive that concern as a reflection of company policy, whether it is formally stated to be so or not.

Figure 17.10
Evaluation of Field Supervisors
Source: Hinze 1976

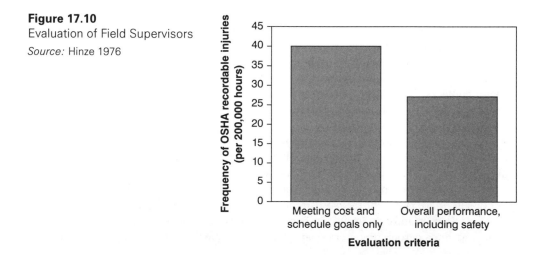

Figure 17.11
What Levels in the Company Review Accident Statistics?

Source: Levitt 1975

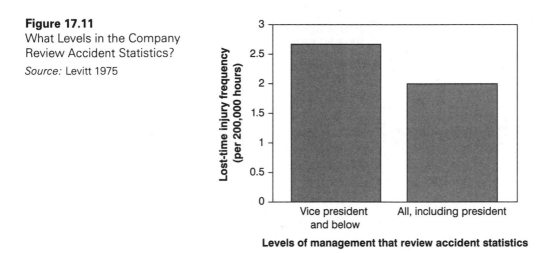

Levels of management that review accident statistics

That perception will then serve as motivation for safety on the job. The results of one study show that the effect on safety is measurable (see Figure 17.12).

From these results it is evident that safety communications, especially from top management, are important. The tone for safety at the project level is dictated to a large degree by the communications that top management has with the field personnel.

A Top-Management Model of Safety

At the beginning of this chapter, an example was developed in which a company grew steadily from a simple one-crew firm to a large business with a $40 million annual volume. The description demonstrated how personal contacts diminished as the firm grew. A basic model of safety performance in a firm was developed by Levitt (1975). In light of the past discussions, the model, shown in Figure 17.13, is self-explanatory.

Figure 17.12
Top Management Communications on Safety with Field Superintendents

Source: Hinze 1976

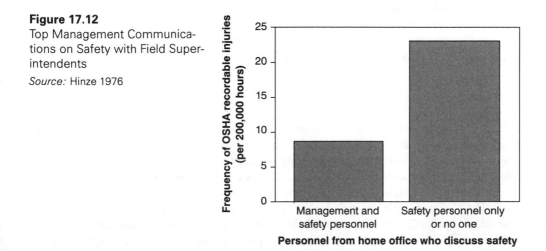

Personnel from home office who discuss safety

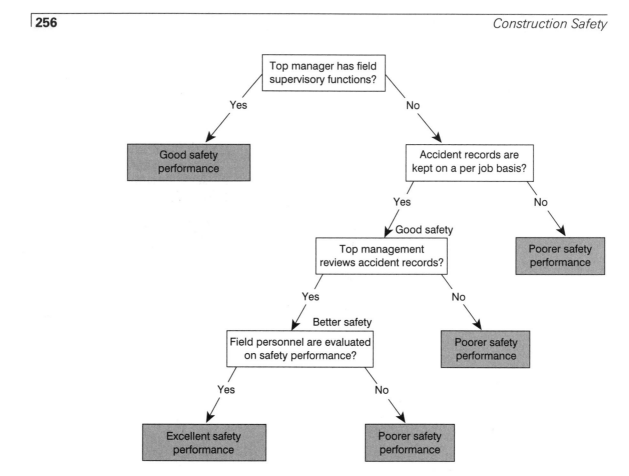

Figure 17.13
A Model of Top Management's Role in Safety
Source: Levitt 1975

Note that in a larger firm the top managers should be directly involved in the safety program. Their involvement should include the review of job safety records and the evaluation of the safety performance of field personnel. Those more formal approaches to safety keep top managers involved in the process.

An Example

There is no set formula for achieving safety in the workplace, because projects have different characteristics and the work force is never the same. The following case involves events in which the owner of a firm played an instrumental role in drastically changing the safety performance of the company. The essential elements of the case are true. Information that would reveal the identity of the contractor has been altered.

The Nelson Construction Company (not its real name) is a general contracting firm based in Denver. The firm, involved in heavy construction projects, has done an annual volume of business of more than $20 million over the past several years. But the president of the Nelson Company—we'll call him George Nelson—discovered several years ago that safety problems were endangering his friends and his profits.

In the spring of 1990, several employees who were Nelson's friends were injured in job-related accidents. Nelson was particularly perplexed that many of the injured workers were the old-timers in the company. One of the injuries resulted in a fatality. The rash of injuries was of such concern to Nelson that he presented the problem to a team of safety professionals. Nelson explained that the company had had a fairly good safety program in years past but suddenly the number of injuries was out of proportion.

The safety professionals had several discussions with Nelson during the fall of 1990 and the spring of 1991 to determine a possible means of improving the company's safety record. A brief survey of the company safety program showed that a deliberate effort had indeed been made at the company level to ensure the safety of the workers.

The company had long maintained a policy of conducting weekly toolbox meetings on the jobs. On major projects, those valued at more than $6–7 million, it was standard policy to assign a full-time safety engineer to the job. The company also held periodic company safety meetings and held prejob conferences at which OSHA safety consultants were active participants.

Model Company

One OSHA compliance officer who was familiar with the Nelson Company discussed the company at a safety workshop. During an informal conversation, the compliance officer casually mentioned the name of the Nelson Company to one of the safety professionals. Ironically, the compliance officer said a study should be made of the company, as he felt that the firm was a model of safety. He cited the prejob conferences to which OSHA consultants were invited as an example. When visiting the Nelson job sites on random inspections, he said, compliance officers seldom found any violations, certainly no serious ones.

According to this compliance officer, the Nelson Company had nothing to worry about. On the other hand, the company president was concerned because many long-time employees were being seriously injured. The discrepancy between the perceptions of the two men (the compliance officer and George Nelson) may be explained by the fact that one was considering the safety intentions of the company together with observations of the physical plant, while the other considered the resulting personal injuries.

Although the worker injuries were primarily of humanistic concern to Nelson, he soon realized that company profits were also being eroded by the injuries. That erosion was evidenced by the increase in the loss ratios, a measure that can be used to gauge the effectiveness of a firm's safety efforts.

For the fiscal years from July 1, 1986, to July 1, 1989, the company's loss ratio averaged 42%. In fiscal year 1989 the loss ratio was 146%, and in fiscal year 1990 it went up to 226%. That meant that for every dollar the Nelson Company paid in premiums, the insurance company had to pay out $2.26 in claims. With the sudden rise in losses, it was no wonder that the Nelson Company was having difficulty in obtaining insurance coverage.

Note that the experience modification rate is based on the claims made over a three-year period that does not include the immediately preceding year. Thus, the experience modification rate of 133% for 1993–94 is based on the losses from July 1989 to July 1992. For 1994–95, the experience modification rate was reduced to 91%.

Poor Communication

One of the problems observed was a lack of clear communication between the insurance carrier and the Nelson Company. As the numerous injuries occurred, the insurance carrier sent regular computerized reports to Nelson. The insurance carrier never mentioned those monthly reports in its other correspondence with him. The reports showed detailed information about each employee injury. Unfortunately, Nelson failed to examine the reports in any detail. Perhaps he assumed that he would not be able to understand the computer printouts even if he examined them.

Worse yet, Nelson later admitted that he did not fully understand how the job injuries would later be reflected in the company's insurance premiums. He was not aware that the experience modification rate (EMR) would have a direct effect on the insurance premiums, nor was he aware of the means by which the EMR was derived. He had somehow felt that the insurance coverage protected the company from any adverse financial effects resulting from worker injuries.

The first step in addressing the problem was to help Nelson fully understand the meaning and value of the insurance reports. Those reports provided information on each claim: the injured party, the project or job, the type of injury, the cost of the claim to date, the amount held in reserve for the claim, whether the case had been closed, and so on. Initially, the safety experts spent time to help Nelson read and extract the most relevant information from the reports. After a brief orientation, Nelson was able to see at a glance which injuries were most costly and how much in reserves was set aside for each case.

The safety consultants told Nelson to try to identify any pattern of job injuries, particularly when several occurred on a single project. In addition, they explained how injury costs would be reflected in future insurance premiums. The explanation of the costs of the job injuries and their subsequent effect on insurance premiums prompted Nelson to make immediate changes within the company. The first change was to obtain a different insurance carrier.

Although the Nelson Company had difficulty getting another insurance carrier, the company eventually found one. Perhaps this change was necessary simply for the sake of change. In addition, however, the new insurance company took a more active role in the company's safety program. Insurance representatives spent time on the job sites to evaluate and analyze problems and potential problems. They also made a careful study of the company injury statistics to see if any trends were developing.

The new carrier carefully explained all administrative details to employees of the Nelson Co. In addition, the insurance company played a stronger role in fighting fraudulent claims. The assistance received from the new insurance carrier should not be interpreted as implying that the prior carrier was not providing worthwhile service. Perhaps the same services were available from the prior insurance carrier. Unfortunately, the Nelson Company had not previously expressed the cooperative spirit so needed for a good insurance carrier–construction firm relationship.

Other changes soon followed. The changes began with the top-level managers in the company, and the field supervisors soon began to follow suit.

A New Title for the President

One problem Nelson recognized was that when a full-time safety engineer was on a project, the project supervisors considered that person to be the only party responsible for safety. Nelson appointed himself chief safety engineer. That action conveyed to the employees that top management considered safety a top priority. The point was made verbally and through carefully prepared memoranda stressing that safety cannot be removed from supervisory duties and responsibilities. Responsibility for safety, in short, could not and would not be delegated in the company. Everyone was responsible for safety. That policy was further emphasized at supervisory meetings.

Up to that time, Nelson had been reducing his role in the company in preparation for taking early retirement. He had been primarily involved in administrative matters and, as a result, seldom visited the job sites. However, with the new emphasis on safety, Nelson became more active in company operations. He made more frequent visits to the job sites. During his visits he addressed safety as a key concern. In fact, he would ask about job injuries on his visits before asking about construction progress. Nelson told employees, "Safety is an attitude," and said that as chief safety engineer he wanted all personnel in the company to "think safety."

The same attitude was conveyed by the vice president, the operations manager, through frequent visits to the various jobs. Like Nelson, he was thoroughly convinced of the importance of safety, and he also emphasized that importance with the job supervisors.

To further emphasize his support for safety, Nelson decided to personally conduct the safety sessions at the annual company meetings.

The education process did not stop at the top management levels. The key people on the jobs were drilled on the need to be safe. One of the key points that Nelson stressed with his supervisory staff was that injuries actually cut into company profits. That was a strong selling point for safety, particularly in the Nelson Company, which for the past 10 years had been providing company stock to its key people. The 20 field supervisors soon realized that the costs of injuries cut directly into company profits and, in so doing, reduced the value of their privately held stock.

It is worth noting that the changes made in the company were primarily mental. The supervisory staff had always been encouraged to take first-aid classes, which were paid for by the company. Seminars on OSHA were also regularly attended. Consequently, there was no need to train company personnel in the technical areas of safety.

Insurance as a Partner

Some other changes were initiated in the company. The company began to conduct a prejob survey on each new job to minimize hazards and to limit property damage and public liability. The new insurance carrier played an active role in the prejob conferences. In fact, insurance was now viewed in a different light. The insurance company began to be considered a business partner. Reductions in losses from injuries were seen as the source of a competitive edge whenever a bid was submitted.

An additional change in the company was to eliminate the separate company safety meetings. Safety was incorporated into all company business meetings. Safety was no longer treated as a separate entity. The responsibility for safety was shifted from one individual to all employees.

The Nelson Company made many administrative changes. What effect did those changes have on the company's safety performance? The answer is that the safety efforts of the company paid off in saved lives as well as dollars. The number of injuries has dropped, and—most noteworthy—the employees have suffered no serious injuries. On the financial side, the loss ratios for fiscal years 1992 and 1993 were held to less than 1%.

Contractor's Safety Record		
Period Covered (July–June)	**Loss Ratio (%)**	**Experience Modification Rate (%)**
1986–87	22.3	86
1987–88	45.1	78
1988–89	59.5	74
1989–90	146.5	84
1990–91	226.5	89
1991–92	58.1	115
1992–93	0.05	134
1993–94	0.09	133

The results are particularly encouraging because the company has grown and diversified its operations, both in types of construction and in geographic area. Growth and diversification are generally associated with increases in job-related injuries. However, this did not hold true for the Nelson Company with its newly implemented safety program.

Additional benefits from the company's excellent safety record were realized through a cash rebate from the insurance company. At one annual company meeting, the insurance company handling the Nelson Company account presented the president with a rebate check for nearly $150,000. Believing in the old Viking philosophy that "those who pull the oars share in the plunder," Nelson turned to the company supervisors and said, "This is yours." The company worked as a team on safety and was to share in the rewards as a team also.

The predominant mechanism of the change was management changes through education—education of the president, of the field supervisors, and of all employees of the company. The chief reason for the success was a company president willing and open to education and motivated to implement the necessary changes. The results were so dramatic and widespread that everyone in the company was made to feel responsible for the positive effects.

Final Comments

Safety begins with top management. This phrase has almost become a cliché. The commitment of top management consists of more than developing a company policy that espouses the virtues of safety. Top managers must show their commitment by becoming personally involved in safety. If top management takes a firm and committed stand on safety, others will recognize it and respond accordingly. The commitment must come from the heart.

Review Questions

1. Why do small construction firms generally have better safety records than do medium-sized firms?
2. Why do large construction firms generally have better safety records than do medium-sized firms?
3. What kinds of pressure can top management impose on construction project personnel that might impair safety performance?
4. When is it advisable to have formal policies on safety?
5. In the Nelson case, what was probably the most important change made in the firm to benefit safety? What other changes also contributed to the improvement in safety performance?
6. Give examples of the role of communication in construction safety?
7. Why might the number of bidders for a contract influence the safety performance on a construction project?
8. Explain how record keeping can assist in the achievement of good safety performance.
9. Give examples of ways in which project control can be exhibited on a construction project, and explain why it might influence safety performance.
10. How can top managers demonstrate their personal commitment to safety?

References

Bachus, R. 1992. "Safety Pays." *Pacific Builder and Engineer* 98, no. 20, 6–12.

Bureau of Labor Statistics. 1994. Workplace Injuries and Illnesses in 1993." USDL-94-600. Washington, D.C.: U.S. Department of Labor.

Hinze, J. 1976. *The Effect of Middle Management on Safety in Construction.* Technical Report no. 209 (June), Construction Institute. Stanford, Calif.: Stanford University.

———. 1977a. "Effective Job Control Improved Job Safety." *National Utility Contractor* 1, no. 3, 23–25.

———. 1977b. "How Dollar Volume Changes a Company." *National Utility Contractor* 1, no. 2, 26–27.

———. 1978a. "Company Concern and Safety Go Together." *National Utility Contractor* 2, no. 8, 12–13.

———. 1978b. "Turnover, New Workers, and Safety." *Journal of the Construction Division, ASCE* 104, no. 4, 409–17.

———. 1978c. "Worker Turnover and Job Safety." *National Utility Contractor* 2, no. 1, 17.

———. 1988. "Safety Payoff." *Pacific Builder and Engineer* 93, no. 9, 12–13.

Hinze, J., and N. Carino. 1979. *A Study of Work Practices Employed to Protect Workers in Trenches.* NBSIR 80-1988. Washington, D.C.: National Bureau of Standards.

Hinze, J., and C. Harrison. 1981. "Safety Programs in Large Construction Firms." *Journal of the Construction Division, ASCE* 107, no. 3, 455–67.

Hinze, J., and D. Maxwell. 1987. "Company Growth and Safety Performance." *Pacific Builder and Engineer* 93, no. 10, 12.

Hinze, J., and J. Pannullo. 1978. "Safety: Function of Job Control." *Journal of the Construction Division, ASCE* 104, no. 2, 241–49.

Hinze, J., and P. Raboud. 1988. "Safety on Large Building Construction Projects." *Journal of Construction Engineering and Management, ASCE* 114, no. 2, 286–93.

Levitt, R. 1975. *The Effect of Top Management on Safety in Construction.* Technical Report no. 196 (July), Construction Institute. Stanford, Calif.: Stanford University.

Levitt, R., and H. Parker. 1976. "Reducing Construction Accidents—Top Management's Role." *Journal of the Construction Division, ASCE* 102, no. 3, 465–78.

Maxwell, D. 1986. "A Safety Survey of Construction Firms in the State of Washington." Unpublished Master's research report, University of Washington.

Peyton, R., and T. Rubio. 1991. *Construction Safety Practices and Principles.* New York: Van Nostrand Reinhold.

Piepho, N. 1993. "The Relationship of Construction Company Characteristics to Safety Performance." Master's thesis, University of Washington.

Reed, D., and J. Hinze. 1986. "A Study of Construction Safety in Washington State, USA." Paper read at IABSE Symposium, Tokyo, September.

U.S. Department of Labor. 1986. *A Brief Guide to Recordkeeping Requirements for Occupational Injuries and Illnesses.* OMB no. 1220-0029 (June).

Safety Personnel

> *Talk safety constantly, because you can lead a goose to water, and if you hold its head under long enough, it's going to get some of it.*

In the staffing of a construction project, some consideration must be given to the safety needs of the project. Safety needs vary, depending largely on the size and type of project.

OSHA's Personnel Requirements

The OSHA regulations stipulate that certain personnel be assigned to construction sites. Such personnel are mentioned in various paragraphs in the standards. Some of the more relevant definitions (from 29 CFR § 1926.32) are the following:

(d) *Authorized person* means a person approved or assigned by the employer to perform a specific type of duty or duties or to be at a specific location at the jobsite. . . .

(f) *Competent person* means one who is capable of identifying existing and predictable hazards in the surroundings or working conditions which are unsanitary, hazardous, or dangerous to employees, and who has authorization to take prompt corrective measures to eliminate them. . . .

(i) *Designated person* means "authorized person" as defined in paragraph (d) of this section. . . .

(m) *Qualified* means one who, by possession of a recognized degree, certificate, or professional standing, or who by extensive knowledge, training, and experience, has successfully demonstrated his ability to solve or resolve problems relating to the subject matter, the work, or the project.

One of OSHA's provisions addresses medical personnel. The provision (29 CFR § 1926.50(a)) states, "The employer shall insure the availability of medical personnel for advice and consultation, on matters of occupational health." Presumably, when a construction project is located near medical services, the employer need only establish contact or set up some type of account with the medical services. However, even on some small projects (those with 10–20 workers) that have a short duration (several weeks to a few months), some contractors stipulate that a specified number of workers have a current first-aid training card. On large projects (those with more than a thousand workers), many firms employ paramedics and nurses, who are assigned to a first-aid station and are asked to address a variety of safety and health issues that arise on site.

The OSHA regulations also address the need to plan for the efficient treatment of any badly injured workers. Section 1926.50(b) states, "Provisions shall be made prior to commencement of the project for prompt medical attention in case of serious injury." That essentially means that the contractor must have a plan worked out in advance to address circumstances that require the immediate attention of a medical professional. Section 1926.50(c) states, "In the absence of an infirmary, clinic, hospital, or physician, that is reasonably accessible in terms of time and distance to the worksite, which is available for the treatment of injured employees, a person who has a valid certificate in first-aid training from the U.S. Bureau of Mines, the American Red Cross, or equivalent training that can be verified by documentary evidence, shall be available at the worksite to render first aid."

Note that the stated personnel requirements represent minimum requirements. Many employers now far exceed the minimum in the staffing they provide.

Safety Responsibility of Job-Site Personnel

Before discussing the particulars of the safety personnel assigned to construction projects, a brief discussion of the role of other personnel on site seems imperative. In particular, what are the roles of the superintendent and the foremen on projects that have full-time safety personnel assigned to them? Do their roles or responsibilities concerning safety change when full-time safety personnel are on site? Although some nuances of their safety activities will probably change when safety personnel are assigned to the project, the fundamental roles of supervisors will not be altered.

The superintendent and the foremen on the construction project should view the safety personnel on site as providing assistance in the area of safety. It would be wrong for these supervisors to view their safety responsibilities as having been delegated to the safety personnel. It must be borne in mind that it is in the accomplishment of the work that injuries generally occur. The supervisors provide the essential guidance and direction for the workers to accomplish their work tasks. If that guidance is provided without regard for safety, there is little that the safety personnel on site can do to prevent accidents. Therefore, the responsibility for safety still rests squarely on the shoulders of the superintendent and the other supervisors. The role of safety personnel is to assist the supervisors in delivering their projects without injuries. The safety personnel are to be used as a "second pair of eyes" to help supervisors in the identification of job hazards.

When there are no full-time safety personnel assigned to a project, it is a common default for the superintendent to be named the authorized person to see that the OSHA regulations are followed. That authorized person is the contact person for OSHA. Who is the authorized OSHA contact when full-time safety personnel are on site? In some firms, the authorized person remains the superintendent. Others designate the job-site safety director to fill the position. Regardless of who carries the "authorized person" label, the responsibility for safety is not delegated or relinquished by those in supervision.

Safety Personnel

Many employers place greater emphasis on the prevention of accidents than on the treatment of injuries. That is, they try to ensure that injuries will not occur on their projects. The adage "An ounce of prevention is worth a pound of cure" may be quite appropriate to describe this emerging safety philosophy.

The staffing requirements for job-site safety may be established to some extent by the construction contract. The following is an example of a contract provision that stipulates that some person must be formally identified as having primary responsibility for safety:

Safety Personnel: The Contractor shall designate a person on his staff to manage the Contractor's safety and accident prevention program. That person must have the authority to properly execute the safety responsibilities of the Contractor on the job site. The designated person will provide a point of contact for the Owner's Representative on matters of job safety.

Safety personnel must perform many different duties to satisfy their safety responsibilities. They keep records of job-site safety performance, as indicated by the occurrence of injuries, near misses, and noncompliance activities. They make regular job-site inspections to provide assurance that employee safety is maintained. Questions of safety or OSHA requirements may also arise on a regular basis. Safety personnel must therefore keep up-to-date on the OSHA regulations, current safety technology, and other safety matters. They may also be involved in worker orientation, and they may be asked to provide training on specific matters from time to time. In more recent years, greater amounts of time have been required for matters related to hazard communication. Project planning is another area in which safety personnel may become involved. In the planning stages of a project, safety suggestions can pay big dividends. Safety personnel, through their knowledge of the hazards associated with different project operations, can offer valuable suggestions in the planning stage of a project.

What is the appropriate safety staffing approach? Some insights were gained from a 1980 study of the top contractors, in which 49 of the largest 100 contractors responded (Hinze and Harrison 1981). Some of the most interesting findings were related to company commitment and the authority granted to the safety personnel. Commitment can be shown in a number of ways. One question asked about the criterion used for determining when to assign a full-time job safety representative or job safety director to a construction project. The responding firms, all with reasonably respectable safety records, differed in the size criterion that was used. The firms with the best safety records had the most stringent size criteria. That is, the firms with the better safety records assigned full-time safety directors to construction projects of varying sizes, typically any projects with more than 100, 200, or 300 workers. The firms that assigned full-time safety personnel to only the very large projects (often only those exceeding 1,000 workers) did not have safety records that were as impressive (see Figure 18.1).

The means by which a job safety director is selected is also important to safety performance. One of the questions asked of the large contractors concerned the person who actually hired the job safety directors. There are essentially two paths by which a job safety director can be selected and hired on a project. One path is through the safety office, and the other is through project management. Note that if the job safety director is hired by someone in management—namely, the project manager or the project superintendent—the loyalties of the job safety director may be biased. That is, his or her judgment may be impaired if safety concerns are viewed as compromising productivity.

Will the job safety director be able to wield a great deal of clout if hired by the superintendent or the project manager? Presumably, one that has the power to hire the job safety director also has the power to fire the job safety director. Figure 18.2 shows the influence of the hiring practices on safety performance. If hired by the safety department personnel, the job safety director will not have his or her judgment clouded by job-site politics to the same extent as when hired by job-site, production-oriented personnel.

When the job safety director is hired by someone in the safety department, the practice makes it clear that safety is important and will not be used as a negotiating issue when productivity questions arise. The same principle can be carried through to the corporate level. The study asked about the person to whom the company safety director reported. It was found that the safest firms were those in which the safety

Figure 18.1
Safety Performance and Criteria for Assigning a Full-time Job Safety Director

Source: Hinze and Harrison 1981

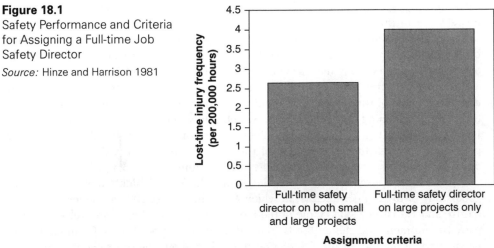

Figure 18.2

Does the Company Safety Director Hire the Job Safety Director?

Source: Hinze and Harrison 1981

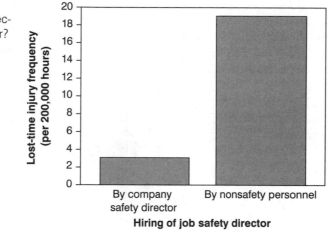

Hiring of job safety director

director reported directly to either the president of the firm or a vice president (see Figure 18.3). Firms in which the corporate safety director reported to a lower-level manager had poorer safety performances. If something is important, it goes directly to the president. If safety reporting must first go to a lower-level manager, the message is clear that safety is not a high priority. The evidence from the study shows that the message has a significant influence on safety performance.

The actual nature of the reporting that takes place varies considerably from firm to firm. Baseline reporting almost always includes a monthly report concerning injuries, summarized on a project-by-project basis. Perhaps the more serious injuries are reported as they occur. Reports may also be provided on any OSHA inspections that have occurred. Other information varies, depending on the nature of the staffing of the projects, the size of the projects, the amount of work that is subcontracted, the types of

Figure 18.3

The Person to Whom the Company Safety Director Reports

Source: Hinze and Harrison 1981

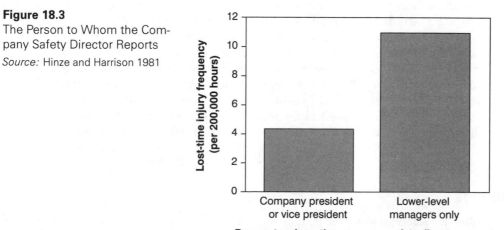

Person to whom the company safety director reports

Figure 18.4
Does the Job Safety Director
Have the Authority to Stop
Unsafe Work?
Source: Levitt 1975

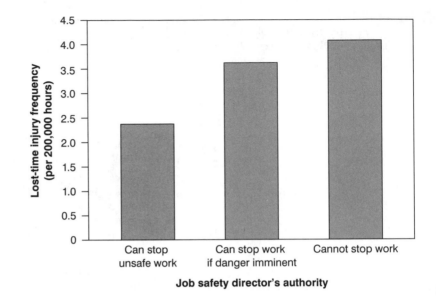

projects being constructed, and so on. At the very least, however, the reports should provide sufficient information for effectively evaluating the safety performance of the various construction personnel on the projects.

An earlier study, which included a smaller sample of 23 construction firms, provides additional ideas on the structuring of the safety staff. In that study, Levitt (1975) used the experience modification rate (EMR) as the primary measure of safety performance. Although the EMR may not always be the best measure of safety performance, especially when firms of differing sizes are involved, some interesting conclusions were reported. The study showed that better safety performance existed in firms that had established safety departments. That result shows the value of company-level commitment to safety. Such commitment is so very important to construction safety.

In findings similar to those of the study described earlier, Levitt found that firms with safer records had their job-site safety inspection reports sent directly to top management. The other (less safe) firms had the reports sent to persons in lower-level positions. It was not clear whether top management ever saw some of the reports.

Levitt's study also showed that firms with better safety records gave the job safety supervisors or safety directors the authority to stop work considered unsafe (Figure 18.4). The job safety director position is not a symbolic position. With the position comes an obligation to assist in the identification of hazards and in the mitigation of those hazards. That obligation cannot be compromised. The proper execution of the obligation entails the necessary authority to accomplish the required tasks.

Final Comments

Although safety cannot ever be fully delegated by supervisory personnel to safety officers, safety personnel can play a valuable role by assisting project managers and superintendents in achieving the zero-accidents goal. It is essential that the safety personnel be given the appropriate authority to properly execute their duties. Safety personnel cannot be regarded as filling symbolic positions; they must be regarded as being at the core of the safety program of the company.

Review Questions

1. What is a good measure of whether the job-site safety officer has the appropriate authority to execute the safety responsibilities on site?
2. For the purposes of good safety performance, what criteria should be used to decide when full-time safety personnel should be assigned to a construction project?
3. Describe the foremen's responsibility for safety when full-time safety personnel are assigned to a construction project.
4. Describe the means by which, according to research studies, a job safety director should be selected and hired on a project.
5. Describe the types of documentation that safety personnel might be expected to maintain.
6. Describe the basic functions of job-site safety directors.
7. Draw an organizational chart that shows the ideal relationship of the company safety director to the other key company personnel.
8. What is the appropriate relationship between the project safety director and the project superintendent?
9. How can the OSHA regulations be satisfied when a construction project is 100 miles from the nearest hospital or medical clinic?
10. At what stage of construction should the job-site safety director be assigned to the project?

References

Hinze, J., and C. Harrison. 1981. "Safety Programs in Large Construction Firms." *Journal of the Construction Division, ASCE* 107, no. 3, 455–67.

Levitt, R. 1975. *The Effect of Top Management on Safety in Construction.* Technical Report no. 196, Construction Institute. Stanford, Calif.: Stanford University.

Levitt, R., and N. Samelson. 1993. *Construction Safety Management.* 2d ed. New York: John Wiley.

Subcontractor Safety

You can subcontract all the work, but you cannot delegate all the safety responsibilities.

The construction industry thrives on the work of specialty contractors, generally referred to as subcontractors. On building construction projects, it is common for 80–90% of the work to be performed by subcontractors. On highway or other heavy projects, the portion subcontracted is generally less, but a significant amount of the work is still performed under subcontract agreements. In fact, on virtually all public works projects, a designated portion of the project funds are set aside for the employment of women-owned businesses (WBEs) and minority-owned businesses (MBEs), firms that tend to offer specialized services.

Contractually, the subcontracting firm typically enters into an agreement directly with the general contractor. Although the owner commonly has the power of final approval of the selected subcontractors, typically the general contractor's first choice is employed on the project. Contractually, the subcontracting firm does not have an agreement with the owner. In fact, the main contract (between the general contractor and the owner) often states this fact very specifically. In essence, the subcontractor is regarded by the owner as an employee of the general contractor. As far as the owner is concerned, the work performed by subcontractors is the same as the work performed by the general contractor. That is shown in the following typical provision:

The Contractor shall not sublet, sell, transfer, assign, or otherwise dispose of the contract or contracts or any portion thereof or of the contractor's right, title, or interest therein without the written consent of the Owner. In case such consent is given, the contractor will be permitted to sublet a portion thereof, but shall perform with the contractor's own organization work amounting to not less than 50 percent of the total contract amount, except that any items designated in the contract as Specialty Items may be performed by subcontract and the cost of any such specialty item so performed by subcontract may be deducted from the total cost before computing the amount of work required to be performed by the contractor with his own organization. *No subcontracts or transfer of contract shall release the contractor from his liability* under the contract and bond. (italics added)

The subcontract agreement may address safety to some extent. It is common for subcontractors to be contractually required to comply with the OSHA regulations, but that requirement does little more than emphasize that safety regulations exist. Safety provisions found in some subcontract agreements are as follows:

Safety. Subcontractor shall comply with all applicable safety rules, regulations, and recognized trade practices for the protection of workers and other persons who may be near the work area. Subcontractor shall also promptly comply with any directive issued by the Contractor or the Owner pertaining to safety and shall participate fully in the Contractor's safety program.

This provision goes slightly beyond the OSHA regulations by including "trade practices." Note that the subcontractor is also obligated to comply with safety-related directives issued by the project owner and the general contractor. In addition, the subcontractor is required to participate in the safety program of the general contractor.

The quoted provision, in its brevity, is similar to the subcontract provision appearing in the American Institute of Architects (AIA) Document A401 (Standard Form of Agreement between Contractor and Subcontractor, 1987 edition). The AIA provision does not acknowledge the general contractor's safety program, but it does include a requirement that the subcontractor notify the general contractor within three days of the occurrence of an injury to an employee or agent of the subcontractor.

The following is another example of a safety provision taken from a subcontract agreement:

Safety. The Subcontractor agrees that he is fully cognizant of the Construction Safety Act of 1969 and the Occupational Safety and Health Act of 1970, including all changes and amendments thereto, and agrees to be responsible for any violation of the provisions contained therein caused by his work operation. No Subcontractor or his employees may use alcohol or drugs on-site. Nor shall the Subcontractor permit the off-site use of alcohol or drugs by any employee to jeopardize the health and safety of other workers or the public. The Subcontractor shall immediately remove permanently from the site any person the job superintendent has objection to on account of alcohol and/or drug use.

The foregoing provision includes a caution about the changing nature of the safety regulations and a statement that the subcontractor is held to the most recent version. The other specifics of the provision relate to the use of alcohol and drugs on the construction project. The following provision, used by a Seattle general contractor, is a modification of the provision in the Associated General Contractors of America (AGC) standard form Subcontract for Building Construction (AGC Document No. 600).

> **Safety.** Subcontractor agrees that the prevention of injuries to workers engaged in the work is its responsibility, even if the Contractor establishes a safety program for the entire project. Subcontractor shall establish and implement safety measures, policies and standards conforming to those required or recommended by governmental authorities, the Contractor, and the Owner, including, but not limited to, any requirements imposed by the Contract Documents. Subcontractor shall comply with the recommendations of insurance companies having an interest in the project and shall stop any part of the work deemed to be unsafe until corrective measures have been taken. Contractor's failure to stop Subcontractor's unsafe practices shall not relieve Subcontractor of its responsibility therefor.

This provision begins with the statement that safety is the responsibility of the subcontractor. In addition to complying with the regulations, the subcontractor is also required to comply with any recommendations offered by insurance companies and any additional requirements stipulated in the contract documents. The contractor retains the specific right to stop any unsafe practices of the subcontractor.

Another subcontract stated the following:

> It is understood and agreed that the Subcontractor will have equipment, workers, and supplies on this project and that the use thereof by the Subcontractor must at all times comply with all local, state, and federal regulations, including OSHA safety regulations. For any safety violations for which claims, fines, or penalties may be levied, assessed, or extracted from the General Contractor, the Subcontractor agrees to reimburse and/or hold harmless the General Contractor on account of any such claim, fine, or penalty which may be paid by the Contractor which arises out of or which is due to any action on the part of the Subcontractor, its agents, employees, or suppliers. Any amounts required to hold the Contractor harmless shall be deducted by the Contractor from any payment due the Subcontractor.

This provision includes a hold-harmless provision, in which the subcontractor agrees to assume any indebtedness that the general contractor may incur as a result of the actions of the subcontractor. Such hold-harmless clauses are becoming more widely used. Not all jurisdictions will enforce such provisions; however, the potential cost associated with such a clause cannot be ignored.

Another subcontract agreement states the following:

> Subcontractor shall comply with all current state and federal safety, air, water, pollution, hazardous waste, and other public health and welfare standards, as well as the requirements of the local authorities, including such standards and requirements which may be imposed or become effective after the execution of this agreement. The Subcontractor shall protect other work which is subject to damage from the Subcontractor's construction activities. This Subcontractor shall not permit any of his employees to work on the job site who is deemed to be a hazard to himself or others for whatever reason.
>
> Any materials brought onto the job site by this Subcontractor, his subcontractor(s), or material supplier(s) that may be considered by any governing authority to be hazardous, toxic, dangerous, or contaminated shall be specifically identified, stored, used, protected, labeled, and disposed of by this Subcontractor in accordance with proper procedures.

> Subcontractor is to notify the Contractor immediately in writing of any injuries to Subcontractor's workers which occur on the project site or are related to work taking place on the site. Subcontractor also agrees to notify the Contractor in writing if any injury results in a claim for workers' compensation benefits or in any other legal action against the subcontractor.

This subcontract provision, while appearing under the heading Safety, is primarily focused on the use of hazardous materials.

Although the owner views the subcontractor as being close to the general contractor's "camp," that is not the perception of most general contractors. The subcontract agreement is typically carefully drafted so as to ensure that the subcontracting firm is clearly an independent contractor and not an agent of the general contractor. That is done largely because the liability of the general contractor would increase if the subcontractor were inadvertently to become an agent of the general contractor. Many general contractors have found that, despite their efforts to ensure treatment of their subcontractors as independent contractors, they were not shielded from liability. Of particular interest are personal injury suits that are filed by or on behalf of employees of subcontractors against general contractors. This phenomenon (suit of the general contractor for the actions of a subcontractor) is specific to certain jurisdictions. That is, such suits have not been successful in all states, because statutory law precludes such suits in some states.

General contractors, because of their in-house capabilities for management, are hired by owners to oversee, direct, and coordinate the construction efforts on their construction projects. Because of their broad knowledge of their projects and because of their control of the various functions carried out on each project, general contractors are increasingly viewed as bearing at least some of the burden of liability incurred through the actions of subcontractors. The OSHA provision on which the broad interpretation is based is 29 CFR § 1926.10, which states that "no contractor or subcontractor contracting for any part of the contract work shall require any laborer or mechanic employed in the performance of the contract to work in surroundings or under working conditions which are unsanitary, hazardous, or dangerous to his health or safety, as determined under construction safety and health standards promulgated by the Secretary by regulation." Note that this says that the general contractor bears a responsibility for "any laborer."

Although subcontractor safety is addressed in many subcontract agreements, in most cases it is addressed in a superficial fashion. Needless to say, the safety performance of subcontractors is a topic that should be of primary interest to all general contractors. With the naming of owners as parties to many lawsuits, it is also becoming increasingly important for owners to be concerned about the overall safety of their projects, including all work performed by subcontractors.

Subcontractor Safety Begins in the Selection Process

A general contractor that has a very good safety record may undertake a new project with the assumption that the same general work procedures will be followed. Perhaps the general contractor can select all subcontractors on the basis of the lowest bid and still have a good safety record on a project. Much lies in the degree of control that the general contractor is able to wield over the various trades workers and the subcontractors. The safety culture of the project must be quickly and effectively embraced by all parties involved on the construction project. That may be difficult for subcontractors who are focused only on maximizing profits, meeting the schedule, and providing the quality that will satisfy the contract obligations. Such firms often regard safety as a luxury for which additional efforts are warranted only when they do not compromise profits, increase project duration, or adversely affect project quality.

To avoid the potential of employing a subcontractor that does not appreciate the continuing need to be concerned about safety, general contractors should carefully select their subcontractors. Safety should be a definite criterion for subcontractor selection.

How can a general contractor identify a safe subcontractor? There are, of course, many "safety experts" who can provide a ready answer for this question. Unfortunately, it is not that easy. Remember that a subcontractor with a history of poor safety performance may be able turn things around and become an exceptionally safe company. Conversely, a firm with a good safety record so far can theoretically end up with a poor safety record. That often happens if a company has gone through a period of tremendous growth or if it has diversified its operations to include work for which little in-house expertise exists. Although such changes may not be commonplace, they do point out that simply looking at past safety performance is a narrow view.

Obviously, the past safety performance of a company should be evaluated. Unfortunately, the past safety performance of a company may not be as easy to evaluate as it may seem. What measure should be used for evaluating the past safety performance of a subcontractor? Different answers may be offered, including the experience modification rate, the loss ratio on workers' compensation, and the injury frequency. Naturally, if all those measures were considered and all yielded the same result, there would be a strong basis on which to make the decision. If the measures are in conflict, however, the decision becomes more complex.

Influence of General Contractors on Subcontractor Safety

Subcontractor safety was the subject of the first safety research effort undertaken by the Construction Industry Institute (CII). (Refer to Chapter 3 for a brief description of the CII.) The study was specifically focused on the ways in which general contractors influence subcontractor safety (Hinze and Figone 1988; Hinze and Talley 1988). No major safety study had previously been conducted on subcontractor safety.

Because almost all projects are completed with the considerable involvement of subcontractors, it seems reasonable for the safety performance of subcontractors to be a major concern of owners and general contractors. That was one of the underlying reasons for CII's support of the study.

The study revealed that there is a difference between medium and large projects in the way to achieve good safety performance. Research findings were indeed different for projects of different sizes. In fact, the research effort actually consisted of two separate studies. One study was of medium-sized projects, and the other was of large projects. The terms *medium* and *large* are not universally defined, so their definitions in the studies will be described briefly as the studies are introduced.

Subcontractor Safety on Medium-Sized Projects

The subcontractors employed on medium-sized projects had the following characteristics:

Annual volume: $600,000 to $25,000,000
Work force: 4,500 to 300,000 worker hours per year

Those size parameters were completely arbitrary. That is, the firms included in the study were not selected on the basis of size. That range happened to be the range in size of the firms included in the study. The subcontractors were in either the San Francisco Bay Area or the Puget Sound Area. Through the study, it was possible to identify practices of general contractors that resulted in better safety performance for subcontractors.

In the study of subcontractor safety on medium-sized projects, safety was most influenced by five broad categories of variables (Hinze and Figone 1988). They are summarized in Figure 19.1 in the order of the strength of their influence on subcontractor safety. Subcontractor safety performance is influenced by all five factors; however, project pressures and project coordination are by far the most important in their impact on subcontractor safety.

Project Pressures

Project pressures were found to have the greatest impact on subcontractor safety performance. Several factors were discovered that contributed to such pressures. They are summarized as follows:

1. The superintendents of the general contractors stated whether or not they felt they were working under pressure. On the projects of those who stated that there was a great deal of pressure, the subcontractors' safety records were poor. Conversely, the subcontractors had better safety records when the superintendents stated there was very little pressure.
2. The schedule status of the project was found to be linked to the safety performance of the subcontractors. The graph in Figure 19.2 illustrates that relationship.
3. When the general contractor's managers emphasized essentially only profits, subcontractor safety declined. Better safety records were noted when profits were mentioned along with other goals.

Figure 19.1
The Relative Influence of General Contractors' Practices on Subcontractor Safety on Medium-Sized Projects
Source: Hinze and Figone 1988

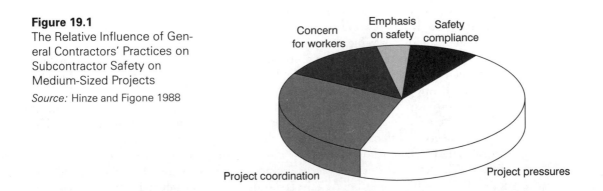

Figure 19.2
Schedule Status and Subcontractor Safety Performance
Source: Hinze and Figone 1988

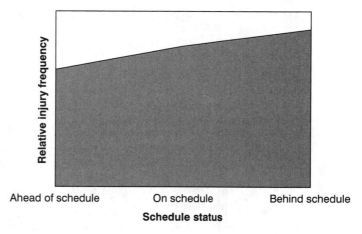

4. When asked about job priorities, the general contractors that responded with only an emphasis on cost and schedule had subcontractors with poorer safety records. Safer records were noted when other priorities, such as safety and quality, were included among the priorities.
5. Subcontractor safety performance was best when the subcontractors were employed on projects on which the general contractors negotiated their contracts. On the competitively bid projects, the subcontractors' safety records suffered. It was also found that when subcontracts were negotiated, better safety performances were realized.

Note that subcontractor safety is related to the overall project status, even though some measures of project status may have seemingly little to do with the relationship between the general contractor and the subcontractor. The key is perhaps that a safe project is not behind schedule and that, in general, when a project is on schedule and within the budget, there is no overriding pressure felt on the job. Job pressure and delayed production are sources of stress.

Project Coordination

The effectiveness of the general contractor's efforts to provide project coordination was found to be directly related to subcontractor safety performance. Projects on which the general contractors were assessed as having good coordination skills were also those on which subcontractors had better safety records.

Many factors influence the ease with which coordination can be provided. To a large extent, the effectiveness of coordination is influenced by such factors as the size and complexity of the project. It was found that the subcontractors on the larger projects had poorer safety records than the subcontractors on the smaller projects.

Note that the safety performances of the subcontractors were also found to be directly influenced by the number of subcontractors employed on the projects. The relative injury frequencies for different numbers of subcontractors are shown in Figure 19.3. The results show a clear association between the number of subcontractors and the safety records of the subcontractors.

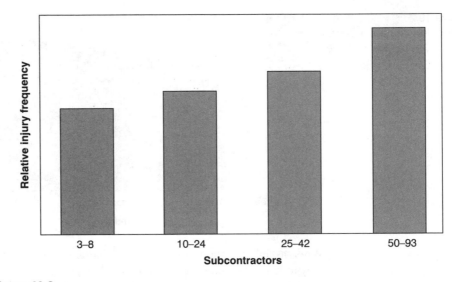

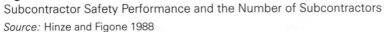

Figure 19.3
Subcontractor Safety Performance and the Number of Subcontractors
Source: Hinze and Figone 1988

It is to be expected that general contractors would want to work with some subcontractors more than others. In fact some general contractors made it a point to hire subcontractors with whom a working relationship had already been established. Working with familiar subcontractors pays off in the area of safety. This finding is not unlike the finding (discussed in Chapter 17) that companies are safer when they retain their employees for longer periods of time. Familiarity is good for safety performance.

Coordination is among the most important issues to subcontractors. They want direction on the project. How can direction be given most effectively? Are subcontractors allowed to have input in the schedule? Are subcontractors informed in advance if there is slippage in the schedule? Are subcontractor constraints reflected in the schedules?

The influence of coordination on safety is considerable. By having a clear directive on when particular services are needed, a subcontractor can focus on delivering those services.

Emphasis on Safety

The general contractor's emphasis on safety is important to subcontractor safety. The importance of safety to a general contractor quickly becomes apparent on a construction site. One way that a general contractor can show the importance of safety is by keeping track of safety. If safety is placed on the same level of importance as quality, time, and cost, subcontractor safety will be improved. Another way that the general contractor can show concern about safety is through daily communications on the project. The daily communication of safety concerns was also found to directly influence subcontractor safety.

Management's role in safety becomes apparent with these findings. There must be "commitment from the top" on safety. If it is heeded, the results will be felt and realized in better safety performance.

Concern for Workers

General contractors who express concern for workers have safer subcontractors. Although the issue of concern was subjectively assessed, it was found to be expressed in the following two ways:

1. The contractors care about the individual needs of workers.
2. The contractors give job orientations to all workers.

Do workers have a voice on the job? Will someone listen to them? Can concerns be addressed seriously to someone in management? Although workers do not run or control projects, they should be recognized as having needs and concerns. Worker orientation for all workers (including the workers of subcontractors) helps job safety. The unknowns that surround a job are sources of stress, and their influence on workers can be reduced through orientation.

Compliance with Safety Regulations

It is important to address the safety conditions that exist at the site. Eliminating hazards is important. The following were noted as being directly associated with better safety records for subcontractors.

1. Projects are specifically monitored for such items as handrails, floor openings, and overhead power lines.
2. Frequent job-site inspections are conducted.
3. Job-site inspections include the work of subcontractors.

Although compliance with safety regulations was not of paramount importance in influencing subcontractor safety, its role should not be considered negligible. The work of subcontractors should be included in job-site inspections. The subcontractors are part of the total project, and their work should not be viewed any differently.

Subcontractor Safety on Large Projects

The second study conducted on subcontractor safety, instead of being an examination of particular subcontractors, was an analysis of large projects being constructed throughout the United States (Hinze and Talley 1988). Although the smallest project was $10 million and the largest was $3.5 billion, those were not typical sizes. Most projects were over $100 million. The projects employed 50—3,000 workers. In this study of large projects, the practices of general contractors were examined. The safety records of subcontractors were compared with those practices to determine which practices had the greatest influence on subcontractor safety.

As illustrated in Figure 19.4, subcontractor safety on large projects is most influenced by

1. the general contractor's strong emphasis on safety
2. the general contractor's effective project coordination

Figure 19.4
The Relative Influence of General Contractors's Practices on Subcontractor Safety on Large Projects
Source: Hinze and Talley 1988

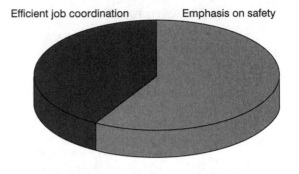
Efficient job coordination   Emphasis on safety

Subcontractor safety was found to be influenced by safety emphasis and project coordination, with the strongest influence consisting of the emphasis on safety on the job. The second most important influence is efficient job coordination. Note that job coordination was also found to be very important for safety in the study of medium-sized firms.

On large projects it was found that virtually all of the following practices are common:

1. A full-time project safety director is assigned.
2. All workers must attend toolbox meetings.
3. Safety is discussed during coordination meetings.
4. Safety is discussed at the prejob conference.
5. The safety performance of the project is monitored.
6. Supervisory safety performance is monitored.
7. Top managers discuss safety on job visits.
8. Supervisors attend separate safety meetings.
9. Bonuses are affected by safety performance.
10. Compliance with safety regulations is required.

Many project managers could examine this list and think to themselves that their firms already do all of the above. The point to be made is that the research study found that almost all large projects use those practices. Since essentially every project employed the practices, no means was available by which to assess the merits of any of them. Thus, it is not clear how much those practices influence subcontractor safety.

Some other practices were found to be directly related to subcontractor safety performance on large projects. They included the following:

1. Subcontractors are required to hold their own toolbox meetings.
2. A safety orientation is given to the employees of all subcontractors.
3. Subcontractor safety programs are carefully reviewed.
4. Subcontractors must submit safety reports to the project managers.
5. Accidents of subcontractors are investigated by project managers.
6. Project managers make special job safety tours.
7. The work of subcontractors is inspected for safety.

Those practices were identified as definitely having a favorable influence on subcontractor safety performance. Note that most of them are safety practices that are implemented with the subcontractor specifically in mind.

Clear direction in performing their tasks is very important to subcontractors. As the research showed, it is also important for subcontractor safety. Some findings were related to the association between project coordination and better safety performance among subcontractors. The project coordination factors that benefited subcontractor safety included the following:

1. The tasks of all crafts and all subcontractors are carefully planned.
2. The coordination skills of the general contractor are highly rated by the subcontractors.
3. The projects are smaller.
4. Schedules are updated whenever necessary.
5. Short-interval (look-ahead) schedules are used to help plan jobs.

Perhaps the most notable finding of the study was that general contractors have a stronger influence on subcontractor safety performance than do the subcontractors themselves. That finding is the bottom line of the study. It emphasizes that the general contractor's role in subcontractor safety is not incidental. In fact, the role is pivotal in determining the success of subcontractor safety on the project.

Final Comments

Contractors are to be commended when they take proactive and positive steps in their operations to ensure the safety of the workers. As research findings suggest, success in safety may go far beyond the actual safety program that an employer might set up. Safety must be regarded as an integral component of the overall operations of a firm. That is especially true where subcontractor safety is concerned. On construction sites, subcontractor safety is considerably affected by the efficiency with which the work activities are coordinated. Supervisors, subcontractors, and the workers want to do a good job, and efforts should be expended so that the flow of work is smooth for all parties.

Review Questions

1. What seems to enhance subcontractor safety, no matter what the size of the project?
2. In what ways can coordination be demonstrated on a project?
3. What factors have the greatest impact on subcontractor safety in medium-sized firms?
4. What factors have the greatest impact on subcontractor safety on large projects?
5. What safety practices or programs were found to exist on virtually all large projects?
6. Explain why safety performance is influenced by different factors on medium-sized projects and on large projects.
7. How might subcontractors experience pressure on a construction project?
8. What type of subcontract provision addressing safety is perhaps the most common one found in subcontract agreements, even though it adds little or nothing to the subcontractor's responsibility for safety?
9. How strong is the general contractor's influence on the safety performance of subcontractors?

10. What selection criteria for subcontractors might allow the general contractor greater confidence in the safety performance to be achieved by the subcontractors?

References

Construction Industry Institute. 1991. *Managing Subcontractor Safety.* Publication 13-1 (February).

Hinze, J. 1987. "Qualities of Safe Superintendents." *ASCE Journal of Construction Engineering and Management.* 113, no. 1, 169–71.

Hinze, J., and L. Figone. 1988. *Subcontractor Safety As Influenced by General Contractors on Small and Medium Sized Projects.* CII Source Document 38. Austin, Tex.: Construction Industry Institute.

Hinze, J., and H. Parker. 1978. "Safety: Productivity and Job Pressures." *Journal of the Construction Division, ASCE* 104, no. 1, 27–34.

Hinze, J., and D. Talley. 1988. *Subcontractor Safety As Influenced by General Contractors on Large Projects.* CII Source Document 39. Austin, Tex.: Construction Industry Institute.

Project Coordination and Construction Safety

Safety is not a pain; injuries are.

Whenever a construction contract is entered into, the elements of cost, time, and quality are invariably included—specifically, that the project is to be delivered in a stated time with the requisite quality and that, for such delivery, the contractor is to be compensated with a specified monetary amount. The time component has been mentioned in other chapters as harboring the greatest potential for increasing pressures on those performing the work.

If a work plan falls behind schedule, the standard reaction is to somehow increase the production effort in order to get back on schedule. When the production effort is increased, accidents have an increased chance of occurrence. That effect demonstrates the need for the work to progress smoothly and in an organized fashion so that the scheduled work activities take place as planned. With the many different tasks involved in most construction projects and with the large number of subcontractors that participate in the construction effort, it is clear that a great deal of coordination is required to deliver projects in the specified period of time.

In this chapter I will present information on how coordination efforts on construction projects are related to safety performance. Only the most relevant information about different research studies is provided in this chapter, as it is the findings that are considered of primary interest here. The reader is invited to review the references if more detailed information on the studies is of interest.

The Importance of Coordination

On most construction projects, the general contractor prepares some type of project schedule. The schedule generally identifies the major activities required to deliver the project, along with the allotted times for the accomplishment of those activities. Schedules are generally prepared with the use of a computer and can be relatively sophisticated. It is increasingly common for projects to be scheduled through the use of computer programs that develop a network diagram of the planned work. Such a diagram is commonly known as a critical-path method (CPM) schedule. Many other programs generate schedules in the form of bar charts. Even some simple and relatively inexpensive scheduling programs have the ability to indicate when certain activities are to be performed by a specific crew or by a particular subcontractor.

Those capabilities of scheduling software demonstrate the widely accepted importance of the need to coordinate the tasks to be performed by different parties. It is important to know how the different tasks are related and how long each task is expected to take. If the tasks are performed in the allotted times, the project will be completed on time. If some tasks are not completed on time, the managers of the construction effort should have sufficient advance notice of the delay so that adjustments can be made to the scheduled activities. That is, if the schedule falls behind, changes must be made in the logistics or in the allocation of resources if the schedule is to be compressed in some way. The value of such schedules is demonstrated well by the inclusion in many construction contracts of a requirement that a project schedule be developed.

Network diagrams, such as CPM schedules, have been widely used for the scheduling of construction activities. Their preparation requires the owner, the contractor, or a scheduling consultant to develop a clear idea of the operations needed, their sequencing, and their timing. As the scheduling model is developed, it may alert the developer to potential problem areas, such as excessive resource demands, and allows that person to manipulate or adjust the schedule to address such problems. When completed, the schedule provides an estimate of the project's duration and specific times during which individual activities will occur. Thus, coordination of the various workers, subcontractors, suppliers, and other resources can be accomplished.

Of the various project management functions, coordination is of particular importance to subcontractors. Subcontractors want to be fully informed when they are to be on the construction site to perform their duties. It can be very costly to a subcontractor to gear up to do work on a project only to find that nothing can be done because other work has not been completed. For example, suppose a drywall subcontractor has been told to show up on the job on a given day to install drywall. So that maximum performance can be achieved, the drywall subcontractor has the Sheetrock delivered to the site the day before the planned work. Then, when the Sheetrock installation begins, the drywallers realize that the specified sprinkler system has not been installed, so the ceiling drywall cannot be installed. Furthermore, they find that the insulation has not been installed in the exterior walls, so even those walls cannot be drywalled. Rather than performing the work piecemeal, the drywall subcontractor angrily withdraws from the project. The general contractor's credibility in coordinating the work has now been tarnished, and the drywaller will be more reluctant to rely on the general contractor in the future.

Subcontractors want direction on the project. When that direction is administered well, the subcontractors tend to profit more, as the work goes more smoothly. All the parties have the same stake in getting the work done. They want to be involved in the effort, and they want to be told exactly when their services will be needed. How can such direction be given most effectively? Are subcontractors allowed to have input in the schedule? Are subcontractors informed in advance if there is slippage in the schedule? Are subcontractor constraints reflected in the schedules? If subcontractors are not properly coordinated, their work will not be performed efficiently. Subcontractors have a need to be informed in advance when their services will be required on the construction site. If they are not informed, productivity will suffer and project delays can be expected.

The coordination effort affects all those involved in the construction effort. Those affected include the various foremen and supervisors of the general contractor, the many suppliers associated with the project, and certainly the subcontractors. How does coordination relate to safety? It will be shown that the coordination effort has a direct impact on safety performance.

Conflict between Scheduling and Safety?

There is an unspoken myth that perhaps schedules cannot be met without compromising safety. If a project falls behind schedule, supervisors who believe the myth may be inclined to reduce their efforts on safety to beef up the production effort. Those with this belief assume that safety compromises productivity and that safety consumes valuable resources. Actually, the reverse is true. This subject has already been addressed in a prior chapter, but it is of such importance that it warrants repeating.

Consider the safety records of superintendents who were rated by their superiors on their ability to meet schedules. As shown in Figure 20.1, the superintendents with

Figure 20.1
The Ability of Superintendents
to Meet Established Schedules
Source: Hinze and Parker 1978

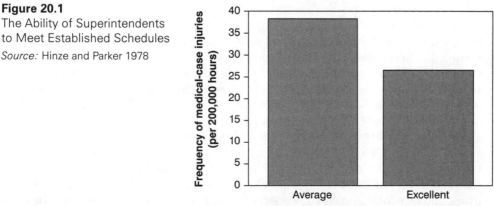

the best ratings for their ability to meet specified schedules were also those with the best safety records (Hinze 1976; Hinze and Parker 1978). Thus, there is no conflict. In fact, it appears that preserving safety and meeting schedules are mutually achievable objectives. It is interesting that the safety records of all the superintendents were not the same, as that would indicate that safety performance is independent of the ability to meet schedules. Instead, safety and success in scheduling appear to be dependent on each other, and they are certainly jointly achievable.

A project that is well organized reduces the pressure and frustration experienced by the workers. Good coordination means the job will proceed smoothly, the necessary tools and materials will be available, and a minimum amount of rework will be required. The workers can concentrate on performing their work, and this concentration facilitates working more safely. In addition, good coordination is an indication of the overall quality of management. Other studies have shown that superintendents who run well-managed projects are the same ones that administer their projects more safely (Hinze 1987; Hinze and Raboud 1988).

Research findings linking safety performance to effective management are sufficiently convincing to support the premise that there is no conflict between achieving good safety performance and meeting a schedule. The findings show that general contractors and their superintendents can simultaneously meet established schedules and have safe projects.

The Relationship of Coordination to Safety Performance

To meet schedules in the construction of major facilities, coordination is of paramount importance. Without coordination, there is chaos. Where there is chaos, delays have a way of increasing at a seemingly exponential rate. Unless the proper steps are taken to get back on track, the project that is off schedule by a small amount can quickly turn into a project that is very much off schedule. If adjustments are not made, the morale of the work force can be damaged. In very bad situations, sabotage of the work may even occur. With the importance of coordination well understood, it is worth examining the relationship between coordination and safety.

In a safety study of 24 high-rise construction projects in Canada, several subcontractor representatives on each project were asked to rate the general contractors on their ability to coordinate the construction work (Raboud 1986). The ratings were then compared with the safety records of the general contractors on those projects. The results of the study are shown in Figure 20.2. The findings, similar to those discussed in the preceding section, were that the general contractors with the better-rated abilities to coordinate construction activities had the better safety records.

Effective project coordination has the objective of organizing the project activities so that all parties (crew foremen, subcontractors, suppliers, etc.) have a clear idea of when they are to start certain activities and when such activities are to be completed. Thus, each party involved in the project knows the answers to the basic questions *what, when,* and *how long.* If everything goes according to the plan, the project will be completed on time.

Figure 20.2
The General Contractor's Coordination Ability

Source: Raboud 1986

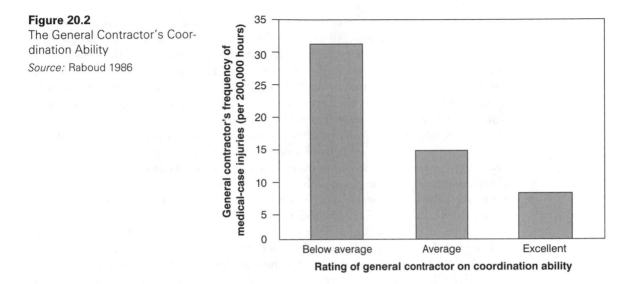

Figure 20.2

A large study of construction safety was conducted on 57 large commercial and industrial projects in the United States, ranging from $10 million to nearly $4 billion (Hinze and Talley 1988). General contractors and subcontractors were involved in the study. Subcontractors were asked about the effectiveness of the general contractors at coordination. The responses were compared with the safety performances of the subcontractors. The results, shown in Figure 20.3, reveal that the safety performances of subcontractors are linked to the coordination efforts of the general contractors.

The results show that the subcontractors experienced better safety on projects in which the coordination abilities of the general contractors were evaluated as being very good or excellent. Note that the injury frequency of the subcontractors who rated the general contractors' abilities as excellent was only 6.6 injuries per 200,000 hours of worker exposure. In general, good safety performance is most readily assured when the coordination abilities of the general contractor are good.

Figure 20.3
Subcontractors' Rating of the General Contractor's Ability to Coordinate the Work

Source: Hinze and Talley 1988

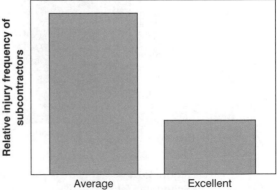

The assessment of the abilities of a general contractor to coordinate construction activities is a subjective one. At the same time, however, subcontractors can give reasonably good evaluations because their work is directly affected by the coordination efforts. If the coordination efforts are poor, then the subcontractor will encounter delays and frustrations caused by not knowing when the construction project is actually ready for work to be done by a particular trade or subcontractor. That problem may result in an activity's running behind schedule.

A more objective, yet more general, question relates to the overall project. For example, if the coordination skills of a general contractor are good, it can be inferred that the project will probably be delivered on or ahead of schedule. For an examination of the relationship of project schedule status to safety performance, general contractors were asked about the project status (Hinze and Raboud 1988; Raboud 1986; Hinze and Figone 1988). The results are shown in Figure 20.4.

The status of the project in relation to the schedule appears to be a fairly reliable indicator of the safety performance that subcontractors might expect. The subcontractors on projects that were ahead of schedule had the best safety records. On the other hand, the subcontractors on projects that were reported to be behind schedule had noticeably poorer safety records. These findings support the theme being established: that effective coordination improves project safety performance.

Project coordination consists of a variety of tasks. On large construction projects, coordination is generally accepted to begin with a schedule, a construction plan con-

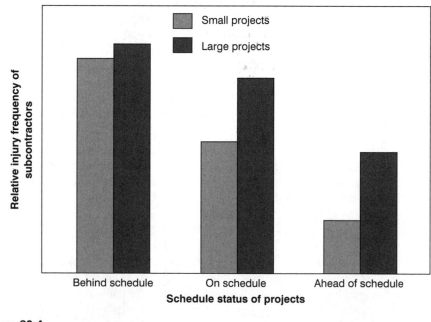

Figure 20.4
Schedule Status
Source: Hinze and Figone 1988; Raboud 1986

Figure 20.5
The Type of Schedule Used
Source: Hinze and Raboud 1988

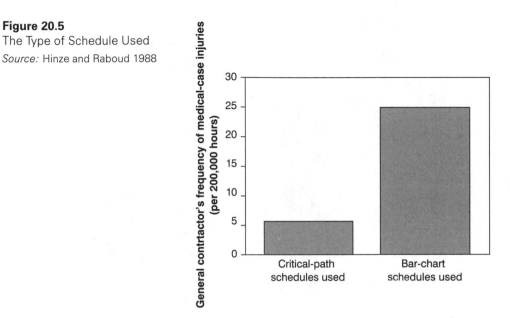

sisting of activities and dates. On large projects the schedule is typically in the form of a network-based CPM schedule or a bar chart. A question was asked in the Canadian study about the specific type of schedule employed on each project (Raboud 1986; Hinze and Raboud 1988). It was discovered that the injury rates of general contractors appeared to be influenced by the type of schedule used (see Figure 20.5).

The results show that the projects using CPM schedules had lower injury rates than did those using the less-detailed schedules, namely, bar charts. The essential differences between CPM schedules and bar charts are the level of detail and the failure of bar charts, generally, to show the relationships among the different activities. Greater detail can be incorporated into CPM schedules, and they are more accurate in portraying the relationship that each activity has to all other activities. Bar charts simply show the times at which activities are expected to occur. Thus, CPM schedules are generally considered more appropriate when projects are more complex.

It is not sufficient simply to have a schedule. If a schedule is to be an effective time management tool, it must be used. A question was asked in the Canadian study to assess the degree to which the schedule was actually utilized as a tool to manage time on a project (Raboud 1986; Hinze and Raboud 1988). The results indicate that the extent of use of the schedule is related to safety performance (see Figure 20.6).

Greater use of schedules appears to pay dividends in safety performance. Note that the safety results examined were the general contractor's safety record and the subcontractors' safety records. The more extensive use of the schedules was associated with better safety performances for both general contractors and subcontractors. The results point to an inference that the management of time is linked to the management of safety.

The findings show that general contractors have a significant influence on the safety performances of their subcontractors. Several of the specific findings related to schedules and scheduling show the extent of the influence that scheduling has on safety performance.

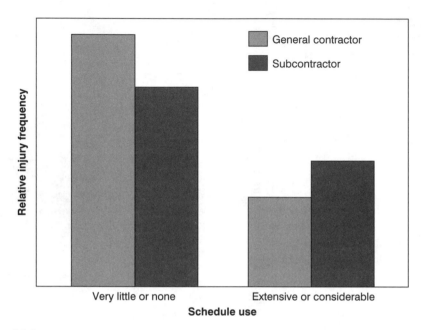

Figure 20.6
The Degree of Schedule Use
Source: Hinze and Raboud 1988

Short-Interval Schedules and Safety

Whenever the topic of construction schedules is brought up in a classroom, the immediate response is to think about project schedules that show, in varying levels of detail, all the activities required to take a project from the start of construction to project completion. The type of schedule envisioned is probably a bar chart or a critical path schedule (either an arrow diagram or a precedence diagram). Those are the "big picture" schedules that are generally discussed in the classroom. Although such schedules are very important, there is another type of schedule that is perhaps even more important, namely, the short-interval schedule.

Short-interval schedules, as the name implies, cover activities that are to take place in the immediate or near future, usually the next two, three, or four weeks. The focus of a short-interval schedule is at the crew level. Sufficient detail is shown on such a schedule to advise the foreman of the tasks to be performed by the crew virtually every day for the period covered. Note that this schedule is quite different from the project-level, or master, schedule, which cannot be prepared with such precision. These short-term schedules, as used on many construction projects, have greater relevance to what is actually happening on a project on a day-to-day basis.

Short-interval schedules are valuable for crew planning, a task that is not feasible with project schedules. It is from the short-interval schedules that the various craft foremen obtain information about the specific tasks to be performed. For example, the project or master schedule may have an activity labeled "construct exterior wooden stairs." The short-

Figure 20.7

Short-Interval Schedules

Source: Raboud 1986

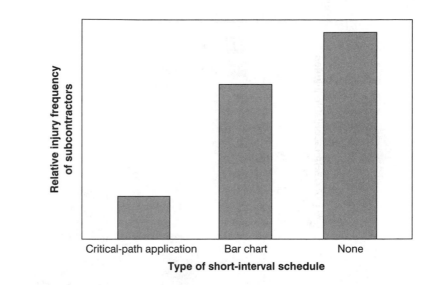

interval schedule will show the same activity, but the activity will be broken down into various components, such as "excavate for footings," "place concrete for footings," "install posts and beams," "build stairs," "erect rails," and "prime and paint stairs." Note that the level of detail is such that the concrete crew work can be planned for a specific day, the carpentry crew work can be planned for a specific period, and the painting crew will also know when its services will be needed. In short, the daily activities occurring on a construction project often revolve around the information provided in the short-interval schedules.

It has already been shown that safety performance is better on projects that use project schedules to a greater extent. Does the use of short-interval schedules have a similar influence on construction safety? As shown in Figure 20.7, findings suggest that not only are short-interval schedules good for subcontractor safety, but the greater amount of detail included in the schedules (as in CPM-based short-interval schedules) also benefits the safety performance of the general contractor (Raboud 1986).

The added detail that may be included in short-interval schedules provides additional guidance to foremen in organizing their crews' activities. The added detail apparently makes the work go more smoothly, by helping the foremen plan the tasks to be performed by individual workers and procure the necessary materials and equipment on a day-to-day basis. Smoother work means less hassle in the workplace, and less hassle is good for safety. Just as greater detail in project schedules is good for project safety, so, too, greater detail in short-interval schedules is good for project safety.

Of course, it must be recognized that having a schedule does not automatically mean that there is universal acceptance and use of the schedule. Some supervisors are quite good at envisioning the tasks that must be completed in the near future. Unfortunately, construction projects, with their bureaucracy and the growing number of government regulations, have become more and more complex. Schedules are tools to help manage. How often are they prepared? Does the frequency of preparation affect safety? Results show that short-interval schedules are prepared with varying frequencies, but as far as safety is concerned, they should be prepared frequently, as shown in Figure 20.8.

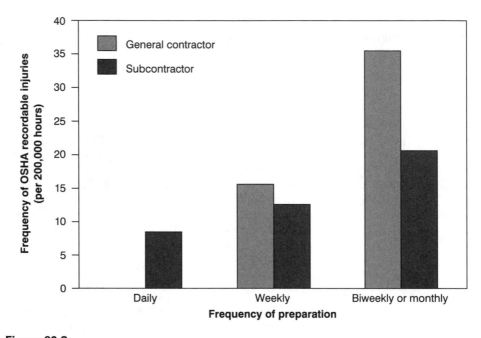

Figure 20.8
The Frequency of Preparation of Short-Interval Schedules
Source: Hinze and Talley 1988

The results (gleaned from a study focused on the safety performances of both general contractors and subcontractors) show the same effect, namely, that safety performance is better on projects where more frequent preparation of the short-interval schedules occurs (Hinze and Talley 1988). The information in Figure 20.8 is particularly interesting in that it shows that both general contractors and subcontractors have better safety records when the short-interval schedules are prepared more frequently. Note that safety performance for subcontractors was particularly good when the short-interval schedules were prepared daily. No general contractors prepared the short-interval schedules on a daily basis.

It must be noted that short-interval schedules are used to plan and organize crew activities on a day-to-day basis. If they are prepared every two weeks or every month, much of the information will contain errors. That is because it is virtually impossible to plan activities so precisely that no foreman will have to make any adjustments to a monthly schedule by the time the month comes to a close. The accuracy will be high for the first few days, but it will quickly diminish as conflicts arise, delays occur, and changes are made. Change is unavoidable, and it is to be expected. Unfortunately, if the schedule information is no longer relevant, it will no longer be used. As time passes and the accuracy of the short-interval schedule diminishes, more and more foremen will use the short-interval schedule less and less. This trend will complicate the coordination effort, as foremen will no longer have a common tool to organize their activities. There will, no doubt, be greater confusion on the construction site, and it will be reflected in a decline in safety performance.

The safety performance of the general contractor and of the subcontractors is better when the short-interval schedules are prepared more frequently. The more-frequently prepared schedules present information that is more relevant to the actual work taking place on a given day. It is this current information that is most helpful to foremen when they coordinate their activities.

Since the short-interval schedules are to be used on a day-to-day basis, it is important that they have the appropriate level of detail and that the information be properly organized and presented. Who is in the best position to prepare such a schedule? The information in Figure 20.9 presents some enlightenment here. Although one might think the superintendent, the scheduling department, and the project manager should be equally adept at developing a short-interval schedule, the differences in safety performances indicate that they are not (Hinze and Talley 1988). Understandably, the superintendent is the closest to the work effort and undoubtedly has the best sense of how the tasks are to be organized. It is interesting that the schedules prepared by the superintendent also resulted in the best safety performance. Perhaps the project manager tends to focus on the big picture and ignores some valuable details, or possibly the project manager does not understand specific nuances of scheduling several different crews—for example, the constraints that limited resources, such as equipment or tools, may place on the amount of work that can be done by a crew or by several crews. It is also possible that short-interval schedules prepared by project managers are prepared to satisfy a contractual requirement and are not relied on for organizing the work activities.

In general, the findings suggest that, for best safety results, short-interval schedules should be prepared frequently and with a high level of detail. The coordination of the daily tasks must be such that work is facilitated. Work is best facilitated when the scheduling information is current. If the short-interval schedules are prepared monthly,

Figure 20.9
The Preparer of the Short-Interval Schedules

Source: Hinze and Talley 1988

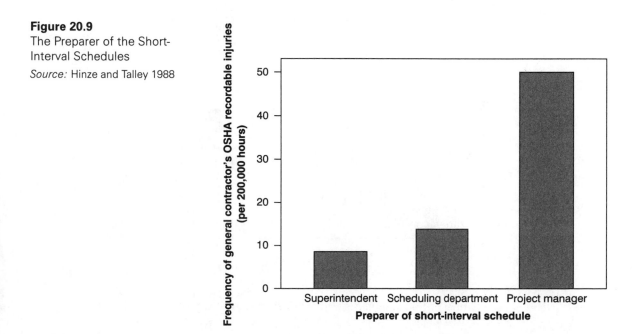

much of the information will be flawed, particularly the information on tasks that are planned later in the month. The schedules appear to have greater relevance when they are prepared by the persons who are closest to the actual field operations.

Project Complexity

Findings presented in other chapters have shown the clear relationship between project size and safety performance. Although much of the increase in injury frequency may be attributed to the growing bureaucracy that accompanies growing project size, a portion of the increase may be the result of the increase in project complexity. Specific measures of project complexity are difficult to establish, but it is generally agreed that more complex projects have greater numbers of specialty contractors or subcontractors. The reason that portions of construction work are traditionally subcontracted is that the work being sublet is beyond the expertise of the general contractor. Thus, specialty contractors are a necessity, and on very complex projects, greater numbers of them are required.

Figure 20.10 is an illustration of the relationship of the number of subcontractors on a project to the safety performance of the subcontractors. As can be seen from the figure, the number of subcontractors required on projects varies considerably. From that it might be inferred that project complexity, too, varies considerably. It is also evident that there is a strong relationship between the number of subcontractors and subcontractor safety performance (Hinze and Figone 1988). Complex projects merit additional attention to safety.

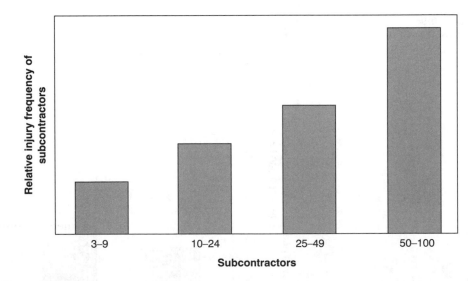

Figure 20.10
The Number of Subcontractors (Project Complexity)
Source: Hinze and Figone 1988

Final Comments

Research findings provide compelling evidence that project coordination and safety performance are closely related. Furthermore, general contractors play a pivotal role in the coordination effort. The importance of coordination applies to schedules of overall project duration and also to short-interval schedules.

Construction workers are task oriented; they want to accomplish their work assignments. If their activities are not properly coordinated with the activities of other crafts, with materials deliveries, or with the work of other subcontractors, frustrations will ensue. These frustrations will be evidenced in reduced worker morale. The ramifications of reduced morale will be observed in reduced productivity and, quite possibly, as the data show, in an increase in the frequency of injuries.

It is common to think of a proactive stance on safety as consisting of the establishment of a thorough safety program, in which worker orientation, personal protective equipment, safety meetings, and similar issues are addressed. Project scheduling also affects safety performance. In some cases it has been shown that the effectiveness with which the work activities of a project are coordinated influences safety performance to a greater extent than do certain elements of safety programs.

Coordination efforts must be maintained at a level of detail that ensures the smooth performance of construction efforts. Much of that detail is lacking in overall project schedules. Successful coordination should include the use of short-interval schedules that accurately reflect the work that needs to be done in the following two to three weeks. Contractors must recognize that coordination is successful only when accurate information is communicated. Thus, it is important to also establish a routine mechanism, such as weekly meetings, by which sequencing and scheduling information can be conveyed to the applicable parties. It is important for all parties on a construction project to have the same understanding of which tasks are most important for the overall progress of the work. When that shared understanding is achieved consistently, an environment will be established in which good safety performance can be realized.

Review Questions

1. Why does the schedule status of a project affect safety performance?
2. Are productivity and safety in conflict?
3. Describe the different measures that have linked project coordination with safety performance.
4. Using the information gleaned from past research, describe a project that might have little need of sophisticated scheduling and might still have a good safety record.
5. Which findings presented in this chapter can be viewed as indicators of job pressures?
6. Explain why the type of schedule used might affect safety performance.
7. What are short-interval schedules?
8. Describe aspects of the preparation and use of short-interval schedules that are conducive to good safety performance.
9. Describe measures of project complexity that have been associated with safety performance. What other measures might be similarly examined that would indicate project complexity?

10. How might one measure the extent of use of a schedule, and why is the extent to which a schedule is used important to safety?

References

Hinze, J. 1976. *The Effect of Middle Management on Safety in Construction*. Technical Report no. 209 (June), Construction Institute. Stanford, Calif.: Stanford University.

———. 1987. "Qualities of Safe Superintendents." *ASCE Journal of Construction Engineering and Management* 113, no. 1, 169–71.

Hinze, J., and L. Figone. 1988. *Subcontractor Safety As Influenced by General Contractors on Small and Medium Sized Projects*. CII Source Document 38. Austin, Tex.: Construction Industry Institute.

Hinze, J., and H. Parker. 1978. "Safety: Productivity and Job Pressures." *Journal of the Construction Division, ASCE* 104, no. 1, 27–34.

Hinze, J., and P. Raboud. 1988. "Safety on Large Building Construction Projects." *Journal of the Construction Division, ASCE* 114, no. 2, 286–93.

Hinze, J., and D. Talley. 1988. *Subcontractor Safety As Influenced by General Contractors on Large Projects*. CII Source Document 39. Austin, Tex.: Construction Industry Institute.

Hinze, J., and F. Wiegand. 1992. "Role of Designers in Construction Worker Safety." *ASCE Journal of Construction Engineering and Management* 118, no. 4, 677–84.

Levitt, R. 1975. *The Effect of Top Management on Safety in Construction*. Technical Report no. 196 (July), Construction Institute. Stanford, Calif.: Stanford University.

Levitt, R., and N. Samelson. 1993. *Safety Management*. New York: John Wiley.

Raboud, P. 1986. "Construction Subcontractor Safety." Master's thesis, University of Washington.

Samelson, N. 1983. *Crew Factors in Safety Performance in Heavy Maintenance Operations*. Technical Report no. 275, Construction Institute. Stanford, Calif.: Stanford University.

Owners and Construction Safety

A construction project doesn't have to cost an arm and a leg.

Owners of facilities being constructed are becoming increasingly involved in construction safety. Their increasing involvement stems primarily from the higher costs of construction that are due to the high indirect costs of worker injuries, the escalating cost of workers' compensation insurance, the increased impact of safety legislation, and the ever-present threat of liability suits. To counter those influences, owners are recognizing the greater benefit of promoting safety on their projects. Safety can no longer be left solely in the hands of construction contractors. Owners must be aggressive advocates of safety in order for significant improvements in safety to occur.

Owners can play a key role in influencing the safety performance that is ultimately realized on construction projects. The nature of the role played by owners begins with the establishment of a clear objective concerning safety. Owners whose objective is to avoid liability tend to shield themselves from suit by including indemnification provisions in the general contract and by distancing themselves in other ways from the actual work being done. Owners whose objective is to avoid OSHA citations will probably do very little, as OSHA citations have little influence on owners. If anything, provisions might be included in the contract whereby the contractor is alerted to specific physical hazards and perhaps guidance is given or requirements are stated for addressing the hazards. Owners whose objective is to avoid injuries are likely to have a proactive and more direct involvement in construction operations.

Owner Involvement in Construction Safety

Once the owner has established a clear philosophical position on safety, that position can be communicated in a variety of ways. An obvious beginning point is to communicate the objective in the bidding documents and the contract documents. It can be further communicated at prebid conferences. Although communication is very important, the owner can and does play an active role in safety in the manner in which contractors are selected. In the private sector, owners have a great deal of control over the contractors hired to perform work. Owners intent on reducing injuries can play a key role by awarding contracts to the contractors they feel will perform safely on their projects.

In the early 1990s, a series of studies were conducted of firms that had large construction budgets. The firms were large private owners who funded such projects as high-rise offices, commercial buildings, retail stores, warehouses, petrochemical plants, heavy process plants, manufacturing facilities, hospitals, and utility projects. A portion of the study consisted of questions related to safety. One question of particular interest asked the owners if they reviewed contractors' safety records before permitting the contractors to bid on their projects. The results, illustrated in Figure 21.1, show that the majority of the owners perform such safety reviews and that the percentage of owners with such policies is increasing each year. It was noted that it was generally the owners with the larger construction budgets that had such policies (Hinze 1991, 1992, 1994a, 1994b).

The trend is clear that owners are getting more concerned about construction safety and that they are beginning to address it in the selection process. It is also clear from the study that owners have particular safety concerns about unknown contractors. The owners with the strongest policies on safety have such requirements as being notified of any major accidents, making independent job-site safety inspections, and peri-

Figure 21.1

Requirement by Large Owners That Contractors Be Reviewed on Safety Before Being Allowed to Bid

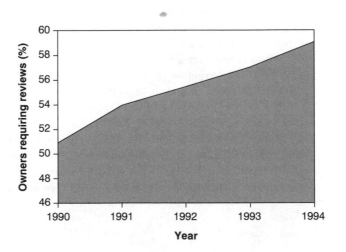

odically reviewing the contractors' injury rates. Some unique owner practices included the following:

- placing company representatives on every construction project
- conducting safety meetings with the contractors
- requiring the contractors to adhere to owner-developed safety practices
- providing contractor safety training
- requiring all contractors to go through safety orientation
- reviewing each contractor's safety program
- conducting regular audits of contractor safety performance
- implementing safety incentive programs on all construction projects

The trend toward increased owner involvement in contractor safety is likely to continue, as 46% of the firms stated that they would be more concerned about safety in the future than they had been in the past. In addition, 47% of the owners stated that they had an increased concern about pending federal legislation related to safety. In addition, 4% stated that safety (not costs, schedules, quality, etc.) was their top construction problem.

Although they represented a minority, nearly 20% of the owners stated that they regarded construction safety as the contractor's responsibility alone. Those owners, as suspected, had more relaxed policies concerning construction safety.

Selecting Safe Contractors

Because of the significant role played by contractors in project safety, it is reasonable and prudent to carefully restrict the selection of construction firms to those that have performed safely in the past. Once the decision is made to award construction contracts only to contractors who have safe job histories, the selection would seem to be a relatively simple task. But what constitutes a good safety record? What measurement or measurements should be used to determine if a contractor has a good safety record? The credibility of anyone with a single measurement for the answer to this question should immediately be put in doubt. The assessment of past safety performance may very well include the consideration of several different factors.

One must fully understand the gamut of measures, along with their strengths and shortcomings, to truly make an informed determination of the safety performance of a contractor. Otherwise, one will easily overlook the disadvantages of a favorite measure. It is most wise to consider several measures of the safety performance of a contractor. Some of the more important ones will be described.

Injury Incident Rates

The commonly used injury incident rate can provide a valid measure of safety. Even this measure has many nuances. The injury incident rate may reflect lost-workday injuries, OSHA recordable injuries, medical-case injuries, first-aid cases, or some other measure. As already discussed, there are shades of gray in the lost-workday case definitions, and even the OSHA recordable injuries and the medical-case injuries are not always the same. Of these measures, the lost-workday incident rate is an indication of injury severity, while the OSHA recordable incident rate relates more to injury frequency. Most injury incident rates include either lost-workday injuries or OSHA recordable injuries. Lost-workday injuries, being more severe, tend to occur with less frequency than do OSHA recordable injuries.

Regardless of the type of injury included in the measure, the incident rate should be based on a constant exposure time. Most measures are based on 200,000 hours of worker exposure. Such measures equate approximately to the number of injuries that occur in a work force of 100 workers over a period of one year. When small firms or projects are to be evaluated on safety, the number of worker hours of exposure will probably be relatively small. For such evaluations, the use of OSHA recordable injuries is preferred, but valuable information can be provided if the lost-workday injuries are included in a separate incident rate.

Even though two companies are being compared on the basis of their injury incident rates, some care must be exercised to avoid biased decisions. For example, one company may have injury incident rates experienced on a remodel project while another firm has injury incident rates based on a project that was new construction. The two projects may not be comparable. Furthermore, the types of work and the nature of the exposures may have been quite different.

If injury incident rates are to be used as a measure of safety, a basis for making comparisons should be established. For example, if the lost-workday incident rate is being used as the measure of safety performance, the incident rate of a particular contractor could be compared with that of another contractor. It must be realized that such a comparison will only identify the "safer" of the two contractors. Perhaps both contractors have unacceptable injury incident rates. Thus, it might be appropriate to set some threshold value for the acceptability of any contractor. The threshold value might be based on an injury incident rate that reflects the industry average. If a firm is truly concerned about safety, the threshold value should be set, not at the industry average, but rather at some percentage of that average. There is some concern that the published industry averages are inflated and that they do not accurately reflect industry performance. Some statistics may be available from workers' compensation insurance carriers, but that information is not generally published. Perhaps the best way to set the threshold value is to use safety performance information obtained on other projects done for the firm.

Experience Modification Rates

One common measure used to assess contractor safety performance is the experience modification rate (EMR) for workers' compensation insurance. The EMR reflects a combination of injury frequency and severity. For many firms, the EMR is a good measure of safety performance. The shortcomings of using EMRs should be understood. A low EMR for a company is a clear indication that the safety record has been good, especially for the three years on which the EMR is based. For large firms, the evidence provided by the EMR is even more compelling. Unfortunately, the EMR does not reflect the nature of the work on which the performance is based. If two companies are compared on the basis of their respective ratings, any discrepancies in their ratings may be more a function of the difference in their sizes than of a difference in their injury records. The discrepancy may also reflect differences in the states in which the firms conduct business, as the figures used in the computation of the EMR vary from state to state.

The equation for the computation of the EMR is as follows:

$$\text{Experience modification} = \frac{Ap + WAe + (1-W)Ee + B}{E + B}$$

where

$Ap + WAe + (1-W)Ee$ = adjusted actual losses

$\quad Ap$ = actual primary losses (summation of costs below \$5,000/injury)

$\quad W$ = weight (provided in state experience-rating-plan manuals)

$\quad Ae$ = actual excess losses (summation of costs above \$5,000/injury)

$\quad Ee$ = expected excess loss [equal to $E(1-\text{discount ratio})$; the discount ratio is provided in state experience-rating-plan manuals]

$\quad E$ = expected losses (equal to payroll × expected loss ratio; the expected loss ratio is analogous to the manual rate, but without the insurance administration cost)

$\quad B$ = ballast (provided in state experience-rating-plan manuals)

Although the formula is essentially the same from state to state, the values of the different variables change from state to state. Thus, the computation of the EMR for a company is unique for a particular state. If a company has experience in two different states, two different EMR computations will be required.

The computation of the ratings is biased in such a way that small firms cannot achieve a rating as low as that potentially attainable by large firms. Although the EMR computation is designed so that a small contractor will not incur huge increases in the EMR because of a single catastrophic loss, the computation similarly prevents safe small contractors from ever achieving very low EMRs. The upper and lower limits of the EMR are not similarly constrained for large contractors. Thus, when two firms of different sizes have good safety records and are compared on the basis of their EMRs, the comparison will be biased in favor of the larger firm.

Another disadvantage of the use of EMRs for assessing safety performance is that the rating is based on dated information, namely, information on injuries that occurred in the three years prior to the immediately preceding year. If a firm has made significant changes in its safety program and has experienced exemplary safety performance in the preceding year, that information will not be reflected in the EMR. It will be reflected in future years only. The data in Table 21.1 illustrate that point.

In the example in Table 21.1, the contractor evidently had a series of years with consistently poor safety records. That history is demonstrated by the four years (1990 to 1993) the EMR was over 1.0. The safety record, measured by the incidences of recordable injuries and lost-workday injuries, was particularly good for two of those years, namely, 1992 and 1993. Note that the EMR of 0.73 for 1996 is based on the losses in three years, 1992–1994, in which good safety records were achieved. For 1997, the EMR will probably increase because of the poorer safety record of 1995. Thus, if the contractor were to be evaluated in 1995 on the basis of injury rates, the assessment would be different from an assessment based on the EMR. A similar conflict in the two assessments would occur in 1996.

Table 21.1

A Comparison of a Construction Firm's Injury Incidence Rates and EMRs over a Period of Years

	Contractor's Safety Record		
Year Covered	Incidence of Recordable Injuries*	Incidence of Lost-Workday Injuries*	Experience Modification Rate (%)
1990	18.2	8.3	115
1991	13.3	8.6	117
1992	9.8	3.3	111
1993	7.6	3.1	107
1994	8.8	2.8	94
1995	16.3	9.4	81
1996	19.5	14.3	73

* Incident rates are based on 100 workers per year or 200,000 hours of worker exposure.

The foregoing discussion demonstrates the dilemma facing those who want to evaluate contractor safety performance by using injury rates and EMRs. For 1995 and 1996, conflicting conclusions would be made.

What if the injury rates of two firms were identical? Would the dilemma suddenly vanish? The quick answer is that a choice between the two companies on the basis of safety performance would be a toss-up. Unfortunately, that might not be true if the assessment of safety performance were made solely on the basis of the EMR. Table 21.2 presents EMRs for three different Oregon companies that do the same type of business (their workers are all in the same trade) and have identical injury incidence rates of 20. That is, on the basis of injury frequency, they are the same. The only differences in their safety performances are in the actual costs of the injuries. Different EMRs for the companies are readily apparent. The primary factors affecting the EMRs

Table 21.2

EMR% As Affected by Hourly Wages, Number of Employees, and Costs of Injuries

	Cost Per Injury				
	(Injury Incidence Rate = 20 Injuries per 200,000 or 1 injury per 5 employees)				
Size of Firms and Hourly Wages Paid	$1,000	$2,000	$10,000	$20,000	$50,000
A: 200 employees $18/hour	55	64	102	128	207
B: 40 employees $18/hour	68	76	104	114	143
C: 40 employees $10/hour	77	90	135	148	187

are the cost per injury, the number of employees, and the hourly wages paid. Even when injury rates remain constant, changes in the costs of injuries and in hourly wages dramatically alter EMRs.

The information in Table 21.2 shows that when the injury incidence rate, the hourly wage, and the cost per injury are held constant, the EMR is lower for firms with larger numbers of employees. That is true only when the injury costs are low; it is reversed when the injury costs are high (exceeding $10,000). Note that a small company with each injury costing $1,000 (Company C) has a slightly worse EMR than a similar-sized firm (Company B) with each injury costing twice as much, or $2,000. Note also that the small firm with wages of $10 per hour and injury costs of $10,000 per injury has a higher EMR than the large firm (Company A) with wages of $18 per hour and injury costs of $20,000 per injury. When the only difference between two companies is in the hourly wages paid, the firm paying the lower wages has the higher EMR.

Table 21.2 shows that EMRs vary even when the injury incidence rates are identical. The difference between EMRs and injury incidence rates is further illustrated in Table 21.3. While Table 21.2 shows variations in EMR when the injury incidence rates are identical, Table 21.3 shows conditions under which the EMRs are the same even though the injury incidence rates and costs differ.

Experts disagree on whether EMRs should be used instead of injury incidence rates. Some tout the value of one while others extol the merits of the other. Clearly, instances will arise where different assessments will be made of a construction firm's safety record, depending on whether the measure is the EMR or the injury incidence rate. There should be reluctance on the part of the owner to use the EMR as the sole measure of safety performance. The EMR is sensitive to the number of employees and the hourly wage rates. Although it might be argued that the injury rates also have disadvantages as a measure of safety performance, they may be more meaningful, especially if separate measurements exist for lost-workday cases and OSHA recordable cases.

Loss Ratio

Another measure of safety performance is the loss ratio. This measure is related to the injuries that have occurred, but rather than the number of injuries, its focus is on their costs. Thus, the severity of the injuries is where the emphasis is placed. The loss ratio is simply the quotient of the costs of claims divided by the amount paid in premiums, or the ratio of the cost of injuries to the cost of insurance. Naturally, if this ratio exceeds 1.0, the costs of claims exceed the premiums, and a poor record is clearly evident.

Table 21.3
Injury Incidence Rate and Cost
Combinations That Result in
Identical EMRs

Company	Injury Incidence	Cost per Injury	EMR (%)
A	3	$50,000	71
B	2.5	$50,000	71
B	5	$10,000	71
C	5	$2,000	71
C	10	$1,000	71

* See Table 21.2 for company descriptors.

The drawback of using the loss ratio is that a single loss can greatly alter the ratio. On the other hand, a low ratio may mean that the injuries are minor or that claims are well managed to keep the losses under control. Note also that a firm with a high EMR and a high manual rate for workers' compensation insurance pays an appreciable amount in premiums. Such a firm, when compared with a similar firm with a low EMR and the same claims costs, would be evaluated as safer if the only measure examined were the loss ratio. If the loss ratio is reviewed with detailed information about the number of claims and their associated costs, a clearer sense can be established of the safety performance of a firm. The loss ratio is related to the EMR to some extent, in that the emphasis is on the severity of the injuries rather than on injury frequency.

Record of OSHA Citations and Fines

Information on OSHA compliance inspections can be very helpful in providing information about a firm's field safety practices. In large firms it might be an especially useful measure of safety. The measure is recommended to augment information provided by other safety measures. The shortcomings of this measure become readily apparent when some consideration is given to how the information is collected. An obvious shortcoming, especially in a small firm, is that the information may be lacking completely, simply because the firm has never had an OSHA inspection on any of its projects. Thus, the information is valuable only if OSHA inspections have been conducted on several different projects.

For example, suppose two firms are being evaluated and each has information on four OSHA inspections. For one firm, the OSHA inspections all took place on the same project. For the other firm, the OSHA inspections occurred on four different projects. For which firm would the OSHA inspections provide better information? That might be difficult to answer. If both firms report good results from their OSHA inspections, is more insight gained? For the firm with inspection information from four projects, the measure of OSHA inspections is more compelling. On the other hand, if the firm with all inspections occurring on the same project plans to use the same project personnel on the upcoming project, the information is more helpful.

Because OSHA inspections are generally infrequent occurrences, this information is not advisable as a sole measure of safety performance. When OSHA inspection information is used to evaluate a firm, care must be taken to distinguish between the different types of violations, especially the serious and nonserious ones. It is almost universally accepted that, if virtually any construction project of any size were inspected on any day, an OSHA violation could be found. Minor violations and nonserious violations should not be ignored, but they should not be the primary measure in an evaluation. To some extent, information on the penalties will be helpful. Unfortunately, the fines are highly variable for seemingly similar violations. Again, OSHA inspection information, when it is available, should be used to augment other safety measures.

Litigation Related to Injuries

Information on litigation is not generally considered a good measure of safety performance. Such information may be more useful as a measure of the success a firm has had in minimizing the consequences of injuries. It may also reflect the success of the contractor's insurance carrier in keeping claims costs to a minimum and perhaps also in fighting fraudulent claims.

An emerging practice adopted by some firms in recent years is the establishment of back-to-work programs for their injured employees. The back-to-work programs are focused on restricted-work or lost-workday cases, in which workers sustain injuries that restrict their ability to work. Instead of having such a worker miss a few days of work, project tasks are set up so that the worker can be gainfully employed and not miss any workdays. In the past, some referred to reassigned injured workers as the "walking wounded." Some allegations have been made that such workers were assigned to meaningless tasks. Assigning workers to easier tasks, even such tasks as counting inventory, may have been frowned on in the past, but there is growing favor for the practice.

As reflected in references to the "walking wounded," the original conception of a back-to-work program was often as a mechanism for averting the consequences of injuries (increased workers' compensation premiums). More recently the philosophies behind the back-to-work programs are more positive, and the programs are regarded more favorably because they help preserve the pride that workers have in their jobs. Even if an injury prevents a worker from doing the typical duties of the trade, a modified work regimen is better than no work at all. Regardless of the various perceptions and connotations associated with such programs, the programs have proven successful for some firms in minimizing recuperation costs and in galvanizing a long-term relationship between the company and the workers.

Information on litigation is generally of value only in a comparison of two very large firms. Despite the constant industry talk about litigation, the frequency of formal litigation is still quite low. If a firm has had one case in the past five years, little insight is really gained from that information. It might be more appropriate to examine the programs that a company implements to maintain project safety and to keep litigation to a minimum.

Performance Records of Key Personnel

As has already been discussed in Chapters 15 and 16, the safety performance on a construction site is determined to a large extent by the supervisory personnel on the job site. Even within a single company, the safety records of the projects may vary considerably, a variation due in large part to the personnel on those projects. If an assessment is to be made of a company's safety performance, it is helpful to consider the specific safety performance records of the key individuals who will be assigned to a particular project. It must be recognized that an evaluation of individuals is probably not likely to occur on a competitively bid project but is more likely to be possible on a negotiated contract. At bid time on competitively bid projects, personnel assignments may not be as predictable as on negotiated projects.

For which project personnel should safety records be evaluated? The key individuals on which the safety evaluations should generally be focused are the primary representatives of the company at the project level, namely, the project manager and the job superintendent. On very large projects with several tiers of job managers, other personnel may also be evaluated. On smaller projects, however, the safety performance evaluation may be restricted to the job superintendent.

Through the consideration of the performance records of key individuals in a firm, it will become apparent that certain employees contribute more to the company's overall safety record than do others. It has been noted by many that superintendents with good safety records on past projects tend to maintain that level of performance on other projects. Unfortunately, those with poor safety records can often be expected to continue to perform in that manner unless specific steps are taken to improve project safety performance.

Project Safety Plan

A concerted effort is needed to provide assurance that good safety performance on a project is attainable. Key personnel, such as the job superintendent and the project manager, are certainly important players in that effort. Company policies can be used to augment and enhance the safety efforts of those personnel. Such policies must be formal to be implemented consistently. Good safety preparation can do much to prepare for a construction project. It is one way of instilling confidence that given procedures will be carried out to ensure good safety performance. The elements of a safety program, described in greater detail in Chapter 6, include job hazard analysis, safety training, worker orientation, a site-specific fall prevention program, and a confined space program. All the elements should be standard operating procedures for a firm, and the practices and policies must be in written form to ensure consistency in implementation. If a firm has a safety program, and if the firm has a mechanism to ensure its consistent implementation, greater confidence can be placed in the selection of the firm for the safe delivery of a construction project.

Contractor Qualification Safety Survey

With the drawbacks of the different measures of safety performance noted, it is obvious that no single measure merits exclusive use for the determination of a contractor's safety record. It is much more appropriate to make the assessment by considering several measures. All the measures have some value, so it seems appropriate to utilize all the measures that the contractor can provide. An example of a survey form is presented at the end of this chapter as Figure 21.2. The form requests information on the various measures discussed.

Starting a Construction Project Safely

If a facility owner screens construction firms for safety performance, a considerable safety benefit will probably be realized on the construction site. It must be realized that the screening process—whether it focuses on injury rates, EMRs, OSHA inspections, supervisory safety records, or past safety programs—generally examines past performance. An owner cannot select a contractor on the basis of past performance and assume that project safety is assured. The owner of a facility wants assurance that the contractor will perform safely on the project to be constructed.

It is through the construction contract that safety can be made an integral part of any construction project. For example, the owner can stipulate certain requirements in the contract to affirm its commitment to safety. Owners often have different ways of expressing themselves in contracts. The contract language, as described in Chapter 10, can be used to provide additional evidence of the owner's resolve to have the project delivered safely. Unfortunately, the contract language can also be so lax as to diminish the importance of safety on the project. Much of the variation in the contracts stems from the advice of legal counsel. It is in the contract that some legal advisers insist that the owner place the responsibility for safety solely on the contractor.

Philosophical differences are evident in some construction contracts. Some companies want to be very assertive about safety in the hopes of having a positive influence on safety performance. Others distance themselves to a greater extent in the hope of avoiding liability. The key word in the phrase "in the hope of avoiding liability" is *hope*. There is a very slim chance that the contract language will help to avoid liability. Many of the liability cases that arise stem from a common law duty on the part of the owner, and therefore the contract language may be ignored by the courts in placing some of the responsibility on the owner. Thus, the best way to avoid liability is to focus on avoiding injuries. The contract should be carefully assembled and worded so that the message is consistent with the owner's philosophy. An owner must carefully assess the basic commitment that the firm wants to make to construction safety, and that commitment must then be reflected in the contract.

An owner, to be actively involved in construction safety, might consider several contractual issues. Many of the issues relate to the safety obligations placed on the contractor. Contract provisions may include the following requirements:

- submittal of a project-specific safety plan
- job hazard analysis
- regular safety meetings with supervisory personnel
- a designated project safety coordinator
- mandatory reporting of accidents, safety inspections, and safety meetings
- inclusion of subcontractors in the safety program
- compliance with the owner's safety guidelines
- establishment of a viable worker orientation program

Although many of these requirements may be recognized as mandatory under the OSHA regulations, their specific inclusion in the contract will demonstrate the extent of the owner's commitment to safety.

Owner Involvement in Site Safety

It is generally assumed that during construction the contractor shoulders most of the responsibility for worker safety. If a contractor has been carefully selected, with safety a criterion, and if the contract contains provisions that stress the importance of safety, the continued involvement of the owner need not be extensive.

If worker safety is truly the objective of the owner, involvement in the safety effort will continue. That involvement is especially important when the construction firm is not fully committed to safety. The most common form of owner involvement in safety during the construction phase is in the monitoring of safety efforts by requiring the submittal of regular (typically monthly) reports. Those reports will surely include the monthly reporting of all injuries, with immediate notification of the owner being required on any serious injuries. Other reports that might be required include inspection reports of safety committees, reports of safety meetings, reports of near misses, accident investigation reports, and reports of safety violations.

The owner may elect to be a more active participant in the construction safety arena. More active participation can be achieved through such means as independent job-site safety inspections by the owner, active involvement in safety meetings, and the establishment of specific project safety rules. Some owners have gotten more directly involved by funding project safety incentive programs. The incentive budgets often reflect the commitment of substantial sums of money.

Designer Selection

The owner's commitment to safety might extend to the selection of designers. Designers might be selected for the extent to which they will address construction worker safety in their designs. Eventually, the owner commitment to safety will be reflected in the design itself. This is admittedly a new philosophy that some owners are adopting, but eventually it will be widely accepted in some sectors of the construction industry.

Owners and Subcontractor Safety

The influence that owners have on project safety extends to subcontractor safety. That influence can be direct if the owner elects to be proactive in the area of safety. For example, for improved subcontractor safety, the owner could do the following:

- require general contractors to evaluate subcontractors on safety (EMRs, injury rates, loss ratios, etc.)
- insist on owner approval of subcontractors, based on satisfaction of minimum standards of past safety performance
- require subcontractors to submit project safety programs

Various other means may be available to owners by which they can actively and aggressively be involved in subcontractor safety. The subcontractors should not be forgotten or ignored. Every party involved in a project should be included in the overall project safety plan.

Final Comments

The owner's involvement in construction safety can pay real dividends through reduced injuries. Before any construction contract is contemplated, owners should assess their commitment to safety. That assessment includes the determination of whether safety is to take priority over the avoidance of litigation. Regardless of whether the concern is for safety or litigation, it behooves owners to carefully screen contractors. The screening should take into account a variety of measures on safety; reliance on a single measure is to be avoided. Furthermore, owners should be active in project safety before the start of the construction effort, and their involvement should be sustained throughout the construction process.

Owners have become increasingly more mindful of the importance of the role they play in worker safety. Owners can help contractors buy into the zero-accidents philosophy. In fact, the very selection of contractors and the contract wording used to ensure safety will encourage contractors to communicate that same message to their employees and subcontractors.

Review Questions

1. What is an important way that several of the large owners (consumers of construction services) currently communicate their resolve to have good safety performances on their projects?
2. What are the primary disadvantages of evaluating a contractor exclusively on the basis of the loss ratio?
3. What are the primary disadvantages of evaluating a contractor exclusively on the basis of the EMR?
4. What are the primary disadvantages of evaluating the safety performance of a contractor by considering the results of OSHA inspections or injury-related lawsuits?
5. Discuss what are probably the best two measures of contractor safety performance when they are considered together.
6. Why have construction contracts historically not been very forceful in including the owner in project safety during construction?
7. What are the positive aspects of back-to-work programs?
8. How might an owner play a positive and proactive role in project safety during the construction phase of a project?
9. If injury rates are used to evaluate a contractor, what should be the benchmark against which the injury rates are compared?
10. Why is it a good practice to obtain specific information about the safety performance records of key personnel who will be assigned to a particular construction site?

References

Bush, V. 1975. *Safety in the Construction Industry: OSHA.* Reston, Va.: Reston Publishing.
Business Roundtable. 1982. *Improving Construction Safety Performance: The User's Role.* Construction Industry Cost Effectiveness Project, Report A-3. New York: Business Roundtable.
Goldsmith, C. 1987. *Safety Management in Construction and Industry.* New York: McGraw-Hill.
Hinze, J. 1991. *A Study of the Construction Activity and Procurement Policies of Major Consumers of Construction Services.* Washington, D.C.: Merit Shop Foundation.
———. 1992. *A Study of the Construction Activity and Procurement Policies of Major Consumers of Construction Services (Study 2).* Washington, D.C.: Merit Shop Foundation.
———. 1994a. *A Study of the Construction Activity Projections for 1994.* Washington, D.C.: Merit Shop Foundation.

————. 1994b. *A Study of the Construction Activity Projections for 1995.* Washington, D.C.: Merit Shop Foundation.

Hinze, J., D. Bren, and N. Piepho. 1995. "Experience Modification Rating as Measure of Safety Performance." *ASCE Journal of Construction Engineering and Management* 121, no. 4, 455–58.

Levitt, R., and N. Samelson. 1993. *Construction Safety Management.* 2d ed. New York: John Wiley.

Petersen, D. 1988. *Safety Management.* Goshen, N.Y.: Aloray.

Peyton, R., and T. Rubio. 1991. *Construction Safety Practices and Principles.* New York: Van Nostrand Reinhold.

Facility Investments, Inc.
5725 Olympic Avenue
Seattle, Washington

Contractor Qualification
Safety Survey

Facility Investments believes that safety, quality, and productivity are of equal importance in the construction of this project. So that we may properly evaluate each contractor's qualifications to perform the work in a safe manner, all contractors must supply the following information to qualify for consideration.

The information provided will be used in the selection process to identify contractors who have an effective loss-prevention program and can adequately control accident costs.

Note: All information provided will be held in confidence. Contractors may be asked to provide verifiable evidence to substantiate the information provided.

I. Contractor Safety Record

1. List your firm's interstate experience modification rate (EMR) for the three most recent years:

Year	EMR
19 ___	___
19 ___	___
19 ___	___

2. Please use your last two years' OSHA No. 200 logs and payroll records to fill in the number of injuries and illnesses recorded and the total hours worked on your firm's construction jobs.

	Last Year: 19 ___	**2 Years ago: 19 ___**
a. Lost-workday cases	___	___
b. Restricted-workday cases	___	___
c. OSHA recordable cases	___	___
d. Fatalities	___	___
e. Employee hours worked (field employees only)	___	___

3. Indicate the types of projects generally constructed by the firm:

___ residential	___ small commercial	___ high-rise buildings
___ manufacturing facilities	___ heavy-process plants	___ liquid-process plants
___ warehouses	___ utility projects	___ electrical work
___ plumbing and heating	___ (other) specify: _____	

Figure 21.2
Example of Contractor Qualification Safety Survey

Safety Survey (cont.)

4. List loss ratios on the firm's workers' compensation policy for the past three years.

Year Covered	Loss Ratio
Last year: 19 ____	_____
2 years ago: 19 ____	_____
3 years ago: 19 ____	_____

5. List the firm's experiences with OSHA inspections in the past three years.

Year Covered	Number of Inspections	Number of Serious Citations	Cost of OSHA Fines Paid
Last year: 19 ____	_____	_____	_____
2 years ago: 19 ____	_____	_____	_____
3 years ago: 19 ____	_____	_____	_____

6. List the firm's experiences with litigation in the past five years.

Years Covered	Number of Suits Filed	Number of Suits Settled in Court	Number of Suits Lost/Settlement Cost
19 ____ to 19 ____			

7. Name the individuals to be assigned to the following positions. Provide information on the safety performances of those individuals or the groups under their supervision.

Project Title	Employee Name	Injury Incidence Rate on Past Projects (per 200,000 worker hours)
Project Manager	_____	_____
Job Superintendent	_____	_____
Job Safety Director	_____	_____

II. Contractor Safety Programs

8. Did the firm develop its own written site-specific safety program for the last project completed:____ yes ____ no

If yes, please provide a copy for this review. (The copy will be returned after the review.)

9. Describe the crew safety (toolbox) meetings conducted by the firm.

Frequency:	____ weekly	____ monthly	____ other: _____
Conducted by:	____ foreman	____ safety director	____ other: _____
Attendees:	____ crew	____ job employees	____ other: _____
Sub's workers:	____ also attend	____ hold their own	____ other: _____
Minutes written?	____ yes	____ no	____ other: _____
Minutes kept:	____ at job site	____ at home office	____ other: _____

If minutes are written, please provide a copy of past meeting minutes.

Figure 21.2
Example of Contractor Qualification Safety Survey (continued)

Safety Survey (cont.)

10. Are safety meetings held for field supervisors? ___ yes ___ no

Frequency:	___ weekly	___ monthly	___ other: _____
Conducted by:	___ proj. mgr.	___ safety director	___ other: _____
Attendees:	___ foremen	___ supts.	___ other: _____
Minutes written?	___ yes	___ no	
Minutes kept:	___ at job site	___ at home office	___ other: _____

If minutes are written, please provide a copy of past meeting minutes.

11. Does the firm have a formal worker orientation program? ___ yes ___ no
    Who is oriented? ___ employees ___ all workers ___ other: _____

If there is such a program, please provide a decription for this review.

12. Are accident investigations made? ___ yes ___ no
    If yes, for what accidents? ___ recordable ___ lost-workday ___ other _____
    Who investigates? ___ supt. ___ safety dir. ___ other: _____
    Distribution: ___ job file ___ home office ___ other: _____

If accidents are investigated, please provide a sample report from the last project.

13. Does the firm conduct job safety analyses? ___ yes ___ no

If yes, please provide a copy from the last project.

14. Does the firm sponsor a safety incentive program at the project level?
    ___ yes ___ no

If yes, who participates: ___ workers ___ foremen
                         ___ supts. ___ other: _____

15. Are field supervisors evaluated on safety performance? ___ yes ___ no

If yes, briefly describe the evaluation procedure and criteria: _____

_____

16. At what levels are records of safety performance maintained?
    ___ foremen ___ project ___ company ___ other: _____

17. Are project safety inspections conducted on a regular basis? ___ yes ___ no
    if yes, how often? ___ weekly ___ monthly ___ other: _____
    Who inspects? ___ safety comm. ___ safety dir. ___ other: _____

18. Does the firm have a drug testing or substance abuse program? ___ yes ___ no
    Who is tested? ___ employees ___ all workers ___ other: _____

If the firm has such a program, please provide a detailed description.

Figure 21.2
Example of Contractor Qualification Safety Survey (continued)

Designer Influence on Construction Worker Safety

Design hazards out, and design safety in.

The past few chapters of this book have concerned primarily those aspects of construction safety that are related to the "people issues," or the human factors, of construction safety. There has already been some discussion of the premise that accidents are the result of unsafe physical conditions, unsafe acts, or combinations of the two. The OSHA regulations address primarily the unsafe physical conditions that contribute to construction worker injuries. The supervisory influence on safety that is of the greatest significance appears to be related to the prevention of unsafe acts. The discussions about the various levels of supervision and management have addressed ways that the human factors can be addressed for good safety results.

The roles of the various parties involved in the construction process have been described. The positions of those parties are illustrated in Figure 22.1.

Of the parties shown, only the designers have not been discussed. Do designers have a role in construction safety? Clearly they do. Do most designers want to be involved in the safety process? Unfortunately, they do not. The motivation to avoid involvement is simple: avoidance of litigation. Designers fear that, if they make decisions to choose project components that are expected to improve construction safety, they will bear a greater liability if an injury occurs as a consequence of one of those project components. Is their logic valid? The question is difficult to answer, as very few

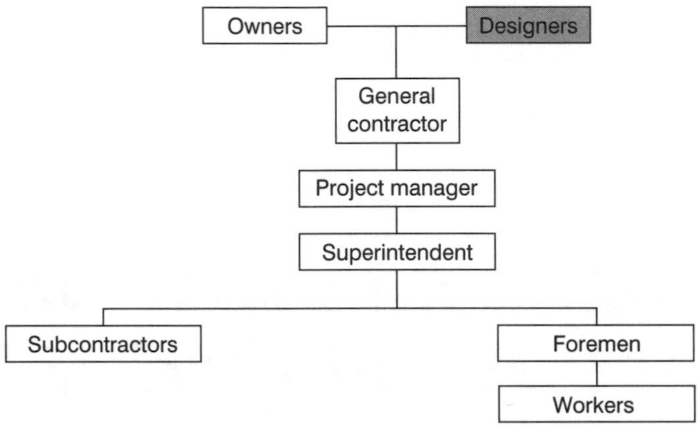

Figure 22.1

Organizational Relationship of Typical Parties Involved in the Construction Process

court cases have addressed this issue. Unfortunately, the legal counselors of architectural design firms appear to be providing almost universal advice to that effect. Is the advice sound, and should it be followed? That is where professionalism comes in. It seems as if a designer would have a moral or professional obligation to alter a design to make it safer for construction workers if major risks were generally known.

Design decisions directly affect construction safety. The way the designers detail connections, select materials, arrange facility components, and generally add definition to a facility design directly influences the way the workers will perform the work. Can the designers contend that they are not responsible for construction safety simply because they do not tell the contractor how to install or assemble the components of the facility? Can the same designers honestly say that they have no idea or general notion of how the contractors generally perform work when only the end result is specified? Clearly such contentions are not reality. Unfortunately, this mindset of pleading ignorance is the most common one.

At the center of the debate about designers and safety is the premise that, when plans dictate the end result and not the "means, methods, techniques, sequences, and procedures," the designer is not liable. If a standard procedure is used to construct a given type of component or facility, it seems likely that designers are familiar with that method. If designers know of a modified design approach for which a safer work method would probably be used, one would expect designers to have no reluctance to change the design. Even in the modified design, the designer could specify only the end result and not the "means, methods, techniques, sequences, and procedures" by which the work will be done. How would the modified design create a greater liability for the designer? One would think that it should not increase the designer's liability in any respect.

Consider the scenario from a slightly different perspective. Suppose the designer did know of a modified design approach for which a safer work method would probably be used. Suppose the modified method was not utilized, and suppose a construction worker was seriously injured while attempting to construct the facility component as specified. Would the designer possibly incur a greater liability because a modified design would have resulted in a safer construction approach? One would think that the failure to exercise the ability to deliver a design that was known to be safer to construct would result in an increase in liability. Case law does not provide clear guidance on this issue. In general, the question to be decided revolves around the exercise of the standard of care that is currently practiced in the profession.

Different scenarios are shown in Figure 22.2, describing a designer's actions in relation to a construction worker injury. In each scenario, the designer specifies only the end result and not the method of construction. In scenario 1, the designer designs a facility component (component A). In scenario 2, the designer designs a facility component (component B) because the designer feels that component B will be safer to install than component A would be. Scenario 3 is similar to scenario 2 except that the designer

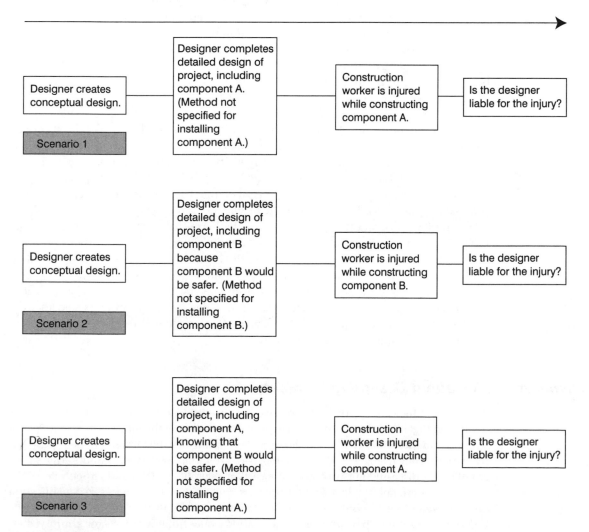

Figure 22.2
Different Designer Decisions and Possible Liability Consequences

designs component A knowing that B would have been safer. In each scenario, a construction worker is injured. Is designer liability equal in the three scenarios?

Clearly, scenarios 2 and 3 would appear to place a greater risk of liability on the designer. That is because in both those scenarios the designer has knowledge of the relative risks associated with components A and B. Note that the designer in scenario 3 knows that a modified approach would be safer but, for some reason, opts for a less safe design. Legal counsel would find it difficult to defend that decision; however, the legal view may focus on the standard of practice. For example, in scenario 2 the issue is one of reasonable care. If the designer has acted in a prudent manner, regardless of the end result, there is no increased liability exposure (*City of Mounds View v. Walijarvi*, 263 N.W. 2d 420 [1978]; *Coombs v. Beede*, 36 A. 104 [1896]; *City of Eveleth v. Ruble*, 285 N.W. 2d 521 [1974]). Perhaps the concern that legal advisers generally have is depicted in scenario 2. That situation may arise if the designer feels that component B would be safer but it turns out to be less safe. It is not an enviable position for the designer, but it is not as adverse as is the situation depicted in scenario 3. The primary difference between scenarios 2 and 3 is that in scenario 2 the designer is trying to opt for the safer design, while in scenario 3 the designer ignores the safety issues that are known. If the designer knows of a safer approach, there is a duty to employ that knowledge in practice in that the professional cannot ignore the information nor fail to take the appropriate steps to address the hazards (*Hanna v. Huer, Johns, Neel, Rivers and Webb*, 662 P. 2d 243 [1983]; *Mallow v. Tucker, Sadler & Bennett, Architects & Engineers, Inc.*, 54 Cal. Rptr. 174 [1966]; *Caldwell v. Bechtel, Inc.*, 631 F. 2d 989 [D.C. Cir. 1980]). Thus, safety is everyone's business. It is especially true when one has knowledge that can influence professional decisions. In the *Caldwell v. Bechtel* decision, the court focused on "Bechtel's superior skills, and its ability to foresee the harm that might be expected to befall the worker. The court saw these as creating a duty in Bechtel to take responsible steps to prevent harm to the worker." Aside from the legal or liability concerns, it should be evident that the moral action would be to select the safer options.

There is another aspect that has not been specifically mentioned. That aspect is that if the designer makes a design decision in which the safer option is selected, the chance of an injury is reduced. If the chance of an accident is reduced, the chance of incurring any liability is similarly reduced.

Owner Attitudes about Designing for Safety

As a result of the liability crisis, owners have greatly expanded their role in ensuring worker safety, and that role can be expected to expand even further in the future. The rising costs of workers' compensation claims and the escalation of litigation claims are not being ignored by owners. They realize that the costs of injuries are ultimately reflected in the cost of construction. As discussed in Chapter 3, those costs are significant (Hinze and Appelgate 1991).

Owners are not helpless when it comes to ensuring safety on a job. Prequalification and the selection of contractors are frequently based, in part, on the contractors' demonstrated safety performance. Information concerning a contractor's injury incidence and experience modification rate (EMR) provides a look at the contractor's past safety performance and can be incorporated into the selection process. In addition, owners can influence job-site safety through their contractual agreements with contractors. By insisting on addressing safety in the contract, an owner increases the probability that the contractor will follow outlined safety procedures. Direct involvement of owners in project safety also promotes safety.

There are some barriers to increased designer involvement in safety. Can safety responsibilities be extended to them? With legal counsel telling designers that they are to avoid addressing matters of safety in their designs, safer designs are not likely to occur. At any rate, design modifications will not occur on the designers' initiative alone. This is where owners can play a pivotal role. Recall that many large private owners now conduct safety audits of contractors before permitting them to submit bids on their projects. In other words, contractors with poor safety records need not apply. Naturally, contractors are inclined to change their practices as they pertain to safety if continued construction contracts are at stake. Can the same strategy apply to designers?

What if owners approached designers with the intent of awarding design contracts to them but insisted that construction worker safety be addressed in the design? Would the designers be inclined to consider the safety consequences when evaluating different design options? If the design contract were at stake, the designer would surely try to accommodate the owner. Is such a request by the owner reasonable? Keep in mind that a lawsuit resulting from a serious injury on a project will most assuredly include the owner of the facility being constructed. That is one reason owners want to hire safety-conscious contractors; that is, they do not want injuries on their projects. Should owners demand any less of their designers?

In two recent studies of the large consumers of construction services, firms with large construction budgets, questions were asked about designers and safety (Hinze 1994a, 1994b). Specifically, the owners were asked, "Does the company ask its designers to consider construction worker safety when preparing designs?" The results of the two studies were similar and are shown in consolidated form in Figure 22.3.

As shown in the figure, 45% of the owners participating in the study stated that designers have never considered construction worker safety in their designs, and 11%

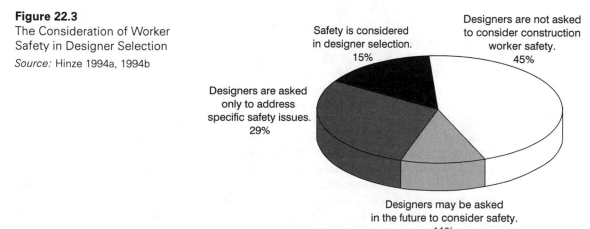

Figure 22.3
The Consideration of Worker
Safety in Designer Selection
Source: Hinze 1994a, 1994b

Safety is considered
in designer selection.
15%

Designers are not asked
to consider construction
worker safety.
45%

Designers are asked
only to address
specific safety issues.
29%

Designers may be asked
in the future to consider safety.
11%

of the owners may consider design safety in the future. The 29% that stated specific safety issues were addressed were obviously concerned about hazards that were already known to them when the designers were selected. An example might be a remodeling project that involves asbestos removal. Of necessity, that hazard would have to be addressed by the designer. Note that 15% stated that designer selection actually took into consideration the extent that designers would address construction safety in their designs. Since those respondents were primarily those with larger construction budgets, those firms are probably more concerned about safety than many owners with smaller construction budgets. In fact, 27% of the firms with construction budgets exceeding $100 million reported that they based their selection of designers, in part, on whether construction safety would be addressed in their designs. With the escalating costs of workers' compensation and with the high liability suit settlements involving owners, it can reasonably be expected that more owners will expect designers to consider construction safety in the design phase.

The third party to the typical general contracting arrangement is the designer. In an effort to limit their exposure to third-party lawsuits, design professionals typically distance themselves from the responsibility for safety during the construction phase. Today's design codes and standards reflect that attitude. Currently, no reference standards exist to show how design decisions could or should be made for the benefit of improved construction worker safety.

Design Decisions That Affect Construction Safety

How can a professional architect or engineer modify the design to enhance construction worker safety? Are there specific design details that can eliminate job-site hazards and reduce the number of injuries and fatalities?

Although the concept may sound bold, many designers do address construction worker safety when making design decisions. That is particularly true of designers employed in design-build or design-construct firms. Such firms are in a unique situation in that failure to address worker safety in the design may directly affect the safety performance of their own workers as they construct the facility. Thus, the design-build firms do not need to be convinced of the value of addressing construction safety in their designs.

Notable changes have been made in the design of steel structures, leading to changes in steel erection practices. Those changes point out the need for more designers to be concerned about safety. "It is the erector who is in the limelight. He is the one who becomes the accident statistic, but all too frequently he has been put into an unnecessarily unsafe situation because of the type of connection he has to make or its location" (Raggs and Cunningham 1988). Others have also recognized that designers could play a valuable role in enhancing construction worker safety. "What may be a simple and acceptable connection by design may present a difficult or potentially dangerous erection problem. Such a detail may lead to a situation where a beam cannot be erected without some loosening of other bolts, whereby what was once stable is now unstable and a potentially dangerous condition exists" (Allen and Lovejoy 1989).

Design-build firms have been most helpful in offering their input concerning design ideas that are beneficial for construction worker safety (Hinze and Wiegand 1992). Unfortunately, a survey of designers revealed that "less than one-third of the design firms address construction worker safety in their designs, and less than one-half of the independent constructability reviews conducted address construction worker safety" (Hinze and Wiegand 1992). From those results, it was concluded that "for safety of construction workers to be addressed by designers on a regular basis or as an integral design function on all projects, a dramatic change must occur in the mind-set of the design profession."

It must be recognized that designers have traditionally not been asked to address construction worker safety in their designs. Thus, the immediate task in the industry is to develop a body of knowledge concerning the myriad design ideas that have been used in the past to make construction sites safer. The task of acquiring information on the many different design ideas has begun with a compilation of the various design approaches that have successfully addressed construction worker safety on past projects. That information has been acquired through the efforts of researchers at the University of Washington on a project funded by the Construction Industry Institute (Gambatese 1996). Surprisingly, some major firms provided design manuals that contained numerous design-for-safety ideas. The information is available to design professionals from the Construction Industry Institute.

Design-for-safety ideas are numerous and quite varied. Some suggestions include the following:

1. Design trenches at minimum feasible depths.
2. Examine valve stems and motor operators on valves during design to determine if they will protrude into walkway areas. Rotate them so as to provide safe passage on stairs and platforms.
3. Design permanent stairs and walkways to be constructed early in the construction phase, so that the use of temporary scaffolding is minimized.
4. Relocate, disconnect, or bury overhead power transmission lines off site to allow safe access and working areas for cranes.
5. Design for cut-and-cover installations instead of tunneling.
6. Group roof and floor penetrations so that the number of openings is kept to a minimum.

Consider the example of the parapet on a flat roof. The Uniform Building Code standards require parapets to be 30″ tall. On the other hand, OSHA regulations require 42″-tall guardrails. Why the discrepancy? Can both standards be accommodated in the design? Refer to Figure 22.4. Note that, with the addition of 12″ of height to the parapet, the construction crews will not have to build an additional guardrail. For this particular design suggestion, the benefits also accrue to the maintenance personnel, who may be required to go on the roof for maintenance checks during the facility operation and occupancy. Over 400 such design-for-safety ideas have been accumulated.

Firms performing similar types of work tend to develop similar suggestions. When designing and constructing comparable facilities, these firms make similar design decisions. Additional ideas, along with the specific rationale for the consideration of each, include the following (Hinze and Gambatese 1994):

1. Suggestion: Pre-fabricate building components in the shop or on the ground, and erect them as complete assemblies.

Figure 22.4
Modifications to a Parapet That Address Construction Worker Safety

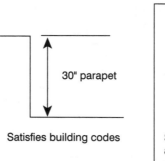

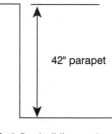

30" parapet

42" parapet

Satisfies building codes

Satisfies building codes and OSHA regulations on guardrails

Purpose: Reduce worker exposure to falls from elevation and struck by falling objects.

2. Suggestion: Design roadways with a wide shoulder to allow room for work crews and equipment to maneuver.

Purpose: Provide an uncongested work site, and distance the workers from moving traffic.

3. Suggestion: In areas that receive significant amounts of snow, place exterior stairs and ramps on the sheltered side of the structure.

Purpose: Reduce slip hazards due to snow and ice.

4. Suggestion: Design columns to have a hole in the web at 42″ above the floor level to support a guardrail cable and provide a connection point for safety lanyards.

Purpose: Since the safety system is built in place, such fabrication details will facilitate worker safety with reduced construction cost and reduced worker exposure.

5. Suggestion: Locate exterior stairs on the south or west sides of the structure.

Purpose: Prevent a slipping hazard due to the buildup of ice and moss from the lack of sun.

6. Suggestion: Minimize the number of building plan offsets. Make the offsets a consistent size and as large as possible.

Purpose: Prevent fall hazards by simplifying the work area for the construction workers.

7. Suggestion: For roadway designs, lengthen the project maintenance life cycle by upgrading the initial project specification standards.

Purpose: Reduce the frequency of maintenance workers' exposure to traffic.

8. Suggestion: Research the history of the project site and the background of any new materials specified for the construction. Include any pertinent information in the contract documents to alert the contractor.

Purpose: Identify hazardous materials and dangerous conditions.

9. Suggestion: Do not allow schedules with sustained overtime.

Purpose: Workers will not be alert if overtime is maintained over a sustained period.

10. Suggestion: Provide, or have the contractor submit, a construction sequence for complicated or unique designs.

Purpose: "Well begun is half done," and any thought to planning the construction work will result in improved construction worker safety performance.

For designers to adequately address construction worker safety, they must first be motivated to do so. The motivation can best be provided by facility owners. In addition, the designers must be educated as to the various ways that design decisions can help construction safety. As mentioned, a significant amount of such information has been compiled (Gambatese 1996) and is available from the Construction Industry Institute.

When all the parties to the construction process focus on construction worker safety, construction work will no longer be so costly in injuries and suffering. The motivation already exists for safety to be addressed by all the parties. With a concerted effort, especially by facility owners, construction workers on future projects will be regarded as unique facility occupants whose safety is to be assured. Once this evolution has occurred, greater industry pride will be a natural occurrence.

Construction Managers and Safety

Designers are typically regarded as agents of the owner. Another party that is often in a similar role is the construction manager. The construction manager's role in safety is similar to that of the designer, so construction managers or construction management firms deserve at least some mention. Construction managers, or CMs, are common parties on many large construction projects. What role do CMs play in construction safety? This is a much debated issue.

As agents of the owner, CMs have historically enjoyed at least some immunity from liability. Unfortunately for the CMs, the times are changing. An examination of court cases that have evaluated the responsibility that CMs have for construction worker safety does not provide any clear direction. There are cases in which the CMs on a particular project had specific responsibilities for safety but were held immune as agents of the owner for injuries incurred by construction workers. Other cases have held CMs liable for construction worker injuries even though their contracts specifically excluded any responsibility for construction safety. In the latter decisions, the courts have elected to ignore the contract language and have relied instead on the common law duty of these professionals. When all the court decisions concerning CMs and safety are examined, a basic conclusion is that the court cases provide no guidance (Hinze and Kusaka 1992). The courts are simply not consistent in their decisions concerning CMs.

The behavior of CMs, as far as construction safety is concerned, should be guided by professionalism. If it is, the CMs will try to address any serious safety hazards they observe. As professionals, they can do no less.

Final Comments

Although few designers are currently willing to admit that they play an important role in construction worker safety, many design-build firms have accepted that role for many years. Those firms see the effect that design decisions have on the safety of construction crews. Being mindful of that effect, designers will become increasingly more sensitive to this issue. Just as owners seek to ensure safety on their projects by selecting safety-minded contractors, owners should do likewise with design firms and insist that their designers address the safety of the construction workers in their design decisions. Many helpful suggestions on how to design for safety have been compiled. As those ideas become publicized and adopted into practice, designers will be playing a more responsible role in worker safety.

Review Questions

1. Why have designers historically not addressed construction worker safety in their designs? Evaluate the merits of those reasons.
2. In what settings are designers particularly sensitive to design decisions that have an effect on construction worker safety?
3. What is perhaps the best way for designers to become motivated to address construction worker safety in their designs?
4. Although designers have not historically addressed construction worker safety in their designs, what dynamics have caused an increase in the practice of addressing safety in the design phase?
5. Develop an example in which the design of one aspect of a facility is made safer for construction workers.
6. If the designer does not direct the "means, methods, techniques, sequences, and procedures" of the work, how can it be argued that the designer has an effect on construction safety?
7. Are construction managers more liable for construction safety if they try to improve it?
8. What common sense rationale can be offered to a designer for selecting the safer of two alternatives?
9. What is the current perception of the extent to which designers address construction worker safety in their designs?
10. How can owners motivate designers to address construction worker safety in the design of their projects?

References

Allen, P., and E. Lovejoy. 1989. "Designing for Safety." *Structural Engineer* 67, no. 5, 83–87.

Gambatese, J. 1996. "Addressing Construction Worker Safety in the Project Design." Ph.D. diss., University of Washington.

Gans, G. 1981. "The Construction Manager and Safety." *Journal of the Construction Division* 107, no. 2, 219–26.

Hinze, J. 1994a. *A Study of the Construction Activity Projections for 1994.* Washington, D.C.: Merit Shop Foundation.

———. 1994b. *A Study of the Construction Activity Projections for 1995.* Washington, D.C.: Merit Shop Foundation.

Hinze, J., and L. Appelgate. 1991. "Costs of Construction Injuries." *Journal of Construction Engineering and Management* 117, no. 3, 537–50.

Hinze, J., and J. Gambatese. 1994. "Design Decisions That Impact Construction Worker Safety." In *Proceedings of the Fifth Annual Rinker International Conference Focusing on Construction*

Safety and Loss Control, University of Florida, Gainesville, FL, October 12–14, 1994, conference coordinated by R. Coble. Gainesville: University of Florida.

Hinze, J., and F. Gordon. 1979. "Supervisor-Worker Relationship Affects Injury Rate." *Journal of the Construction Division* 105, no. 3, 253–62.

Hinze J., and A. Kusaka. 1992. "Safety Programs and the Construction Manager." Discussion paper. *Journal of Construction Engineering and Management* 118, no. 3, 629–30.

Hinze, J., and H. Parker. 1978. "Safety: Productivity and Job Pressures." *Journal of the Construction Division* 104, no. 1, 27–34.

Hinze, J., and D. Tally. 1988. "Subcontractor Safety As Influenced by General Contractors on Large Projects." CII Source Document 39. Austin, Tex.: Construction Industry Institute.

Hinze, J., and F. Wiegand. 1992. "Role of Designers in Construction Worker Safety." *Journal of Construction Engineering and Management* 118, no. 4, 677–84.

Morpurgo, S. 1992. "Accident Prevention at Dam Construction Sites." *International Water Power and Dam Construction* 44, no. 8, 13.

Raggs, R., and J. Cunningham. 1988. "Safety and Efficiency in Steel Construction—The Broadgate Experience." *Civil Engineering* (London), May, 35.

Smith, G., and R. Roth. 1991. "Safety Programs and the Construction Manager." *Journal of Construction Engineering and Management* 117, no. 2, 360–71.

U.S. Department of Labor. Occupational Safety and Health Administration. 1990. *Analysis of Construction Fatalities—The OSHA Data Base 1985–1989.* November. Washington, D.C.

KEY TERMS

Accident: unplanned event, generally with negative consequences, that may or may not be associated with property damage or an injury

Authorized person: a person approved or assigned by the employer to perform a specific type of duty or duties or to be at a specific location or locations at the jobsite

Census of Fatal Occupational Injuries (CFOI): program established by the Bureau of Labor Statistics in 1992 to accurately document the number of fatalities occurring in different industries

Competent person: an individual who is capable of identifying existing and predictable hazards in the surroundings or working conditions which are unsanitary, hazardous, or dangerous to employees, and has authorization to take prompt corrective measures

Death rate: ratio of the number of worker deaths per 100,000 workers employed for one year

Employee: every laborer (one who performs manual labor or labors at an occupation requiring physical strength) or mechanic (worker skilled with tools) under the Construction Safety Act regardless of the contractual relationship which may be alleged to exist between the laborer or mechanic and the contractor or subcontractor who engaged him or her

Experience modification rating: multiplier applied to the manual rate paid on workers' compensation by a firm, based on its history of workers' compensation claims, reflecting both injury frequency and injury severity

Injury frequency: ratio of the number of injuries incurred per 200,000 hours of worker exposure or per 100 full-time workers employed in one year

Lost workday injury: a work-related injury of an employee in which the employee experiences either days away from work (absence from the job for medical treatment or recuperation), days of restricted work activity (inability to perform his or her normal job duties over a normal work shift), or both.

Material safety data sheet (MSDS): written or printed material concerning a hazardous chemical that contains information on its identity (including common names), its ingredients (if a mixture or compound), the material or materials in it that are known to be hazardous, physical and chemical characteristics of the hazardous chemical, its physical and health hazards, symptoms of exposure, any medical conditions generally recognized as being aggravated by exposure to the chemical, the primary route of entry, the OSHA permissible exposure limit, precautions to be taken during handling and use, and steps to be followed upon exposure

Medical case injury: worker injury requiring the services of a physician

Near miss: incident involving no injury and no property damage, but high potential for such occurrence

Occupational Safety and Health Administration (OSHA): agency created by the Occupational Safety and Health Act (OSH Act) to promulgate safety and health standards, enforce compliance with the safety regulations, and monitor industry safety performance

Qualified person: a person who by reason of experience or training is familiar with a particular operation to be performed and the typical hazards involved

Recordable injury: a work-related injury of an employee resulting from an event on a construction site and requiring treatment by medical personnel or causing loss of consciousness, restriction of work or motion, or transfer to another job

Zero accidents: philosophy adopted by some companies in which the goal is to have no worker injuries

Index

abatement, 72, 78, 79, 80, 104
absenteeism, 176, 179, 182
acceleration, 39
accessibility, 224
accident, 2, 4–7, 11–17, 19–25,
    31–32, 42, 43–44, 49–51,
    53–54, 59, 62–64, 73, 91,
    101, 102, 106, 109, 110,
    115, 118, 137, 155–157,
    161, 164–167, 173, 175,
    176, 186, 191, 193, 196,
    197, 203, 204, 232, 265
accident, defined, 6, 7
Accident Facts, 3, 4, 5
accident free (See zero accidents.)
accident prevention, 6, 7, 8, 11, 23,
    49, 101, 102, 106, 155,
    156, 157, 161, 166, 197,
    265
accident prone, 11, 12, 13, 14, 15,
    16, 42
accident proneness theory, 11, 12,
    13, 14, 15, 16, 17
accident statistics, 3, 4, 5, 43
accounting, 64, 68, 107
adjustment stress theory, 15, 16, 17
age, 13, 42, 174, 207
agriculture, 3, 5, 72
ahead of schedule, 237
alcohol, 15, 105, 159, 173, 174, 180,
    181, 272
ambulance service, 50, 109, 164
American Institute of Architects,
    272
American Red Cross, 264
anger, 225
annual meeting, 259, 260

annual summary, 191
appeals procedure, 79
area director, 79, 80
Associated General Contractors,
    273
assumption of risk, 1
attitude, 15, 24, 25, 65, 175, 203,
    227, 228, 254, 259
authorized person, 75, 263, 265
awareness, 1, 2, 24, 151, 156, 170

behind schedule, 213, 239
bid projects, 251
bidding, 57, 65
biological clock, 37, 38, 39
biorhythm cycles, 42, 43, 44, 45, 46
blanket testing, 107, 175, 176
bonus, 147, 149
builders risk insurance, 53
Bureau of Labor Statistics (BLS), 3,
    4, 244

camaraderie, 211
causes of accidents, 2, 7, 11–28, 44,
    88, 90
Census of Fatal Occupational
    Injuries, 3, 4
CFR (See Code of Federal Regula-
    tions.)
chain of custody, 179
chain-of-events, 11, 21, 23–27
change in the work, 7, 8, 22, 174,
    178, 182, 209, 250
channels of communication, 253
checklists, 102, 115, 122, 125–132,
    156, 157, 159

chief executive officer, 243
circadian rhythm, 37, 38, 39
citations, 1, 77, 79, 81, 86, 88, 92,
    95, 100, 304
cleaning up, 32
clear instructions, 209
closing conferences, 79
cocaine, 173, 181
Code of Federal Regulation, 72–75,
    88, 93, 94, 96, 125, 129,
    130, 134, 175, 263, 264
coding, 91, 92
cohesive crews, 113, 211
cold temperatures, 36, 37, 105, 117,
    160, 226
commitment, 100, 101, 106, 107,
    118, 120, 149, 150, 155,
    201, 203, 212, 227, 243,
    251, 252, 254, 265, 267
commitment of top management,
    100, 120, 203, 243, 252
common law, 1
common sense, 237
company philosophy, 99, 135, 139
company policies, 16, 23–25, 50,
    104, 144, 152, 175, 179,
    180, 196, 209, 210, 220,
    243, 249, 251, 252, 254,
    273
competent person, 75, 103, 158,
    162, 263
competition, 20, 214, 222, 239, 240
compliance inspections, 78
compliance officers (See OSHA
    compliance officers.)
concrete, 6, 35, 36, 52, 90, 91, 96,
    117, 160, 167

confined space, 74, 101, 104, 105, 117, 134, 156, 160, 167, 168, 171, 306
Construction Industry Institute (CII), 55, 56, 181, 203, 275, 319, 321
construction managers, 49, 54, 321
construction methods, 156
construction safety, 7, 85, 111, 139, 151–154, 157, 159, 169, 170, 182, 196, 235, 237, 238, 251, 252, 267
construction schedule, 136
contract documents, 112, 151, 152, 155, 273
contributory negligence, 1
control, 16, 24–27, 49, 52, 74, 82, 102, 104–106, 110, 134, 136, 152, 156, 160, 161, 168, 177, 179, 202, 205, 214, 225–227, 232, 235, 238, 247–250
coordination, 25, 49, 277, 278, 283–295
corporate policies, 23
corrective measures, 25, 75, 79, 118, 119, 120, 162, 263, 273
cost overruns, 238, 239
cost ratios, 60, 61
cost reimbursable, 57, 61
cost reports, 113, 222, 254
court cases, 314, 321
court decision, 76, 78
crack, 173, 181
crane, 52, 89–92, 104, 117, 132
crew size, 6, 53, 226, 227
crew supervisor, 191
criminal charges, 65
critical days, 42–46

daily visits, 253
Davis-Bacon Act, 75, 264
deadline, 16, 21
death rate (See fatality rate.)
dehydration, 36
delegate, 102, 156
demonstration program, 81
designated individual, 168
designer, 25, 27, 169, 308, 313–322

dinners, 113, 139
direct costs, 50, 52, 55–58, 60, 65
disincentives, 144–146, 170, 171
disputes, 20, 175
distractions theory, 11, 17–21, 23, 208
documentation, 119, 123, 137
drinking water, 36, 209
drowning, 90
drug abuse, 20, 176, 178, 181
drug abuser, 176, 178
drug testing, 108, 162, 174–182, 207, 312
drugs, 15, 20, 105, 108, 159, 162, 173–182, 207, 272
dust, 116, 118, 188, 189, 197

educate and persuade, 133
education, 21, 74, 75, 81, 86, 87, 93–96, 103, 113, 134, 158, 164, 259, 260
electric shocks, 82
emergency plan, 103, 109, 164, 165
emergency temporary standard, 76
emphasis on safety, 170, 259
Employee Assistance Program, 180
enforcing the regulations, 72
engineers, 53, 73, 167, 172, 196
entrainment, 38, 39
equipment damage, 6, 53
exams, 137, 210
experience modification rating, 51, 109, 149, 257, 258, 267, 275, 300–304, 310, 316
exposure to hazards, 13–15
eye protection, 66, 105, 107

facility owners, 2, 151, 204
fall protection, 23, 95, 104, 105, 160, 226
falls, 2, 19, 23, 82, 89, 91, 95, 104, 105, 117, 118, 160, 226, 231, 257
family, 16, 22, 39, 56, 64, 65, 139, 143, 222, 232
fatalities, 2, 3, 5, 8, 82, 85, 88–90, 95, 174, 185, 186, 310
fatality frequency rate, 3, 4
fatigue, 15, 16, 32, 108, 162
Federal Register, 76

feedback, 119, 164, 192, 215, 246
fellow worker, 12, 14, 16, 53, 62, 63, 142, 173–175, 211, 212
fellow worker doctrine, 1
field supervision, 23, 106, 161, 252, 254, 259, 260
field visits, 246
field work, 246, 252
fines, 1, 24, 72, 77, 79, 80, 86, 112, 273, 304
fire, 40, 50, 90, 93, 94, 103, 104, 105, 116, 158, 160, 165, 266
first aid, 52, 53, 54, 74, 95, 103, 105, 109, 134, 143, 158, 159, 164, 186, 188, 197, 210, 259, 264
first aid cases, 188, 197
first aid classes, 259
first aid courses, 103, 158
first aid facilities, 103
first aid injuries, 52, 143, 210
first aid procedures, 74, 134
first aid supplies, 109, 164
first aid training, 105, 159
first-line supervisor (See foreman.)
flagger, 166
floor openings, 106
focused inspections, 82
follow-up inspection, 78, 81, 119, 146, 193
follow-up testing, 175, 176, 180
follow-up treatment, 59, 61, 62, 64, 65, 188, 189
foreman, 6, 24–26, 55, 63, 99, 104, 106, 109, 113, 136, 139, 146–148, 161, 168, 204, 213, 219–227, 232, 235, 236, 238, 239, 246, 264
formal complaints, 120
fraud, 67, 68
fraudulent claims, 35, 258
frequency of injuries, 41, 44, 51, 85
Friday, 34, 35, 240
full moon, 40

gang meetings, 135, 202
general duty clause, 1, 71, 72, 154
general foreman, 25, 26

geographic region, 8, 182, 260
gimmick, 143, 144
goals, 6, 14, 15, 64, 104, 147, 149,
          173, 180, 202, 203, 220,
          222, 238
goals-freedom-alertness theory, 11,
          14–17
good faith, 79, 80
good managers, 233–235
goodwill, 56, 215
guardrails, 93, 94, 96, 226

hard hats, 66, 105, 159, 160, 167
harmful substance, 74, 134
haz com (See hazard communica-
          tion.)
hazard communication, 75, 76, 87,
          95, 104, 158
hazard identification, 106, 115, 116,
          124, 160, 161
hazards, 2, 3, 5, 12, 17, 19, 21, 24,
          71, 72, 74, 75, 80–82, 92,
          95, 102, 103, 106,
          115–121, 123, 124, 133,
          134, 156, 157, 158,
          160–162, 166, 167, 185,
          209, 226, 259, 263, 265,
          268
headgear, 36, 167
health care facility, 40, 53
hearing protection, 105
heat exhaustion, 36, 226
heroin, 173
hidden, 40, 52, 54, 55, 58
hold harmless (See indemnifica-
          tion.)
hot temperatures, 36, 117, 226
hourly wages, 53
hour of the day, 31–33
housekeeping, 24, 105, 159, 160

ice, 36, 143
ideas, 41, 63, 92, 116, 202, 209, 223
image, 65, 177
imminent danger, 120, 163
inadequate instruction, 25, 100
inadequate planning, 25, 113
incentive, 50, 51, 64, 141–143, 144,
          146, 147, 149, 150, 170,
          171, 177, 182, 197

incident reports, 191–193
indemnification, 100, 111, 151, 166,
          169, 170–172, 273, 297
independent contractor, 186
indirect costs, 52–54
Industrial Revolution, 1
injuries, 85, 175, 193, 238
injury rate, 4, 5, 176
injury report, 43, 57, 110, 164
injury statistics, 2–6
inspection, 24, 59, 73, 77–79, 81,
          82, 107, 108, 111, 120,
          122, 123, 136, 154, 155,
          157–159, 162, 163, 165,
          169, 198, 248, 267
inspection tour, 107, 122
instruction, 25, 100, 167, 209
insurance carrier, 51, 60, 112, 123,
          124, 189, 258, 259, 260
insurance company, 35, 51, 123,
          189, 257, 258, 259, 260,
          273
insurance premiums, 2, 50, 51, 53,
          65, 68, 112, 170, 204, 257,
          258, 303, 304, 305
investigation of accidents, 2, 24, 25,
          43, 54, 59, 61, 62, 63, 81,
          104, 110, 157, 159, 165,
          191, 193–196, 280, 308,
          312

jet lag, 38
job hazard analysis, 103, 116–120
job orientation, 210, 232
job safety director, 266, 268
job security, 16
job termination, 146

key personnel, 209, 305, 306

labor agreement, 31, 209, 226
lack of sleep, 15, 16, 22
late starts, 182
laws and regulations, 26, 151, 153
lawsuit, 172
learning curve, 251
levels of management, 23, 109, 213,
          250, 252
liability, 2, 15, 23, 27, 58, 64, 65,
          110, 111, 151, 166, 169,

          170, 172, 175, 177, 259,
          272, 274, 297, 307,
          313–316, 318, 321
liability crisis, 2
liability insurance, 2
lighting, 39, 116
litigation, 2, 100, 151, 193, 304,
          305, 308, 311, 313, 316
lockout, 104, 105, 160
loss of consciousness, 188
loss ratio, 51, 52, 109, 257, 260,
          275, 301, 303, 304, 308,
          311
lost productivity, 59, 205
lost time injuries, 5, 55, 57, 58,
          60–63, 65, 109, 142, 144,
          147, 148, 164, 170, 186,
          189, 191, 196, 197, 310
loyalty, 112, 147, 212, 213, 247
LSD, 173
lunar cycle, 39–42

macho, 13, 100
management tools, 221
manager, 25, 26, 49, 54, 99, 106,
          107, 121, 122, 136, 139,
          140, 149, 175, 196, 201,
          203, 204, 209, 213, 221,
          231, 233–235, 246, 248,
          249, 253, 256, 259, 266,
          267
managerial qualities, 234
manual rates, 50
marijuana, 173, 174, 181
master schedule, 113
material damage, 6, 53
material handled, 192
Material Safety Data Sheet, 104, 159
media, 54, 59
medical case injuries, 57–63, 65,
          196, 299
medical personnel, 264
medical treatment, 53, 54, 58, 63,
          109, 110, 164, 188
mental diversions, 15
merit program, 82
middle manager (See
          superintendent.)
middle managers, 99, 231
mining, 3, 5

mission, 100, 101, 155

mitigation, 268

mock OSHA inspections, 122, 123, 197

modified work plan, 305

Monday, 6, 34–36, 134, 135

moods, 40

moral, 110

morale, 25, 56, 65, 178, 205, 215

motivation, 13, 222, 223

National Institute of Safety and Health (NIOSH), 72

National Safety Council (NSC), 3–6, 135, 196, 197

nature of work, the, 6, 8, 15, 19, 135

near miss, 7, 108, 111, 121, 138, 144, 165, 176, 177, 192, 194, 197, 198, 266, 309

negative reinforcement, 144

negligence, 65

new hires, 104, 175, 210, 220, 221, 232

new moon, 40

new workers, 23, 208–210, 213, 220, 221, 232, 250, 252

newsletter, 113, 204

noise, 15, 116, 118

noncompliance, 166, 167, 265

number of bidders, 251

Occupation Safety and Health Act (OSH Act), 1, 2, 71–82

Occupational Safety and Health Administration (OSHA), 3, 71–74, 76–82, 85–89, 90, 92, 93–96, 100, 102–105, 108, 109, 111, 116, 120–124, 134, 143, 148, 151, 154–158, 160, 162, 163, 164, 167, 169, 170, 171, 175, 185, 186, 188, 189, 191, 193, 197, 207, 210, 240, 257, 259, 263, 264, 265, 267, 272, 273

Occupational Safety and Health Review Commission (OSHRC), 72, 80

onerous, 169

orientation, 8, 21, 24, 49, 53, 103, 104, 133, 158, 202, 209, 210, 220, 221, 232, 252, 258, 265, 266, 279, 280, 295, 299, 306, 307, 312

orientation of new hires, 104

OSHA compliance officers, 72, 77–80, 82, 92, 95, 108, 120, 124, 163, 257

OSHA consultation, 80, 81, 82, 120, 121

OSHA inspections, 77–80, 163

OSHA log, 78, 186–189, 191, 198

OSHA poster, 77, 78, 186

OSHA recordable injuries, 109, 143, 186–191, 240, 310

OSHA recordkeeping, 185, 197

OSHA regulations, 72, 73, 74, 76–78, 80–82, 86–92, 95, 100, 103, 105, 121, 134, 155, 157, 158, 160, 163, 175, 186, 207, 210, 263, 265, 272

OSHA standards (See OSHA regulations.)

outside work, 6

over budget, 202, 238

overhead power lines, 90

owner, 2, 25–27, 58, 59, 102–104, 107–111, 148, 149, 151, 152, 154–165, 167, 169–172, 201, 204, 243, 245, 248, 250, 253, 256, 265, 271–274, 297–313, 316–318

owner involvement, 162, 297–313, 307, 308

pace of work, 32, 35

paradigm shifts, 203

peak level, 32

peak production, 35

periodic testing, 175, 176

personal attention, 226

personal needs, 214, 233, 235

personal problems, 12, 15, 211, 223

personal protective equipment, 116, 119, 159

phase of work, 103, 106, 157, 158, 160, 163

picnics, 113

poor design, 25

poor managers, 233–235

positive reinforcement, 15, 144, 215, 221

posting requirements, 80, 123

praise, 215

preconstruction conference, 102, 167

premium, 2, 50, 51, 53, 65, 68, 112, 157, 170, 204, 257, 258, 303, 304, 305

prequalification, 170

prescription drugs, 173

preselection of physicians, 66, 67

president, 72, 139, 149, 201, 203, 204, 213, 243, 248, 250, 252–254, 256–260, 267

pressure, 16, 174, 213, 214, 222, 223, 236–240, 251, 253, 276–277

pride, 147, 205

proactive, 5, 6, 26, 151, 152, 166, 205

production huddle, 135

productivity, 17, 20, 25, 32, 36, 53–56, 59, 65, 174, 179, 205, 210, 212, 215, 237, 239, 240, 266

productivity and safety, 17, 18, 19, 65, 237

profit margin, 65, 251

profits, 55, 65, 113, 251

progress payments, 103, 157

project activities, 113, 156, 202

project control, 110, 247

project design, 23, 103, 204

project designers, 204

project engineers, 175, 231

project layout, 209, 232

project manager, 25, 26, 106, 107, 121, 122, 136, 139, 140, 149, 175, 196, 203, 204, 209, 213, 231, 246, 248, 266

project planning, 23, 214, 253, 265

project schedule, 117, 202, 209

project visit, 81, 252

property damage, 7, 101, 110, 155, 164, 259

protect, 2, 72, 91, 154, 155, 166, 167, 169, 273

public hearings, 76

quality, 14, 15, 82, 168, 176, 177, 179, 202, 212, 213, 247, 254

rain, 116

random testing, 108, 175, 177, 179, 180

reassign, 224

recognition, 1, 74, 103, 109, 123, 134, 139, 147, 158, 221, 252

recording, 193, 248

reduced productivity, 56, 215

regulatory personnel, 54, 123

rehabilitation, 108, 110, 176, 180

rehiring, 110

replacement, 12, 24, 53, 56, 59

reprimand, 144, 146

reputation, 56, 205

research studies, 12, 16, 55, 221, 232, 244

respect, 113, 214, 223

responsibility, 1, 2, 25, 26, 27, 49, 73, 74, 77, 100, 101, 111, 134, 153–156, 158, 162, 163, 165–167, 169, 171, 197, 201, 227, 235, 259, 260, 264, 273

responsibility for safety, 2, 26, 155, 166, 201, 259, 260, 264

rewarding work, 7, 14, 15, 212, 249

risk, 12, 13, 51, 53, 81, 92, 106, 113, 161, 167, 171, 208, 232

roofs, 88, 89, 91, 226

roving superintendent, 246

rulemaking, 76

safety and productivity, 18

safety awards, 140, 141, 144, 146, 202

safety awareness, 24, 170

safety belt, 106, 107

safety budget, 107

safety bulletin board, 104, 159

safety committee, 79, 105, 107, 121, 122, 124, 160, 198, 309

safety conference, 103, 158

safety culture, 101, 201–205, 232

safety departments, 266, 267

safety dinner, 139, 140

safety director, 63, 102, 139, 203, 265, 266, 268

safety expert, 258

safety gimmicks, 202

safety guidelines, 104, 144

safety infractions, 121, 136

safety inspections, 24, 107, 108, 111, 120, 122, 123, 136, 157–159, 162, 163, 165, 169, 267, 312

safety issues, 42, 55, 121, 156

safety legislation, 1, 2, 151

safety literature, 210

safety meetings, 34, 103, 106, 116, 120, 122, 123, 133–136, 137, 139, 140, 157–159, 161, 168, 192, 202, 209, 252, 257, 260, 312

safety nets, 105, 160

safety officer, 136, 157, 165

safety personnel, 124, 140, 263–269

safety philosophy, 100, 155, 265

safety professionals, 54, 257

safety program, 99–113, 122, 134, 141, 144, 155–158, 160, 161, 165–167, 172, 181, 196, 201, 207, 243, 252, 256–258, 260, 272, 273, 280, 281, 295, 299, 301, 306, 307, 311

safety programs, 99–102, 104, 106, 108, 110, 112, 113, 122, 134, 141, 144, 155–161, 165–167, 172, 181, 196, 201, 207, 243, 252, 256, 257, 258, 260, 272, 273

safety records, 5, 6, 8, 82, 135, 144, 147, 164, 185–198, 211, 212, 215, 221, 232–234, 237, 244, 247, 251, 253, 254, 256, 257, 260, 266, 267

safety representative, 103, 158, 266

safety shoes, 105

safety standards, 101, 109, 111, 154, 155, 169

safety studies, 196, 235, 254, 255

safety violation reports, 116, 197

sanctions, 144

sanitation, 104, 105, 122, 125, 154, 160

satisfaction, 144, 211–213, 215, 221

Saturday, 41

scaffolding, 24, 66, 86–89, 93–96, 106, 129

scene of the accident, 193

schedule, 6, 63, 64, 110, 113, 115, 117, 136, 164, 202, 209, 213, 237, 239, 247

schedule of activities, 115

schedule of values, 117

season, 36, 37, 41, 44

selecting a general contractor, 25, 299–306, 310–312

selecting a subcontractor, 274, 275

sensitivity, 235

serious hazard, 17, 18

serious injury, 7, 175, 193

serious violations, 79, 92, 93, 95, 120, 163

severity of injuries, 51

shift work, 37, 39

short interval schedules, 290–294

site visit, 78, 81, 113, 121, 248, 252

sleep, 15, 16, 38, 39, 40

small employer, 80

smoking, 105, 159

snow, 36

speed limits, 105, 159

stairways, 93, 94, 96

Standard Industrial Classification, 185

star program, 81

state-plan states, 80

statistics, 2, 3, 5, 13, 34, 36, 43, 64, 72, 73, 95, 170, 188, 198, 207, 244, 258

stop work, 55, 79, 243, 247, 267

stranger, 211

stress, 11, 15, 16, 21, 27, 39, 146, 208, 209, 211, 213, 222, 224

subcontractor, 58, 73, 75, 104, 106,

108, 111, 153–155, 157–159, 161, 162, 170, 264, 271–281, 308

substance abuse, 16, 20, 104, 107, 162, 173–176, 178–182, 207, 312

substance abuse programs, 107, 108, 162, 179–182

substance abusers, 107, 173–175, 180–182, 207

suggestions, 113

summer, 36, 37, 226

sun, 36

superintendent, 25, 26, 62, 63, 73, 99, 103, 122, 135, 136, 147, 149, 158, 191, 202, 209, 213, 231–240, 246, 248, 264, 265, 266, 272

supervisor, 6, 16, 54, 110, 133, 152, 165, 168, 191, 192, 209, 222, 227

supervisory personnel, 61, 65, 124

supervisory skills, 223

supplementary record, 189–191, 198

supplier, 155, 273

symbolic, 102, 268

tailboard conference, 135

tardiness, 176

task accomplishment, 17

temperature, 15, 36, 38, 117

testing for reasonable cause, 175, 176

Thursday, 35, 36, 135

tides, 40

time costs of injuries, 49, 52, 55, 60, 63–65, 68

time of year, 36, 37

timing of injuries, 31, 32, 36

tool box, 52, 63, 133, 280, 311

toolbox meetings, 106, 137, 138, 161

top level, 243

top management, 99, 100, 120, 123, 149, 197, 201, 203, 204, 243–261, 267

total quality management, 202

traffic control, 104, 105, 152, 160, 168

traffic supervisor, 152, 168

training, 7, 8, 13, 23–25, 49, 53, 59, 72–77, 79, 81, 82, 86, 87, 93–96, 100, 103, 104, 105, 115, 116, 118, 119, 121, 134–137, 157–159, 164, 167, 180, 192, 196, 202, 209, 219, 223, 236, 252, 259, 264, 265

transportation cost, 109, 164

trenching, 78, 90, 104, 160, 185

true costs of injuries, 49–68

Tuesday, 35

turnover, 7, 8, 174, 178, 182, 250, 251, 252

unemployment, 240

unknowns, 208, 209, 213, 232

unsafe actions, 100, 137

upper management, 110, 120

valium, 181

variance, 15, 16, 76, 77

ventilation, 74, 116, 167, 168

veteran worker, 209, 213, 221, 232

violations, 24, 76, 78–80, 88, 92, 93, 95, 116, 120, 143–145, 163, 169, 179, 197, 198, 272

voluntary protection programs, 81

waning of the moon, 40

watchful eye, 221

waxing of the moon, 40

weather, 36, 37

Wednesday, 34–36, 135

weekly safety meeting, 63, 133, 192, 209, 280

welding fumes, 118

willful violations, 80, 88

wind, 116, 143, 158

within budget, 237, 238

work delays, 205

work hazards, 12

work procedures, 101, 116, 211

work zones, 167

workday, 33, 57–63, 65, 134, 148, 170, 186, 189, 191, 196, 224, 246

worker behavior, 23, 122, 146, 174, 204, 222

worker competency, 73

worker exposure, 4, 12

worker safety, 1, 2, 26, 27, 65, 76, 92, 100, 117, 118, 146, 152–156, 166, 168, 170–173, 197, 208–210, 219, 220

worker training, 23

workers' compensation fraud, 66, 67, 68

workers' compensation insurance, 1, 35, 50, 51, 52, 151, 177, 182, 186, 188, 189, 197, 205

working relationship, 25, 113, 210

worry, 15, 20, 21, 257

zero accidents, 5, 6, 64, 173, 203